WATER SECURITY

WATER SECURITY

Conflicts, Threats, Policies

Dr. JAMES A. TINDALL
Dr. ANDREW A. CAMPBELL

Library of Congress Cataloging-in-Publication Data
Tindall, James A.
Water Security: Conflicts, Threats, Policies/Dr. James A. Tindall and Dr. Andrew A. Campbell
p. 452

ISBN-10:0-9817037-0-4
ISBN 13: 978-0-9817037-0-1

Cover design (front, back, spine) by Manoj Sharma and Indyahub (www.indyahub.com).

Published by DTP Publishing, Denver, Colorado

Printed in the United States of America by CreateSpace a DBA of On-Demand Publishing, LLC — a division of the Amazon group of companies.

10 9 8 7 6 5 4 3 2 1

ISBN-10:0-9817037-0-4
ISBN 13: 978-0-9817037-0-1

Dedication

To the heavy lifters in security and intelligence; the real change agents and creative minds, whose work often remains unnoticed and underappreciated.

Tribal Water Symbol

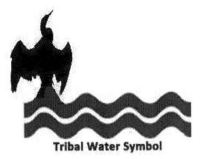

CONTENTS

Preface

Whether economically, environmentally, or socially, there is no greater threat to international security or individual quality of life than scarcity of water. Water distribution systems extend over vast areas and are therefore vulnerable to a wide array of risks. These dangers are many — from increasing global population to man-made, natural, and technological hazards. Disruption of water supplies can threaten the delivery of vital human services, endanger public health and the environment, cause mass casualties, and threaten population sustainability, social stability, and national and homeland security. Devising concepts and counter measures to protect water supplies will assist the public, policy makers, and planners at all levels of government to develop solutions for national and international water-security and sustainability issues.

A cooperative and concerted effort between policy makers, planners, managers, the public, science agencies, law enforcement, and security and intelligence agencies is required to develop solutions to water-security threats. From supply and sustainability to critical infrastructure, intelligence, and physical security; from public and higher education to institutional capacity building and a focus on 'needs based' water consumption are but a few critical areas we must address. No single issue impacts all people as directly as water security — the entire global community is a stakeholder.

Dr. James A. Tindall and Dr. Andrew A. Campbell
August 2011
Denver, Colorado USA
Melbourne, Australia

Disclaimer

The opinions and comments offered and discussed in this book are solely those of the authors and do not represent the views, policy, or opinions of any federal agency, private corporation(s), or the U.S. Government. Mention of a specific tool, software, or other product does not affirm endorsement of the item(s) discussed nor of the agency or private firm that markets or manufactures said item(s). Finally, the reference of a specific corporation, firm, or government agency does not constitute author endorsement of them or endorsement by the agency(s) for which the author(s) work.

Sponsors

This book was sponsored by the TinMore Institute (www.tinmore.com), a global resources think tank that provides companies and corporations with leading knowledge required for current and future competitive outperformance through timely analysis and forecasting and solutions for complex global resource problems.

Appreciation is given also to Transnational Resources Development Associates (www.transrda.com) who foster global resource development and sustainability for developing nations in the areas of agriculture, energy, emergency management, healthcare, manufacturing, security, and water. The authors are grateful for their support.

Executive Summary

This book represents an overview of the significant interdependencies in water security and its important role in the lives of people throughout the global community. What is water security? "Water Security is the protection of adequate water supplies for food, fiber, industrial, and residential needs for expanding populations, which requires maximizing water-use efficiency, developing new supplies, and protecting water reserves in event of scarcity due to natural, [man-made], or technological hazards."[1]

By definition the subject is highly complex and covers many areas through interdependency with critical infrastructure — the systems that drive life and the economy, which include energy, transportation, agriculture and food, public health, defense industry, and others. Water also is complexly interdependent with many other areas such as transboundary resources and political issues, national and international security, emergency preparedness and incident planning, policy, and many others. The security implications of water-related issues are fundamentally characterized by the uncertainty they introduce with respect to overall water availability, water security, food security, economic sustainability, and social stability. Terrorist, natural, and technological hazards also play an important role in mitigation of failure of water systems and how policy is implemented to account for these hazards. Although many countries such as the U.S. have invested and devoted substantial economic resources to dams, reservoirs, water conveyance systems, storage, flood control defenses, and other distribution systems, a growing population will inevitably increase this cost. Water is the primary driver that allows economic sustainability and has long been a source of conflict — from the Wild West days in the United States to current peace process endeavors in the Middle East. Aptly stated, nothing is more important than water and its security excepting life itself.

In this century new challenges to water security and national security will likely manifest themselves more frequently. Security convergence and operational resilience are examples of public and

---

[1] J. Tindall, and Campbell, A., "Water Security-National and Global Issues," ed. National Research Proram (Denver: Government Printing Office, 2010).

private sector components that will be vital for ensuring continuity of operations. In this sense, water security and other security measures should be thought of as sustainability, not merely physical elements — there can be no security without sustainability. The fundamental key will be to maintain security processes that are flexible and adaptable and that incorporate continuity goals and strategies. These processes should be based on an all-hazards approach that considers disruption from the primary hazards — anthropogenic (terrorist or manmade), natural, and technological. There are four major future security implications: (1) to hedge against uncertainty; (2) to curtail outdated and less useful security concepts; (3) to explore new security concepts and be rapidly adaptable; and (4) to adapt through time via changing technologies. These implications will be applied against relations with not only current security issues, but also far more significant issues that relate to water security and critical infrastructure, mass sustainability, and the primary hazards that can affect them. Addressing these issues requires a heightened flexibility and adaptability that could prove problematic for hierarchal organizations. Thus, water-security issues reflect much more than management, planning, and policy.

Both energy and water security has become a national and global priority. The continued security and economic health of a country depends on a sustainable supply of both because these two critical natural resources are so closely linked. The production of energy requires large volumes of water while the treatment and distribution of water is equally dependent upon readily available, low-cost energy. For example, electricity production accounts for over 40 percent of all daily freshwater withdrawals in the United States; the indirect use of water (home lighting and electric appliances) is approximately equal to direct use (watering lawns and taking showers).

Current trends of water use and availability indicate that meeting future water and energy demands to support continued economic development will require improved utilization and management of both resources. Primary concerns include (1) increasing populations that require more food and energy (which will cause direct competition between the two largest water users for limited water resources — energy and agriculture); (2) resource needs for economic expansion (projections indicate the U.S. will

require an additional 393,000 MW of new generating capacity — equivalent to about 1,000 new 400 MW plants by the year 2020, which is unlikely to occur); (3) potential environmental and ecological restrictions on the use of water for various purposes; and (4) potential terrorist attacks on power grids and water-treatment and distribution systems. The ability to meet increasing demand for affordable water and energy is being seriously challenged by these and other emerging issues; this is true for almost all countries. As an example, a terrorist attack or other hazard occurrence against a national water supply could disrupt the delivery of vital human services, threaten both public health and the environment, potentially cause mass casualties, and likely weaken social cohesion and trust in government, resulting in grave public concern for national and/or homeland security. A threat to continuity of services is a potential threat to continuity of government since both are necessary for continuity of operations. To exacerbate matters, water infrastructure is difficult to protect — it extends over vast areas and ownership is overwhelmingly nonfederal (approximately 85 percent). Although counter measures are being established for enhanced physical security, improved coordination among stakeholders, and risk assessment and vulnerability analysis, the vastness of these systems leaves them weakened. A key issue is the proportionate additional resources directed at public and private sector specific priorities. A large portion of this work is focused on water quality and supply.

Globally, unsafe water, inadequate sanitation, and improper hygiene cause illness and death from disease on a large scale. Improving these conditions can lead to better health, poverty reduction, and sustainable socio-economic development. However, many countries are challenged to provide these basic necessities, which have left and continue to leave people at risk for water, sanitation, and hygiene (WASH)-related diseases. Generally, water and public health revolve around safe water, good sanitation and hygiene and their education in six areas: (1) community systems (water safety plans, assessment and development); (2) sanitation and hygiene (toilets, hygiene, sewer and wastewater treatment); (3) diseases and contaminants (waterborne, sanitation, and hygiene related); (4) household treatment (safe water systems and storage); (5) travelers' health (safe drinking and recreational water and injury

and illnesses); and (6) educational resources (publication, Internet, etc.). These are additional, yet significant aspects of water security.

A growing population is beginning to strain global resources, particularly water. Water stress affects 44 percent of the world's population. The United Nations Environment Programme (1999) projected that by 2050 nearly 5 billion people will be affected by freshwater scarcity. Currently, over one billion people in the world lack access to improved water supplies and 2.6 billion people lack adequate sanitation — the two issues are interdependent — water is needed for sanitation and lack of it promotes disease. On a global scale, the health burden accompanying these interdependent conditions results in about 5,000 child deaths daily, mostly from diseases associated with lack of access to good quality drinking water, sanitation, and good hygiene.[2] The disparate distribution of water also makes it difficult for resource and economic scarce areas such as the Middle East, Pakistan, Afghanistan, Northern Africa, and others to cope. The three general areas necessary for improved water-related public health problems include (1) good quality drinking water; (2) adequate quantities of water for food production, health, and hygiene; and (3) sustainable sanitation processes. Although these issues may seem trite, their effects on the local or regional area are a security concern and illustrated by the rising number of conflicts over water resources around the world.

For large cities, simultaneous shortages of food, water and power, created in large part by water shortages, could dramatically destabilize mass population sustainability, security, and governance, which make water security and supply issues a matter of national stability. The most pressing water-supply issues facing almost all cities are increasing population and urbanization — the primary causes of water shortages. Population growth in arid regions dramatically reduces available water supplies from both ground and surface waters. Examples include Phoenix, Las Vegas, and Denver in the U.S., as well as other cities that are located in semi-arid to desert conditions. Within the U.S., cities are short of water, especially in the arid West where the Colorado River supports about 22 million people, is drawn upon by seven states, supplies such cities as Los

---

[2] M. Schomaker, "Guidelines on Municipal Wastewater Management," ed. UNEO/WHO/HABITAT/WSSCC (The Hague: WSSCC, 2004).

Angeles and San Diego, California; Las Vegas, Nevada; Phoenix, Arizona; and Denver, Colorado and also provides large volumes of water for agriculture. The situation is similar for the Indus River system that supplies parts of China, India, and Pakistan; the Jordan River supplying Israel, Jordan, and Syria; and other world regions. A worst case scenario is Lake Chad in Africa, which has been depleted 95 percent in the past 40 years.

The effects of global water and distribution shortages are potentially catastrophic, creating mass civil unrest, food shortages, and large-scale failure of industry and, thus, society. The end result could dramatically destabilize security and governance, especially if the current poor global economic outlook persists. Water supply is therefore a matter of national stability and security for all countries and is the reason most countries have sought to harness water and the energy it provides. As an example, construction of Hoover Dam was one of the greatest undertakings in human history considering its scale and scope, the manpower necessary to achieve the project, and its economic and social impacts. The waters impounded behind Hoover Dam in Lake Mead have played an integral role in the burgeoning of agriculture and urban development in the American Southwest — providing water to about 22 million people and hydro power to about 7 million. The Colorado River is the lifeblood of this region and Hoover Dam is, quite literally, the heart of it. All of the major cities and the majority of the agricultural lands would not exist without the security of water reserved in Lake Mead. Therefore, management and mitigation of stored water will become increasingly significant as a function of rapidly increasing population and increasing demand.

The centralized nature of such projects, coupled with substantially increasing resources, needs to facilitate a viable and renewable source of water and power, and pose a liability to the future security and sustainability of a region. Total reliance on the entrapment of water in a hot and arid climate regime utilized by millions of people and large agricultural investments is generally not a sustainable endeavor. Additionally, these issues pose a significant threat to the security of critical resources (access to water, food, and power) due to a non-redundant water supply.

The zones most directly at risk from failure of such systems are those areas directly dependent on it for critical resources, regardless

of geographic location. Examples could include Hoover Dam in the U.S., Three Gorges Dam in China, and Tarbela Dam in Pakistan. For agricultural areas that depend on these resources, a failure of the system would be catastrophic, causing simultaneous security risks to our basic needs as a society — water, food, and energy. This would occur through failure to provide municipal and industrial water needs; agricultural water needs (loss of a reliable supply of resources would have both local and national impacts); clean electrical power; and economic losses (which would cause a significant downturn in production and loss of jobs with cascading failures into the supply chain and other critical infrastructure that would have a severe rippling effect through the nation). Failure also would affect energy, commodity, and food prices extensively, as well as have other unseen effects (not discussed here due to sensitivity and security issues).

The security risks to critical resources are overly relevant because of the number of people and agricultural lands that are directly and solely dependent on resources provided either directly or indirectly from large-scale water projects. Additionally, any clear and present resource security risks are likely to occur simultaneously to a large population, causing deprivation of critical resources with almost no alternatives available for substitution — posing a significant security risk to the entire population at large. As more people compete for finite resources, sustainability will likely fail at some juncture and many people will be unable to meet basic resource needs. However, it is difficult to predict and gauge the exact effects of such an event to the local and national environmental and economic landscape, generally because an event of this magnitude and scope has not yet been experienced. However, it could be assumed that this event would cause large-scale disruption, both locally and nationally — the duration of the residual effects of this event would not be short lived.

The major mechanisms of failure for large water projects, dams, etc., would include earthquakes and terrorist attacks, as well as technological failure. The likelihood of a terrorist attacks remains the highest probability of dam inoperability and would likely occur due to contamination from biological agents such as Anthrax, Botulism, or others, through chemical agents, such as Nerve (G and V agents), biotoxins (Ricin, Digitalis), etc. Bio-agents would cause the most immediate damage through poisoning water, especially an

agricultural water supply. Other terrorist threats could potentially rely on explosives of various types and/or technology such as cyber attacks of industrial control and Supervisory Control and Data Acquisition systems (SCADA).

Industrial control systems (ICS) that manage critical infrastructure such as flow of water, energy transmission, communications and so forth are moving to general-purpose computer hardware and software in ever increasing numbers for cost efficiency and centralization of control. Yet best practices for information technology that shares many of the same components do not always work for industrial control systems and in some cases can be harmful. Common products and practices such as the Java programming language, virtualization, desktop security tools, remote access, standard network topology, commercial off-the-shelf operating systems and lax password policy have the capability to cause more damage than good, creating increased vulnerability of these systems to hackers. Industrial control systems should defy information technology and embrace read-only operating systems, network segmentation, security through simplicity, and, above all, set higher standards for employees who manage and maintain computer systems. These control systems must have unique policies and procedures, patch procedures, security software, and employees who understand the differences between information technology and industrial control systems — all while working on the same general-purpose computer hardware. The information technology and industrial control system worlds should never come together. Their objectives, consequences, and fates are too far apart.

Natural and technological failures also represent dire threats to these systems and/or projects. Regardless, the shadow cast by the limited resources and growing populations poses an urgent dilemma to the future security of many nations and could have a profound effect on national security. For example, the importance of interdependencies among critical infrastructures is well recognized — the economic sustainability and prosperity, security, and social well being of countries depend on infrastructure reliability. Although the surface interdependencies are more easily understood, the complex underlying interdependencies are understood by a scant few. This failure to understand the complexities and the cascading failures and resulting disruptions among infrastructures will decrease the effectiveness of response and recovery efforts during man-made, natural, or technological hazards, or may result in common cause failures that leave planners and emergency response personnel unprepared to effectively deal with operational continuity and the impacts of these disruptions.

Interdependencies among infrastructure can generally be categorized into four components: (1) cyber; (2) physical; (3) logical; and (4) geographical. Additionally, water and wastewater systems have interdependencies with other infrastructure that are unique and that must be understood when developing and conducting vulnerability assessments, response and recovery plans, and security and sustainability.

Gaps in understanding the analytic capability of infrastructure and related systems are apparent in the context of analyzing multiple scenarios of possible events that involve interdependence between one or multiple infrastructure and related components within even one system. Each linkage between systems is important. The types of failure that can occur within infrastructure include (1) cascading; (2) escalating; and (3) common cause. Infrastructures are also linked to varying degrees, which influences vulnerability and response requirements, resiliency, and operational considerations. ICS, deregulation, business mergers, and related components can dramatically affect both the economic and business aspects of the infrastructure environment and have become an important part of infrastructure that is rarely discussed, even though these components can all significantly affect water security. Unfortunately ICS have also led to the introduction of new vulnerabilities, particularly cyber attack from both terrorist and criminal elements. Compounding these factors has been the increase of legal and regulatory issues, increased environmental regulations, government investment decisions, and public health and safety concerns. All have served to influence infrastructure operations and interdependence. The importance of the crucial role of water is profound. Water infrastructure and shortages have a cascading detrimental effect on all facets of economic, public health, social areas, the political arena, transportation, trade, and interdependencies between various industries — these are the non-surficial complexities that scant few understand.

Compounded with water is its requirement by agriculture to feed a growing population — without water, agriculture is impossible. Risks and vulnerabilities due to the three primary hazards also link directly to agriculture. For example, attacks against agriculture are not new, and have been conducted throughout history both by nation-states and by sub-state organizations utilizing biological weapons. At least nine countries (Canada, France, Germany, Iraq, Japan, South Africa, United Kingdom, United States and former USSR) have documented agricultural bioweapons programs during some part of the 20th century. Four other countries (Egypt, North Korea, Rhodesia and Syria) are believed to have or have had agricultural bioweapons programs.[3] Although individuals or sub-state groups have used bioweapons against agricultural or food targets, only a few can be considered terrorist in nature. In 1952, the Mau Mau (an insurgent organization in Kenya) killed 33 head of cattle at a mission station using African milk bush (a local plant toxin). In 1984, the Rajneesh cult spread salmonella in salad bars at Oregon restaurants to influence a local election.[4]

The most effective biological weapon agents would be highly infectious, communicable, and lethal; efficiently dispersible; easily produced in large quantities; stable in storage; resistant to environmental degradation; and lacking vaccines or effective treatments. Biological agents may be targeted directly against humans through injection or topical application; deployed against agricultural crops, livestock, poultry, and fish; applied as a contaminant of food or drinking water; disseminated as an aerosol; or introduced through a natural vector such as an insect.

Authorities may be persuaded that a disease outbreak is natural, providing cover or plausible deniability to biological terrorists. An example is the recent E-coli outbreak in Europe during May-June 2011 that spread to the U.S., which has thus far managed to control it. According to European scientists, the source of the outbreaks is unknown and potential causes have ranged from Spanish cucumbers to vegetables from other countries. At the time of

---

[3] Jim Monke, "Agroterrorism: Threats and Preparedeness," ed. Congressional Research Service (Washington DC: Library of Congress, 2004).
[4] Ibid.

this writing more than 2,400 people have become ill and 23 are dead.[5]

Linking water security to agriculture from an agroterrorism perspective, there are a number of threats to drinking water: improperly disposed chemicals; animal wastes; pesticides; human wastes; wastes injected deep underground; and naturally-occurring substances that can all contaminate drinking water and also food, either deliberately or accidentally. Likewise, drinking water that is poorly treated or disinfected that travels through an improperly maintained or sabotaged distribution system can also pose a health risk.

Naturally occurring outbreaks of diseases signal the devastation that could result from a carefully choreographed intentional or accidental event. Examples include the recent Foot and Mouth disease epidemics in Taiwan and Great Britain, swine cholera in the Netherlands, and infection of Florida citrus trees with citrus canker, which aptly demonstrate the vulnerability of living targets to biological pathogens and the economic chaos that can result from an outbreak — intentional, accidental, or natural.

Distribution systems are among the most vulnerable physical components of a drinking-water utility, as well as the computer systems that manage critical utility functions; treatment chemicals stored on-site; and source water supplies. Two key factors appear to constitute overarching vulnerabilities: (1) a lack of the information individual utilities need to identify their most serious threats and (2) a lack of redundancy in vital system components, which increases the likelihood an attack or failure could render an entire utility inoperable.

In regard to anthropogenic threats to water security, supplies, and sustainability, the most serious terrorist threat to a water supply is the flight or sudden emergence of simultaneous and coordinated black-swan. A coordinated 'black swan' terrorist attack on the U.S. water supply, dependent on severity, could involve a reordering of defense priorities to the maintenance of civil order within the continental United States. An example of such a scenario is given in

[5] Lisa Baertlein, "Major E.Coli Outbreaks Decline, Salmonella Up," *Reuters U.S. Edition*(2011), http://www.reuters.com/article/2011/06/07/us-ecoli-usa-idUSTRE75675K20110607.

chapter 1. Also, a paradigm case of a terrorist 'black swan attack' was the three day terror attack on Mumbai from 26-28 November 2008. In 1993, Bin Laden declared war on America and stressed his commitment to 'the defeat of the U.S. economy." By 14 September 2003, Bin Laden claimed the success of the 9/11 attacks. Not surprisingly, Al Qaeda and other terrorist group's psychological warfare strategists have an impressive sociological understanding of the vulnerabilities of western target societies, including the importance of the relationship between consent and legitimacy of government.

Since the 2001 terrorist attacks, the FBI has identified and interviewed Al Qaeda supporters who planned attacks against U.S. water supplies and plans, particularly Hoover and TVA Dams. A successful attack would potentially be catastrophic. It should also be presumed that the U.S. is not the only target country. A cascading attack on water infrastructure would disrupt and in some cases destroy key storage and distribution nodes. The chaotic consequences would ensure that government priorities would be diverted to terrorist induced socio-economic dislocation, a form of Al Qaeda induced Hurricane Katrina. Simultaneous co-coordinated attacks on targets across a country would complicate the attack picture. For example, in the U.S. alone there are over 5,700 facilities and structures vital to American national security and economic well being. A terrorist attack against a single vulnerable high-value infrastructure target of over 5,000 key nodes would exhibit many of the characteristics and consequences of a natural disaster, including social dislocation, disorientation and panic, widespread anomie and social disorganization, threats to public order, public health crises, and possible epidemics.

A water infrastructure attack would likely be executed in four stages: (1) intelligence collection; (2) distraction and diversion of security forces; (3) attack by U.S. indigenous person(s); and (4) use of bio-agents as weapon of choice to poison large supplies. Terrorists have demonstrated operational interests in various water systems around the world. The best tool to defeat them is likely counterintelligence. Internal counterintelligence (CI) programs are essential to counter a wide spectrum of insider threats ranging from targeted terrorist moles within the target infrastructure to employees, contractors, and sub-contractors who may have direct or

indirect affiliations to foreign intelligence services, or terrorist patron states, and individuals with untraceable or unverifiable familial tribal ethnic connections to pro-terrorist groups, organizations, or regimes. As an example, a paradigm CI failure occurred in May 2009: a California Water Service Company (CWSC) employed Abdirahman Ismael Abdi, a non-U.S. citizen who was holding a British passport and working on a fraudulent H1B visa. Employed as an auditor at CWSC in San Jose, California, and using his electronic key card, he gained access to the secure electronic gate at the CWSC parking lot, and then used the computers of two CWSC employees to send over $9 million dollars to three separate accounts in Qatar. Terrorists are the primary counterintelligence threat to many countries. Such attacks on water systems have four operational advantages: (1) technical and human assets in the form of "home grown" jihadists; (2) secure human and technical clandestine communications; (3) clandestine assets in Islamic Diasporas; and (4) the ability of its engineering elite to inflict a single spectacular attack on water infrastructure, which could wreak massive damage to social cohesion and the economy. Terrorist threats exacerbate the already stretched thin lines of water security.

In addition to manmade threats, natural threats pose a significant problem for water security. An example is wildfires, which can cause major disruptions of the water supply for a city due to debris flow and other processes and thus play a major role in water security. The primary post-fire pathways for the transport of various constituents are mudslides and erosion — often termed debris flow. This flow carries nutrients down slope into streams and reservoirs to varying degree. The effects of wildfires should not be underestimated. In recent years a large number of fires have been anthropogenic (intentionally or accidentally lit). It should be noted that terrorists consider fire a strategy to achieve operational and economic objectives against their enemies. For example, although not known to be specifically terrorist associated, approximately half of Australia's 20-30,000 bush fires are deliberately lit; the same is true in the U.S. and other countries.

The effects of large wildfires can be catastrophic, costing millions of dollars in damage, destroying thousands of acres of land and the environment, and lasting effects on the economy, agriculture, the environment and other sectors. Wildfires can

significantly affect water security through destruction and disruption of infrastructure, supply and distribution, rail and truck transportation, air traffic, power supply and transmission, and can cause public health and environmental hazards resulting in severe economic damage, loss of life, and loss of animal species. Additionally, timber exports and pharmaceutical supplies can be affected.

To further compound water-security concerns, there are other issues of equal or greater importance including transboundary, emergency preparedness and planning, water economics, and policy. Transboundary water resource issues and disputes are those that cross one or more international borders. The term 'water war' has often been used to describe disputes regarding water use. The divergence between nations concerning economics, infrastructure, and political orientation has complicated transboundary water sharing. Poor use and management of already limited water resources provides evidence of problems at each level of government: (1) State level — lacking sufficient supplies; (2) National level — competing demands between sectors; and (3) International level — threats between nations sharing transboundary resources. Examples of transboundary water issues include multiple entity competition for water, the stronger antagonist controlling water resources (through military or economic means), use of propaganda to justify control, threat of water terrorism, and economic development disputes.

During transboundary disputes regarding the Danube River in Europe, it was discovered that the public consultation process and working with all stakeholders brought more rapid results. There appears to be several factors that have been the driving force for transboundary cooperation in Europe specifically including: (1) a large gradient in economic development; (2) major political changes in Central and Eastern Europe after 1991; (3) transformation of legislation and administration of former East Bloc countries; (4) water pollution and environmental degradation; and (5) International River, i.e., used for navigation. It remains to be determined whether or not China and its neighbors, Israel and its neighbors, and other regions can utilize the European model as a framework for their respective transboundary issues.

From a historical setting, the mode of cooperation has shifted from bilateral agreements to basin-wide agreements. For transboundary problems it is likely that water and environment relation actions will likely be based on implementation of precautionary principles, utilizing best available techniques and practices, controlling pollution at the source, requiring the polluter to pay, and regional cooperation and information sharing. For conflicting areas such as China and its relation with Pakistan and India, as well as Southeast Asia, and for the Middle East, water-security issues threaten basic national interests. Both the quantity and distribution of water throughout these countries and their neighbors represent significant challenges to social and economic sustainability. Population growth increases demands on water supply, causing problems with the environment, salt-water intrusion, economic development, public health, and other issues. All of these nations are already under some form of water stress that minimally threatens economic sustainability from the individual fisherman to the entire country, threatening disruption of economic and agricultural activity in the most vulnerable areas.

As a highlight, China's very survival, particularly its economic sustainability, is growingly threatened by water-security and water-supply issues. About 23 percent of its population lives in western regions where glacial melt provides the principal dry season water source. This continually diminishing resource is creating an emergent competition among users. Also, the Indus River system, with headwaters in Tibet, has become a significant problem that could potentially erupt into conflict with Pakistan and India. Because China, Pakistan, and India are nuclear armed, a solution to transboundary water issues for this area is critical. The Indus River has been a source of conflict between China, Pakistan, Nepal, Bangladesh, and India for centuries. The use and overuse of water, territorial claiming of water resources, damming and water distribution are resulting in more grievous water conflicts. Specific regions such as the Mekong, Indus, and Ganges also will likely be more severely impacted with time in regard to water stress, and being transboundary in nature will likely strain the capacity of Chinese institutions and policy frameworks. China's national security also will be in jeopardy in event of dire water stress, forcing greater cooperation or potential hostility with its surrounding neighbors and even the U.S. because of strategic

concerns over water and food security as well as economic sustainability. Transboundary water issues seriously affect and impact water security and other global issues, especially sustainable economic development, human health, and food production.

Developing new water resources to help resolve transboundary water problems will require technological solutions that increase water supplies such as desalination, waste-water reuse, and so forth, but also, effective management of current resources such as transferring water from wet to dry zones. These types of measures will require significant financial investment.

Within-country water issues are just as important as transboundary issues, especially for emergency services and response, where different levels of government, public authorities, and private sector interests need to collaborate for the national good, i.e., most commonly during severe natural disasters. Generally, a lack of standards continues to undermine the vast majority of a nation's water systems and local government emergency planning and complicate water-security implementation. There is an obvious difference in a national approach to protecting water infrastructure compared to the approach of local and state governments — the low-probability high-consequence Federal approach and the high-probability low-consequence local approach complicates collaboration and response. However, this issue is more appropriately addressed through policy.

Water economics also is one of the greatest challenges to water security. The world is facing a global crisis for resources; energy prices are soaring, creating unexpected consequences for water-supply issues, commodity prices, and food production. When discussing water versus a national economy, it is important to understand three basic areas: (1) the relation between the overall economy and the water sector; (2) the physical, social, and economic nature of water; and (3) the pros and cons of alternative approaches to water policies for public use and policy issues related to an economic organization of water resources, such as water pricing, and their management.

Four primary types of economic benefits of water use include (1) commodity; (2) water assimilation; (3) aquatic and wildlife habitats; and (4) recreational. Also, individuals obtain commodity benefits from water through use for cooking, drinking, and

sanitation. Agriculture and industry gain commodity benefits by using water for production for foodstuffs and manufacturing. This type of use represents private goods from water through production activities, but also represents rivals in consumption. An economic organization of the water sector has generally been split into either market or government entities. Along with attempts to organize have come many market and government failures, many of which have related to economic structure and irrigation. Almost every country relies on a mix of market policies and government interventions to manage water resources. In the U.S., while the free market competitive system is often viewed as the most efficient system for allocation of resources, market imperfections and fluctuations on occasion can accentuate income disparities.

The outputs of non-market activities for water are difficult to define and the inputs that produced them are difficult to measure. Regardless, water economics is complex; the resource is extremely interdependent with other sectors and due to scarcity in many areas around the globe, development of supplies and pricing are a primary focus. Because of these critical issues, water is a national-security problem.

Pricing water is also difficult, initially stemming from increasing populations that need more; concentration of these populations in locations that over time are further removed from the resource; increased pollution requiring more costly treatment; and industrialization that has led to the connection of all homes connected to public water and sewer systems. The pricing of water should consider both the level and structure of prices. A pricing structure should consider at least four requirements: (1) a price sufficient to recover costs; (2) a price fair to all users; (3) pricing that provides incentives for conservation; and (4) a price that is efficient and administratively feasible.

A primary principle in water economics is that there is a demand for water of differing qualities. Also, the largest costs in the water sector are borne by the development of storage, transportation, distribution, and treatment systems. Innovative and forward thinking approaches of water management are needed to ensure sustainability of such large systems. Economic principles also must be explicitly integrated into management. Development of a basic framework that could serve as a starting solution would include

numerous parameters such as (1) recovering costs; (2) utilizing/developing tools for economic analysis; (3) putting costs and benefits into proportion; (4) implementing pricing policies for droughts and water scarcity; (5) implementing analysis of management and economics; and (4) assessing a 'true' value for water.

The shorter the supply of a natural resource, the more important it is to have an institutional structure for efficient allocation among stakeholders for current and future needs. The general economic system views water as either a common property resource to be freely shared or as a good to be priced and traded in the market. Neither approach ensures sound water management and economics because many functions, services, and values of water are not used or traded in the market. These include the value of aquatic environments (a habitat for biodiversity), recreational values of water, use as a transportation medium, role in waste treatment and manufacturing, role of water in displacing and transporting materials and contaminants, and more.

Because of these many issues, there has been much discussion about water being undervalued around the world. Although many nations are focused on water issues, many also lack the capital investment to develop and implement needed water systems for supply and treatment. Conceptually, water can be priced directly or indirectly. Direct pricing involves setting prices and charges payable from use, reuse, and disposal of water — by users. Indirect pricing relies on applying a wide variety of mechanisms that reveal the cost of using water and associated resources. The latter is more difficult, but compares interdependencies with other sectors and through economic analysis and other tools could suggest a more true value for water within a locale, region, or country.

It should be noted that externality (effects of an economic transaction that extends beyond the actors in the transaction) charges work in both political and social contexts when there is reasonable acceptance of the principle of 'polluters and users pay.' In a social climate that supports economic development regardless of impacts across the water cycle and sector, an externality charge is difficult to implement. Thus, within such a framework, it is important that externalities associated with potable water, reuse, and wastewater be treated consistently. Typically, any framework used

would be designed to facilitate a rational investment in potable water, reuse water, and wastewater, which incorporates the full costs of production and effects of the environment into account. For large projects, public investment is likely always a requirement due to total cost and environmental consequences. Failure to adequately address water economics will imperil national security.

Finally, critical questions arise about water and other resource and policy issues regarding water security and use. What are the roles of local, state, Tribal, and Federal governments in water resources development and management? Who should pay, and how much? What agencies should be involved? Should existing projects be revamped or re-operated? What agency should be in oversight control for security from a sustainability perspective? The list is endless, but sound policies can alleviate major future problems.

Within a management context policy is generally presented as a formal, written statement. Policy analysis can aptly be defined as a systematic analysis of policy options. Alternately, policy management is a comprehensive umbrella that concerns a specific effort to improve capacity to manage policy, perform good policy analysis, and facilitate cooperation in policy processes. Generally, policy development can be improved in two ways: (1) upgrading policy-making processes, which can involve improved policy process management and restructuring organizations; and (2) establishing improved broad-scope policies that guide the substance of discrete policies. Regardless of policy type or approach, specific circumstances will likely need specific process requirements. A problem with many international type policy process models is that they provide for the policy analysis phase in great detail, not for guidance regarding events that lead up to the analysis phase.

A variety of underlying issues separate to the policy itself and should be recognized. These include policy reform, political processes, time-frame opportunities, internal processes, process development, forward thinking, involvement of multiple stakeholders and other criteria.

Atop a policy sets a governance cycle, generally a four-step process, but one that can be highly complex in relation to execution. Governance cycles generally follow (1) a review phase; (2) a policy development phase; (3) a reform phase; and (4) an implementation and control phase. When implementing functions of the governance

cycle, it is important to emphasize, especially for sectors as complex as water, fit within the country's national development framework and thus, with governing laws consistent with the constitution. It is also important to begin with the macro level. Once the basic phases of policy development are accomplished, a review cycle must regularly monitor and evaluate implementation of policy, which may need to be adjusted through time in terms of legislation, resources management, etc., along with cross-cutting issues such as intra-governmental cooperation and interaction.

Inclusive within policy development is defining and having a clear understanding of what policy is and what it is not, that it is dynamic, requires political endorsement (particularly for a national policy), and that a specific process (and style) is necessary for writing policy. A policy will require an overall description and reference framework. Ideally, it will contain primary or main policy principles that provide an overall framework such as water use, water management, fostering participation, etc. The policy needs to be sufficiently detailed so that it covers a comprehensive range of issues that integrate the whole. It is also important to address global concerns such as water security and global systems for water-scarce regions.

Perceptions of natural resources have changed greatly since the 1990s. Consequently, fundamental economic measures taken by governments to meet their water deficits will differ widely from the water rhetoric and declared water policy. Interdependent within global perspectives is the fact that water is recognized as an economic resource, which contradicts user expectations and various religious claims that water should be a free entitlement. Within this environment, water that was free for agriculture is not based on user-pay scenarios. Two economic principles — allocation and productive efficiency — are particularly relevant to water allocation and management because they comply with the sound principle of increasing returns to water. Unfortunately, the subject of the reallocation of water generally results in intense political reaction from those who perceive they might lose by the change. However, these ultimately need to be reflected in policy.

Other factors that are of great importance in water security globally are the close relations between a national water gap and that nation's food gap. The greatest management challenge in

attempting to steer the political economy of water is how to access sufficient water to meet staple food needs — a growing problem. Water is a major factor of production in agriculture, and its relative availability in different climatic zones ensures that some economies have a significant advantage in food-staples production. The contrast in the capacities to produce food surpluses is given stark expression in the world trade figures. In the decades since the middle of the twentieth century, agricultural sectors of industrialized economies located in the temperate climatic regions have progressively increased their productivity in grain production.

All of these global issues, including environmental resources and development for sustainability, as well as legal issues (particularly transboundary water sharing) create growing complexities for water security.

Acknowledgments

The authors would like to thank Kathleen R. Binns for editing this entire manuscript from both a narrow and broad-scope approach in a persistent and tireless effort to make it the best in its field. We also express thankful appreciation to Steve Steckel for contributing Chapter 12 and for his significant knowledge as one of the foremost experts in the U.S in the areas of IT and ICS security, data-base controls, and related fields. Also, we gratefully acknowledge William H. Austin, one of the top three emergency managers in the U.S. for contributing Chapter 14 and his exceptional expertise with combined water and emergency response units and systems.

The authors express sincere gratitude to Senator Gary Hart for his specific and logical comments regarding international issues of water security and foreign affairs, as well as appreciation to the following for helpful comments, opinions, and suggestions for various portions of water security and related subject matter — Dr. Dewayne Branch, Dr. Ashton Robison Cook, Maria Johnson Figueroa, and Emily Wade.

About the Authors

James Tindall, Ph.D.,

Dr. Tindall was raised on Big Cypress Reservation in the Florida Everglades and has worked in a variety of positions including: Chief Strategist; Chief Technology Officer; federal scientist for a national research program; and as Vice President for a large consulting firm. A veteran of the U.S. Army with experiences in intelligence and explosives, he holds B.S., M.S., Ph.D., and M.A. degrees — the latter in International Security Studies from the U. S. Naval Postgraduate School, where he won Outstanding Thesis award. He has performed extensive work in S&T relevant to global security, business management and leadership, and sector interdependencies involving water, energy, agriculture and food, and commodity supply lines, as well as public policy, critical infrastructures, and their cascading failure effects at country and global scales, especially related to economic effects. His work also has included intelligence, forecasting resource changes, business and security strategy, social networks, vulnerability analysis, risk assessment, operational resiliency, and continuity of operations. Dr. Tindall also has participated in the Middle East Peace Process and worked extensively in these areas nationally, in China, Europe (Germany, Hungary, and Romania), and Latin America in El Salvador, as well as for large city governments in Brazil, Chile, Guatemala, and Nicaragua. He served as a technical advisor for Romania on environmental protocols in that country's attempt to join the European Union, which was successful in January 2007. Academically, he has served as major professor and chair for 28 graduate students who received their M.S. and Ph.D. degrees under his tutelage, mentored over 1,000 upper level and graduate students, and counseled and advised more than 400 professionals. In the spirit of entrepreneurship, he also has founded and run several small businesses. Contact: assist@drtindall.com.

Andrew A. Campbell, Ph.D.,

Dr. Campbell graduated with first class honors and the university prize in social sciences (Phi Beta Kappa) in Victoria, Australia, receiving his Ph.D. in social sciences on the study of Max Weber and political ethics. He specializes in threat analysis and counterintelligence in the context of hostile foreign intelligence services and the global terrorist threat that includes special interests in cross cultural and comparative studies of deception and counterintelligence methodology. Currently completing his second Ph.D. on hostile intelligence services methodologies, he is published widely in specialist journals. Dr. Campbell is .a former Australian intelligence analyst and now directs a private consultancy. His lifelong work in counterintelligence, counter espionage, and counter-terrorism (CI-CE-CT) has and continues to be of great value, providing significant, unique, and forward thinking insights to the intelligence community at large. He has served as a mentor to numerous professionals in international intelligence and the issues involved that affects the national security of the United States, as well as international security and stability of countries around the world. Dr. Campbell has been at the forefront of CI-CE-CT, investigating the multifaceted nature of threats to the Western world and the United States of America in particular. Most recently the proliferation of Diasporas in Western target countries, their divided loyalties, and their personal and organizational links to clandestine foreign intelligence organizations and their derivation from conspiracy infused cultures, poses an unparalleled internal and global security threat. Dr. Campbell works extensively in this area to help defend and protect Western and U.S. interests, which is increasingly under, not only sustained terrorist attack as part of a clash of civilizations, but also in the war against intelligence organizations that has generally been conducted from within seeking to neutralize intelligence capability and capacity. Working with a variety of organizations and agencies, his specific work is withheld for security reasons.

PART I: CONFLICTS IN WATER RELATED ISSUES

CHAPTER 1: Water Security – A Primer

Introduction

This chapter is an overview of water security and the significant role it plays in the lives of people throughout the global community.[6] "Water Security is the protection of adequate water supplies for food, fiber, industrial, and residential needs for expanding populations, which requires maximizing water-use efficiency, developing new supplies, and protecting water reserves in event of scarcity due to natural, [man-made], or technological hazards."[7]

By definition the subject is highly complex and covers a great many areas through interdependency with critical infrastructure — those systems that drive life and the economy, which include energy, chemical industry, transportation, defense industry, public health, agriculture and food, and others. The security implications of water-related issues are fundamentally characterized by the uncertainty they introduce with respect to overall water availability, water security, food security, economic sustainability, and social stability. Although many countries such as the U.S. have invested and devoted large economic resources to water conveyance systems, storage, flood control defenses, reservoirs, dams, and other distribution systems, a growing population will inevitably increase this cost. Additionally, water also is complexly interdependent with many other areas such as transboundary resource and political issues, national and international security, emergency preparedness and incident planning, policy. Water is the primary driver that allows economic sustainability and thus fosters countries, cultures, and politics. Water has long been a source of conflict — from the Wild West days in the United States to current peace processes endeavors

---

[6] **Note:** *portions of this chapter were extracted from J. Tindall, and Campbell, A., "Water Security-National and Global Issues," ed. National Research Program (Denver: Government Printing Office, 2010).*

[7] Tindall, "Water Security-National and Global Issues."

in the Middle East. Aptly stated, nothing is more important than water and its security excepting life itself.

Water security is an industry that suffers and will continue to suffer from cognitive dissonance, i.e., a threat to self concept. As an example, the belief that Lake Mead or some other lake or reservoir will run dry of water is incompatible with the belief that good water management will solve our water problems. Understanding only the surface issues and that all possible scenarios derive from them is in conflict with the belief that the complexity of underlying issues related to cascading failure can cause more catastrophic failures than anticipated — a black swan event. The problem of cognitive dissonance arises because it is easier to make excuses and rationalize than it is to change behavior. Because water security is critical to human survival it is necessary to guard against cognitive dissonance, specifically at management levels.

Potable or clean freshwater availability is crucial to life and economic, environmental, and social systems — it sustains good health and quality of life. Earth's water is recirculated through the atmosphere to the subsurface via the hydrologic cycle; globally, however, the amount of freshwater is finite and makes up only 2.5 percent of Earth's water — locally to regionally, freshwater supplies are small and widely distributed, often creating a climate of contention for water resources and security. At local to regional levels, freshwater availability depends upon precipitation patterns, changing climate, and whether the source of consumed water comes directly from desalination, precipitation, and surface and/or groundwater. At a local to national level, threats to securing potable water sources increase with increasing population and economies. Driving a greater water demand are increasing living standards and urbanization, which increase average per-capita water consumption. Often, disruptions in sustainable supplies and distribution of potable water, as well as conflicts over water resources (often influenced by land use, human population, use patterns, technological advances, environmental impacts, management processes and decisions, transnational boundaries, etc.) become key security issues for local to national government officials. Consequently, Water Security is one of the key trends most likely to influence future global security.[8] Water

[8] J.A. Tindall, "Expected Key Trends Likely to Influence Global Security," *Global*

security is becoming ever more important due to population growth — global population tripled during the 20th century and demand for water increased nine-fold.[9]

Often the term global security is mentioned, yet is not defined. Perhaps the best definition available has been developed by the think tank, TinMore Institute (2010)[10]: "Global Security is "The peaceful intercourse of all nations for a parallel advancement of individual to societal well being and quality of life and, the actions taken by nations to guarantee shared sustainability, safety, and continuity that challenges mutual security." Threats and hazards to Global Security evolve from a Man-Made (Anthropogenic), Natural, Technological Triad and might include such actions as disruption of natural or commodity resources; failed or failing states; pandemics (swine flu or others); climate change; mass population migrations; civil unrest; and other unsuspected or surprising disturbances to national peace."[11]

Water Security should play a critical role in government planning — professionals should consider water shortages, stressed resources, poor water quality, distribution of potable water to users, and many other issues in water security, management, and sustainability. However, the roles of Water Security professionals are underscored by the uneven global distribution of freshwater and local to regional freshwater deficits caused by extraction exceeding available recharge — sustainability. Additionally, when water consumption exceeds 10 percent of renewable supplies, the source of supply is considered stressed. Where adequate and sustainable supplies influence health, food production, and economies, the demand for water grows fastest in areas of the world experiencing freshwater scarcity — where quality of life is minimal. Adding further stress to quality of life issues are inadequate sanitary living conditions coupled with contaminated water that could result in cancer, liver and kidney damage or failure, nervous system disorders, damage to

---

Security Affairs and Analysis (GSAAJ) 2, no. 3 (2008).

[9] D. Hinrichsen, Robey, B., and Upadhyay, U.D.,, "Solutions for a Water-Short World," in *Population Information Program*, ed. Johns Hopkins School of Public Health (Baltimore: Johns Hopkins, 1997).

[10] TinMore Institute, "A Definition of Global Security,"(2010), http://tinmore.com/security-def.php.

[11] Ibid

the immune system, birth defects, and water-borne diseases.[12] Additionally, certain naturally occurring water-borne chemicals are suspect carcinogens, such as arsenic in Bangladesh and West Bengal, India, where problems associated with high arsenic levels arose due to switching from surface to groundwater sources. Generally, regions of high density populations stress water resources; adding to this problem, increasing populations occur in areas where natural hazards — earthquakes, hurricanes, floods, and droughts — are most severe and known to disrupt potable water distribution.[13] Militarily, water resources and security are a primary component of environmental warfare; however, this text will not discuss significant details in that area.

Millions of people lack access to adequate potable water supplies and Government Officials are unable to appropriately manage and assess water resources due to insufficient information and knowledge. Furthermore, the United Nations[14] states that approximately one billion people are deprived of potable water due to mismanagement and depletion of water resources. Humans need drinking water daily, but deprivation of water, combined with the large volumes of water needed for food production lead to increased water-resource conflicts and negative effects on security. Without increasing water use or proper prioritization, it is unlikely that sufficient food can continue to be produced to meet the demands of global population growth.

Unfortunately, stressed and/or unsustainable resources, poor water quality, disrupted distribution and resulting destabilized population centers are becoming global trends, especially in large urbanized areas, often resulting in local to regional water shortages, provoking water-use problems and conflicts. Water shortages and increasing conflicts between supplies, distribution, and use and management signify the need to develop and impose processes for mitigating Water-Security issues. This necessitates that Water-Security Professionals and Water Resource Managers be called upon

---

[12] United Nations, "The Millennium Development Goals Report," (United Nations Department of Economic and Social Affairs, 2010).

[13] Hinrichsen, "Solutions for a Water-Short World."

[14] United Nations, "Water for People-Water for Life," in *The United Nations World Water Development Report* (Paris: United Nations, 2003).

to provide solutions to potential future problems; they must also be skilled in multiple disciplines. Problems in water security areas continue to grow; currently, 44-percent of the world's population faces water stress. The UN projects that by 2025 global freshwater stress on water use will increase significantly owing to increasing population , especially in northern Africa, Eurasia, the Middle East, and even the United States; and by 2050, nearly 5-billion people will be affected by freshwater scarcity.

Table 1: The Water Threats and Hazards Triad: The most common hazards affecting water supply and sustainability (Tindall and Campbell, 2009).

Man-made (Anthropogenic)	Natural	Technological
Terrorist*	Climate Change	Infrastructure Failure
War and Civil Unrest	Hurricanes	Hazardous Chemicals and Biological Material Events
Population Growth	Earthquakes	Malfunctions of IT and Equipment
Human error and poor assessment and resource allocation	Tsunamis	
	Droughts	
	Floods	
	Wildfires	
	Landslides	
	Volcanoes	

*Includes foreign and domestic cyber and industrial sabotage, particularly against/including SCADA (Supervisory Control and Data Acquisition) control systems.

Because most future population growth in the U.S. is projected to be within water-stressed areas, demand and distribution will likely remain a problem. Thirty-four percent of water is extracted for irrigation (in other countries agriculture water use is about 70 percent), but 47 percent of the water is consumed for other uses, particularly thermoelectric plant cooling in which water is returned back to the environment.[15]

Water-Security strategies depend upon appropriately jointly developed and implemented Water-Management plans and practices. Also, Water-Management practices necessary for Water Security must include plans for potable-water sustainability, proper waste-water and waste-disposal methods, distribution, water-use priorities, and water-resource development, as well as protection of storage and conveyance systems. Commonly, in developing countries, water supplies often are restricted by disparate water distribution, poor infrastructure, insufficient water quantity and quality, and excessive cost issues. Nevertheless, developing appropriate practices should be a first priority if public health and quality of life are to improve while reducing security concerns.[16] [17] Additionally, combined plans and practices must be designed to enhance economic development, deny instability, and address challenges to regional and international security. In this regard, local and national Water Security strategies improve foreign relations as related to transboundary water disputes and nationalist, minority, and ethnic aspirations that value the symbolic states' access to water.

The development and mitigation of Water-Security processes follow the Water Threats and Hazards Triad (WTHT) and represent common types of hazards affecting water supply and sustainability. As an example, an occurrence of a WTHT component against critical water infrastructures could prove disastrous to water supply and sustainability from a local to regional or national level.[18] From a

---

[15] S. Hutson, Barber, N., Kenny, J., Linsey, K., Lumia, D., and Maupin, M., "Estimated Use of Water in the United States in 2000," (Reston: Government Printing Office, 2004).

[16] J. Tindall, and Campbell, A., "Water Security - Nation State and International Security Implications," *Disaster Advances* 2, no. 2 (2009).

[17] Nations, "Water for People-Water for Life."

[18] Tindall, "Water Security - Nation State and International Security Implications."

Homeland Security perspective, an evaluation of these three primary-hazards reveals risks and vulnerabilities to the population at large: a net assessment — an 'all hazards' approach — in addressing water-security and protecting finite potable-water resources against various threats. WTHT components are a pressing concern for Public (Government) and Private (Corporate) Officials.

Terrorism – A Man-made Hazard:

Man-Made threats against water supplies and distribution systems currently are a major concern and much time is spent by agencies to prevent such attacks. Most likely, prior to the 9/11 terrorist attacks, Mohamed Atta scouted Hoover Dam as a potential, future target according to the FBI.[19] Such an attack would have been economically catastrophic to the U.S. and denotes why the U.S. Intelligence Community is working with federal agencies regarding critical water-resources and their security (see chapters 1, 7, 8, and 10). Additionally, Al-Qaeda strategists acquired manuals on water treatment and distribution systems that potentially could be used to plan an attack on these types of water systems. Although various experts have stated that the death of Usama Bin Laden ultimately means the death of Al Qaeda, it is in the end irrelevant since Al Qaeda likely will have already passed along gleaned information to other terrorist groups. About 50 terrorist groups are in operation worldwide, which includes potential terrorists groups not now recognized, but may soon be. It would be a fatal flaw to believe that terrorist groups do not share information and tactics and that they are all singular in purpose. Thus, terrorism is likely to increase, and enhanced technology complications, such as operations controlled by Supervisory Control and Data Acquisition (SCADA) valves that can be accessed via the Internet, make water systems more vulnerable. Similar type controls/valves are found in the electric power grid and nuclear plants, where nuclear power generation requires water for cooling. Also such an attack would be interdependent with energy, other resources, and hazards interdependence and would be

---

[19] Quinn Tamm, "Hoover Dam, Boulder City, Nevada, Mileage Review: Las Vegas, Nevada," (Las Vegas: Federal Bureau of Investigation, 2004).

considered a 'Black Swan' event. A potential terrorist attack is therefore illustrated.

Case Study: Potential Terrorist Attack Scenario against the Water Sector

The following potential terrorist attack is based on recent intelligence analysis and assessment of terrorist and drug cartel capabilities. The facilities, functions, and data are real; however, facility names and specific locations have been changed for security reasons.

The Enemy

Carlos Decena was in a constant rage after increasing drug-enforcement pressure from the U.S. and Mexican governments against the Los Zetas Cartel led to a raid that resulted in the death of his brother, wife, and son. With an almost unlimited army of drug smugglers and assassins at his command, Carlos vowed revenge. Having progressively shifted his business interests toward human rather than drug trafficking, Carlos was unconcerned about possible reprisal. He knew two primary things about his U.S. adversary: they were not agile enough to successfully defeat his tactics and strategy (they won only small victories on occasion); and constant bickering among law enforcement and intelligence agencies to justify funding clouded accurate intelligence assessments, which is why the Americans had not been able to prevent the 9/11 attacks — it was an inherent weakness he could use to advantage. Further, without border enforcement, the drug trade and sprouts of terrorism flourished on both sides of the border, which had allowed him and his co-conspirators to achieve their current capacity.

Three years previously, the Los Zetas cartel had assisted several Al Qaeda operatives in crossing the U.S./Mexico border with a variety of explosives, RPGs, and bio-weapons. He knew that anthrax was one of those bio-weapons. Since that initial meeting, Carlos had provided assistance many times. He also had discovered that Al Qaeda had worked with the Sinaloa Cartel before working with Los Zetas, and he speculated the terrorists already had a substantial arsenal cached in the United States. The cooperation of these groups provided the perfect opportunity for Carlos to strike. He developed a

strategy against U.S. targets based on discussions with Al Qaeda and intelligence they had gathered on U.S. critical infrastructure predating the 9/11 attacks. Carlos combined that knowledge and intelligence with his own, which was much more than the two countries' governments would admit.

Carlos had witnessed the failures of various terrorist operatives in the U.S. and knew they were insufficiently skilled and unprepared. He would not make the same mistake with the operatives of the new strategy; thus, in addition to training already received, for four months the 30 handpicked operatives selected for RPG, explosives, and other duties, were trained in all aspects of their missions and put through rigorous combative physical training at a secret Los Zetas training facility in Mexico. Each RPG operative was able to consistently hit moving and stationary, mock jeep-sized targets during darkness with great proficiency out to 200 yards using a European developed night-vision sight. Since nearly all operations would be in darkness, the handpicked operatives trained extensively for night operations. Also, each individual was capable of backpacking 60 pounds of equipment over tortuous terrain at an average pace of 8-15 minutes per mile for distances up to 10 miles (about 15 kilometers). The operatives studied schematics, locations, and facility and target layouts, and developed contingent response scenarios for 'what if' situations. Mockups of each facility were done to scale so each team could rehearse in real time overcoming obstacles such as fences, guards, etc. While not Navy Seals, they were conditioned and highly capable.

Each operative would carry a suppressed AK-47 and suppressed pistol for personal defense and each 2-4 man team would include a dedicated automatic-weapons specialist during mission execution and escape and evasion. Each RPG operative would carry one launcher and 6 HEAT (high-explosive anti tank) rounds. The launcher would be disposed of as soon after the attack as feasible, but the night vision device would be removed and used to maneuver during the escape and evasion phase. All drivers would additionally be equipped with night-vision goggles to avoid detection. All equipment was to be handled with gloves only to avoid individual trace by the FBI.

The operational goal was to cause economic devastation on a large scale and induce fear. The first step would be to initiate a diversionary attack that would keep law enforcement occupied while the remainder of the plan was carried out — multiple simultaneous attacks. In addition to working with the original Al Qaeda group, Carlos also joined forces with Al Qaeda in the Arabian Peninsula (AQAP); both groups had proven track records of mounting international operations. He met with his counterparts of Al Qaeda and AQAP — Muhamad Saif and Al-Madani Hazawiri respectively. Carlos mused how a common enemy made for successful collaboration. The brazenness of cartel members coupled with the technological and planning skills of Al Qaeda constituted a formidable foe.

All primary targets would be attacked simultaneously on 27 February 2012. Due to average precipitation events, this timing afforded the greatest likelihood of very wet conditions according to 50 year historical records. As the plan crystallized, Carlos had his own men cross the border with additional supplies Al Qaeda and AQAP operatives would need to carry out the mission and cache them in secure drug houses. Cartel members would provide basic logistics using code words, pre-assigned meeting times and places in typical terrorist cell-network procedures. Both Al Qaeda groups would provide explosives experts for the main targets; all were professional engineers who had obtained engineering degrees from various U.S. universities. All placed explosives would be wired with pre-paid cell phones that would be set off at distance with confirmed visual surveillance. In key target locations, Al Qaeda and AQAP operatives had moved in over a year earlier and went about daily activities — avoiding suspicion.

The Attack

Nearing the fateful day, the attack had begun much earlier with no fanfare; evidence of its effects had just struck. E-coli had been detected in numerous communities throughout the U.S., particularly in California and New York. A few days earlier, at 2 a.m., a crop-dusting plane had taken off from a small dirt runway about 40 miles northeast of the Valley of Zamora, Michoacán, Mexico with 3,000 pounds of E-Coli laden liquid. The experienced pilot wore night-

vision goggles as he sprayed commercial strawberry fields that would be harvested the same day for shipment to the U.S. Recent cutbacks in USDA inspectors and incentives ensured the fruit would get through. It was the time of year that almost all strawberries shipped to the U.S. were grown in Mexico with the majority of imports coinciding with the February attack date. These are the strawberries packed into clamshells bearing the familiar industry names and found in all major supermarket chains when it is not strawberry season in the U.S. As the outbreak spread, it was difficult to determine the origin, much like the May 2011 outbreak in Europe. The outbreak, as most agroterrorism attacks likely would, appeared accidental; intelligence agencies, CDC, USDA (U.S. Department of Agriculture) inspectors, and law enforcement groups were working overtime to track the outbreak's origin and avert a public-health disaster.

Coincidentally, a small group of AQAP operatives dropped off the interstate in the desert southwest U.S. This was a popular place for weekend outdoor getaways, and dirt bikes were popular; the area included farms, so agricultural equipment was a common sight. The operatives had scouted the place for weeks. Behind them they towed a small flatbed, canvas-covered trailer. Underneath the canvas was a small, three-seat, crop-dusting helicopter capable of 90 mph and 210-mile trips. The group of operatives worked their way down the dirt roads toward Bunkerville Ridge into a remote area in a shallow ravine filled with juniper. The location was desolate — no houses for miles; they were about 40 miles from the target reservoir. Just after dark, they donned protective gear, uncovered the helicopter and loaded it with the bio-weapon — the pilot, utilizing night vision goggles, made his way to about midway up the reservoir, quickly dumped his liquefied load in one short burst, and returned about an hour later. The operatives loaded the helicopter back on the small trailer, covered it, and, again utilizing night vision goggles, made it back to the interstate just prior to midnight and headed for a short layover before moving to the next target — a power plant. It was Wednesday, February 22.

That same morning, Kahleed boarded the Desert Star, train number 4 in Los Angeles, heading eastbound to Chicago. The bomb

was already onboard; the train would arrive at its destination in 43 hours.

In Louisiana, Acme Chemicals was shipping chlorine (used by industries in large quantities to treat wastewater) by tanker cars to Chicago and other locations where trains would pass through the northeast corridor. Al Qaeda and Los Zetas operatives lay in wait equipped with chemical masks, in Fairfax, Philadelphia, and New York. Obtaining the shipping schedules had not been difficult; there was no shortage of disgruntled employees or disillusioned Americans. The tanker cars in these locations were struck by RPG-7s utilizing 2-man teams with standard HEAT rounds capable of penetrating 260 mm (10 inches) RHA (rolled homogeneous armor) — more than sufficient to penetrate a chlorine tanker. All targets were within a 150-yard range and on portions of the track where the trains moved slowly. Each team lay in wait like a sniper — all locations had been and were under continued surveillance. One-half mile up track from each attack location, the rails were wired to explode to derail the train, which would ensure chlorine gas escaped over a larger area if the RPG attack did not derail the train. If the train were derailed due to the initial attack, the rail would be exploded after first response personnel arrived on scene. All targets would be at the specified location about 2 a.m. MST.

In a major rail yard in Chicago, operatives waited to explode an incoming chlorine tanker with explosives, which would close the yards to all operations. This would guarantee that most rail traffic was halted for several days due to chlorine gas leakage and fear of additional attacks. A shortage of chlorine for wastewater treatment would be assured.

In the northeast U.S., operatives had taken residence in a small rural home about one year earlier and had drilled into a major aqueduct that supplies a large populace with about one-half of its drinking water supply. The aqueduct leaked so much that it had been leaking into the basement of the home for some time. The home was already crumbling due to age and neglected repair, and the explosive charge would surely collapse it. As the water drained from the aqueduct further toward major cities, multiple locations would automatically collapse due to lack of buoyancy support from water flow, totally cutting the supply, likely for months.

In the northwestern U.S., several charges had been planted in weak areas of selected levees along portions of two adjoining rivers in a major agricultural area. The levees were over 100 years old and weak. Most of the surrounding delta is below sea level by as much as 15 feet. A report from the Army Corps of Engineers and the Federal Emergency Management Agency indicated a 60 percent chance of a levee breach in the fastest-growing populated areas, which would halt all development and inundate the surrounding area including local airports and adjacent towns, with about 12 to 20 feet of water. One to three breaches in the correct locations would cause cascading failures of many others. A levee breach would render the delta unstable, initiating further levee failure and subsequent flooding and also allowing saltwater intrusion into the delta, which is compounded by water diversions that remove 40 percent of the freshwater flowing into the delta. A breach would cause saltwater to be pulled south, flooding a natural water-storage area with 300 billion gallons of salt water. The storage area provides water for 23 million people to the south via aqueducts; it would be forced to shut down and operate on freshwater reserves. Ensuing water rationing could perhaps stretch reserves for 6 to 12 months. However, the delta would not return to normal for 2 to 3 years, which could leave agricultural areas to the south a wasteland — all water users would be forced to significantly reduce water use. Because agriculture and energy are the largest water users the results would be dire.

The earthen portion of a dam in the southeastern U.S. was another strategic target; it was exploded with shaped charges — the dam was at capacity due to heavy rains and subsequent flooding, much like the flooding of spring 2010. The dam controlled flow along a major river and was about 150 miles northeast of a population of one million. The dam had been a problem for years, almost since construction; along with its adjacent reservoir it resided upon a Karst bedrock foundation. Rain and snowmelt water contains dissolved carbon dioxide from the atmosphere, which, in solution, forms a weak carbonic acid. That acid attacks the limestone rock dissolving it, and thereby leading to the voids (empty spaces) within the rock formation. The water pressure of a reservoir above such a foundation exerts substantial hydraulic pressure that easily dislodges the cementing clays that are in the cracks and void spaces causing severe

weakening of the earthen dam and also results in large amounts of seepage.

Carlos had studied his targets well. He knew that failure would result in water quickly rushing through; cutting a trough about 600 feet wide and 200 feet deep, allowing the river to flow uncontrolled — at about 40 feet per second, the unstoppable wall of water would take about three days to reach the major population base, which would be buried beneath 20 feet of water. Because the dam is also a hydroelectric facility, a widespread loss of power occurred along with loss of communications, and response ability. Smaller towns along the route to the major population center were flooded as well. Heavy rains erased evidence of the operatives, making it almost impossible to track the terrorists. This was a well-developed strategy executed with purpose to achieve their goal.

One of the final targets, to stop water conveyance, was the power grid in the Southwestern United States. It was chosen due to its remoteness, general weakness, and the large cities such as Los Angeles and Las Vegas the grid services. Four power plant targets were chosen. The first two plants had relatively easy access and were only ten miles apart. The megawatt (MW) output of each plant is 2,270 NFC (nameplate capacity or, normal maximum output) from five generators and 1,848 MW from four generators. The combined annual total is 28.1 million MWh (mega watt hours). The other power plant targets were not far distant and had a three-generator output of 2,409 MW (17 million MWh annually) and four-generator output of 2,318 MW (14.8 million MWh annually). All plants were attacked at precisely 2 a.m. MST using four-man teams. The primary targets were the generators adjacent to the switch yard of the plants. Remaining HEAT rounds from each RPG-7 were fired into the nearest boilers or turbines--or approaching security vehicles that may not have been taken out prior to the RPG attack. Time allowed for each attack from initiation of first firing was just under two minutes. One plant was approached from the water side, which is remote and unrestricted.

Two days after the attacks the following newspaper article appeared:

The Nation's Daily
Wednesday February 29, 2012

Terrorist Attacks Pale 9/11 in Destructive Results

By CLIVE JOHNSON

A continuing saga - yesterday, Al Qaeda and Al Qaeda of Arabian Peninsula (AQAP) claimed responsibility for the recent wave of terrorist attacks.

It has been confirmed that the E-coli outbreak in the U.S. was a result of poisoning strawberries in Mexico. Then, on February 27 at dusk, a passenger train originating in Los Angeles exploded at a Chicago terminal killing 305 people and injuring 200 others. Darkness created confusion and disorientation as emergency responders worked feverishly. At about 4 a.m. EST, a chlorine tanker in a nearby railway yard exploded halting rescue efforts, forcing evacuations from homes, and killing over 1,000 people so far as a result of chlorine gas escape.

Tragically, three chlorine tankers and the trains pulling them derailed in Fairfax, Philadelphia, and New York, causing mass evacuations with over 2,000 dead in those locations at last report. Out west, four power plants were attacked, destroying their generators and some boilers. The northernmost power plant damage resulted in power shut off to eight western states. While no immediate loss of life has been reported, the systems will be out of commission for at least several weeks, potentially months, and may be at minimal production for the near future. Los Angeles and other major southwestern cities will be forced to endure rolling blackouts for an indefinite time. According to an FBI spokesperson, transformers at about two dozen power substations in the northeast and southwest had been shot with what appeared to be 50 caliber armor piercing rounds, destroying them; several transformers would require four to six months for replacement, making it necessary to re-route power.

In the northwest, a network of levees was destroyed, flooding a major city and adjacent regional airport with 20 feet of water and destroying a natural delta, inundating it with sea water. The delta and adjoining reservoir supply water to over 20 million people to the south. The agricultural sector will receive no water as reserves will be targeted for the human population at large. The affected area will become a wasteland. In the southeast, a dam was destroyed resulting in flooding of a large metro area greater than one-million in population with 15 feet of water and four smaller towns. Death tolls in both locations and damages have not yet been assessed.

Meanwhile, a bio-weapons material, unidentified at this time, has caused the death of hundreds in the southwest and has been tracked to a large reservoir, which has been shut down and may be out of operation for two to three years. The water and hydropower from the reservoir comprises about 50 percent of the regional use — effects on transportation, agriculture, business, public health, and other areas will likely be catastrophic and cannot yet be measured. It also affected agriculture in the region; all agricultural operations have been closed per government order.

The scope of the attack, based on analysis from the Department of Homeland Security appears to be centered on the water sector and its interdependence with other critical infrastructure and the economy. An anonymous source said the agency had been warned of such large-scale attack events since the 9/11 attacks, but neglected to act on mitigation efforts because they did not believe terrorists had the capacity and capability to carry out such a multiple-pronged attack. Unlike other terrorist attacks, which the U.S. appeared to be fortunate to prevent or halt, each of these individual attacks appears to have been successful. Ironically, not one terrorist has been captured and intelligence and law enforcement agencies have no leads. They are now classifying the series of attacks as Black Swan Monday.

Based on a comparative analysis of the 2003 New York City blackout that affected eight states and 45 million people for only two days, and which caused $7 to 10 billion in damage, TinMore Institute estimated damage amounts for the series of terrorist attacks at about $1.4 trillion but, as with most catastrophic events, suggests the amount is likely to climb, far surpassing effects from the 9/11 attack.

From other sources, it appears the terrorists crossed the U.S./Mexico border near the Tohono O'odham Reservation in Arizona. For years Tribal leaders have petitioned the federal government to help them beef up their law enforcement capabilities, themselves warning of such a possibility. The formation of over 30 drug gangs within the tribe has not helped matters. Elsewhere, Congressman Ortiz of New Mexico is sponsoring a bill to completely close the U.S./Mexico border at all non-official crossings, completing the border fence, and immediately enforcing all immigration and employment laws. "If we had already fulfilled our responsibility as we promised, this tragedy would have been averted. It's truly tragic that it requires a nation to experience such a reprehensible event to do what should have already been done. What are we going to tell the victims' families?" . . . .

Intelligence reports and capability analysis from within the U.S. and from other countries suggest that such an attack is entirely feasible and that several terrorist groups have not only the capability and weapons, but the financial means to carry them out. As an example, the U.S. Department of Homeland Security warned (July 2011) thousands of U.S. utility plants that they could be the targets of "violent extremists." Factually, such individuals have obtained insider positions "and might use those positions to wage physical and cyber attacks on behalf of Al-Qaeda.[20] Officials found evidence among materials recovered during the May 2011, U.S. military operation in Pakistan that killed Usama Bin Laden. The report further stated, "Based on the reliable reporting of previous incidents, we have high confidence in our judgment that insiders and their actions pose a significant threat to the infrastructure and information systems of U.S. facilities."[21] In 2010, U.S. officials arrested an alleged Al-Qaeda recruit — the American man had worked at five U.S. nuclear power plants in the Pennsylvania area after passing federal background checks.

This potential attack illustrates the dependency of water on other sectors. What would be the results be of a successful attack? What might the public expect? Generally, a variety of areas would be affected, but only a few will be discussed for the case study. These areas would include power generation, water supply, transportation, communication, industry, and security.

[20] B. Ross, Schwartz, R., and Chuchmach, M., "New Terror Report Warns of Insider Threat to Utilities," *ABC News The Blotter*(2011), http://abcnews.go.com/Blotter/terror-alert-warns-insider-threat-infrastructure/story?id=14118119.

[21] Ibid

The damage to power generation facilities would likely be difficult and costly to repair. The initial outage could cause a reboot of system computers for other infrastructures that could result in many cascading failures, and power plants would automatically go into safe mode to prevent damage due to potential overload, taking them essentially offline. All homes, businesses, and industries not immediately affected would be required to reduce consumption.

A loss of power would cause loss of water pressure, which can cause potential contamination due to back flow, as well as reduce capabilities of emergency response groups such as firefighters to effectively respond. Boiling-water advisories would be likely since water treatment plants and wastewater systems would be unable to adequately treat water. Restaurants in affected areas would be closed due to potential health hazards from spoilage and possible contaminated water. Many wastewater treatment facilities have no backup power supply, which can cause dumping of raw sewage into local waters. The 2003, New York City blackout serves as an example

Transportation electric-rail systems such as those in Los Angeles, New York, and other locations would be stopped until power could be restored. Passenger screenings at airports would be affected and might cause the airport to temporarily close; in addition, electronic ticketing, baggage claim, facility services, and other airport businesses would also be affected. All of these impacts will result in flight delays and backups at other airports. All night-time landings will be halted. Gas stations will be unable to pump gas, leaving automobiles and transport trucks (semi's) without fuel. Some cars will drive until they run out of gas and will be abandoned, hindering traffic. Stop lights in affected towns and cities will stop, creating congestion and accidents. Gas prices would soar exorbitantly in affected areas since supply would be very limited. Affected oil refineries would be shut down, creating further pressure on gasoline supplies and potentially create a broader energy emergency.

Communications will slow. Cell phones and similar devices will only work until the battery goes dead with no power to recharge. Backup generators at cellular sites will run out of fuel and then the cell tower will cease operating, leaving only land lines for communication — and these will be quickly overwhelmed. Cable television, radio, and Internet communications will stop, excepting dial-up modems, which predominantly exist in rural areas. This will limit public information and cause mass panic. Also, depending on Internet backbone services, Internet communications well outside the immediately affected areas could be impacted.

Industrial services, manufacturing plants, and other organizations directly in the affected area will be immediately closed or work slowed due to supply problems. For those factories that produce parts for other sectors, supply lines will be interrupted, creating a shortage. The need to conserve energy until power is completely restored will result in minimal output of manufactured goods and services. Pharmacies in immediately affected areas will be forced to close, likely causing life threatening events for critical medications for illnesses such as diabetes, high blood pressure, mental illness, epilepsy, and so forth. Hospitals, which could face a personnel shortage, will also be affected within the facility, by water problems, transportation hassles, and myriad other problems.

In regard to security, looting will likely require large amounts of overtime by law enforcement and emergency response personnel. Traffic congestion due to traffic light outage will cause delayed response, and streets may be crowded with workers unable to get home or to shelter, further increasing gridlock. The use of candles due to blackout conditions will cause fires that could spread quickly if response is delayed due to cascading problems related to traffic gridlock. Emergency generator failure for some groups could cause severe communications and emergency number services problems.

Damage costs will soar due to lost production, loss of work for many workers, overtime wages for others, food spoilage in major grocery stores, and indirect costs due to other factors. For example, some companies will resort to complete shutdown, which will disrupt deliveries to customers and from suppliers and thus, loss of commodities. Because of the just-in-time production scheduling that is timed to meet planned production and minimize or eliminate cost of inventory, almost every sector that provides products to consumers, from the local grocery store to the auto-supply store, will face potentially serious product shortages. Grocery stores that are open will quickly empty of supplies, as will many other stores. Produce and similar goods will quickly perish. Because the average logical supply chain is 1,500 miles from source to consumer in the

U.S., elasticity of operations will be gone and critical shortages of food, medicines, gas, and other products will be likely. Additionally, for some manufacturing plants such as chemical, oil, or steel, flaring of products can occur, creating massive clouds of smoke, potentially harmful.

This potential attack illustrates that policy must be stronger (see chapter 16) and should involve more stakeholders than the usual, such as law enforcement and intelligence agencies, defense groups, and others because of the critical nature of the resource. The attack demonstrates interdependency due to 'geographic concentration' (the physical location of critical assets in sufficient proximity to each other that they are vulnerable to disruption by the same, or through successive regional events). As an example, over 38 percent of the U.S. chlorine production is located in coastal Louisiana and over 35 percent of U.S. freight railcars pass through Illinois, primarily around Chicago. Business interruptions, mass evacuations, and other economic interdependencies abound as well. This scenario represents but a mere fraction of catastrophic events that could result from interdependent, cascading events of a hazard disruption of water and potentially related sectors.

Natural Threats to Water Security

Hurricanes — Hurricane Katrina (2005) caused large loss of life, ruptured levees, and created serious environmental and water quality consequences.

Earthquakes — Scientists predict a major earthquake will hit Los Angeles in the future, an event that could sever (1) the Colorado River Aqueduct, and/or (2) the California Aqueduct supplying water from Lake Mead in Nevada. These two distribution systems supply potable water to 18 million residents within metropolitan Los Angeles.

Wildfires — The short and long-term effects of wildfires should be serious considerations for any water-security program. This may be particularly true due to 100 years of fire suppression in the U.S., where large fires burn about 6,000,000 acres in drier years (National Interagency Fire Center). The Hayman Fire in Colorado in 2002, the largest fire in Colorado's history (138,000 acres), seriously degraded the water quality of Cheeseman and Strontia Springs Reservoirs —

primary water sources for metropolitan Denver, which required eight million dollars over four years to remove debris, replace culverts, build sediment dams, and seed slopes for restoration. For instance, deforestation of hillsides by fire promotes flooding and debris flow during wet periods.

Contaminants — Heavy rains and flooding could create particularly severe water contamination problem that can be fatal. E-coli infiltrated water pipes following torrential rains in Walkterton, Ontario, Canada; 7 people died and over 2,300 became seriously ill after contracting food-poisoning bacteria.[22] In 1993, dozens died and an estimated 400,000 developed chronic illnesses due to the parasite cryptosporidium, which contaminated the water supply of Milwaukee, Wisconsin, after heavy rainfall.[23]

Climate Change — Water Security strategies need also to include events related to extreme drought. In 1995, a severe drought spread from central, eastern, and western Texas and New Mexico into Arizona and parts of California, Nevada, Utah, Colorado, Oklahoma, and Kansas. Interdependent impacts of the drought were dramatic — water restrictions increased in many cities, forcing residents to cut usage about 25 percent; winter wheat conditions in 19 states were very poor; wind and insect damage significantly affected crops; a shortage of hay throughout the region reached disastrous proportions, forcing ranchers to sell cattle at the lowest prices in ten years; and agricultural losses for cotton, wheat, feed grains, cattle, corn and agriculturally related industries such as harvesting, trucking, and food processing in Texas alone reached five billion dollars.[24] Economically, reduced supplies of irrigation water led to decreased vegetable production with related job and income losses; food prices increased as much as 22 percent in response to the lower production levels for milk, meat, produce, and other foodstuffs; and prices for

---

[22] Kim Vicente and Klaus Christoffersen, "The Walkerton E. Coli Outbreak - a Test of Rasmussen's Framework for Risk Management in a Dynamic Society," *Theoretical Issues in Ergonomics Science* 7, no. No. 2 (2006).

[23] P.S. Corso, Kramer, M.H., Blair, K.A., Addiss, D.G., Davis, J.P., and Haddix, A.C., "Cost of Illness in the 1993 Waterborne Cryptosporidium Outbreak Milwaukee, Wisconsin," *Emerging Infectious Disease* 9, no. 4 (2003).

[24] D.A. Wilhite, and Vanyarkho, O., ed. *Pervasive Impacts of a Creeping Phenomenon* (London: Routledge Press,1999).

gasoline, diesel, and liquefied petroleum rose 15 percent above previous levels. Fires raged throughout the region and in Colorado alone burned 262,009 ha (647,440 acres). Total regional drought impacts were estimated at $10–15 billion, although it is difficult to quantify many social and environmental impacts.[25] This extended drought demonstrates the significant level of vulnerability, the diversity of impacts, and the effects such impacts can have on a myriad of water-security risks.

Technological Hazards

Technological hazards include, but are not limited to, biohazards and hazardous materials incidents and nuclear power plant failures. Generally, little or no warning precedes these incidents. Victims may not know they have been affected until years later. For example, health problems caused by hidden toxic waste sites — Love Canal, near Niagara Falls, New York — surfaced years after initial exposure. Perhaps the most well known is the Chernobyl nuclear reactor disaster, April 1986 in Ukraine, that resulted from a low-power systems test and subsequent severe release of radioactivity following a massive power excursion that destroyed the reactor.

Hazards Interdependence

Understanding the interdependency and complexity of water to other life-support systems (critical infrastructures) is important. The interconnectedness of these threats and the crucial role water plays in life systems is illustrated in Figure 1.1, which shows three levels of critical infrastructure in order of importance (Levels 1 to 3). Level 1 Critical Infrastructure is one of the three most important (Level 1, Figure 1.1). If a natural disaster were to affect water infrastructure, failures would potentially occur in all levels — cascading failure. Depending on the intensity and duration of a disaster, all Level 3 Critical Infrastructures could be affected. The interdependence of agriculture & food production (Level 3: Figure 1.1) is particularly vulnerable to water shortages from all infrastructure levels — production to distribution.

---

[25] Ibid.

Energy generation is often dependent on water — hydroelectric power generation requires a constant water supply, as is the case with the Hoover Dam in the U.S. and the Bhakra Nangal Dam in India. All nuclear power plants require a steady source of water for cooling. Failures of one Critical Infrastructure could adversely affect others, especially agriculture & food and public health (Figure 1.1). For example, if water levels in a reservoir fall because of drought, there is insufficient water to turn turbines and generate electricity; an example of cascading failure. To strengthen water-security strategies and processes, a dual strategy is necessary that will (1) monitor infrastructure and supplies and (2) assess, understand, and manage water resources to avoid the threat of water related security and conflict concerns. Also, effective monitoring of water scarcity, energy, and environmental degradation can aid water managers. In the Homeland Security arena, intelligence estimates also should factor water security into threat assessments and consider the need for creating specialized water security data-collection platforms.

Water Security Activities

International agencies, such as the World Bank, are well aware of the seriousness of Water-Security issues and the history of water conflicts and consequences on humans. Since ancient times, water has been used as a weapon through the destruction of water resources and distribution facilities.[26] However, conflicts within and between countries in attempts to secure ample clean water still occur. As an example, a noted editor of a leading Pakistani paper stated: "If, in order to resolve our water problems, we have to wage nuclear war with India, we will."[27] Such statements demonstrate how water-use and actual or perceived ownership conflicts may create social and political disorder and serious security risks to a region or a country and international law has proven inadequate in defending the equal use of shared water supplies. Often, such conflicts become

---

[26] Herbert C. Young, *Understanding Water Rights and Conflicts* (Denver: BergYoung, 2006).

[27] Tufail Ahmad, "Nuclear War over Water Disputes between India and Pakistan?," *Kashmir Global*, July 20 2009.

zero-sum disputes and involve cultural, tribal, or religious, and regional and/or transnational victims.[28] Further increasing tensions, the control of water supplies are viewed as symbolizing superiority or advantage over a real or imaginary enemy.

Figure 1.1: U.S. Threat Schema denoting basic interdependencies between critical infrastructure key resources (Source: author; used by permission).

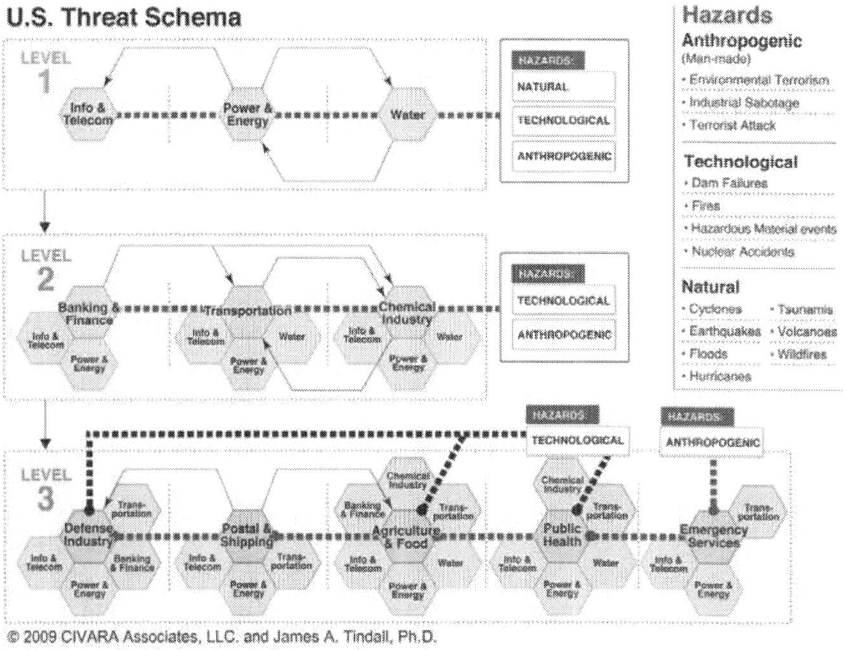

A few examples of water security issues and conflicts include: An International Alert identified 46 countries with a combined population of 2.7 billion in which both climate change and water-related crises may create a high risk of violent conflict;[29] whereas 56 countries represent an additional 1.2 billion people at high risk of political instability.

---

[28] Tindall, "Water Security - Nation State and International Security Implications."

[29] Dan Smith, and Vivekananda, Janani, "A Climate of Conflict: The Links between Climate Change, Peace and War," *International Alert*(2007), http://aquadoc.typepad.com/waterwired/files/climate_conflict.pdf.

A 2004-2006 Somalia/Ethiopia dispute over water wells and pastoral lands left nearly 250 people killed and many more injured. A three-year drought led to the violence, aggravated by the lack of effective government and central planning.[30]

In African Burkina Fasso in 2007, declining rainfall led to growing clashes among animal herders and farmers with competing water needs.[31] Two thousand people (including 1,400 children) were forced to flee their homes because of water disputes.

U.S. agencies, such as the Department of Energy, Department of Defense, Federal Bureau of Investigation, National Oceanic and Atmospheric Administration (NOAA), Environmental Protection Agency (EPA), Department of Homeland Security (DHS), and others, understand and acknowledge the importance of Water Security and the results of neglect to the Nation and individual States. These agencies are attempting to effectively link water security to critical infrastructure protection (CIP) and intelligence gathering capabilities through merging the intelligence cycle (plan, collect, process, analyze, and disseminate information — 'intelligence fusion' in center, right diagram - Figure 1.2), intelligence sources, and fixed assets of critical infrastructure (dams, facilities, operations, road and water ways, etc.). Although increasing in complexity, CIP also considers detection, prevention, response, and mitigation as interdependent components of this process (center outer and left upper (green) diagrams - Figure 1.2), thus increasing complexity. The process effectively merges intelligence sources and assets, and CIP, as well as considering organization type for both collection and/or security (Figure 1.2, bottom left). Additionally, further effectiveness is achieved by adding resource data and information collected and analyzed by other federal agencies such as NOAA, NASA, and others. Merging the intelligence cycle, intelligence sources, critical infrastructure assets and their protection, resource data and other information is a complex process (Figure 1.2); however, implementation is crucial for protecting billion-dollar infrastructures

---

[30] BBC News, "Dozens Dead in Somalia Clashes,"(2004), http://news.bbc.co.uk/2/hi/africa/4073063.stm.

[31] United Nations Office Commissioner for Human Rights, "Burkina Faso-Innovation and Education Needed to Head Off Water War," ed. United Nations Office for the Coordination of Humanitarian Affairs (Rome: United Nations, 2008).

like Hoover Dam and favors a strategic rather than tactical approach. The entire process also incorporates security convergence, operational risk management, operational resiliency, and other factors that will not be discussed.

Figure 1.2: Critical Infrastructure Protection (CIP) within the Intelligence Process (Source: Author, used by permission).

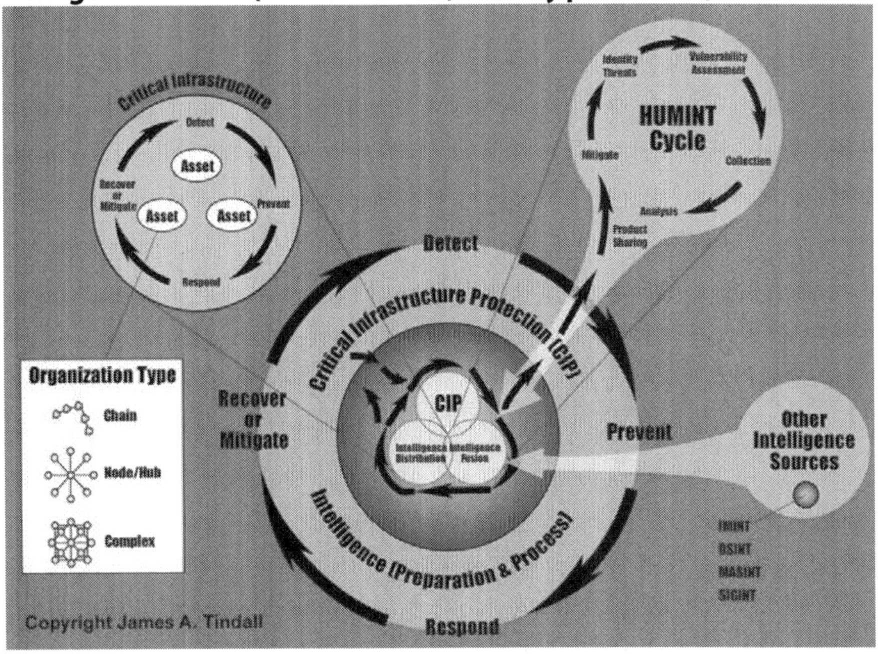

Both the federal government and private sector should anxiously engage in efforts to improve the understanding and effective management of water resources around the globe to help address scientific and management concerns regarding water resources supply, sustainability, protection, and security. Investigation of the complex interdependency of water with life-support systems such as power and energy, agriculture and food, and public health and how these are affected by natural disasters should likely be at the top of the priority list. These systems and/or assets, very vulnerable to the water threats and hazards triad, are essential for public health and safety, the functioning and sustainability of society, the economy, and the security of nations. Various federal agencies such as NOAA, NASA, DOE, DOI, and others continue to

examine interdependencies of ecosystem functions, energy and water, and integrated information (information coupled from multiple fields of science) of all hazards to develop solutions to water-security problems. The goal is to create new products, such as mathematical models, that increase resource security and are useful for reducing loss of life and property, as well as environmental risks, and their impact and relations on and to other fields of science such as climatology, hydrology, ocean sciences, seismology, volcanology, geology, biology, etc. A primary goal is to reduce the vulnerability of people and communities at risk from hazards by working with partners throughout all sectors of society. As an example, the TinMore Institute (www.tinmore.com), a global resources think tank, has developed methods that forecast climate, water, and energy use, as well as consequences on economic, production, and related sectors for seven years forward, which is a significant risk mitigation tool and will help in this area.

Conclusions

Water Security is of primary importance, from local to national levels, and is necessary to promote global stabilization and increased quality of life. Local to Global Officials influential in decision-making processes realize and acknowledge the need for secure water sources. Water security and sustainability problems related to climate change, desertification, growing populations, disparate water distribution, man-made threats, as well as distribution management and hazards, particularly wildfires, are increasing stress on global water supplies. Water conservation methods and operations and technology such as new dams, cloud seeding, desalination plants, and underground water storage will likely be insufficient to meet the demands of a growing global population and increased energy and agricultural demands which are resulting in increased tension between individuals and nations. Because water supplies are finite, the potential for water-related conflicts are likely to increase and become more acute. The need for transboundary water sharing, which has been a constant source of contention since territorial times in the arid Western U.S. and recently in the drought-stricken Eastern United States, and in the Middle East, is now a global issue.

The study and development of strategies and counter measures to ensure water sustainability and security requires a fusion of scientific and analytical skills and tradecraft, as well as increased awareness by the public, resource managers, and government entities. Programs, including those promoting institutional capacity-building and networking, education for research, continuing professional education, and other activities targeting training and increasing knowledge for citizens demonstrate the fusion of water with national security. The U.S. military is at the forefront of these issues providing higher-level education and training, most notably at the U.S. Naval Postgraduate School. National security planners, analysts, and agencies are increasingly studying the challenge of threats to water supplies and infrastructure from hazards and transnational terrorists.[32, 33] One example is the Water Infrastructure Security Enhancements (WISE) Project funded by EPA, an effort to get all water utilities serving populations of more than 3,300 to voluntarily perform vulnerability and risk assessments and take preventive measures against possible attacks and other hazards.

The U.S. government could provide world leadership on water security and sustainability issues through science, education, and international programs. Research activities within various federal agencies are well suited to solve many scientific, technical, management, and integrated problems encountered within this area and myriad interdependencies among other sectors. Universities and research institutes could further promote and develop water security as a distinct discipline, thus expanding public education; intelligence agencies should be further tasked to integrate water-security issues and define them within the context of national security. A cooperative and concerted effort between the public, policy makers, planners, managers, science agencies, security and intelligence groups, and law enforcement will be required to develop solutions to water-security threats. Ensuring and protecting water supplies is a complex issue that is critical to national and international security interests and the health, welfare, and security of all.

---

[32] Claudia Copeland, "Terrorism and Security Issues Facing the Water Infrastructure Security Sector," (Washington, DC: Library of Congress, 2009).
[33] Carl Behrens, and Holt, Mark, "Nuclear Power Plants-Vulnerability to Terrorist Attacks," (Washington, DC: Library of Congress, 2005).

CHAPTER 2: Water and Global Security: Key 21st Century Trends

Executive Summary

In this century new challenges to security likely will manifest themselves more frequently. Aspects such as security convergence and operational resilience are examples of public and private sector components that will be vital for ensuring continuity of operations. In this sense, security should be thought of as sustainability, not merely physical elements — there can be no security without sustainability. The fundamental key will be to maintain security processes that are flexible and adaptable and that incorporate continuity goals and strategies. These processes should be based on an all hazards approach that considers disruption from the primary hazards — man-made (anthropogenic), natural, and technological (see chapter 1). There are four major security implications: (1) to hedge against uncertainty; (2) to curtail outdated and less useful security concepts; (3) to explore new security concepts and be prepared to be rapidly adaptable; and (4) to adapt through time via changing technologies. These implications will be applied against relations with not only current security issues, but far more significant issues that relate to water security and critical infrastructure, mass sustainability, and the primary hazards that can affect them. Addressing these issues requires a heightened flexibility and adaptability that could prove problematic for hierarchal organizations.

The new global landscape and the effects of economic, trade, social, and other issues, particularly water security, power and energy, and agricultural and food production in relation to the overall scope will likely result in reaching and perhaps surpassing operational resiliency boundaries much faster, which could result in a rapid cessation of operations. In such an environment, being able not only to respond, but also to anticipate and diffuse problems before they reach the point of collapse, will be of paramount importance to agency, government, and organizational security to maintain continuity of operations. Therefore, it would seem pertinent that the relation of strategic, complex issues that can affect continuity of operations from an all-hazards approach be well understood. An excellent example is the British Petroleum oil leak in the Gulf of Mexico that began in April 2010. How far-reaching will the environmental effects be? How will this affect the U.S. national economy since within about two months the fishing, shrimp, and recreational industries were catastrophically affected? More importantly, what are the ramifications on U.S. Homeland Security?

Introduction

This chapter reviews the critical security issues, challenges, and threats that may likely emerge over the next five to 12 years. The security and responses of a government, agency, or other organizations will be influenced by key trends in global economic and commerce transformations, resource shortages such as food and water, changes in security from the physical to the technological, and trends in technology direction, as well as strategic goals.

In this century, new challenges to security will manifest themselves on a more frequent basis than in the past due to population growth, which causes greater security needs and increases risks and vulnerabilities. For the near term, probable opponents include organized crime, terrorists, or nation states who can successfully counter security solutions directly; challenges related to critical infrastructure security from various hazards; and large-scale effects on resource sustainability such as water, agricultural, and other resource scarcity. These could cause unconventional security situations reaching beyond current security and other defense role plans developed for issues such as military intervention during times of civil unrest.

An organization must be prepared to counter many direct and indirect threats to security. Because today's threats are not necessarily the same as future threats, current security solutions likely will be ill-suited to sustain continuity of operations. Security convergence (the convergence of physical and information security including complex interdependencies of many components throughout all organizational functions and departments) and operational resiliency (the ability to adapt to risk that affects its core

operational capacities: business processes, systems and technology, resources, and people) are examples of components that may become vital to ensure continuity of operations. Future adversaries will learn from the past and will likely confront us in very different ways, using means that will defeat or circumvent existing and new technologies or processes.[34]

New challenges will emerge not only in regard to current security issues but stemming from changing natural, geopolitical, demographic, social, and economic drivers. Even a small group of individuals with relatively modest capabilities and budget could have a significant impact on an organization or government. For example, what consequences would a bio attack on Hoover Dam cause since it provides water to about 22 million people and electricity to about seven million? Natural disasters of a variety of magnitudes and intensities could also have catastrophic consequences as was demonstrated by Hurricane Katrina. Technological disasters such as the British Petroleum oil leak in the Gulf of Mexico in 2010, Chernobyl, and similar disasters will have far-reaching and long-term consequences.

The fundamental key is to include and maintain security processes that will be both flexible and adaptable and that incorporate continuity goals and strategies. These processes should be based on an all-hazards approach that considers all possibilities of disruption from the primary hazards (man-made, natural, and technological). The very context of security will alter dramatically in the future as more advanced methods and technologies are developed to sustain continuity of operations. As an example, technologies that relate to Supervisory Control and Data Acquisition (SCADA) controls for infrastructure systems have already increased our vulnerability. Inclusive in this must be the development of strategies for the unanticipated such as a Black Swan event so that security maintains a proactive rather than reactive posture. Also, it should be noted that development of new technologies could make us even more vulnerable due to cyber warfare and other issues.

---

[34] B. et al. Jackson, *Aptitude for Destruction, Volume 1: Organizational Learning in Terrorist Groups and Its Implications for Combating Terrorism.* (Rand Corporation, 2005 2005).

Sustainability of agencies, corporations, governments, and countries are more important than the physical security process as a whole. This is well illustrated by the current global economic crises, as problems relating to employment and shortage of resources, particularly water and food, spread. Failure to anticipate these challenges and to change security processes commensurately could inexorably result in erosion of the ability to protect organizations and people. The majority of security efforts in the past and presently generally include a focus on guards, gates, and guns (the 3Gs model), but these physical security methods are ineffective against advanced technology used in terrorist and criminal activities. For example, rather than break in and steal property, organized criminals and terrorists are utilizing computer technology to hold firms at ransom and steal identities, as well as for other reasons. An example is a denial of service (DOS) attack in which a firm's servers are attacked by another server in an attempt to create an overload, or a distributed denial of service attack (DDOS) where multiple servers are used to attack simultaneously. The attack could also be achieved by infection with a virus that requires an encryption key to unlock. A ransom is then demanded to stop the attacks so the firm can get the encryption key and continue operations. These codes are becoming more malicious and more difficult to stop and have forced many firms to pay millions of dollars.[35]

Related attacks include cyber attacks on critical infrastructures such as the power grid and on SCADA systems that control flow of water and its distribution. However, sustainability of security personnel, knowledge, and other defense systems and processes are lagging. Examples include protection of critical infrastructure, but more importantly the sustainability of large masses that affect continuity in not only the affected areas but quite possibly stabilization of a region. For example, climate change could increase the dependency of developing countries on imports and exacerbate existing focus of food insecurity in many countries around the world.[36] Food insecurity is a partial result of water security from

---

[35] ZDNet Staff, "Beware of Ransomware, Firm Warns," *ZD Net*(2006), http://news.zdnet.com/2100-1009-6097741.html.

[36] Amgad Elmahdi, "Wbfs Model: Strategic Water and Food Security Planning on National Wide Level." (IGU-2008 Water sustainability commission),

various natural causes including climate change, mismanagement of water resources, and lack of developing new supplies, resource sustainability, and so forth. These problems exist and are escalating. Agriculture and food production is intensely interdependent with water management and its security. The impact is generally observed in four areas: (1) food availability (including production and trade); (2) accessibility; (3) usefulness; and (4) stability of supply, which is generally associated with water availability. Food and water-security systems are diverse in scale, structure, and time, making them difficult to protect.

More importantly, management of this now global-security system is very complex due to the uncontrolled nature of man-made, particularly terrorism, and natural hazards. The assessment of the effectiveness of management decisions is difficult due to interdependencies and complexity of water-systems components (agricultural, environmental, physical, and socio-economic). Further complexity could occur in instances where water and food resource management is decentralized and performed by multiple management entities.

Key Trends Affecting Security

There appear to be four key trends that are parallel and interrelated and that continue to drive changes for security: (1) geopolitical, (2) demographic and social, (3) globally interrelated markets, and (4) technological.

The geopolitical revolution prompted the collapse of the Soviet Union and the emergence of China as a major global economic actor. It significantly impacts manufacturing, economics, energy and water use, and other areas in developed economies. And, sustainable partnerships with Middle East allies and global economic and national security impacts due to violence in areas such as Iraq and Afghanistan and spill over into adjacent countries and regions. Demographic and social pressures on public and natural resource systems, especially agricultural production and water — with special emphasis on water security — add to the complexity of security

---

http://works.bepress.com/amgad_elmahdi/24.

issues. These changes have become dramatically apparent in the Darfur region of the Sudan, in northeast Africa[37], the Middle East, and the Americas and are beginning to cause shifts in both resources and global tensions that could ultimately impact security (the security of large-scale populations) for many global corporations and governments. This impact is due to interdependent effects within the economy, political and business partners/cooperators, accompanying and corresponding trade and economic issues, the growing scarcity of global resources (food, water, and energy), and the systems they directly affect. The emergence of a global, interdependent marketplace has stretched the capability of present security infrastructure. The Internet has paved the way for much of this emergence and continues to change at almost an exponential rate[38]. Technology has transformed industry-based economies into information-based economies and revolutionized global manufacturing bases, defense and other industry supply chains, labor markets, SCADA controls for critical infrastructure, and other interdependent systems.

These key trends should be used in strategic security, policy, and organizational actions taken by major corporations and governments. The current global economic state is a key example of interdependence between the four trends. Intertwined significantly within this trend is governmental policy directed at critical resources, but which is poorly developed with little strategic direction or focus and very partisan — for example, the energy crises in regard to oil and alternative fuels, as well as water and its sustainability and security. The decisions made today about strategic security direction, whether as a corporation or a government, will have tremendous future implications.

[37] Irin News Staff, "Sudan: More Displacement Amid Continuing Violence in Darfur "(2007), http://www.alertnet.org/thenews/newsdesk/IRIN/17ac4df0d56400f5b6341a7b17024e02.htm.

[38] Steve Schifferes, "How the Internet Transformed Business "(2006), http://news.bbc.co.uk/1/hi/business/5235332.stm.

Geopolitical Trends

For a specific case in point, the satellite states of the former Soviet Union have become more disparate as they compete for manufacturing and energy bases and with near neighbors in the Middle East, even as groups of states seek to join together in regional or other interstate arrangements to further common political and economic interests — the European Union (EU) is an example.[39, 40] From an organizational perspective these present security risks, challenges, and opportunities; from a policy standpoint, serious problems could arise from governance and decisions about resource management. To illustrate, the EU imports about one quarter of its gas from Russia, 80 percent of which is distributed through a system that crosses the Ukraine. Russia and Ukraine have had problems in the past regarding apportioning debts and assets, military disputes, and ethnic Russians.[41] As an example, in January 2009, Russia shut off all gas supplies to Europe through Ukraine, leaving more than a dozen countries scrambling to cope during a winter cold snap. Prime Minister Vladimir Putin publicly endorsed the move and urged that international observers be brought into the energy dispute. The effects of the gas cutoff reverberated across the continent, where some countries have substantial reserves and others do not. The EU accused both nations of using consumers as pawns in their quarrel, and tens of thousands of people, mostly in Bulgaria, were without central heating. What effects would occur in the EU if Russia, due to a more serious issue with the Ukraine, cut off natural gas supplies?

On a broad scale, in addition to the typical security challenge, new challenges could arise based upon conflict of race, religion, political ideology, or economic status that might increase operational and security risks. Iraq, Afghanistan, and other areas around the world are good examples. A downturn of the global economy could exacerbate global-security problems and greatly expand the number of affected areas. As a brief example, more people are moving from

---

[39]Derek Hunns, *Russia and Nato* (Intellect, Ltd, 1997).
[40]R.J. Krickus, "The Presidential Crisis in Lithuania: Its Roots and the Russian Factor ", ed. East European Studies at the Woodrow Wilson International Center for Scholars (2004).
[41]Staff, "The Post-Cold-War War: Strained Relations between Russia and Ukraine," *The Economist* (1993).

passive to active roles in terrorism in Britain,[42] and throughout the EU terrorists are becoming more difficult to profile.[43] This is due to recruitment of disgruntled European Union (EU) citizens with government policies – such a scenario will likely spread to the U.S. and other countries. Terrorists and terrorist leadership will become more difficult to profile and recognize — Usama Bin Laden's death was the most recent catalyst in this direction.

These issues alone, notwithstanding natural and technological hazards, will serve to further tax security forces, along with strategic goals and initiatives. The role and importance of multinational corporations within the security arena will grow as government policy, business opportunities, and the number of commerce transactions abroad continues to expand. Regardless of services, security risks will inevitably rise and exert growing influence on the global community, national governments, and corporations.

As a corporation or government, these developments have implications on an approach to security solutions, partnerships, supply-chains, trade agreements, the environment, food and water security, and other issues, which pose a series of significant security-related questions:

- What risks will be posed to the corporation or government policy in regions that control scarce resources, but may have plentiful labor or lack of it? The partial answer to this question may be forthcoming within the next two to three years as a result of China's growing water shortage and how it could affect neighbor countries such as India and Pakistan and U.S. foreign policy.
- How would a firm deal with an anti-nation alliance against its country of origin, which may affect the private company or government agency? An example of such

[42]M. Jordan, "Britain's Mi5 Warns of Rising Terror Threat: Spy Agency Aware of 200 Cells, Chief Says " *Washington Post*(2006), http://rjrcos.blogspot.com/2007/03/britains-mi5-warns-of-rising-terror.html.

[43]C. Whitlock, "European Terrorists Are Becoming Harder to Profile " *The Day.com*(2007), http://www.theday.com/re.aspx?re=a41fe4d5-201d-4cad-b59b-148d0b263625.

an alliance is the five nations who have associated themselves with the Presidents of Venezuela and Iran, Hugo Chavez and Mahmoud Ahmadinejad, respectively, against the U.S.[44] These alliance countries currently include Bolivia, Peru, Ecuador, Guatemala, and Venezuela, as well as outside influences from Iran and Cuba. And, the number of countries in the alliance is likely to grow, causing significant security concerns for the U.S. and its allies throughout Latin America. U.S. troop deployment to Latin America on an expanded scale in the next five years is highly likely.

- What effect would such an alliance have on a government or one of its agencies, or an organization that has partners or cooperators in the alliance region?
- What effect would it have on regulations such as ITAR (International Traffic in Arms Regulations), FOCI (Foreign Ownership, Control or Influence), FCPA (Foreign Corrupt Practices Act), import and export due diligence, or other legal, compliance, or policy issues? Clearly, an organization or government should not overlook the importance of those with whom they have partnerships or alliances because the security risks could be high and the consequences dire. This is primarily because political, economic, or trade developments in the countries where partners reside could have considerable and wide interdependent effects on strategic goals.

Consequently, security solutions, both short and long term, related to these questions and to other issues, will be affected. The necessity of transformation from the 3Gs security model to the more advanced, interdependent security convergence, operational risk management, and operational resiliency model would seemingly become more important because the latter can function more efficiently and effectively with large-scale strategic issues, mass

---

[44] S. Johnson, "Trash Talk at the U.N. Chavez's Delusion," *National Review Online*(2006), http://article.nationalreview.com/?q=YTY3YzFhMjdjZmQ4ODQ3MmVjYzY5ZDYzYjdhNTMwYjc=.

sustainability, policy issues, and related factors that influence continuity of operations.

Demographic and Social Trends

Paralleling and influencing political developments are social and demographic trends that threaten to outstrip the ability of many countries and regional economies to adapt with trade partners and corporations. These trends include rapid population growth in regions ill-prepared to absorb it, refugee migration and immigration, chronic unemployment, and intensified competition for resources — notably energy, food, and water. As an example, China, while growing continuously in economic terms, is facing what may become a grim water crisis that could seriously jeopardize mass sustainability. This crises is being created by three main factors: (1) water distribution patterns and climate change; (2) pollution (manmade and natural); and (3) industrial and population increases. As these three factors intensify, the demand for water will exceed supplies and negatively affect water security — not only in China, but possibly its surrounding, nuclear-armed neighbors — India and Pakistan; this will likely result in global repercussions and significant changes to U.S. foreign policy.

The world's poor and developing countries face the greatest rates of population increase and the related challenge of providing jobs, health care, decent living conditions, and requisite social services, but also have many economically viable resources for the global marketplace. However, in preparation for participation to provide various goods and services, these countries face many challenges, which include sustainability from a security perspective. Challenges will be especially serious in urban areas that are already experiencing acute shortfalls of services. Such developments could trigger recurrent humanitarian crises characterized by famine and disease and heightened civil unrest that may require extensive security involvement and other responses by the international community — Ethiopia and Sudan are examples.[45] The problem is

---

[45] *P. et al. Webb, "Drought and Famine in Ethiopia and Sudan: An Ongoing Tragedy," Natural Hazards 4, no. 1 (1991).*

that a flattening global landscape is having such an effect that current areas of stability or instability may be reversed in the near future (3 to 5 years) so that now stable economies and countries become much less stable whether through resource shortages, economic issues, or other problems. These situations could become particularly acute in event of steepening global recession or depression. Examples of cultural and political revolutions (mostly violent) in past history demonstrate how quickly operational and business environments can change. The economic collapse of Greece in 2010 is a clear example. Even natural disasters such as Hurricane Katrina suggest the need for greater preparedness from an operational resiliency perspective. How will business or governmental partnerships be influenced in such affected regions? How will natural hazards affect commodity supply chains that are extended around the globe, where partners and allies are in many different countries and for which continued regulatory and compliance issues, intermingled with the auspices of national security, are increasing?

ECONOMIC TRENDS

Closely tied to the challenges developing from these demographic and social trends are the effects of the expanding global marketplace. U.S. citizens, businesses, and non-government organizations (NGOs) have moved into every corner of the globe.[46] This same process is occurring in other countries whose citizens, businesses, and NGOs have operations within and outside their respective countries. Multinational corporations continue to gain economic power and political influence, posing not only opportunities for business growth, but also security challenges to the firm — and to governments, who may react by enforcing more stringent regulations that affect organizational growth and security. One example would be trade and economic sanctions such as those longstanding between the U.S. and Cuba. Even though they may become more difficult to implement and enforce — what would be

[46]K. Davis, "Flat or Spiky? The Paradox of How the Flattening of the Global Economy Encourages Spikes of Economic Activity and Population Concentration " (Mid-America Manufacturing Technology Center2006).

the effect on corporate gains, policy, or programmatic issues, and are backups in place for related security solutions? Conjointly, the flow of private capital into the less-developed world can be a force for positive change. The explosion of communications and information accessibility will influence political, cultural, and economic patterns and expanded employment bases, perhaps profoundly.

Critical resources such as water and arable land will likely become scarcer than oil, exacerbating political, economic, and ethnic tensions, which will present risks for corporations, NGOs (non government organizations), government agencies, and militaries through massive civil unrest. One of many examples occurred in Sri Lanka, where fighting broke out in Trincomalee as a result of a dispute over water supplies, leaving many to wonder if the entire country would be drawn into civil war.[47] Without a sustainable water supply there can be no long-term economic development, which is the driver of finance regardless of geography.

Another example of tensions caused by scarce resources is portrayed in Israel. The waters of the Sea of Galilee have served as a source of conflict between Israel and its neighbors for centuries. The 1967 War with Syria was considered by many to be a war over water: "I can promise that if there is not sufficient water in our region, if there is scarcity of water, if people remain thirsty for water, then we shall doubtless face war" said Meir Ben Meir, Former Israeli Water Commissioner. The Jordan Valley is not unique — along the Nile, Tigris, and Euphrates exists a danger of conflict over water. Palestinians gathering water from a spring in their village use one quarter as much water as their Israeli neighbors.[48] Strife continues over whether or not Israel will return access to rivers or underground water supplies with the return of lands such as the West Bank.[49] The scarcity of water keeps Israel, Jordan, Syria, and other neighboring countries in a constant state of tension. Nabil Sha'ath, the Palestinian

---

[47] S. Dissanayake, "Water and War in Sri Lanka," *BBC News Online*(2006), http://news.bbc.co.uk/2/hi/south_asia/5239570.stm.
[48] M. Ja'as, "Infrastructure Development after Oslo B in the West Bank Governates of the Palestinian National Authority," *Water Science and Technology* 42, no. 1-2 (2000).
[49] D. Nazer, Siebel, M., Van Der Zaag, P., Mimi, Z., and Gizjen, H., "Water Footprint of the Palestinians in the West Bank," *Journal of the American Water Resources Association* 44, no. No. 2 (2008).

Authority's Minister of Planning and International Co-operation, insisted that the Israelis need to rethink their agricultural practices, "They've got to change their crops, cut down on citrus, cut down on rice," explains Mr. Sha'ath.

Water in the Middle East has a long history. Post-WW I, Israel wanted Sykes-Picot borders altered to include the Jordan River, Lower Litani, east coast of the Sea of Galilee, and Lower Yarmouk headwaters and tributaries.[50] These borders affect Palestine, southern Lebanon, Syria, and the Jordan Valley. Efforts to secure these water sources fell short because French opposition blocked them. By the end of World War II, accommodating a growing Palestinian and Jewish population became critical. Israel's "War of Independence" followed in 1947-48, which assured water sovereignty as well. Several regional water-sharing proposals failed in part because Israel coupled them to recognizing the Jewish state. Israel's National Water Carrier project began in the late 1950s and through the early 1960s; it became the country's largest water project — to transfer Sea of Galilee northern water to highly populated areas in the center and south and to facilitate efficient water use.[51] Neighboring Arab states viewed the project as a hostile act — they responded with their own diversion plans. Reciprocally, Israel viewed these diversion plans as a national-security threat and confrontation followed. Israel targeted the National Water Carrier and retaliated against Syrian construction sites, and thus, the 1967 war resulted. The Prime Minister of Israel, David Ben-Gurion, had previously warned that Israel and Arab neighbors would battle over strategic water resources and determine Palestine's fate. A well-documented perspective regarding Israel and its 'Water Wars' has been written by Godesky.[52]

This issue will likely become more contentious in the future as population throughout the Middle-East region increases, distribution infrastructure continues to deteriorate, and water shortages grow. This could be particularly catastrophic due to links between terrorist groups in various countries in the region and the heavily armed

---

[50] Stephen Lendman. *Drought and Israeli Policy Threaten West Bank Water Security.* Global Policy Forum (in press).
[51] Ibid.
[52] J. Godesky, "Israel's Water Wars,"(2006), http://anthropik.com/2006/08/israels-water-wars.

nature of potential combatants.[53] Based on current events of the Shiite militant group Hezbollah bringing down the Lebanese government (January 2011) and whether they will retain control, relations with the U.S., Israel, and other Middle East neighbors could have dire security consequences. Despite this, water security is crucial for the entire region and could serve as a strengthening common bond between Israel and its neighbors. Thus, securing and preserving water supplies against manmade, natural, and technological threats is essential. This example serves as a reminder that security trends go far beyond physical security, borders, and armed combatants. Further, the combined complexities are both highly interdependent and intricate.

Finally, perceived disparities of wealth, where vast riches are controlled by relatively few countries, could also create tension and present political and moral challenges for businesses and governments caught in the middle. As an example, in some countries bribes are common place, but for businesses in the U.S., strict internal controls prohibit this.[54] The key legislation is the FCPA. How will this affect global security practices of U.S. agencies and the military and American business organizations, as well as foreign governments and other corporations?

Technology Trends

Technology is playing an ever-increasing and imperative role in security policy, governance, and solutions. Robotics and unmanned vehicles will likely become a part of everyday life; nano-technology has the potential to radically alter every manufacturing process from computer systems to defense technology and household goods. Information technologies will play a preeminent role in communications, global manufacturing, security, and other industries. A critical technology could be advancement in energy technology such as cold fusion that could catapult the globe from

---

[53] J. Tindall, and Campbell, A., "Water Security-National and Global Issues," ed. National Research Proram (Denver: Government Printing Office, 2010).

[54] BISNIS, "Bisnis, Foreign Corrupt Practices Act Antibribery Provisions (Business Information Service for the Newly Independent States)," (Washington DC: Government Printing Office).

dependence on depleting petroleum reserves or enhanced development in solar, wind, and geothermal energy technologies. Technological advances will also lend themselves to more lethal and destructive weapons that can be utilized by criminals and terrorists, presenting even greater risks and vulnerabilities. In the hands of these groups, foreign or domestic, new weapons offer frightening security prospects to all entities, not only in terms of immediate physical threat, but also in destruction of large distribution and life-sustaining systems that comprise critical infrastructure.

Apparently, since the advent of the dot-com era, the world has been in the grip of rapid technological advances in everything from surveillance and detection technologies to space-borne telecommunications.[55] With a new cycle about every 18 months, the rapid rate of new and improved technologies is a defining characteristic of this era and of future change and will likely have an indelible influence on new security strategies, operational concepts, and tactics that organizations and governments and their agencies employ from the programmatic to the strategic level. If security and continuity functions do not maintain a change of pace equal to that of the technological revolution it is very likely that vulnerabilities and risks will increase dramatically.

Cyber security issues and Internet crimes have accompanied technological advances in a way that was not foreseen. Both criminal and terrorist groups invest heavily into technology as a means to steal funds from bank accounts, hack into critical infrastructure such water distribution systems and power grids, practice identity theft, and so forth. Coupling technology advances with terrorist goals and objectives is helping them to rapidly gain an advantage in this area. The advantage is so acute in various sectors that law enforcement and other fail safes are rapidly nullified. Quite frankly, criminal and terrorists groups pay armies of cyber-hackers to achieve their goals and, according to IT experts, governments and corporations, are rapidly losing this battle.

---

[55]Online Spectrum, "Terror: What's Next? Five Years after 9/11, Technology's Role against Terrorism Is Still Murky " *IEEE*(2006), http://www.spectrum.ieee.org/sep06/4426.

Future Security Considerations

Depending upon environmental disasters, wars, epidemics or pandemics, and technological breakthroughs — any plausible world future could fundamentally alter the local to global security environment. Current key trends point toward at least one of two types of world futures with various consequences. However, any future will likely experience the necessity for continued and well-thought out strategic-security processes. Two future examples include: (1) conventional balance as has been experienced until now, but one where a hostile alliance is posed against a particular nation or region, such as the Venezuela Alliance against the U.S.; and (2) a future of unending crises in which there are deteriorating global economic conditions coupled with the breakdown of international, corporate, NGOs, and institutions. These include interdependent effects regarding critical resources such as energy, water, food, and even armed gangs such as those in large cities and the drug cartels in Latin America. An example of the latter is the growing tensions and violence along the U.S./Mexico border.

The latter future appears to be currently emerging as the dominant future due to economic global downturn, but at the same time can be combined with future 1. Increasing energy prices, higher food prices, and a continuing credit crisis (beginning in the U.S. as heavy mortgage losses, ongoing in 2011, and a substantial credit crisis) has led to the drastic bankruptcy of large and well established investment and commercial banks around the world. The inability of the U.S. and other countries to control government spending and develop an environment favorable for small and large businesses to create jobs will exacerbate this issue. Perhaps more importantly, several global trends have emerged that are important from a security perspective. These trends include: (1) High Prices (the prices of many commodities, notably oil and food, are rising so high they could cause genuine economic damage, threatening stagflation and a reversal of globalization, as well as mass civil unrest). (2) Trade (the credit crunch is making it difficult for exporters to obtain letters of credit, which could cause a further rise in prices and eventually shortage of goods). (3) Inflation (In February 2008, Reuters reported that global inflation was at historic levels, and that domestic inflation

was at 10-20 year highs for many nations.[56] Inflation was also increasing in developed countries,[57] but remained low compared to the developing world, but it is now slowly increasing again); (4) Increasing Unemployment (The International Labor Organization (ILO) predicted that at least 20 million jobs will have been lost by the end of 2009 due to the crisis — mostly in "construction, real estate, financial services, and the auto sector," bringing world unemployment above 200 million for the first time.[58] The number of unemployed people worldwide could increase by more than 70 million in 2011 as the global recession intensifies (this number extrapolated from data given).[59] The rise of advanced economies in Brazil, India, and China increased the total global labor pool dramatically; add to that the increasing and uncontrolled illegal immigration from countries such as Mexico. Recent improvements in communication and education in these countries have allowed workers to compete more closely with workers in traditionally strong economies, such as the United States and Europe. This huge surge in labor supply has provided downward pressure on wages in developed countries and significantly contributed to unemployment.[60] In the U.S. alone unemployment has hovered at 10 percent for 2009 through beginning 2011. Perhaps more importantly, these changes could be greatly aggravated by increasing global unemployment with a resulting social unrest that could prove extremely difficult for national security — both local and national response forces. This will be particularly true if ensuing water scarcity continues, with interdependent climate change effects, causing

---

[56]Johnson Plumberg, S.C., "Global Inflation Climbs to Historic Levels," *International Herald Tribune*(2008), http://www.iht.com/articles/2008/02/12/business/inflate.php.

[57]EurActiv, "EU Slashes Growth Forecast, Foresees Inflation Surge " EurActive(2008), http://www.euractiv.com/en/euro/eu-slashes-growth-forecast-foresees-inflation-surge/article-170470.

[58] Staff, "Financial Crisis to Cost 20 Million Jobs: Un " *Express India*(2008), http://www.expressindia.com/latest-news/Financial-crisis-to-cost-20-mn-jobs-UN/376061/.

[59] UN, "global unemployment remains at historic high despite strong economic growth – un " un news(2007), http://www.un.org/apps/news/story.asp?newsid=21335&cr=unemployment&cr1.

[60] T. Palley, " The Global Labor Threat,"(2005), http://www.tompaine.com/articles/2005/09/29/the_global_labor_threat.php.

reduced food production that could result in inflation of food prices and scarcity so severe that city-wide riots occur. One example of this includes conditions in Kenya where, "Rocketing food prices — some of which have more than doubled in two years — have sparked riots in numerous countries recently. Millions are reeling from sticker shock and governments are scrambling to staunch a fast-moving crisis before it spins out of control. From Mexico to Pakistan, protests have turned violent"[61]; and (5) Policy Responses (Because national security is closely tied to commerce, trade, and the economy, it is the author's opinion that the financial phase of the crisis beginning with the mortgage crises in the U.S. will likely spread globally and possibly lead to emergency interventions in many national financial systems as the effects linger for several years. This is plausible particularly for the U.S., China, India, and the EU as they are strong trading partners whose combined trade and economic health are closely linked and could result in global repercussions).

Conventional Balance Future

A global condition in which a traditional balance of power exists and in which a hostile regional alliance or a single nation such as China, Russia, or even Iran rises to challenge the United States and EU or other global influencers of power represents a conventional balance. The Latin America alliance described previously is an example; thus, this world future may already be upon us but is merging into an unending crises future. In response to such a future a governments and organizations will likely be required to adapt new security relationships and enter into new alliances, trading, and partnerships to balance and counter new security challenges. This implies that both governments and large corporations will be required to develop a greater capacity for adaptability, flexibility, and operational resiliency. Will a hierarchal organization be able to adapt? Examples of this future also include the formation of an all-Asia or all-Latin America trading bloc similar to the EU and possibly other large groups centered on opposing the political, economic, and cultural

---

[61] V. Vault, "The World's Growing Food-Price Crises," *Time Online*(2008), http://www.time.com/time/world/article/0,8599,1717572,00.html.

influences of the West, primarily the U.S. Increased security spending worldwide will be a prominent feature of this future, as well as military spending — this is occurring today in Iraq, Afghanistan, India, and other countries.[62] However, the great majority of future security spending by both corporations and governments will likely be on more strategic issues such as security convergence processes, operational risk management, risk assessment, and related processes because these will ensure operational resiliency and continuity of operations. Overriding all will be the sustainability of resources, particularly power and energy, water, and food. Additionally, many states and criminal groups (including terrorists) could have acquired weapons of mass destruction (WMDs) and the means to deliver them. If terrorists do not possess or obtain WMDs, they still possess highly toxic chemicals and bio agents such as anthrax, thallium, and even Ebola. Although ethnic and humanitarian tensions will likely still exist, their relative significance in the international system could possibly be reduced due to the resurgence of nation-state conflict. Consequently, good security processes could position organizations to defend against all hazards and risks.

Unending Crises Future

The unending crisis future is that in which deteriorating global economic conditions are coupled with the breakdown of international institutions and organizations, water and its security, transportation, and other critical infrastructures due to a weakened economic state. The key critical infrastructures in this case would be telecommunication, power and energy, and water, with possible catastrophic effects on agriculture and food production if power and water are significantly affected, i.e., become scarce. Weakened nation-states, non-state organizations, corporations, and coalitions could fight over scarce resources. The current "water wars" are a good example.[63] [64] Government, nation-state, and corporate alliances will

---

[62]P. Stålenheim, Perdomo, C., and Sköns, E., ed. *Chapter 8: Military Spending*, Sipri Yearbook 2007: Armaments, Disarmament, and International Security (Sockholm: Stockholm International Peace Research Institute,2007).

[63]J. Sachs, "War Climates "(2006), http://www.globalpolicy.org/socecon/hunger/environment/2006/1023sachsclimate.

likely be fluid, unpredictable, and opportunistic. Nationalism and ethnic hatreds could form violent independence movements in Latin America, Asia, South Asia, and the Middle East, which has happened in many areas throughout history and recently in Bosnia and Rwanda.[65] [66] Pivotal states — countries whose fate determines the survival and success of the surrounding region and ultimately the stability of the international system — will likely be in crisis. The list currently includes Mexico, Brazil, Algeria, Egypt, South Africa, Turkey, India, Pakistan, and Indonesia, but could be modified and extended with time. Virtual narco-states (host states dominated by drug organizations – Mexico and Columbia are examples) exist in regions of Latin, South, and Central America and Southeast Asia. Already, the drug wars along the southern border of the U.S. with Mexico are growing dire, affecting regional security policy, economics, and hatred of the U.S. political class due to inept management and ineffective policies.

Weapons of mass destruction and other high-tech weapons and their means of delivery could become more easily available to those who have the money to buy them. Unchecked massive migrations and failing municipal infrastructures will accelerate urban chaos as municipal populations increase, causing subsequent strain on critical infrastructure and distribution systems, particularly power and water, and also economic strain due to increasing unemployment and subsequent reduced tax revenues from local to national levels. This can be seen today in "sanctuary" cities and states within the U.S. that are having difficult economic problems as a result of such influx, primarily due to illegal immigration by Mexican nationals.[67, 68] It is likely that the United States and Europe could be in

---

htm.

[64] J. and Campbell Tindall, A., "Water Security - Nation State and International Security Implications," *Disaster Advances* 2, no. 2 (2009).

[65] CRS, "Crs Summary: A Resolution Expressing the Sense of the Senate Regarding the Massacre at Srebrenica in July 1995 Sponsored by Senator Gordon H. Smith," ed. Library of Congress (Washington DC: Government Printing Office, 1996).

[66] William Ferroggiaro, "The U.S. And the Genocide in Rwanda 1994: Information, Intelligence and the U.S. Response," *National Security Archive*(2004), http://www.gwu.edu/~nsarchiv/NSAEBB/NSAEBB117/index.htm.

[67] Staff, "Illegal Immigrants Cost Millions in N.J. Tax Dollars," *Press of Atlantic City*(2008), http://www.pressofatlanticcity.com/156/story/58524.html.

danger of losing most of their resolve and ability to influence international events as countries such as China, Russia, Iran, and alliance countries against NATO and the West become more influential due to global resource distributions, economics, and security dilemmas. This loss of resolve is also due to the war against intelligence organizations that has generally been conducted from within by "civil libertarians", anti-U.S. groups, self appointed experts, and radicalized lawyers seeking to neutralize intelligence organizations by proliferating the dominant message that Western societies are not worthy of defense in which the concept of "national security" and "patriotism" are constantly derided as "social constructs." Western societies with their emphasis on pluralistic tolerance are being subverted by those who despise and wish to destroy those values and institutions. Boundaries of tolerance have been greatly pushed, but must be reinstated. The recent withdrawal strategy of Britain from Iraq may signify the beginning of this type of world future;[69] this may also be especially true due to a U.S. withdrawal from Iraq.

In this future, the U.S. public, as an example — perceiving little chance of influencing the chaos abroad — may become preoccupied with domestic security and the economy as non-state actors increasingly penetrate the United States with illegal drugs, terrorism, weapons of mass destruction, transnational crime through and across the southern U.S. border with Mexico and maritime boundaries, as well as across the northern border with Canada and, then across virtual boundaries, as Internet crime continues to grow. Economically this type of world future is being clearly evidenced by the failure of Greece due to government mismanagement resulting in subsequent civil unrest, the ensuing fall of Hungary, and the difficult financial positions of Portugal, Spain, Italy, and France at the time of this writing.

---

[68]D.A. Coleman, "Why Borders Cannot Be Open" (paper presented at the XXIV General Population Conference, Salvador da Bahia, Brazil, August 24, 2001 2001).
[69]Staff, "U.K. To Start Iraq Withdrawal (Cbs News, February 21, 2007 [Cited February 28, 2007]); Available from http://Www.Cbsnews.Com/Stories/2007/02/21/World/Main2496920.Shtml.

Implications

Considering these trends, the possible world futures and strategic environments that may be faced, several implications emerge. The nation-state, although still the dominant entity of the international system, is increasingly affected by the growing power of multinational corporations and international organizations, transnational encroachments on national sovereignty, and demographic pressures that stress the abilities of governments to meet their citizens' needs. The addition of organized criminal groups and terrorist organizations to this mix, as well as possible significant social unrest due to poor global economic conditions and disparate global resources distribution creates an uncertain future. This is especially true in developed cultures with better economic status and thus, access to viable clients such as Europe and particularly the U.S. that are experiencing a severe economic downturn and significant growth of gangs.[70] [71] [72] Consequently, new organizations and even country level strategic-alliance structures may develop that reflect concerns about these evolving challenges, while less relevant alliance relationships will decline. The inability or failure of the U.S. government to deal with the current drug-war driven crises along the U.S./Mexico border is an example.

Technology, geopolitical developments, and economic and social trends will likely alter the realities of today and most certainly impact future security trends and processes. However, it is likely the real test will be caused by water-security issues due to shortages and distribution patterns and the consequent affects on food and agricultural production, and power and energy problems. As an example, resulting from these problems is the plausibility that within the U.S., specific government agencies could face far-reaching programmatic and policy change(s) forced by new international water resource issues and assignments related to world-wide water

---

[70]K. Evering, "House Bill, Fbi Target Gang Violence," *American Observer*(2005), http://observer.american.edu/Apr20/web_pages/gang.htm.

[71]R. Delgadillo, "Going Global to Fight Gangs," *Los Angeles Times*(2008), http://www.latimes.com/news/opinion/la-oe-delgadillo18-2008aug18,0,1640811.story.

[72]T. Cone, "Mexican Drug Gangs Invade U.S. National Forest Land," *Denver Post*(2008), http://www.denverpost.com/nationworld/ci_10698914.

problems and shortages and overall water security. Those agencies equipped to cope with such complex issues may have their entire role adjusted and modified from a forcing of global and therefore, national security concerns, despite the fact that such an agency is not intelligence or defense related. Examples could include NASA, NOAA, EPA, and others. Additional agencies in the U.S. such as the Department of Energy, as well as a variety of global governments, may be tasked with extra duties they were not originally organized to fulfill, but which their expertise greatly qualifies them for as a result of these complex issues and cascading problematic effects. This same scenario could play out with other countries around the world.

The range of possible outcomes is impossible to predict with certainty. Each will present unique conditions, many very different from those of today. The central challenge to security structure is to move forward in a manner that enables effective response to risks, whether from the programmatic level of a company or agency or the strategic level of a nation. This strongly suggests a hedging approach for preparing for the future. Therefore, there are likely four major security implications: (1) to hedge against uncertainty; (2) to curtail outdated and less useful security concepts; (3) to explore new security concepts and become rapidly adaptable; and (4) to adapt to and with changing technologies. All of these could, and likely will, be applied against relations with not only security issues of current concern, but far more significant issues that relate to critical infrastructure, mass sustainability, food, water and energy security, and the hazards (anthropogenic, natural, and technological) that affect them. For best results, current security capabilities could be both maintained and advanced where possible as adaption proceeds to reduce near-term risks. For long-term risks, knowledge about evolving challenges and competitors will likely yield a better understanding of security needs and requirements. During this time a continued adaptation of improved, strategic security processes and policy would be prudent.

Conclusions

Many other areas should be considered for future security, operational success, and continuity of operations, but there is insufficient room in this book to treat them. A partial list might include a broad security approach that allows adaption of future alliances to new security environments, considering new avenues of interoperability with partners, institutionalizing innovation and change, incorporation of security convergence processes, and for large organizations, pursuing avenues that create resiliency and adaptability.

The challenges an organization or government are apt to be confronted with in the future differ substantially from those of the past simply because of the global landscape that allows even small firms and countries to compete effectively with goliaths. The recent downfall of Lehman Brothers, an economic giant, who had done business for 158 years, is a key example.[73] The collapse of the Soviet Union and advent of the Internet appears to have begun an unstoppable process that has changed the major fault lines of international business and governmental policy, security, specific agencies responsible for critical resources, and geopolitical systems around the globe. Concurrently, ongoing technological revolution in computers, through hardware and software innovations, and social networking has restructured government alliances, global business and economic patterns and promises to dramatically alter government, corporate, and security operations. Increasingly, sophisticated high-tech weapons promise to multiply advanced attack capabilities for anyone with the money to buy them, with the two potential adversaries being organized crime and transnational terrorists who currently appear to be financially, rather than ideologically, motivated. Existing and emerging security challenges are occurring in an international environment where commercial, financial, cultural, and communication links often transcend geographic borders, creating strong interdependencies and domino failure or success effects. But perhaps most critical, intertwined among all of these complex issues is the greater complexity of global resources, such as water, food and energy, and how they relate to the overall strategic security issue at corporate, local, regional, national, and global levels.

---

[73] L. Story, and White, B., "Lost Chances Marked Lehman's Downfall," *International Herald Tribune*(2008), http://www.iht.com/articles/2008/10/06/business/lehman.php.

New technologies have diminished the importance of geographic distance but increased the importance of time and, consequently, the ability and necessity to respond quickly to emerging problems. This would imply that addressing such issues will require a heightened flexibility and adaptability, which likely will prove problematic for hierarchal organizations. The need is for a proactive approach and not a reactive one, but such has not been forthcoming from government or large NGOs. The new global landscape and the effects of economics, trade, social, and other issues, particularly water security, power, and agricultural and food production in relation to the overall scope could likely result in reaching operational resiliency boundaries much faster and with dire consequences if resiliency breaks. This would result in a rapid cessation of operations and even discontinuity of government. In such an environment, being able not only to respond but also to anticipate and to diffuse problems before they reach the point of collapse will be more important than ever before to organizational security and continuity of operations. This also implies that the relation of strategic, complex issues of hazards, critical infrastructure, and others that can affect continuity of operations be well understood. We are moving further from traditional conflict scenarios — the future will witness an increasing trend toward resource wars and environmental warfare.

Tribal Water Symbol

CHAPTER 3: Nation-State and International Security Implications

Executive Summary

A terrorist attack such as poisoning and sabotage of the national water supply and water-quality infrastructure of the continental United States could disrupt the delivery of vital human services, threaten both public health and the environment, potentially cause mass casualties, and pose grave public concern for homeland security. Most significantly, an attack on U.S. water resources would weaken social cohesion and trust in government. A threat to continuity of services is a potential threat to continuity of government since both are necessary for continuity of operations. Water infrastructure is difficult to protect, as it extends over vast areas across the U.S. and for which ownership is overwhelmingly nonfederal (approximately 85 percent). Since the 9/11 attacks, federal dam operators and water and wastewater utilities have established counter measures. These include enhanced physical security; improved coordination between corporate ownership, Department of Homeland Security, and local law enforcement; and research into risk assessment and vulnerability analysis to ensure greater system safety. A key issue is the proportionate additional resources directed at public and private sector specific priorities. Agencies that have the scientific and technological ability to leverage resources, exploit integrated science approaches, focus on interdisciplinary practices, utilize informatics expertise, and employ a wide use of evolving technologies should play a key role in water security and related issues.

Introduction

Problems involving water security have a global effect. Water supplies and water distribution systems represent potential targets for terrorist activity in the U.S. because of the critical need for water in

every sector of our industrialized society.[74] As a result, water security should be of grave concern, not only for Homeland Security, but also for international security and sustainability. This chapter focuses on the interdependence of water resources that are critical for water security, which include distribution systems security; anthropogenic (human induced or resulting from human activities) threats and hazards; water as a trigger for tension, conflict, and terrorism; natural and anthropogenic hazards; the water/energy link — interdependence with food, transportation, and security; health issues and security; key themes for water security; and future policy direction. Finally, water is regarded symbolically as the source of life, essential for human survival and regarded as a 'human right.' Water is linked to sanitation, agriculture, industrial production, and health. Large-scale contamination, be it a chemical or biological agent, must be factored into counter-terrorism (CT) planning and threat scenarios.

In addition to security of water-distribution systems, other problems are associated with water security. For example, the conflict or potential of water scarcity is analogous to the more publicized current economic struggle over oil. Without oil, necessary goods and services, including water, cannot be transported especially on a sustainable level for population security. Ninety-seven percent of the world's water is within the oceans and seas; the remainder is mostly held in ice caps or other unattainable sources. Only about one percent of global water is liquid and fresh, ninety-eight percent of which is groundwater.[75] Currently, there are approximately 7,000 cubic meters of renewable water supply per person per year, which should provide ample water for a population three times the current size.[76] [77] This statistic does not factor in any skewed distribution or attainability issues and factors relating to climate change. More importantly, these figures do not include the substantial risks posed by natural disasters and man-made attacks, nor do they include such

---

[74] Patricia Meinhardt, "Water and Bioterrorism: Preparing for the Potential Threat to U.S. Water Supplies and Public Health," *Annual Review of Public Health* 26(2004).
[75] Howard Perlman, "Where Is the Earth's Water Located?," (2008).
[76] T.E. Reilly, Dennehy, K., Alley, W., and Cunningham, W. , "Ground-Water Availability in the United States," ed. USGS (Reston: Government Printing Office, 2008).
[77] Herman Bouwer, "Integrated Water Management for the 21st Century: Problems and Solutions," *Journal of Irrigation and Drainage Engineering* 128, no. 4 (2002).

issues as sustained drought conditions and the relationship between energy use and water supply. Natural disasters that affect water supplies could provide opportunities for terrorist attack. Government concern might be diverted to the water supply problem.

Part 1: Water Usage

There is no economically viable solution for distribution of water in scarce areas with little infrastructure such as parts of Latin America, Africa (Darfur as an example), and other geographic locations. Desalinization plants, ship and truck transportation, and other methods are not feasible under current economic constraints for these locations. This is especially true for most countries outside the U.S., Europe, and Japan who have both governance and financial-resource problems. Therefore, remaining water supplies become a limited and valuable resource that must be properly managed to sustain future economic development.

The critical role of water security is underscored by the global distribution of fresh water — distribution is not uniform. The majority of Africa and many other countries south of the equator suffer from an insufficient water supply, while water-rich countries such as the United States and Canada have a more abundant supply, which is subject to increasing population and climate-change factors. Projections indicate that by 2015, central and North Africa, China, India, and parts of Europe may have critical water shortages similar to those now occurring in Darfur. The outlook for 2025 indicates similar trends, but with economic water scarcity spreading globally south to include many Pacific-island groups and Australia, as well as parts of South America and Mexico, which are currently suffering from water shortages.

The United States uses 291.0 billion cubic meters of water for industrial purposes, 35.8 billion cubic meters of water domestically, and 120.9 billion cubic meters of water for agricultural purposes.[78] This estimate does not include water used for the irrigation of golf courses and landscapes or the recharging of groundwater aquifers, which required more than 160 billion gallons of reclaimed water in

---

[78] Hutson, "Estimated Use of Water in the United States in 2000."

California alone, nor does it consider water used for other purposes; total use, considering all sources, is about 408 billion gallons per day or 563.7 B m^3 per year.[79]

Seventeen percent of the world population is deprived of clean drinking water. This is due to the increasing deterioration of underground sources which supply water unsuitable for human consumption in numerous areas of water-scarce regions.[80] Lack of sanitation and purity leads to many critical health issues. Thus, availability of usable water is a primary global issue. As world populations realize that their water supply is a limited resource, many tensions and even violence may rise at the local, national, and international levels — by 1993, more than 60 countries on six continents faced disputes over water rights.

Water Distribution Systems and Security

Water-distribution systems security currently includes:

- **Auxiliary power and communication systems protection, including SCADA (Supervisory Control and Data Acquisition)**
- **Backflow prevention and cross-connection control programs**
- **Cameras, alarms, motion detectors, water quality monitors and bio-detection**
- **Defensive boundary fencing and signage**
- **Emergency responder communications plan**
- **Leak audits and leak-detection programs**
- **Water links to energy, agriculture, and other complex systems**
- **Protection of pump stations, wellheads, storage tanks, fire hydrants, and power supplies**
- **Public awareness campaigns**
- **Security lighting, patrols, guards, and tamper-resistant locks, chains, doors, and hatches**
- **Vulnerability Assessments and Risk Reduction**
- **Water quality sampling and testing protocols**

---

[79] S. Hutson, Barber, N., Kenny, J., Linsey, K., Lumia, D., and Maupin, M. , "Estimated Use of Water in the United States in 2000," (Reston: Government Printing Office, 2004).

[80] Mohammad-Abdul-Kareem Al-Sofi, "Water Scarcity-the Challenge of the Future," *ISI Web of Knowledge*(1994), http://portal.isiknowledge.com.

The federal government has built hundreds of water projects, primarily dams and reservoirs, for irrigation development and flood control, with municipal and industrial water use (M&I) as an incidental, self-financed, project purpose. Many of these facilities critically interact with the nation's overall water supply, transportation, and electricity infrastructure. The largest federal facilities were built and are managed by the Bureau of Reclamation (Bureau) of the Department of the Interior and the U.S. Army Corps of Engineers (Corps) of the Department of Defense.

Bureau reservoirs, particularly those along the Colorado River, supply water to approximately 25 million people in southern California, Arizona, and Nevada via Bureau and non-Bureau aqueducts. Bureau projects also provide water to nine million acres of farmland and other municipal and industrial water users in 17 western states. The Corps supplies water to thousands of cities, towns, and industries from the nine-and-a-half million acre-feet of water stored in its 116 lakes and reservoirs throughout the country, including service to approximately one million residents in the District of Columbia, Arlington County, and the City of Falls Church. The largest federal facilities also produce enormous amounts of power. For example, Hoover and Glen Canyon Dams on the Colorado River represent 23 percent of the installed electrical capacity of the Bureau of Reclamation's 58 power plants in the West and 7 percent of the total installed capacity in the Western United States. Similarly, Corps facilities and the Bureau's Grand Coulee Dam on the Columbia River provide 43 percent of the total installed capacity in the West (25 percent nationwide). After the 9/11 terrorist attacks, security began to be tightened for these type facilities and distribution networks, but some worry it may not be adequate.[81] Some security measures have sparked controversy. On July 8, 2008, the Denver Water Board closed the road over Dillon Dam in Summit County, Colorado, citing a variety of security concerns. This action moved officials from Summit County, three affected local municipalities, and the local fire and

---

[81] G. Winter, and Broad, W.J., "A Nation Challenged: The Water Supply; Added Security for Dams, Reservoirs and Aqueducts," *New York Times*(2001), http://query.nytimes.com/gst/fullpage.html?res=9F01E7DC133AF935A1575AC0A967 9C8B63.

rescue department to file a suit in the state district court to force reopening of the road.[82]

Anthropogenic/Terrorist Threats

There are minimal and maximal threats to water distribution systems which include

Minimal Threats:

- **Disruption of operating or distribution system components, power, or telecommunications systems,**
- **Electronic control systems (SCADA-supervisory control and data acquisition); and physical damage/sabotage to reservoirs and pumping stations.**

Maximum Threats:

- **A loss of flow and pressure would raise threat levels that could hinder firefighting efforts; the fire is the form of terrorist attack.**
- **Sabotage, covert insertion of contaminants or biological agents inserted into water supply infrastructure could result in catastrophic consequences.**
- **Destruction of a large dam could result in catastrophic short-term flooding and loss of water storage and potential loss of life. For example, the destruction of Hoover Dam would affect 25 M people in the Southwestern U.S. and have disastrous business, economic continuity, and public security consequences.**
- **Bioterrorism or chemical threats could deliver massive contamination by small amounts of microbiological agents or toxic chemicals, and could endanger the public health of thousands, particularly children and the elderly. Examples include anthrax, Cryptosporidium, Escherichia coli 0157:H7, Clostridium botulinum, Bacillus anthracis, and other common microbes. However, there are more**

[82] Stratfor, "Another Dam Threat," *Stratfor Weekly*(2008), http://www.stratfor.com/weekly/another_Dam_threat.

exotic threats that should also be investigated. For example, it has been reported that the Ebola virus can be transported via attachment to water particles in the air.[83]

Detection and Treatment Vulnerability

Radioactivity and insidious bio-hazards are not generally listed for detection in treatment plants because of technological inabilities. Currently, toxic compounds such as cyanide are easily detected by colorimetric methods. (Colorimeters measure the absorbance of particular wavelengths of light by a specific solution and are used to determine the concentration of a known solute in a given solution.) Cyber attacks on computer operations can affect an entire infrastructure network because the majority of SCADA controls are run by computers, which generally have some access port to the Internet.[84] **An attack might take control of the SCADA and remotely open/close valves, causing disruptions of various types. Additionally, hacking attacks against water utility systems could result in theft or corruption of information or denial and disruption of system-wide service.**

Sustaining secure water systems is critical for national security, national morale, and social order. A massive failure by government could breach public faith and severely impede access to unrestricted water/wastewater use. Various federal agencies such as the DOE, EPA, NOAA, and others could assist with threat evaluation, where interdisciplinary capabilities in environmental science, human health, cyber-infrastructure, and informatics strategies are available. In other countries such as India, the Ministry of Water Resources could fulfill such capabilities, but in Great Britain, it may require both the Department of Energy and Climate Change (DECC) and the Department for Environment, Food and Rural Affairs (DEFRA).

Response to Water Security Issues

An excellent case of proportionate response to water security issues within the U.S. is the Water Security initiative proposed by the

---

[83] Qasim Rajpar, "Dam Building Zeal Sparks Controversy," *Asia Water Wire*(2006), http://asiawaterwire.net/node/361.

[84] Richard Preston, *The Hot Zone, a Terrifying True Story* (Anchor Books (Random House), 1995).

EPA. The Water Security (WS) initiative is the U.S. Environmental Protection Agency (EPA) program addressing the risk of intentional contamination of drinking water distribution systems established in response to Homeland Security Presidential Directive 9, under which the Agency must "develop robust, comprehensive, and fully coordinated surveillance and monitoring systems, including international information, for...water quality that provides early detection and awareness of disease, pest, or poisonous agents."

The EPA water-security initiative involves: (1) developing designs of systems for timely detection and appropriate response to contamination incidents; (2) testing and demonstrations of warning systems; and (3) developing practical guidance through outreach programs to promote adoption of effective warning systems.

However, a wider threat spectrum includes risks posed by earthquakes, tornadoes, hurricanes, and terrorists to operations, distribution, and collection. Hurricane Katrina in 2005 and Hurricane Ike (Galveston, Texas) in 2008 are recent and powerful examples of threats posed by natural hazards. The impact of a natural disaster, a terrorist attack, or an unanticipated accident can result in disrupted water treatment, damage to the infrastructure, water shortages, and service interruptions due to distribution and other problems. The safety and security of drinking water and wastewater utilities requires proactive measures.

Physical/Resource, Terrorist Threat, and Consequences

The FBI recently claimed that members of Al-Qaeda scoured the Web searching for methods of gaining control of water supply facilities and wastewater treatment plants through the computer networks used by U.S. utility companies.[85][86][87]

---

[85] Kevin Coleman, "Protecting the Water Supply from Terrorism," *Directions Magazine*, January 16, 2005 2005.

[86] Carl Cameron, "Feds Arrest Al Qaeda Suspects with Plans to Poison Water Supplies," *U.S. & World Breaking News*(2002), http://www.foxnews.com/story/0,2933,59055,00.html.

[87] Fox, "Fbi Warns of Potential Poison Attacks," *U.S. & World Breaking News*(2003), http://www.foxnews.com/story/0,2933,96416,00.html.

The terrorists were particularly interested in the target studies of Supervisory Control and Data Acquisition (SCADA) systems available on multiple SCADA-related Web sites and information on water supply and wastewater management practices in the U.S. and abroad. SCADA systems are used in flow distribution systems to control valves, flow rates, etc., at unmanned facilities from a central location. These systems are generally connected through dedicated communications channels that link a control center to remote terminal units that control water pumps and other equipment. In Harrisburg, Pennsylvania, an infected laptop (compromised via the Internet) gave hackers operating from outside the U.S. access to computer systems at a water treatment plant, which could have had grave consequences were the hackers not detected.[88] There have also been verbal threats against U.S. water supplies. Abu Mohammed al-Ablaj told the London-based al-Majallah magazine that al-Qaeda does not rule out using Sarin gas to poison drinking water in the U.S. and Western cities.[89] Whether such a threat is credible should be evaluated by the nation's human health and science agencies which, due to long established public trust, may greatly reduce panic conditions.

Even accidental water contamination has proven deadly. Seven people died and more than 2,300 became sick after bacteria (E-coli) infiltrated water pipes following torrential rains in Walkterton, Ontario, Canada.[90] In 1993, dozens died and about 400,000 became very ill when a rare parasite named cryptosporidium tainted the water supply of Milwaukee, Wisconsin.[91]

Some commentators believe that risks to water systems are small because of the logistics required to introduce sufficient quantities of agents to cause widespread harm. However, this threat reduction may be too sanguine, as the relevant characteristics of a biological agent's potential as a weapon include its stability in a

---

[88] Bob Sullivan, "How Safe Is Our Water?," *MSNBC Staff and Wire Reports*(2002), http://www.jupiterionizers.com/catalog/article_info.php?tpath=16&articles_id=48.
[89] Robert McMillan, "Hackers Break into Water System Network,"(2006), http://www.infoworld.com/article/06/11/01/HNhackwatersystem_1.html.
[90] NewsMax, "Al-Qaeda Threat to U.S. Water Supply," *NewsMax Wires*(2003), http://archive.newsmax.com/archives/articles/2003/5/28/202658.shtml.
[91] Staff, "Walkerton Report Highlights," *CBS News Online*(2002), http://www.cbc.ca/news/background/walkerton/walkerton_report.html#one.

drinking water system, virulence, culturability in the quantity required, and resistance to detection and treatment. Dependent upon the chemical or biologic agent used, this benign assessment of logistics is naïve.

A number of water-supply specialists also concede that the country's 54,065 public and private water systems are vulnerable. Stanford professor Richard Luthy, chair of the Water Science and Technology Board of the National Research Council, in Congressional testimony said, "Although recognized in the past, the vulnerability of our water systems to deliberate acts has not received sufficient attention. The reasons include the fact that simply developing and maintaining our existing water system received primary attention."

The testimony is valid as the U.S. water infrastructure, as well as many other countries, is old, with some components — distribution pipes, valves, etc., not to mention the treatment plants — exceeding 100 years. The U.S. water distribution systems are in serious need of repair and upgrades. Upgrading these systems across the U.S. would cost billions of dollars. For example, the Hoover Dam cost about $165 million to build in the 1930s; construction costs today would minimally be about four billion dollars. Water distribution systems are a delicate balance of interlocking components that includes the water supply system (dams, reservoirs, wells, etc.), water treatment system, and the water distribution system (pipes, pumps, storage tanks, etc.). These systems are aging and in urgent need of upgrading for hardening against terrorist attacks.

Part 2: Water Resource Conflict – Form of Global Disorder

The struggle between countries to secure a clean source of water is a potential catalyst for war. Environmental degradation, water scarcity, and violent conflict can create social and political disorder and serious security risks. From a national security perspective, it is critical that water scarcity, energy, and environmental degradation be effectively monitored to ensure essential water demand can be met. Water shortages are a global issue. "Water Wars" cannot be dismissed. International law has proven inadequate in defending the equal use of shared water

supplies in some parts of the world, as rapid global population growth has greatly increased the demand for water.[92]

Water as a necessary resource is analogous to oil. Water is becoming a very valuable commodity, yet freshwater resources are unevenly distributed among developing countries. Water scarcity has triggered desperation in countries that lack access to water. This desperation often cannot be resolved by negotiations. Military force may be used to obtain adequate water supplies. Water has very rarely been the trigger in international conflicts, but it is often factored into tensions due to its economic importance.[93] Development regarding transboundary issues where this may occur in the Middle East, China, Pakistan, and India are discussed in more detail in chapter 13.

Driving Factors for Water as a Trigger to Possible Violent Action

High population growth, rising consumption, pollution, and poor water management represent the most significant threats, as do climate change and lack of development of new supplies. The latter is often related to poor water-management practices. The lack of adequate energy to power water supply and distribution is becoming an increasing concern worldwide.

International Alert (2007) reported that Great Britain identified 46 countries (with populations of 2.7 billion people) in which both climate change and water-related crises will create a high risk of violent conflict.[94] Another 56 countries (representing an additional 1.2 billion people), are at high risk of political instability.[95] Throughout history, destruction of water resources and distribution facilities has been used as a weapon against the enemy.

---

[92] Michael H. Kramer Phaedra S. Corso, Kathleen A. Blair, David G. Addiss, Jeffrey P. Davis, and Anne C. Haddix, "Cost of Illness in the 1993 Waterborne Cryptosporidium Outbreak," ed. Center for Disease Control (Washington DC: Government Printing Office, 2003).

[93] Adel Darwish, "Middle East Water Wars,"(2003), http://news.bbc.co.uk/2/hi/middle_east/2949768.stm.

[94] Tindall, "Expected Key Trends Likely to Influence Global Security."

[95] Smith, "A Climate of Conflict: The Links between Climate Change, Peace and War."

In 597 B.C., Nebuchadnezzar breached the aqueduct that supplied the city of Tyre in order to end a long siege.[96]

Chiang Kai-sheck (1938) ordered the destruction of dikes along the Yellow River that controlled water during flood stages so that he could flood areas along the river threatened by Japanese invasion.[97]

During WWII, German hydroelectric dams were routine targets.

During the Vietnam War, many dikes were destroyed by bombing activities that resulted in the death of 2-3 million as a result of both drowning and starvation from the effects.[98]

In 1999, water-supply wells were contaminated by the Serbs.[99]

Case Studies: Water and Conflict

In many conflicts, water has been the trigger for tension, hostility, and terrorism. Most cases stem from four root causes: (1) water scarcity; (2) development disputes; (3) military targets/goals; and (4) terrorism. Following are brief examples of international cases.

1967: During a conflict between Israel and Syria, Israel destroyed the Arab diversion works on the Jordan River and occupied the West Bank and also the Golan Heights, which controls the Banias tributary to the Jordan River. The basis of this conflict was that of military target and tool.[100]

---

[96] Dan Smith, and Vivekananda, Janani, "A Climate of Conflict: The Links between Climate Change, Peace and War," *International Alert*(2007), http://aquadoc.typepad.com/waterwired/files/climate_conflict.pdf.

[97] Herbert C. Young, *Understanding Water Rights and Conflicts* (Denver: Burg Young Publishing, 2003).

[98] M. Wilder, and Wilder, T.S., "The Stanley-Wilder Saga 1862-1962: Letters and Papers from China by Charles Alfred Stanley and George D. And Gertrude S. Wilder, Part Five (1939-1962)," (1962).

[99] Yves Lacoste, "An Illustration of Geographical Warfare: Bombing of the Dikes on the Red River, North Vietna," *Antipode, Universit de Paris, Volume 5, NO: 2, PG: 1-13, 1973:1467-8330, 0066-4812* 5, no. 2 (1973).

[100] Sasa Markovic, "Serbia: Airing Grievances," (Transitions Online, 2004).

1986: Lesotho and South Africa had a development dispute and also hidden military goals; however, Lesotho defense forces, with support from within South Africa, Lesotho reached agreement with South Africa for water from the Highlands of Lesotho. This came after 30 previous years of unsuccessful negotiations, although there is still disagreement as to how much factor water played in the conflict.[101]

1990: In South Africa, due to a development dispute, the Pro-apartheid council cut off water supply to the Wesselton Township, home of 50,000 blacks, following the protests resulting over miserable sanitation and living conditions.[102]

1999: In what has been classified as a development dispute and terrorism, farmers from Hebei and Henan Provinces fought over limited water resources. Heavy weapons, including mortars and bombs, were used and nearly 100 villagers were injured. This involved residents from Huanglongkou Village, Shexian County, Hebei Province, and Gucheng Village, Linzhou City, Henan Province. Many homes and facilities were damaged at an estimated loss of one million $US. [103]

1999: NATO closed water supplies in Belgrade, Yugoslavia, and bombed bridges on the Danube River to disrupt navigation.[104]

2002: In the U.S., papers seized during the arrest of a Lebanese national who had moved to the U.S. and became an Imam at a Islamist mosque in Seattle included instructions on poisoning water sources from a London-based Al-Qaeda recruiter. The FBI issued a

---

[101] P. Wallenstein, and Swain, A. , *International Fresh Water Systems as a Source of Conflict and Cooperation*, ed. Kurt R. Spillmann & Günther Bächler, vol. 14, Environmental Crisis: Regional Conflicts and Ways of Cooperation, Environment and Conflict Project (Zürich & Bern) (Zurich & Bern1997).

[102] A.E. Mohamed, "Joint Development and Cooperation in International Water Resources: The Case of the Limpopo and Orange River Basins in Southern Africa," in *International Waters in Southern Africa (2001)* (Tokyo: UN, 2001).

[103] Staff, "Villagers Fight over Water Resources," ed. Citation provided by Ma Jun (China Water Resources Daily, 2002).

[104] Luis Ramirez, "China's Sichuan Province Tense in Aftermath of Violent Anti-Dam Protests," (Voice of America News, 2004).

bulletin to computer security experts around the country indicating that al-Qaida terrorists may have been studying American Dams and water-supply systems in preparation for new attacks. They specifically sought information on water supply and wastewater management, not only for the U.S., but also internationally.[105]

2004-2006: In a water-scarcity dispute between Somalia and Ethiopia, at least 250 people were killed and many more injured in clashes over water wells and pastoral lands. A three-year drought led to the violence due to limited water resources, aggravated by the lack of effective government and central planning.[106]

2007: Between Burkina Faso, Ghana, and Cote D'Ivoire, declining rainfall led to growing clashes between animal herders and farmers with competing water needs. As early as August 2000, people were forced to flee their homes by fighting in Zounweogo province.[107]

Post 9/11 Terrorist Attacks and Plans

After the 9/11 terrorist attacks on the World Trade Centers, the FBI issued a series of warnings regarding possible terrorist attacks against American targets, specifically the nation's water utilities. The information was discovered in documents in Afghanistan.[108] However, as early as 1990, the U.S. Air Force, during Operation Desert Shield, began considering the effects of terrorist attack on water supplies because of an incident of unintentional food and water poisoning relating to Clostridium botulinum. Major Mike Linschoten stated, "In late September 1990, during Operation DESERT SHIELD, a RIVET JOINT mission was scrubbed and airborne battlefield command and control center was reduced to 50 percent combat effectiveness

---

[105] UNEP, "The Kosovo Conflict: Consequences for the Environment and Human Settlements. ," ed. United Nations Environment Programme and United Nations Center for Human Settlements (Habitat) (Nairobi: UN, 1999).

[106] MSNBC, "Fbi Says Al-Qaida after Water Supply,"(2002), http://www.ionizers.org/water-terrorism.html.

[107] BBC, "Dozens Dead' in Somalia Clashes," *BBC News World Edition Online*(2004), http://news.bbc.co.uk/2/hi/africa/4073063.stm.

[108] Abdul-Hameed Bakier, "Jihadis Discuss Means of Poisoning the Water Supply of Denmark and Great Britain," *Terrorism Focus* 5, no. 32 (2008).

for one week; surveillance coverage was lost, seriously degrading the mission."[109] Because national economies, especially those of developed countries such as the U.S., are increasingly reliant on critical infrastructure systems, particularly water, significant safeguards are necessary. And, while water supply systems have been evaluated for vulnerability, most of these systems are susceptible to terrorist attach through the distribution system by either physical or cyber methods. An asymmetric attack against the U.S. or other country could be catastrophic short term. While many terrorist operations against water resources and vital infrastructure targets have been successfully neutralized in Western countries due to sensitivity of sources, methods, and possible concern with "copy cat" attacks, they have not received media attention. However, a number of cases have been publicized, including—

2002: In Rome, Italy, Italian police arrested four Moroccans allegedly planning to contaminate the water supply system with a cyanide-based chemical, targeting buildings that included the U.S. embassy. Authorities believed the group had ties to Al-Qaeda.[110]

2005: FBI discovered a computer belonging to a person with indirect ties to Usama bin Laden that contained architectural and engineering software related to dams and other water-retaining structures[111] (Note: while this documentation is classified, it is highly likely that the software mentioned in this report relates to SCADA systems — a cause of great concern). This issue is discussed along with solutions in chapter 12.

2006: In Sri Lanka, in an act of terrorism, Tamil Tiger insurgents cut the water supply to government-held villages in the northeastern part of the country. To control the violence, Sri Lankan government

---

[109] CDI, "Securing U.S. Water Supplies," *CDI Terrorism Project*(2002), http://www.cdi.org/terrorism/water-pr.cfm.

[110] Donald C. Hickman, "A Chemical and Biological Warfare Threat: Usaf Water Systems at Risk," ed. USAF Counter proliferation Center (Air War College, Air University, 2003).

[111] BBC, "Cyanide Attack' Foiled in Italy," *BBC News Online*(2002), http://news.bbc.co.uk/hi/english/world/europe/newsid_1831000/1831511.stm.

forces launched attacks on the reservoir where the insurgents were located.[112]

2008: A major Jihadist Internet forum posted a terrorist plot to use chemical and biological agents to poison water in Great Britain and Denmark. The plot was intricate, following steps to collect intelligence, distract and avoid security forces, employ a fair-skinned and blonde Jihadist to execute the attack, and use a highly toxic chemical. The forum posts became quite extensive, suggesting numerous attack strategies, including explosives and a wide variety of toxic substances.[113]

Conclusions

A terrorist attack such as poisoning and sabotage of the national water supply and water-quality infrastructure of the continental United States could disrupt the delivery of vital human services, threaten both public health and the environment, potentially cause mass casualties, and pose grave public concern for homeland security. Most significantly, an attack on U.S. water resources would weaken social cohesion and trust in government. A threat to continuity of services is a potential threat to continuity of government since both are necessary for continuity of operations. Water infrastructure is difficult to protect, as it extends over vast areas across the U.S. and for which ownership is overwhelmingly nonfederal (approximately 85 percent). Since the 9/11 attacks, federal dam operators and water and wastewater utilities have established counter measures. These include enhanced physical security; improved coordination between corporate ownership, Department of Homeland Security, and local law enforcement; and research into risk assessment and vulnerability analysis to ensure greater system safety.

A key issue is the proportionate additional resources directed at public and private sector specific priorities. Agencies that have the scientific and technological ability to leverage resources, exploit

---

[112] Coleman, "Protecting the Water Supply from Terrorism."
[113] BBC, "Water and War in Sri Lanka,"(2006), http://news.bbc.co.uk/2/hi/south_asia/5239570.stm.

integrated science approaches, focus on interdisciplinary practices, utilize informatics expertise, and employ a wide use of evolving technologies should play a key role in water security and related issues.

Water conservation methods and operations and technology such as new dams, cloud seeding, desalination plants and underground water storage will almost certainly be insufficient to meet the demands of the growing global population. Because water availability is finite, which will increase the potential for conflict among existing and new users, it is probable that competition will increase and will result in constant litigation and tension over water resources. The need to share water from rivers that cross state and country boundaries has been a constant source of contention since Territorial times in the arid Western U.S. and recently in the drought-stricken Eastern U.S. Transnational terrorists/jihadists have demonstrated their operation interests in attacks against water infrastructure in many countries, including the U.S., and many planned and intercepted missions have demonstrated a high degree of operational imagination. British-based analysts have recently drawn attention to the high degree of involvement of engineers in jihadist terrorists groups, including those of Usama bin Laden and Mohamed Atta, leader of the 9/11 attacks.[114]

The study of terrorist threat to water supplies will require a fusion of scientific and analytical tradecraft skills — failure to develop such skill sets could prove catastrophic to the homeland security of the United States.

[114] Diego Gambetta, and Hertog, Steffen, "Engineers of Jihad," *Sociology Working Papers* 2007-10(2007).

Tribal Water Symbol

CHAPTER 4: Energy — Water Interdependence

Executive Summary

Energy and water security has become a national and global priority. The continued security and economic health of the United States or any country depend on a sustainable supply of both energy and water because these two critical natural resources are so closely linked. The production of energy requires large volumes of water while the treatment and distribution of water is equally dependent upon readily available, low-cost energy. In 2000, irrigated agriculture and thermoelectric generation withdrawals of fresh water were approximately equal in the U.S. Electricity production requires about 190,000 million gallons of freshwater per day, accounting for over 40percent of all daily freshwater withdrawals in the U.S. In many regions of the U.S., the indirect use of water (home lighting and electric appliances) is approximately equal to direct use (water lawns and taking showers).

Current trends of water use and availability indicate that meeting future water and energy demands to support continued economic development will require improved utilization and management of both energy and water resources. Primary concerns include:

- Increasing populations require more food and energy; this will cause direct competition between the two largest water users (energy and agriculture) for limited water resources.
- Population growth and economic expansion projections indicate the U.S. will require an additional 393,000 MW of new generating capacity (equivalent to about 1,000 new 400 MW plants) by the year 2020, which is unlikely to occur.
- Potential environmental and ecological restrictions on the use of water for power generation such as the removal of hydroelectric dams, restrictions on cooling water withdrawals, and cooling water use for nuclear power plants to protect aquatic species and habitat and the environment.

- **Potential terrorist attacks on power grids and water treatment and distribution systems.**

The nation's ability to meet the increasing demand for affordable water and energy is being seriously challenged by these emerging issues. This is true for almost all countries.

Introduction

Energy policy and related issues are an acknowledged facet of the global community. Energy is needed to convey water; water is required to generate energy. For decades, the U.S. and other countries have failed to develop energy policies that reduce reliance on foreign energy, especially petroleum-based products, and at the same time promote a diverse supply of reliable, affordable, and environmentally sound energy. While the U.S. has often considered an energy policy, no formal policy has been implemented. Further, the BP oil leak in the Gulf of Mexico in the summer of 2010 was a serious detriment to cutting dependency on foreign oil and energy supplies. Oil has allowed the world's burgeoning population to continue to grow. When oil first became a common commodity around 1900, the world population was about two billion; today that population is over six billion. Without the use of oil for extensive monoculture agricultural production and supply through trucking and shipping, the world would have a much smaller population. Despite the growing scarcity of these resources, governments fail to develop policy that will mitigate what may become the greatest catastrophe the world has known — the failure of both energy and water systems on a large scale, which will happen for a variety of reasons.

The continued security and economic health of countries, particularly the U.S., depends on a sustainable supply of energy. More importantly, energy policy must be connected to a sustainable water policy because these two resources are inexorably linked. Energy and water are Level 1 critical infrastructures; the most important of all infrastructures (see chapter 1). These are the life-sustaining systems that drive our economies and affect every part of life, as well as individual quality of life. Current trends in global population growth, energy and water use and their availability indicate that meeting

future energy and water demands to support continued economic growth in a globalization scenario will require the utilization and management in an unprecedented manner of dual resources — energy and water.

In absolute terms, neither energy nor water is in strictly short supply regionally or globally. Instead, both are disparately distributed, particularly in developing nations. What is in short supply is affordable energy and clean, affordable water. At the same time, energy is beginning to compete with agriculture as the largest user of water. A steadily increasing population will significantly increase this competition. Failure to develop sound policies for joint water and energy management and use will jeopardize homeland and national security as well as foreign policy. Both energy and water are growing security threats for the 21st century. Already, cities such as Singapore are treating waste and sewage water for use as drinking water. Cities in the U.S. such as Los Angeles, San Francisco, Las Vegas, and Phoenix are examining this same methodology for possible use. On the energy side, California consistently utilizes rolling blackouts to conserve energy during peak use, a practice which has spread to other populated states such as Texas. The demand for both resources is beginning to outstrip supplies.

Although a dual resource, tensions related to water are increasing and have significant implications for U.S. national security. For example, the Indus River System is in a state of heightened tensions between India and Pakistan. There are those who claim that armed conflict over water resources has never and will never happen. However, this was exactly the cause of the 1967 war between Israel and Syria — the water dispute between the two countries for control over the Jordan River triggered that conflict. The instability in the Middle East lingers as a result of this issue. Furthermore, a continuation of these conflicts could subject the U.S. and its allies to energy blackmail from the rich oil producers of the Middle East and the major corporations who hold the majority of oil rights in those areas. A brief chronology of water conflict is given in chapter 3.

A steadily increasing global population is placing greater demand on energy and water resources. In turn, this will necessitate the need for increased agricultural outputs on a global scale, which will increase competition for energy and water resources. If this

happens, regional stability and national security will be decreased. As an example, in terms of dual use, the water levels of Lake Mead, which is controlled by Hoover Dam, are only 15 feet above critical shortage levels (1,075 feet) at the time of this writing. If the use rate continues, that critical level will be reached by summer 2012 (see Figure 4.1).

Figure 4.1: Lake Mead water level - 1937 to May 18, 2011 (Source: U.S. Bureau of Reclamation - The database is located at http://www.usbr.gov/lc/region/g4000/hourly/mead-elv.html).

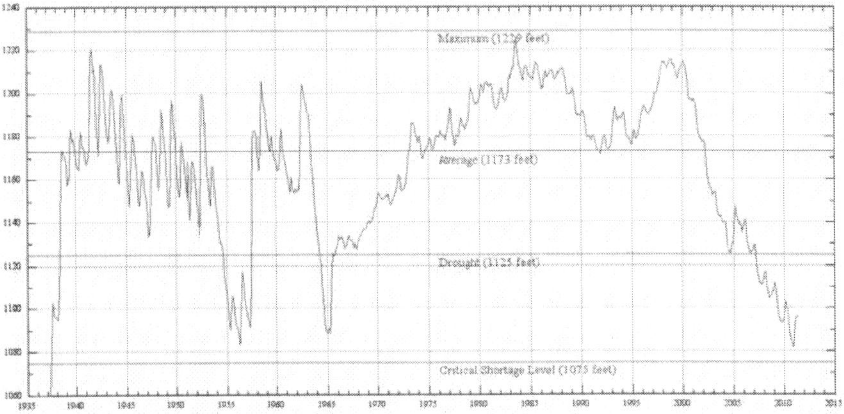

When the critical shortage level is reached, water flow through the dam will cease, as will hydroelectric output. The water from Lake Mead, which is supplied by the Colorado River System, represents half of the water used by metro Los Angeles. The water of Lake Mead is used by 22 million people; seven million people use the hydroelectric energy produced by Hoover Dam turbines. If this critical shortage level is reached, severe consequences will result for the U.S. as a whole, especially economically. In recent years, water levels in Lake Mead, which is fed by the Colorado River, have been about 100 feet lower than historic levels. This drop is primarily a consequence of increasing populations in Los Angeles and Las Vegas, reduced flows in the Colorado River due to a sustained 12-year drought in the Southwest, and other competing uses such as agriculture. It would therefore appear we face a conundrum. Building more power plants will further strain and affect freshwater supplies; constructing larger

delivery systems to meet the needs of growing populations will increase energy demands. Further, Hoover Dam could be particularly vulnerable to a bio-terrorist attack or an earthquake.

There is no redundant supply for this system or for many similar systems around the world, and factually, terrorists already possess the necessary chemicals that require minimal logistics to poison this and other large systems. Although many experts have stated the logistics required to carry out such an attack are virtually impossible, they are in error — depending on the bio-agent used logistics are far less sophisticated and extensive than have been suggested. As an example, it would require only 22.5 pounds of one specific agent to achieve success; this small amount could be easily carried in a backpack or other innocuous container.

Colorado is not the only state in the U.S. facing linked energy and water problems. In June 2008, the state of Florida announced it would sue the U.S. Army Corps of Engineers in regard to the Corps' plan to reduce water flows from reservoirs in Georgia that flowed into the Apalachicola River; this river runs through Florida from the Georgia-Alabama border. Florida's concerns were environmental, that the restricted flow would threaten a variety of endangered species. However, Alabama also objected because they feared that reduced flows might force the Farley Nuclear Plant near Dothan, Alabama, to shut down. Nuclear plants require large quantities of water to cool their reactors (to be discussed later). The state of Georgia had been hit hard by a sustained drought, causing a drop in water levels of rivers around the state, which could have also forced Georgia to shut down its own nuclear power plants. Tensions between these states became much heightened. At one point, a Georgia state legislator suggested that Georgia move its northern border one mile further into Tennessee, citing a problematic land survey dating back to 1818.

This is a firsthand example of the competitive use among water, energy, and the environment — excluding agriculture, which uses vast quantities of water — and how calamitous circumstances could become for large numbers of people and the consequential need for sound policy implementation. Water and energy are required for modern societies to sustain growth. Water is the most important resource since is it necessary to sustain life, but without

energy, food cannot be grown, homes, offices, or schools powered, nor can communications work effectively. A growing population will create demands on these resources at a faster pace than in the past and with consequences that will likely be both unanticipated and disastrous. And, without back-up for most of these systems, various economic, health, and other effects could linger for years.

While these strains between energy and water require sound management and policy development at the local level, especially in water-stressed areas such as the Southwest U.S., relations across boundaries of countries (termed transboundary issues) become ever more important and may likely become the key to preventing potential armed conflict. Water quality concerns, availability and sustainability, border issues, climate change, increasing populations, and growing demands for these resources are creating tough challenges. If, for example, the U.S. and its allies are determined to sever dependence on foreign oil for energy and security concerns, what will this imply for water resources?

Currently there is no cohesive approach since the Department of Energy is concerned more about energy issues than water, assuming there will be sufficient water resources for energy needs; and other agencies, such as NOAA and NASA, only collect water data and are not involved in policy, while the Environmental Protection Agency regulates its quality. The latter looks primarily at water and not at energy and thus, for the most part, all three work separately and discontinuously in closely related areas of these problems; failure to link the criticality of these resources and develop joint policy will likely lead to sustainability issues. Perhaps it will be necessary to form a Department of Water within the U.S. Government, which would be far better economically than nationalization of the U.S. water infrastructure. And, continued failure to develop a national energy policy will likely cause a backlash of results that cannot be escaped. Since other energy sources lag far behind the use of oil and are too expensive for the general population to afford, when oil becomes too costly or in critically short supply, the U.S. lifestyle and that of the world will necessarily shift dramatically and irreversibly.

The energy-water link creates many problems, whether looking at carbon emissions from transportation and their reduction, plug-in cars and their increased energy requirements, or biofuels and

the large quantities of water required to grow them, and scaling these issues nationally and globally becomes a complex strategic issue. The choice for one energy use versus another will require an abundant, dependable, and affordable water supply — oil is not a substitute for drinking water. This chapter will focus on energy-water interdependencies and the primary requirements of the energy industry for water resources and how energy processes affect them.

Energy — Water Interdependencies

Water is a vital and integral element for the development of U.S. and global energy resources and utilization. It is used in energy-resource extraction, refining and processing, and transportation. All of these are vitally interdependent because of their relation to critical infrastructure (see chapter 1). For example, water plays an integral role in electric-power generation, where it is used directly in hydroelectric generation and extensively for cooling and emissions scrubbing in thermoelectric generation. In calendar year 2000, thermoelectric power generation accounted for 39 percent of all freshwater withdrawals in the U.S., or about the same as water withdrawals for irrigated agriculture (34 percent — withdrawals are water diverted or withdrawn from a surface-water or groundwater source).[115] Water withdrawals for thermoelectric power are dominated by power plants that return virtually all withdrawn water to the source and account for 3.3 percent of total freshwater consumption (3.3 billion gallons per day) and represented over 20 percent of non-agricultural water withdrawal.[116] Although this water is returned at a higher temperature and with other changes in quality, it remains available for future use. A number of power plants, including most of those built since 1980, withdraw much less water but consume much of what they withdraw through the process of evaporative cooling, which causes greater pressure on water supplies.

The latest U.S. Census Bureau projections estimate a population increase of 70 million in the next 25 years. Using this estimate, the Energy Information Administration (EIA) predicts

[115] Hutson, "Estimated Use of Water in the United States in 2000."
[116] Ibid

electricity demand to grow by about 50 percent.[117] This projection assumes current laws, regulations, policies, technological progress, and consumer preferences will continue through the projection period. Much of this growth is expected to occur in the Southeast, Southwest, and Far West U.S., where water stress is already prevalent. Additionally, these determinations do not factor in potential destruction by transnational or domestic terrorist groups. Further, nearly all of these systems have no supply redundancy. Once they are destroyed, supply is permanently interrupted until infrastructure is completely rebuilt.

Following current trends for U.S. withdrawal rates, the consumption of water in the electric industry could grow substantially. Although increased demand for water would provide an incentive for technologies that reduce water use, it is unlikely that these technologies would prevent water shortages that are likely to occur if only through general climate changes in which cyclic droughts are common. While technologies are available that can reduce water use in the electric industry, including alternative cooling for thermoelectric power plants, wind power, and solar photovoltaics — economics, policy, and environmental factors have limited implementation. In contrast, water use in the extraction and processing of transportation fuels is relatively small. However, as the U.S. seeks to replace imported petroleum and natural gas with fuels from domestic sources, such as biofuels, synfuel from coal, hydrogen, and oil shale, the demand for water to produce energy fuels will likely grow significantly.

Case Study: Water for Energy Production — the Roan Plateau

Domestic growth of natural gas and oil shale development will probably continue to be increasingly concentrated in the western U.S. One of the more important areas is the Roan Plateau in northwestern Colorado, which has large amounts of both natural gas and oil shale (a rock that contains kerogen, a precursor to

---

[117] EIA, "Annual Energy Outlook 2006: With Projections to 2030," (Washington, DC: Energy Information Administration, 2006.

conventional crude oil generally associated with marine lakes). The Office of Technology Assessment estimated that the amount of water used for oil shale production would range from 2.1 to 5.2 barrels for each barrel of oil.[118] Current operations processes required three barrels of water for each barrel of oil. The Bureau of Land Management (BLM) used a daily production of 350,000 barrels/day (denoted as bbl/day); projections for the entire planning area are 2.5 million bbl/day. This level of production would require 740,000 acre-feet of water annually (241 billion gallons or enough to provide the annual water needs of 3,569,049 U.S. residents). In 2002, this figure was updated to 21 trillion cubic feet (tcf). Further, BLM estimates that the Roan Plateau alone (an area of approximately 77,000 acres) holds 15.4 tcf, which is enough energy to heat four million homes for 20 years, with leases worth as much as $1.3 billion for Colorado.[119]

Findings suggest such large sums of money are not conductive to good decision making for policy development and implementation. For example, will the revenue from energy production be thought more important than life-sustaining water, which will be used in exorbitant quantities? One may not need to look further than the BP oil leak in the Gulf of Mexico, in which it appeared that the rights of the oil company surpassed the desires of a presidential administration and trumped established environmental regulations. Is this the future?

The increasing domestic, agricultural, and environmental water demands and the strain these place on freshwater resources can limit growth in energy supply as a result of competition between these sources. Since 1980, few new dams or reservoirs have been built; freshwater surface withdrawals have leveled off at about 260 billion gallons per day. Many regions around the world, but particularly in the U.S., depend on groundwater to meet increasing water demands; however, declining groundwater tables could severely limit future water availability. Some regions have

---

[118]Oil Shale and Tar Sands Resource Management Plan Amendments to addrress land-use allocations in Colorado, Utah, and Wyoming and Programmatic Environmental Impact Statement BLM, 2008.

[119]BLM, "Blm Roan Plateau Eligibility Report for the National Wild and Scenic Rivers System," ed. Bureau of Land Management (Washington DC: Government Printing Office, 2002).

experienced a severe drop in groundwater levels (as much as 300 to 900 feet) during the past 50 years due to water withdrawal from aquifers because of a greater rate of withdrawal than the rate of natural recharge. This is a widespread, global problem. As an example, a commonly used aquifer that provides water to metropolitan Denver, Colorado, is the Dawson aquifer. Annual withdrawal rates from this aquifer are about 85 cm per year while the natural recharge rate is only 1.5 cm per year, or 56 times less than the withdrawal rate.[120]

A 2003 General Accounting Office study showed that most state water managers expect either local or regional water shortages within the next 10 years under average climate conditions.[121] For drought conditions, more severe water shortages would be expected. This will likely become a recurring problem since many regions experience cyclical droughts. With each succeeding cycle, groundwater levels are generally reduced and surface water supplies during drought periods often decline dramatically; this will increase water stress and cause greater competition between users, energy production, and resources. Further, water shortages will greatly affect energy and food prices as cascading failures begin to occur throughout these systems. Because the average food supplies are trucked 1,500 miles from production areas, food prices could soar out of control and become the number one spending priority for the majority of the population.

Depending on the water quality needs such as cooling of nuclear power plants, freshwater supplies can be augmented with degraded/brackish water or waste water. For example, the Palo Verde Power Plant (nuclear), 45 miles west of Phoenix, uses treated sewage from several nearby municipalities (this plant produces 3.2 GW annually and serves four million customers).[122] Water quantities

---

[120] R.G. Rayolds, Moore, J.E., and Barkmann, P.E., "Groundwater Mining of Bedrock Aquifers in the Denver Basin - Past, Present, and Future," *Environmental Geology* 47, no. 1 (2004); J.E. Moore, Rayolds, R.G., and Barkmann, P.E., "Groundwater Mining of Bedrock Aquifers in the Denver Basin - Past, Present, and Future," *Environmental Geology* 47, no. 1 (2004).

[121] GAO, "Freshwater Supply: States' Views of How Federal Agencies Could Help Them Meet the Challenges of Expected Shortages," (Government Accounting Office, 2003).

[122] Kate Galbraith, "Treated Wastewater for Thirsty Power Plants," *New York Times*,

available for distribution are dependent on the water qualities needed for each use. Increased use of brackish or degraded water may be required in some areas if water users can accept the quality limitations or can afford the cost of energy and infrastructure for water treatment. Many areas around the coastal U.S. and other countries already face the recurring problem of salt-water intrusion. This is due to increased population in these areas that creates greater demand for groundwater supplies. The groundwater is withdrawn, creating less pressure than that provided by the adjacent salt-water table — this pressure difference (greater pressure on the salt-water side) promotes salt water intrusion into freshwater supplies. This is a common problem along coastal areas.

Energy-Water Link

Energy production requires an abundant, predictable, and reliable source of water. However, good quality water is already in short supply throughout much of the U.S. and the world — especially in water-stressed areas. Agriculture uses approximately 70 percent of total water in the U.S., which compares similarly to other countries and, if people wish to eat, there is little that can be done to trim agricultural consumption long-term — due to population increase, agricultural productions must dramatically increase. However, this will cause increased pressure on both water and energy supplies and resources.

The electricity industry ranks second as the largest user of water. Electricity production from fossil fuels and nuclear energy requires 190,000 million gallons of water per day (39 percent of all freshwater withdrawals in the U.S., with 71 percent attributed to fossil-fuel electricity generation).[123] Coal, the most abundant fossil fuel, accounts for 52 percent of U.S. electricity generation; each kWh (kilowatt hour) generated from coal requires the withdrawal of 25 gallons of water. However, this is far less than water use needed for extraction of oil from oil shale. For U.S. citizens, this implies that indirect use of water (home lighting and electric appliances) is approximately equal to direct use (drinking water, water lawns, and

November 4 2008.

[123]Hutson, "Estimated Use of Water in the United States in 2000."

taking showers). According to the 2001 National Energy Policy, population and economic growth in the U.S. alone will require 393,000 MW of new generating capacity by the year 2020. This will further strain U.S. water resources. To supply this demand would require 1,000 new, 400 MW power plants or, about 70 trillion gallons and 88 trillion gallons for fossil/biomass/waste and nuclear power plants, respectively. How much water is that? To illustrate, Lake Mead requires about two years of annual flow from the Colorado River to fill the reservoirs to capacity, which is about nine trillion gallons. Thus, additional power plant water requirements, for fossil/biomass/waste plants, would be enough to fill Lake Mead about eight times.

This scope is difficult for most to comprehend. Additionally, given current economic problems across the nation and within all states, construction of these facilities is very unlikely, which means decreasing energy supplies per capita. It would therefore appear that the most probable solution will be strict limits on energy and water use and/or rolling blackouts to provide necessary supplies. This will help conserve both resources. Continued lack of a formal energy policy, which should be joined to a water policy, will only exacerbate this process. However, due to political self interests, party partisanship, and related issues, it appears unlikely the U.S. will develop an effective energy policy; after all, the efforts first began in 1930 and yet no policy exists.

There is a problem with this scenario, which underscores whether a stable, affordable supply of water will exist to support future U.S. electricity demands and continued economic development at a time when additional jobs are greatly needed:

- **U.S. and global populations are expected to increase significantly; accessible freshwater supplies will not. These supplies are finite; two of the few options to increase or supplement these water supplies are desalination and drinking water treated from city sewage and wastewater as is done in Singapore. The latter is unappealing to most Americans.**
- **Energy necessary for treatment and distribution of water accounts for about 80 percent of its cost; an insufficient supply of affordable energy will have a negative impact on both the price and availability of water. Increasing gas**

prices will have a dramatic impact on water availability and pricing.

- **Population migration and increase in relation to energy demand do not always coincide with water availability. For example, during the 1990s in the U.S., the largest regional population growth, 25 percent, occurred in one of the most water deficient regions, the mountain west.**
- **Water availability is a serious issue in water-stressed regions of the U.S., particularly in the southeast, where population has increased by nearly 14 percent since 1990. In comparison, the water-rich northeast has experienced only a two percent population growth.[124] In other countries such as Darfur, Jordan, and Israel, this problem is more aggravated. Figure 4.1 illustrates population growth in water-stressed areas of the U.S. compared to those with more plentiful water supplies.**
- **An increasing population will require more electricity and more food. More food requires more energy from fossil fuels and more water for crop production. This will create serious competition between the nation's two largest water users for limited water supplies (energy and agriculture). For example, ethanol produced from corn requires nearly 2,500 liters of water to produce one kilogram (300 gal per lb) of ethanol. And, in the U.S., corn commonly is grown in areas experiencing a 20 to 50 percent growth in population. This combination changes irrigation and crop management practices and significantly stresses water resources. Similar trends occur globally.**
- **Proposed restrictions on the use of water for power generation to protect fish and other aquatic organisms could result in both increased costs of electricity and potential energy shortages. This may be especially true since 'green' advocates are calling for the dismantling of existing dams. A line will be drawn — either man is more**

[124] U.S. Census Bureau. Population Estimates program, Population Division.

important or fish and other aquatic life are. Who will make this choice and what will the consequences be?

The critical interdependence between water and energy is inseparable; one resource cannot exist in an industrial economy without the other. Also, the interdependence between these critical infrastructure and others, as well as economic industries and sectors is far deeper than most imagine. If the serious threat of population growth and competition between these resources is not frightening, it should at least be of grave concern.

Figure 4.1: U.S. population growth in water-stressed regions (Source: Energy Analysis Office).

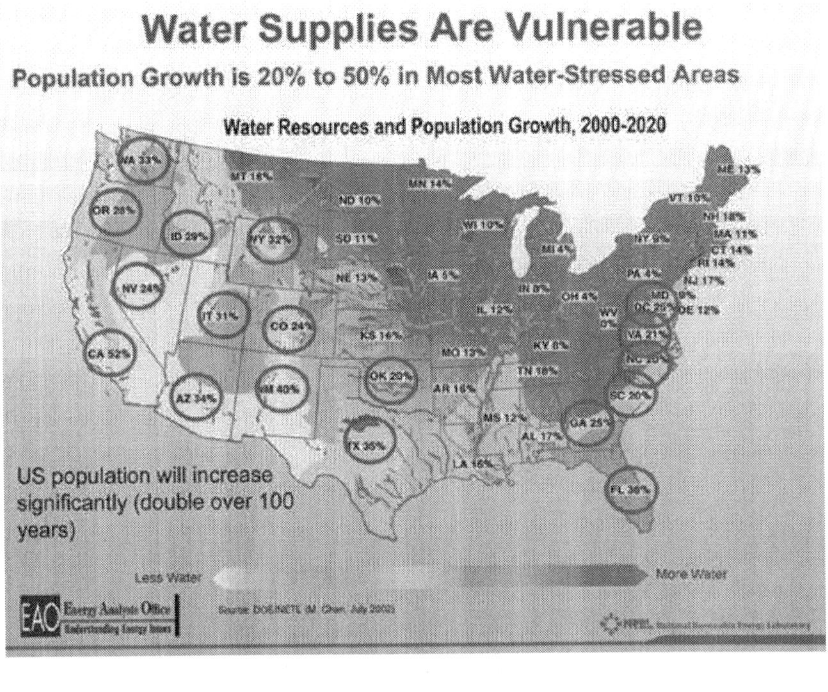

Demands from Energy on Water Resources

Because of increasing population, trends in increased energy use, water stress, and reduced water availability, and increasing water demand indicate the U.S. and the world will continue to confront issues related to the development, management, and utilization of

both resources. Increasing global populations will increase demand for direct use of water, as well as for energy and agricultural production. Historically, water withdrawals for domestic supplies have grown at about the same rate as the population. However, during the 20th century, while global population increased three fold, demand for water worldwide increased six fold.[125] New technologies, conservation efforts, public education, and other measures must be implemented to ensure adequate energy and water supplies. Continuing to use the technology of evaporative cooling for power plants as an example, consumption of water for electrical energy production could more than double by 2030, i.e., to 7.3 billion gallons per day.[126] In the U.S., consumption by the electric industry alone could equal the entire country's 1995 domestic water consumption. This amount would be in addition to water use for extraction and production of transportation fuels from domestic sources, as well as cyclical drought problems, agricultural use, and other needs. In the future, we can expect less freshwater, not more, to be available.

The availability of adequate water supplies has an impact on the availability of energy. Concurrently, energy production and generation activities affect the availability and quality of water. Energy and water, due to interdependence, must be managed together to maintain reliable energy and water supplies or severe shortages of both could occur. Examples include low water levels from drought and competing uses that can and limit the ability of power plants to generate power.[127] Additionally, water levels in aquifers in many regions of the U.S. have declined significantly, increasing energy requirements for pumping, and, in some cases, leading to ground

---

[125] WWC, "Water Crises," http://www.worldwatercouncil.org/index/php?id=25; World Water Council, "Water Crisis," World Water Council, http://www.worldwatercouncil.org/index/php?id=25.

[126] S. Forbes, Hoffmann, J., and Feeley, T., "Estimating Freshwater Needs to Meet 2025 Electricity Generating Capacity Forecasts," ed. National Energy Technology Laboratory (Washington DC: Government Printing Office, 2004); Sarah Forbes Jeffrey Hoffmann, and Thomas Feeley, "Estimating Freshwater Needs to Meet 2025 Electricity Generating Capacity Forecasts," ed. National Energy Technology Laboratory (U.S. Department of Energy, 2004).

[127] Staff, ""Bpa Outlines Impacts of Summer Spill on Transmission System," *Columbia Basin Bulletin*, January 13, 2006 2006; Basin Bulletin, "Bpa Outlines Impacts of Summer Spill on Transmission System," *Columbia Basin Bulletin*, January 13 2006.

subsidence issues, i.e., sinkholes. Further, lack of water for thermoelectric power plant cooling and for hydropower that can limit generation has the potential to increase demand for technologies that reduce the water intensity of the energy industry.

As population increases, the demand for energy will continue to grow. The EIA projects that demand for energy supplies from 2003 to 2030 will grow as follows: petroleum, 38 percent; natural gas, 20 percent; coal, 54 percent; nuclear power, 14 percent; and renewable energy, 58 percent. Demand for electricity from all sources is projected to increase by 53 percent. [128]

Freshwater withdrawals exceed precipitation[129] **in many areas across the U.S. The shortfalls are most dramatic in the Southwest, the high plains, California, and Florida. Population growth in these regions between 2000 and 2025 is estimated to be 30 to 50 percent.**[130] **This growth will place an increased demand on both water and energy. EPRI estimates that most of the western shoreline of Lake Michigan has water demand above available precipitation.**[131] **For example, groundwater levels along the southwestern shores of Lake Michigan have declined hundreds of feet since predevelopment and by 1980 had reached maximum withdrawals of up to 900 feet near Chicago.**[132] **Levels are declining as much as 17 feet per year in some locations.**[133]

---

[128] EIA, "Annual Energy Outlook 2006: With Projections to 2030."

[129] Note: portions of this chapter have been extracted, modified, and updated from agency reports to reflect current trends and circumstances.

[130] P. Campbell, "Population Projections: States, 1995-2025, Current Population Reports," ed. Economics and Statistics Administration (Washington DC: U.S. Department of Commerce, 1997).

[131] EPRI, "Water and Sustainability (Vol. 3)," in *U. S. Water Consumption for Power Production — the Next Half Century* (Electric Power Research Institute, 2002); — — — , "Water and Sustainability (Volume 3): U. S. Water Consumption for Power Production — the Next Half Century," (Electric Power Research Institute, 2002a).

[132] J.R. Bartolino, and Cunningham, W.L., "Groundwater Depletion across the Nation," ed. U.S. Geological Survey (Reston: Government Printing Office, 2003); J.R. Bartolino and W.L. Cunningham, "Groundwater Depletion across the Nation," ed. U.S. Geological Survey (Government Printing Office, 2003).

[133] Staff, "Lake Michigan's Wild West Coast: Looking for Water Laws and Order, Code Red in a Blue Water Basin," (Michigan Land Use Institute, 2003); Michigan Land Use Institute, "Lake Michigan's Wild West Coast: Looking for Water Laws and Order, Code Red in a Blue Water Basin," (2003).

Energy Requires Water — Impacts on Water Quality

Water is used throughout the energy industry for resource extraction, refining and processing, electric power generation, storage, and transport. The energy industry also can impact water quality via waste streams, runoff from mining operations (generally mine tailings), produced water from oil and gas extraction (such as from coal-bed methane), and air emissions that may affect downwind watersheds. Examples of these interactions of energy and water are shown in Table 4.1. Large energy facilities such as power plants, mines, and refineries can have a significant impact on local water supplies and water quality. For example, water withdrawals for thermoelectric power generation alone are comparable to water withdrawals for irrigation. While each represents about 40 percent of U.S. water withdrawals (water that is diverted or withdrawn from a surface-water or groundwater source), energy production returns the majority of withdrawn water. In 1995, all but about 3.3 billion gallons per day (three percent of the 132 billion gallons per day of freshwater withdrawn for thermoelectric power plants) was returned to the source. Although this water was returned at a higher temperature and with other changes in water quality, it remains available for future use. In contrast, of the 134 billion gallons per day withdrawn for irrigation in 1995, 81 billion gallons per day were consumed by evaporation and transpiration (60 percent); another 25 billion gallons per day (19 percent) were reported as lost in conveyance; this would be loss in infiltration to groundwater and some evaporation; it would not be immediately available for future use.[134] However, due to recharge rates, water used for irrigation (that which is not used by plants), i.e., leaked through the conveyance process or evaporated, will eventually become available for future use as governed by recharge rates and hydrologic cycle. In the case of recharge rates, since they are generally slow, withdrawal rates could always be in excess of recharge, causing a growing water deficit.

Another area that relates to energy use, logistics, etc., is the water needed for standing armies, i.e., the military during war and conflict occupation. Their water use is substantial, but will not be focused on in this report.

---

[134] Hutson, "Estimated Use of Water in the United States in 2000."

Water Use and Thermoelectric Power Generation

Thermoelectric power generating technologies using steam to drive turbine generators require cooling to condense the steam at the turbine exhaust. These plants receive heat from a variety of sources, including coal, nuclear, natural gas, oil, biomass (e.g., wood and crop waste), concentrated solar energy, and geothermal energy. The amount of freshwater required for cooling is significant (59 billion gallons of seawater and 136 billion gallons of freshwater per day).[135]

Table 4.1: Interaction of Water to Energy Processes

Energy Element	Link to Water Quality	Link to Water Quality
Electric Power Generation		
Thermoelectric (fossil, biomass, nuclear)	Water required for cooling[1] and scrubbing	Thermal and air emissions can impact surface-water quality and ecology
Hydroelectric	Reservoirs have huge evaporation losses	Can impact water quality, temperatures, and ecology
Solar Photovoltaic's and Wind	None during operation	
Energy Extraction and Production		
Oil and Gas Exploration	Water required for drilling, completion, and fracturing	Impact on shallow groundwater quality
Oil and Gas Production	Large volume of produced, impaired water[2]	Produced water can impact surface and groundwater supplies
Coal and Uranium Mining	Mining operations usually generate large quantities of water	Tailings and drainage can impact surface and ground-water quality
Refining and Processing		
Traditional Oil and Gas Refining	Water needed for refinement processes	End use can impact water quality
Biofuels and Ethanol	Water needed for agricultural production and refining	Refinery requires waste-water treatment

135 Ibid.

Synfuels and Hydrogen	Water needed for synthesis or steam reforming[3]	Wastewater requires treatment
Energy Transportation and Storage		
Energy Pipelines	Water needed for hydrostatic testing	Wastewater requires treatment
Coal Slurry Pipelines	Water needed for slurry transport; water not recycled	Wastewater requires treatment
Barge Transport of Energy	River flows and stages impact fuel delivery; time and cost	Spills or accidents may impact water quality
Oil and Gas Storage Caverns	Slurry mining of caverns requires large quantities of water	Slurry disposal impacts water quality and ecology

[1]Includes geothermal (steam) and solar electric plants.
[2]Impaired water may include contaminants or be saline; production of Coal-bed methane is a good example.
[3]Steam reforming is the conversion of methane into hydrogen and carbon monoxide in reaction with steam over a nickel catalyst.

About 31 percent of current U.S. generating capacity is composed of thermoelectric generating stations (older plants prior to 1970) using open-loop cooling; water is withdrawn for cooling then discharged back to the source. This discharged water is heated through the cooling process; being heated, it can lead to about 1 percent enhanced evaporative loss to the atmosphere.[136] Although not consumed, the availability of large volumes of water for cooling is critical to plant operations. Additionally, the intake and discharge of large volumes of water by these plants have potential environmental consequences. Aquatic life can be adversely affected by impingement (entrapment on intake screens), entrainment (sucked into the cooling water system), and by the discharge of warm water back to the source. Existing open-loop cooling systems may have several more decades of service life and therefore continue to represent a significant

[136] EPRI, "Water and Sustainability (Volume 4): U.S. Electricity Consumption for Water Supply & Treatment-the Next Half Century," (Electric Power Research Institute, 2002b); "Water and Sustainability (Volume 3): U. S. Water Consumption for Power Production — the Next Half Century."

demand for water, though an increased value of water could provide an incentive for cooling improvements that need less water.

Most thermoelectric plants installed since the mid-1970s are cooled by evaporation of the cooling water.[137] Water is pumped in a closed loop through a cooling tower or a cooling pond. These systems withdraw less than five percent of the water withdrawn by open-loop systems, but most of the water withdrawn is lost to evaporation. Total freshwater consumption for the thermoelectric power industry was 3.3 billion gallons per day in 1995.[138] This represents only 3.3 percent of total U.S. water consumption, about 100 billion gallons/day, but is nearly 20 percent of nonagricultural consumption.

Water Power Generation Use for Hydroelectric

Hydroelectric power is also an important part of the electrical industry in the U.S. because it plays an important role in stabilizing the electrical transmission grid and in meeting peak loads, reserve requirements, and other ancillary electrical energy needs. It is unique because it can respond very quickly to changing demand. In addition to the U.S., hydroelectric power generation is an important part of electricity generation in Europe, parts of the Middle East, China (particularly the Three Gorges Dam), and other countries. Within the U.S. it supplied about 6 to 10 percent of generated power between 1990 and 2003.[139] A primary hazard associated with hydroelectric power is that its production varies significantly with water availability (the less water available, the less electricity generated), which can depend upon weather patterns and local hydrology, competing water uses, such as agriculture, flood control, water supply, recreation, and in-stream flow needs such as for navigation and aquatic environments. In this regard, system failures that begin to cascade can have a significant consequence, and a terrorist attack or catastrophic natural hazard such as an earthquake can cause ramifications that could affect the entire country.

---

[137] EIA, "Steam Electric Plant Operation and Design Report," (Energy Information Administration, 2004).

[138] Hutson, "Estimated Use of Water in the United States in 2000."

[139] EIA, "Annual Energy Review 2004," (Energy Information Administration, 2005).

Hydroelectric plant design and operation is highly diverse; projects vary from large, multipurpose storage reservoirs to run-of-river projects that have little or no active water storage. About 85 percent of critical infrastructure in the U.S. is owned by the private industry, but in the case of hydroelectric production, almost one half is federally owned; the other half consists of nonfederal projects that are regulated by the Federal Energy Regulatory Commission (FERC). However, being of smaller scale, there are ten times more non-federal hydropower projects in the U.S. than federal projects. The average water flow through hydroelectric turbines is 3,160 billion gallons/day — about ten times the withdrawals of water from rivers.[140] This water is not categorized as withdrawn water since it remains in the river and is, therefore, generally used multiple times by successive dams.[141] Because of this, reservoir operation can reallocate water releases relative to natural flows. Hydropower projects, such as Lake Mead associated with Hoover Dam near Las Vegas, involves large storage reservoirs; evaporation of water from these reservoirs can represent a significant consumptive use. An estimated, annual average loss for U.S. hydroelectric reservoirs is 4,500 gal/MWh; annual electricity generation is about 300 million MWh.[142] Total evaporation losses are estimated at 3.8 billion gallons per day, but due to multiple use, hydroelectric power is not the only cause of evaporative losses. This evaporation occurs from reservoir surfaces as well as from water use.

Water Use for Energy Extraction and Fuel Production

Water consumption for energy extraction and fuel production is categorized within the industrial/mining industry.[143] Although large amounts of water are used in the conventional extraction of resources, more water is used in conversion into useful

---

[140] Hutson, "Estimated Use of Water in the United States in 2000."

[141] The USGS serves the U.S. by providing reliable scientific information to describe and understand the Earth; minimize loss of life and property from natural disasters; manage water, biologicical, energy, and mineral resources; and enhance and protect quality of life (www.usgs.gov).

[142] EIA, "Annual Energy Review 2004."

[143] The USGS categorizes water sources for various purposes.

forms of energy, whether for converting coal or uranium to electricity as described above or converting petroleum into fuels such as gasoline or diesel. This will likely become very problematic in the future as population increases and forces a natural competition between the energy and agricultural industries for available water resources. This also implies that the threat of a terrorist-attack scenario could be significantly more devastating with time. Refinery use of water for processing and cooling is about 1 to 2.5 gallons of water for every gallon of product. The United States refines nearly 800 million gallons of petroleum products per day, representing about 1 to 2 billion gallons of water per day for the refining process.[144] Natural gas processing and pipeline operations consume an additional 0.4 billion gallons per day. Water is used in the mining industry to cool or lubricate cutting and drilling equipment for dust suppression, fuel processing, and re-vegetation when mining operations and energy extraction are completed. The total water estimated for use in coal mining varies from 1 to 6 gallons per million British thermal units (MMBtu), depending on the source of the coal.[145] When combined with 2003 coal production data (EIA, 2006), total water use for coal mining is estimated at 70 to 260 million gallons per day. Oil shale (the case of the Roan Plateau was mentioned earlier) is another potential domestic source of oil. Based on increasing oil demands and prices, opportunities may exist for significant expansion in the future. But, because oil shale resources are predominantly located in water-stressed areas, development may be constrained by water availability and cost.

Biofuels currently provide about 3 percent of U.S. transportation fuel, with more than 130 ethanol and biodiesel plants in operation, producing over four billion gallons of biofuel each year.[146] The most water-intensive aspect of biofuel production is growing the feedstock, with water consumption for refining generally similar to that for oil refining. When the feedstock is corn or soy (used to make ethanol and biodiesel, respectively) and grown on irrigated land, water consumption per gallon of fuel produced can

---

[144] — — —, "Annual Energy Outlook 2006: With Projections to 2030."

[145] M.S. Lancet, "Distribution and Material Balances of Trace Elements During Coal Cleaning" (paper presented at the International Coal Preparation Conference, 1993).

[146] RFA, "Ethanol Industry Outlook 2006," (Renewable Fuels Association, 2006).

exceed the water consumption for refining by a factor of one thousand.[147] Considering that costs to produce $1 USD of Ethanol are actually $1.30, this is a poor use of water resources since the virtual water represented by the feedstock production represents a costlier resource use.

Initial extraction of conventional oil and gas requires minimal consumption of water. However, significant quantities of water (termed produced water) are extracted with the oil and gas. The quality of produced water can range from nearly fresh to hyper saline; the majority is as saline as seawater. As oil wells age, enhanced recovery techniques are used to extract additional oil, which involve injection of water or steam into the well; some are very water-intensive. Water consumption ranges from 2 to 350 gallons of water per gallon of oil extracted, depending upon the recovery enhancement process. Most of the water used for these purposes is not otherwise usable.[148] Most produced water associated with onshore production is injected back into the producing zones to enhance production or into other formations well below any usable groundwater resources.

Produced Water Volumes during Energy Extraction

In 1995, oil and gas operations generated about 18 billion barrels of produced water (49 million gallons per day), compared to total annual petroleum production of 6.7 billion barrels of oil equivalent (both onshore and offshore production, including crude oil, natural gas, and natural gas liquids production).[149] Produced water varies in quality; with treatment, some may be used for other purposes. Today, the amount of water produced per well varies greatly. For example, water produced by coal-bed methane

---

[147] USDA, "Farm and Ranch Irrigation Survey," ed. National Agriculture Statistics Service (U.S. Dept of Agriculture, 2004).

[148] API, "Overview of Exploration and Production Water Volumes and Wast Management Practices in the United States," ed. ICF Consulting (American Petroleum Institute, 2000); P.H. Gleick, "Water and Energy," *Annual Reviews Environmental Resources* 19(1994).

[149] API, "Overview of Exploration and Production Water Volumes and Wast Management Practices in the United States."

extraction can vary from 7 barrels of water per barrel of oil equivalent in the San Juan Basin (Colorado and New Mexico) to approximately 900 barrels of water per barrel of oil equivalent in the Powder River Basin (Wyoming and Montana).[150] In the Powder River Basin in Wyoming, coal-bed methane produced waters substantially increased soil salinity, making it difficult for vegetation to extract nutrients for plant growth, which affects water resources, the environment, and farmers in the region with serious problems likely to manifest within the next decade.[151]

Energy Processes — Impacts on Water Quality

Oil and gas production that is not adequately managed and monitored can contaminate surface water and shallow aquifers through drilling and production operations or from spills of produced hydrocarbons or brackish water. Refining and processing of oil and gas can generate by-products and wastewater streams that, if not handled appropriately, can cause water contamination. Fuel additives, such as methyl tertiary-butyl ether (MTBE), that have been used to reduce air emissions have also emerged as potential groundwater contaminants.

Energy resource mining and processing, such as coal and uranium mining and oil shale development, can contaminate surface and groundwater. Runoff from both main mine operations and tailings piles can significantly reduce soil and water pH levels and increase heavy metals concentrations in mine drainage water, termed acid-mine drainage. Additionally, runoff from oil shale residue can wash into surface waters and byproducts from in-place extraction methods can impact groundwater quality. An increased interest in U.S. uranium supplies has led to the reopening of some older mines in New Mexico and Utah. By doing so, these mines could generate three to five million gallons of water a day that would need to be

---

150 C.A. Rice, and Nuccio, V., "Water Produced with Coal-Bed Methane," ed. Water Resources Division (Reston: USGS, 2000); C.A. Rice and Vito Nuccio, "Water Produced with Coal-Bed Methane," ed. Water Resources Division (U.S. Geological Survey, 2000).

151 M. Stearns, Tindall, J.A., Cronin, G., Friedel, M.J., and Bergquist, E., "Effects of Coal-Bed Methane Discharge Waters on the Vegetation and Soil Ecosystem in Powder River Basin, Wyoming," *Water, Air, and Soil Pollution* no. 168 (2005).

properly disposed. Water from some abandoned mines must be pumped and treated to prevent contamination of surface waters.[152] This requires more energy and more water. Additionally, water used for pipeline testing, coal slurry pipelines, and solution mining for oil and gas storage caverns creates a range of contaminants that can pollute fresh or coastal water sources if not adequately managed. Hydroelectric plants can impact water quality and river ecology in several ways by changing water temperatures and dissolved oxygen and nitrogen levels in downstream waters and by changing natural flow characteristics of rivers, thereby impacting aquatic ecology. All of these issues can become problems associated with water and public health (see chapter 5).

Supplying Water Requires Energy

Satisfying U.S. and global water needs requires energy for supply, purification, distribution, and treatment of water and wastewater. About four percent of U.S. power generation is used for water supply and treatment.[153] Electricity represents approximately 75 percent of the cost of municipal water processing and distribution.[154] The major difference between water uses among regions is in the amount of energy used to supply water for agriculture. In general, per capita non-agricultural use of energy for water is similar region to region. However, within regions, there can be substantial variation in energy requirements for water supply and treatment, depending upon the source, the distance water is conveyed, and local topography. California is an interesting case study in electrical consumption and illustrates the cost of long-distance water conveyance. California uses about five percent of its electricity

---

[152] C.B. Cecil, and Tewalt, S.J., "Coal Extraction-Environmental Prediction," ed. Water Resources Division (Reston: USGS, 2002); C. Blaine Cecil and Susan J. Tewalt, "Coal Extraction-Environmental Prediction," ed. Water Resources Division (U.S. Geological Survey, 2002).

[153] EPRI, "Water and Sustainability (Volume 4): U.S. Electricity Consumption for Water Supply & Treatment-the Next Half Century."

[154] C. Powicki, "The Water Imperative," *Electric Power Research Institute* (2002).

consumption for water supply and treatment, which is substantially above the national average.[155]

Energy for Water Supply and Conveyance

Supply and conveyance can be the most energy-intensive portion of the water delivery chain. If the water source is groundwater, pumping requirements for supply of freshwater from aquifers varies with depth: 540 kWh per million gallons from a depth of 120 feet, 2000 kWh per million gallons from 400 feet.[156] These energy needs increase in areas where groundwater levels are declining, such as in large or mega-city areas.[157] Energy requirements to pump water from surface waters can be negligible for users located close to the source, with increased requirements with distance. In California, water is conveyed from Northern California up to 400 miles via the State Water Project to the cities of Southern California. Energy savings can be realized when wastewater streams are made available for reuse, rather than conveying freshwater over long distances, as demonstrated in the example of the Palo Verde nuclear power plant. Additionally, long-distance conveyance introduces enhanced security risks for both resources and for the people who rely upon them.

Energy for Treatment and Distribution

Generally, groundwater requires minimal energy for purification, while surface water requires more. Also, energy requirements for distribution and collection vary depending on system size, topography, and age. Older systems often require more energy because of older infrastructure and less efficient equipment. In both the U.S. and internationally, this infrastructure, at least for established cities such as New York, San Francisco, Beijing, New Delhi, and others is over 100 years old and in bad repair. Water leakage through distribution systems in such cities and in most cities is about

---

[155] CEC, "2005 Integrated Energy Policy Report: Committee Draft Report," (California Energy Commission, 2005).

[156] R. Cohen, "Energy Down the Drain: The Hidden Costs of California's Water Supply," (National Resources Defense Council, 2004).

[157] A mega-city has been defined as having a population of 10 million or more persons.

20 percent, substantially increasing energy conveyance and delivery costs and, of course, increasing water quantities.

Energy consumption associated with water use is greater than energy consumption for supply and treatment. Activities such as water heating and washing and drying clothes require 14 percent of California's electricity consumption and 31 percent of its natural gas consumption. Most of that use is residential. Both water and energy can be conserved through the use of appliances such as low flush toilets, energy saving bulbs, and other technologies that reduce use. Even old technologies, still in use today, such as clothes lines in rural areas, could save enormous amounts of energy.

Future Energy Demands — Water Supply and Treatment

Population growth is creating an increased demand for water pumping from greater distances and greater depths. Therefore, as freshwater supplies become more limited, treating water from alternative sources will increase energy demand and costs. Additionally, emerging water treatment requirements, such as those for arsenic removal and emerging contaminants, are becoming more stringent. In 2050, per capita energy requirements are expected to be largely unchanged, except in the industrial and agricultural industries. Energy for public and commercial water supply and treatment are expected to grow with population, with an average increase for the U.S. of about 50 percent between 2000 and 2050. It remains to be seen how much it will cost to treat water containing emerging contaminants. However, due to their pernicious nature, the cost will likely be high. Emerging contaminants are generally the products not used but excreted from our bodies into wastewater systems and that are not currently treated for their removal. Examples of emerging contaminants include caffeine and a wide range of medications prescribed for patients as well as over the counter drugs such as cold medicines and so forth.

Water Shortages and Impacts on Energy Infrastructure

The U.S. energy infrastructure depends heavily on the availability of water and there are multiple problems concerning water availability and value due to growth from competing demands. Most state water managers expect shortages of water over the next decade, since water supply issues are already affecting many existing and proposed energy projects. In some regions, power plants have been required to limit electricity generation because of insufficient water supplies. Citizens and public officials concerned about the availability of water have opposed new high-water-use energy facilities, suggesting clear incentives for using lower water intensity designs in future energy-infrastructure developments. And yet, alternative energy such as wind, solar, and geothermal are limited in their availability to fill the gap in this area. The forms of energy are geographically specific and while large in areas of origin — wind in the northeast, solar energy in the southwest, etc. — conveyance over the distances needed for providing additional energy supplies is not economically viable with current technology. This is because Joule's Law states that the amount of energy lost is in proportion to the squared value of the current voltage. For example, for an electrical current voltage in a circuit of 110 volts, the electrical current lost is a factor of 10. To illustrate this concept, attach a standard 100 foot (30.5 meters) power cable and plug it into a lamp with a 100 watt bulb. If nine more 100 foot extension cables between the lamp and the power outlet are attached, the total distance the electricity would need to travel is 1,000 feet (304.8 meters). Due to the amount of electrical current lost while traveling this distance, there would not be enough power available to light the 100 watt bulb. In contrast, while power stations emit huge mega-watt amounts of power, these stations are also used by many, many consumers, which serves to illustrate the conveyance distance and use limitations.

Compounding the uncertainty regarding supply is the lack of current data on water consumption. Steady or declining rates of water withdrawal do not necessarily imply steady or declining consumption. For example, communities have responded to water shortages, in part, by increasing water re-use for such non-potable (not drinkable) uses as irrigation for parks and recreation, replacing lawns with native grass species, and so forth. Diverting wastewater effluent

from return flows to consumptive uses reduces the need for water withdrawal but does not reduce the rate of water consumption. Following are some examples:

1. **Browns Ferry Nuclear Power Plant, part of the TVA complex on the Tennessee River, often experiences warm river flows, such that the temperature of the water at the plant's cooling intakes often approaches or exceeds the Alabama water quality criterion of 86 °F, nearly the plant's discharge limit of 90 °F.**[158]
2. **Low water on the Missouri River leads to high pumping energy, blocked screens, lower efficiency, load reduction, or shutdown at power plants.**[159]
3. **Arizona rejected permitting for a proposed power plant because of potential impact on a local aquifer.**[160]
4. **University of Texas researchers said power plants would have to curtail production if 20th century drought conditions recurred.**[161]

National water availability and use has not been comprehensively assessed in 25 years, but current trends indicate that demands on U.S. water supplies are growing. Water use in relation to energy demand and production processes is also a problem due to lack of policy linkage. The nation's capacity for storing surface-water is limited, resulting in significant groundwater depletion. Conjointly, population growth, urbanization, and pressures to keep water in streams for fisheries and the environment are placing new demands on freshwater supplies. The potential effects of oscillating drought cycles and weather patterns associated with cyclical climate change also create uncertainty about future water availability and use.

---

[158] T.R. Curlee and M.J. Sale, "Water and Energy Security" (paper presented at the Universities Council on Water Resources, Washington DC, 2003).

[159] J.R. Kruse and A. Womack, "Implications of Alternative Missouri River Flows for Power Plants," (Washington DC: Food and Agricultural Policy Research Institute, 2004).

[160] Water News, "Idaho Denies Water Rights Request for Power Plants," *U.S. Water News Online* 2002.

[161] Clean Air Task Force, "Wounded Waters: The Hidden Side of Power Plant Pollution," (Boston: Clean Air Task Force, 2004).

Water-Management Challenges

Managing water resources requires balancing the competing needs for water with availability of supplies and storage capacity. Reservoirs store water to mitigate the effects of seasonal and annual variations in supply. Water resources are managed to meet the needs of many uses, including irrigation, recreation, hydroelectric power, downstream communities, industry, thermoelectric plants, and in-stream uses, such as navigation, fisheries, and wildlife habitat. Effective policy measures will be required (see chapter 16). As a case study, the Colorado River system provides an example of the challenges of management to meet competing needs. The river system provides a wide range of public benefits: navigation, flood damage reduction, affordable electricity, water quality, water supply, recreation, and economic growth, as well as water to California, principally Los Angeles (50 percent of its needs) and Mexico.

Each of these benefited areas wait in line as a wide variety of stakeholders want the system managed to serve Colorado interests first since the water originates there. Many similar examples occur around the world, including the Indus, Nile, Jordan, and Danube Rivers. For these systems, one of the greatest impacts, especially on surface water, is drought, which affects all stakeholders. Even high precipitation provides no guarantee of adequate water if inflow from precipitation does not coincide with demand. For example, snow pack provides 75 percent of the water supply in the West and is a key part of water storage for cities such as Denver, Colorado. Reservoirs on the middle and lower Colorado River basin can store several times the annual river flow, while reservoirs on the Columbia River can store only about 30 percent of annual flow. When warm temperatures cause rain instead of snow or snow melts earlier, Columbia River reservoirs lack the capacity to store early inflow. Consequently, water must be released early and is not available for later use. The best management tool for such circumstances would be a hydrospheric model — a combined hydrology and climate model of the region that could accurately predict both processes at least seven years forward. The TinMore Institute (www.tinmore.com) has recently developed such a model).

Long-term cyclical changes in precipitation patterns and the effect on flows in rivers and the operation of reservoirs and hydroelectric plants are a major concern to the energy industry. For example, the 2001 drought in the Northwest significantly reduced hydroelectric power production, leading to the loss of thousands of jobs in the energy-intensive aluminum industry.[162] Such loss of hydroelectric power affects not only total power generation, but also power reliability. Because the level of output from hydropower can be quickly changed, it is used to provide peaking power when demand is highest. Peaking capability is especially valuable in the summer, when high temperatures and high humidity can reduce generation efficiency from thermoelectric plants. In the absence of hydroelectric power, peaking needs are being met in most cases by natural gas. Further, besides the water-energy interdependence there are greater economic concerns at many levels — job loss is only one. Lack of peaking power could result in short and possibly longer-term business cessation with coinciding economic effects.

There is a significant incentive to decrease water quantities used by the energy industry. When warm weather or low flow leads to high water temperatures at the plant inlet, power plants may need to reduce generation to avoid exceeding discharge temperature limits specified in plant operating permits, which reduces electricity output. This can be particularly problematic if it occurs during peak demand. In a few cases, low flows, other environmental concerns, and increasing water value are providing incentives for the replacement or upgrade of open-loop cooling systems with new cooling systems to achieve water-efficient and economical generation of power. If surface waters are severely constrained by drought, plant water supplies could be impacted, especially if priority rights or water sharing is imposed.

Groundwater Concerns

Almost 40 percent of water provided by private water suppliers in the U.S. is from groundwater sources, serving 90 million

---

[162] Washington State, "Washington State Hazard Mitigation Plan," ed. Emergency Management Division (Washington Military Department, 2004).

people in all 50 states; another 40 million are self-supplied with groundwater.[163] Some aquifers are adjacent to surface waters; when these aquifers are drained, levels of adjacent surface waters decline, and some riverbeds empty. Other aquifers are isolated from surface waters. Recharge of these aquifers can be very slow, and the water that is being pumped may have taken decades or centuries to accumulate. This is a global problem. The visible impact of over-withdrawal occurs in some areas as the land surface sinks (subsidence) when the underlying water is withdrawn. The sinkholes that have remained in Florida, as reported in the news, are an example.

If the rate of withdrawal exceeds the rate of recharge, then through time, water must be pumped from ever greater depths, increasing energy costs and risking aquifer depletion and possible loss of water supplies. As aquifers are drawn down, water quality is degraded, often yielding brackish waters that require treatment before additional use. Table 4.2 illustrates some typical examples of declining groundwater levels.

Table 4.2: Examples of Declining Groundwater Levels (Source: Bartolino and Cunningham, 2003).

Region	Groundwater Decline
Long Island, NY	Water table declined, stream flows reduced, salt water moving inland
West-central Florida	Groundwater and surface water declining, salt water intruding, sink holes forming
Baton Rouge, LA	Groundwater declining up to 200 feet
Houston, TX	Groundwater declining up to 400 feet, land subsidence up to 10 feet
Arkansas	Sparta aquifer declared "critical"
High Plains	Declines up to 100 feet, water supply (saturated thickness) reduced over half in some areas
Chicago-Milwaukee area	Groundwater serving 8.2 million people has declined as much as 900 feet, declining 17 feet/yr
Pacific Northwest	Declines up to 100 feet

163 Hutson, "Estimated Use of Water in the United States in 2000."

Tucson/Phoenix, AZ	Declines of 300 to 500 feet, subsidence up to 12.5 feet
Las Vegas, NV	Declines up to 300 feet, subsidence up to 6 feet
Antelope Valley, CA	Declines over 300 feet, subsidence over 6 feet

Addressing Future Water Needs Related to Energy

A number of technologies in various stages of development have the potential to reduce water use per unit energy for power generation. These technologies will not likely be deployed until they are economically feasible — based on changes in water value and availability. Potential options for meeting future energy production and generation needs with reduced water use intensity are identified in Table 4.3. A range of electric-generating technologies, including water use for fuel extraction and processing are compared to pros and cons.

Table 4.3: Technology of power generation versus pros and cons of implementation

Technology	Opportunity[1]	Gap
Advanced Cooling (for thermoelectric power plants)	Reduced Water Use	Costs, complexity, hot weather performance, scalability to larger plant size
Combined-Cycle Gas Turbines	Water Use reduced 50percent	Fuel cost increase, increased dependence on gas imports, coal technology validation
Renewable Electric Power	Reduced water use, carbon-free, provides peak power needs	Costly, implementation and/or manufacturing capacity. For some technologies there is intermittent need for storage at high

		penetration
Oil Shale	Large domestic resource	Costly, competes with water use (especially in water-stressed areas), technology required to mitigate environmental impacts
Renewable/Alternative Fuels	Renewable, carbon-free/neutral domestic fuels and fuel from domestic coals and gas	Costs, technology, high water use for bio-fuel production
Maximizing/Increasing Current Water Supplies	Understand supply, utilization, and sector use and dependency.	Educating the public, incomplete consumption data, water storage for future use, cyclic drought, policy, planning, management, coordination

[1]The amount of water required for manufacturing and construction of energy facilities, such as the water used in manufacturing the components of, or to construct, a power plant are not included.

The power generation technologies mentioned in Table 4.3 will only briefly be explained.

Advanced Cooling for Thermoelectric Power Plants

The amount of water used to condense steam from steam-driven turbine generators (per unit electricity output) depends on the type of cooling system and the efficiency of the turbine. Turbine efficiency increases as the difference between the steam temperature and the condensing temperature increases. Plants with higher efficiencies require less cooling per unit energy produced and, therefore, less water. Coal plants operate at higher temperatures than today's nuclear plants, so coal plants require less water than current nuclear plants. One approach to reduce water use in thermoelectric plants is to replace the evaporative cooling towers in closed-loop systems with dry cooling towers cooled only by air, but this reduces plant efficiency. Plant efficiency is higher for plants using evaporative cooling than for plants using dry cooling, especially in a hot, arid climate.

Over the course of a year, the output of a plant with dry cooling will be about 2 percent less than that of a similar plant with evaporative closed-loop cooling, depending on the local climate. However, in the hottest weather, when power demands are highest, plant efficiency may decrease by up to 25 percent.[164] Decreased plant efficiency means increased fuel use and increased emissions, which could provide greater incentives for other efficiency and emission control technology improvements. As the value of water increases, there is increased need and value for technologies that reduce water and energy use, especially to meet peak demand on hot days, when dry-cooled systems lose efficiency.

Dry-cooled systems impose a cost penalty ranging from two to five percent to 6 to 16 percent for the cost of energy compared to evaporative closed-loop cooling.[165] The fact that the cost penalty is highly dependent on the value placed on the energy that is not generated and must be replaced when the weather is hot and demand is high. Dry cooling is best suited to wet, cool climates (not the dry, arid climates of the West where water is most scarce). As of 2002, dry cooling had been installed on only a fraction of 1 percent of U.S. generating capacity, mostly on smaller plants.[166]

Combined-Cycle Gas Turbines

Natural-gas-fired combined-cycle gas turbines use (withdraw and consume) about half as much water as coal-fired plants and have been deployed in large numbers in recent years. The gas turbines in these plants provide two-thirds of their power generation. The hot exhaust from the gas turbine is used to generate steam, which drives a steam turbine to provide the

---

[164] DOE, "Energy Penalty Analysis of Possible Cooling Water Intake Strucgture Requirements on Existing Coal-Fired Power Plants," ed. National Energy Technology Laboratory (Argonne National Laboratory, 2002).

[165] CEC, "Comparison of Alternate Cooling Technologies for California Power Plants: Economic, Environmental and Other Tradeoffs," ed. Public Interest Energy Research (California Energy Commission, 2002).

[166] Ibid

remaining generation. Water use is reduced because only the steam turbine requires condensate cooling. In recent years, simple-cycle and combined-cycle natural gas turbine plants have provided much of the new generating capacity installed in the U.S. However, as natural gas prices increase, it is likely there will be fewer installations of these plants. As with the natural-gas combined-cycle plants, water use is lower than for conventional thermoelectric plants, although, some water is consumed in converting coal to syngas.[167]

Renewable Electric Power

A variety of renewable energy technologies consume no freshwater during operation; these technologies include:

- **Geothermal hot water (binary) systems that are air cooled**
- **Ocean energy systems**
- **Run-of-river hydroelectric**
- **Solar dish-engine**
- **Solar photovoltaic's**
- **Wind**

Additionally, existing reservoirs that do not currently have hydroelectric capacity are candidates for power generation. To reduce impacts on the aquatic environment, these plants could use fish-friendly turbines. Of these technologies, wind is currently being installed in the largest quantities, with more than 6300 MW of capacity installed in the United States.[168] Solar photovoltaic systems installation is also expanding rapidly, with approximately 400 MW installed through 2004. Generation of electrical power by these low water use technologies can help offset power generation from more water-intensive technologies.

Although geothermal, hydropower, solar thermal power with integrated storage, and biomass power can provide dispatchable

---

[167] T.J. Feeley and M. Ramezan, "Electric Utilities and Water: Emerging Issues and R&D Needs" (paper presented at the 9th Annual Industrial Wastes Technical and Gegulatory Conference, San Antonio, Texas, April 13-16 2003).

[168] DOE, "Installed U.S. Wind Capacity, Wind Powering America," (U.S. Dept of Energy, 2005a).

power (power that can be turned on/off or on demand at request of power grid operators); other technologies, such as wind and solar photovoltaic, are both regional and intermittent and must be backed up by other generating systems. Thus, as a sole source of energy they are inadequate at replacing these plants or coal powered energy sources. Connecting modest amounts of intermittent renewable sources to the grid has not been shown to undermine U.S. power grid stability. Both solar and wind have the potential to improve grid operation by providing power when it is most needed, during the hottest/windiest part of the day. Implementation of solar and wind technologies may also increase the need for energy storage.

Oil Shale

Many types of U.S. current transportation fuels are derived from imported petroleum. An approach being considered to reduce dependence on foreign sources of energy is to increase the development and use of domestic energy sources. Unfortunately, most energy extraction and processing operations require huge amounts of water. The U.S. is estimated to have two trillion barrels of oil in the form of oil shale deposits, which is more than triple the proven oil resources of Saudi Arabia. Due to high development costs, oil shale is not widely produced in the U.S., but is increasingly being considered as foreign oil imports prices rise and supplies become intermittent. However, the cost of water — over seven trillion barrels of water — to extract this oil may be too great a price to pay because it would be at the expense of all other water users, particularly agriculture, which is already suffering inadequate supplies resulting in decreased production for a growing population.

Initial recovery work is focused on mining and above-ground processing that consumes two to five gallons of water per gallon of refinery-ready oil.[169] To reduce foreign dependence, providing 25 percent of U.S. oil demand would require 400 million to one billion gallons of water per day. Because oil shale resources are

---

[169] J.T. Bartis, "Oil Shale Development in the United States: Prospects and Policy Issues," (Washington DC: Rand Corporation, 2005).

predominantly located in water-stressed areas, development will likely be constrained.

Renewable and Alternative Fuels

Biofuels provide about three percent of U.S. transportation fuels and are considered a potential domestic source for producing significantly larger volumes of transportation fuel.[170] The most water-intensive aspect of biofuel production is growing the feedstock. For the common feedstock (corn and soybeans) used to make ethanol and biodiesel respectively, water consumption is quite high. The production of ethanol is particularly detrimental to water capacity; it can shift the effects and economy of agricultural production since it may be grown in favor of other foodstuffs that reduce useable consumption of food, but also increases agricultural water use. Production of alternative fuels, such as synfuel from coal or hydrogen from methane, also requires water (up to triple the requirements for water consumption in petroleum refining). Virtually every alternative will require as much water as refineries consume now, if not substantially more.

Increasing and Extending Water Supplies

The U.S. has national programs to develop its vast water resources. Programs by the Bureau of Reclamation, the Army Corps of Engineers, and other federal and state agencies have enabled the U.S. to harness surface water resources of the country's river systems; control floods; store water for agricultural, industrial, and domestic uses; and generate hydroelectric power. In parallel, programs through agencies like the U.S. Bureau of Reclamation, U.S. Army Corps of Engineers, and so forth have allowed states to exploit tremendous groundwater resources and monitor and manage surface water flows to achieve more efficient use of water. The ability to easily expand freshwater availability is limited.

The rate of water withdrawal has increased with the affluence increase of society through most of the last century but has leveled off and even declined in recent years. However, many

---

[170] DOE, "Multiyear Program Plan, 2007-2012," ed. Energy Efficiency and Renewable Energy Office of the Biomass Program (U.S. Dept of Energy, 2005b).

signs indicate that consumption may be outpacing available supplies: aquifers are declining, stored water levels are low, and communities are seeking to improve access to water supplies, in part through desalination and re-use of water. The best courses of action cannot be accurately determined without detailed water use and consumption data, which are lacking. Although residential water use is currently less than the past decade due to better technologies, the increasing use of water supplies resultant to increasing population will override this effort long term as we continue to use water in vast quantities.

Several factors have affected the availability and use of freshwater supplies: decreased water storage capacity because of reservoir sedimentation, requirements to limit water level fluctuations within the reservoir (for recreation or aesthetic reasons), or requirements to meet downstream flow targets for fish and wildlife needs. Another type of storage is the natural storage of moisture in snow pack. Past climate trends suggest that snow packs are decreasing over time and annually are melting earlier.[171] The decreased storage of water in snow packs will limit the reliable yield of river systems that derive much of their flow from the melting of snow pack. However, new data suggest we may be going into a cooling phase climatologically and this may increase snow-pack storage.[172]

Artificial recharge and aquifer storage and recovery are approaches that can increase reliable supplies by purposefully augmenting recharge with excess surface water (or treated effluent) in times when it is readily available, and then withdrawing water when needed. However, significant energy is required to treat and inject water and then to pump it out when that water is needed. There also are efficiency questions; not all of the water injected can be withdrawn. There are a variety of geochemical problems that can arise from the mixing of surface water and groundwater in an aquifer. These problems can result in the long-term decline in the effectiveness of these storage systems.

---

[171] U.S. Senate Committee on Commerce, Science, and Transportation, *The West's Snow Resources in a Changing Climate*, 2004.

[172] E.H. Moran, and Tindall, J.A., "Part 1: Magnetic Intensity and Global Temperatures: A Strong Correlation," *Global Security Affairs and Analysis (GSAAJ)* 1, no. 2 (2007).

Desalination

Options to expand freshwater supply include use of impaired water such as brackish groundwater or seawater. These waters can be converted to drinkable water through desalination, which requires more energy than typical public water supplies, but may be offset as energy prices continue to rise. Energy requirements for desalination are similar to the requirements for pumping water long distances via projects like the California State Water Project. Additionally, produced water from conventional oil and gas production is usually saline. Depending on quality, produced waters can be used with minimal cleanup for non-potable applications such as irrigation, power plant cooling, and industrial and domestic uses. If the water is more heavily contaminated, treatment and disposal following applicable laws and regulations may be the only alternative. Re-use/recycle reduces withdrawal rates and pumping costs but may increase energy needed for treatment. Long-term water and energy conservation measures represent an opportunity to stretch both resources. Reducing water consumption can save energy for water supply and treatment as well as for heating water and can reduce water requirements to the energy industry.

Conclusions

To sustain a reliable and secure energy future that is cost effective, environmentally sound, and supports economic growth and development, energy and water challenges must be immediately and effectively addressed. Rather than only an energy policy, lawmakers should immediately consider a dual water-energy policy. This includes consideration of the impact that water policies and regulations have on energy supplies and demands, and the impact energy policies and regulations have on water demands and availability. Properly quantifying and valuing energy and water resources will enable the public and private sectors to better balance energy and water needs for all users and to develop strategies and approaches to enhance future energy security and sustainability.

Collaboration on energy and water resource planning is needed among federal, regional, and state agencies as well as with industry and other stakeholders. The lack of integrated energy and water planning and management has impacted energy production in many basins and regions across the U.S. For example, in three of the fastest growing regions in the country, the Southeast, Southwest, and the Northwest, new power plants have been opposed because of potential negative impacts on water supplies.[173] Recent droughts and emerging limitations of water resources has many states, including California, Texas, South Dakota, Wisconsin, and Tennessee, scrambling to develop water-use priorities for different water-use industries.[174] Collaboration between stakeholders and regional and state water and energy planning, management, and regulatory groups and agencies are critical. These efforts will ensure proper evaluation and valuation of water resources for all needs, including energy development and generation.

Often, polices or regulations developed to support or enhance one area, such as increasing domestic energy supplies can have unintended negative impacts on water resources. System-level evaluations by stakeholders and government agencies can be used to assess the impact of current or proposed natural resource policies and regulations and improve future energy development and water availability.

When the energy infrastructure is evaluated in a system context compared to water, agriculture and food, and other critical infrastructures, significant improvements in energy and water conservation can often be realized through implementation of innovative processes or technologies, co-location of energy and water facilities, or improvements to energy, water, and other infrastructures. For example, past investments in the water infrastructure by creating dams and surface-water reservoirs in the U.S. have significantly improved water availability. Increased competition for water resources among different users will grow; ways to reduce these conflicts through coordinated infrastructure and policy development would be beneficial.

Due to emerging trends in energy and water resource availability and use, the U.S. will continue to face issues related to natural resource planning and management. Available surface water supplies have not increased in 20 years, and groundwater supplies are

---

[173] News, "Idaho Denies Water Rights Request for Power Plants."

[174] Force, "Wounded Waters: The Hidden Side of Power Plant Pollution."

decreasing. Ensuring ecosystem health will further constrain freshwater supplies. At the same time, continued population growth and migration to areas with already limited water supplies will likely create both water and energy shortages, at least on a sporadic basis, particularly in the arid Southwest and in the Southeast. Based on current water markets and values, the growth in energy demand, along with stricter environmental regulations on cooling water withdrawals, could double water consumption for electric power generation over the next 25 years, consuming as much additional water per day as would be used by 50 million people or more. Additionally, changes in energy strategies in the electricity and transportation industries could further increase water consumption and the value of freshwater supplies.

A continual assessment of regional and national energy and water issues and concerns and the identification of appropriate interactions and coordination approaches with federal and state energy and water agencies will become more necessary. Further, we must address energy and water-related issues surrounding adequate energy and water supplies as well as the optimal management and efficient use of both energy and water.

Finally, most of these systems are not redundant; that is, they have no back up. The failure of any one of these systems could be potentially devastating from a resource, human health, and economic perspective. Therefore, a broad, all-hazards approach to protect these systems from terrorist attacks such as cyber hacking, bio-attack, and other, as well as additional natural and technological hazards, is a necessary and substantial part of the policies implemented to ensure the sustainability and security of energy and water systems. Broad participation will be necessary from user communities, policy and regulatory groups, economic development organizations, industry associations, government agencies (federal, state, tribal), and many others to help address problems and develop and implement good-use policies.

CHAPTER 5: Water and Related Public Health Issues

Executive Summary

Globally, unsafe water, inadequate sanitation, and improper hygiene cause illness and death from disease on a large scale. Improving these conditions can lead to better health, poverty reduction, and sustainable socio-economic development. However, many countries are challenged to provide these basic necessities to their populations, which have and continue to leave people at risk for water, sanitation, and hygiene (WASH)-related diseases. Generally, water and public health revolve around safe water, good sanitation and hygiene and their education in six areas, which include (1) community systems (water safety plans, assessment and development); (2) sanitation and hygiene (toilets, hygiene, sewer and wastewater treatment); (3) diseases and contaminants (waterborne, sanitation, and hygiene related); (4) household treatment (safe water systems and storage); (5) travelers' health (safe drinking and recreational water and injury and illnesses); and (6) educational resources (publication, Internet, etc.).

Global population tripled during the 20th century, and demand for water increased ninefold.[175] This increase in population is beginning to strain global resources, particularly water. Water stress affects 44 percent of the world's population. The United Nations Environment Programme (1999) projected that by 2025, global freshwater stress owing to increasing population on water use will increase significantly, especially in northern Africa, Eurasia, the Middle East, and even in the United States, and by 2050, nearly five billion people will be affected by freshwater scarcity.

Currently, over one billion people in the world lack access to improved water supplies and 2.6 billion people lack adequate sanitation.[176] Unfortunately, the two issues are interdependent. Water

---

[175] Hinrichsen, "Solutions for a Water-Short World."

[176] UNICEF, "Progress for Children: A Report Card on Water and Sanitation," ed.

is needed for sanitation and lack of it promotes disease. On a global scale, the health burden accompanying these interdependent conditions results in about 5,000 child deaths daily, mostly from diseases associates with lack of access to good quality drinking water, sanitation, and proper hygiene.[177] While some countries and regions in the world are improving in these areas, the disparate distribution of water makes it difficult for resource and economic scarce areas such as the Middle East, Pakistan, Afghanistan, Northern Africa, and others. The problem is also increasing in Asia, where an estimated 675 million people lack improved quality drinking water.[178] The three general areas necessary for improvement include (1) good quality, safe drinking water; (2) adequate quantities of water for food production, health, and hygiene; and (3) sustainable sanitation or water treatment processes. Although these issues may seem trite, their affects on the local or regional area are cause for security concern since, as mentioned in chapter 1, the number of conflicts over water resources around the world is rising.

Introduction

Developed nations are being confronted with water and public health problems. Historically conveyed water to residences and businesses in these countries is generally believed to be accompanied by improved hygiene and thus a reduction in disease. However, a steady deterioration of conveyance systems for water is becoming a more severe problem. Cities such as San Francisco, New York and many others have systems or parts of them that are over 100 years old. Conjointly, most of these systems leak about 20 percent of the water pumped through them and are now vulnerable to intrusion and contamination that could contribute to endemic and epidemic waterborne diseases. As an example, the total number of reported waterborne disease outbreaks in the U.S. has decreased since 1980; however, the proportion of waterborne disease outbreaks associated with problems in the distribution systems is increasing.

UNICEF (2006).

[177] M. Schomaker, "Guidelines on Municipal Wastewater Management," ed. UNEO/WHO/HABITAT/WSSCC (The Hague: WSSCC, 2004).

[178] UNICEF, "The State of the World's Children," (New York2004).

From 1971 to 1998, 30 percent of 294 outbreaks in community water systems were associated with distribution system deficiencies, causing an average of 194 illnesses per outbreak.[179] This has been the single most important cause in disease outbreaks. As water distribution infrastructure continues to age, the number of outbreaks will likely increase from protozoal, parasitic, bacterial, viral, and other sources and organisms. Top priorities that should be addressed for water-related public health issues are listed in Table 5.1.

Table 5.1. Priority Areas in Water and Public Health (not listed in order of priority).

Lesser Developed Nations	Transition Economies	Developed Nations
Absent or deteriorating infrastructure	Deteriorating infrastructure	Disinfection byproducts
Education in hygiene and sanitation	Failing technologies	Molecular Techniques
Emerging pathogens	Surveillance	Opportunistic pathogens (and the CCL)
Personnel/Operator Training	Source water quality	Chemicals (agricultural and industrial)
Source water quality and quantity	Disinfection byproducts	Emerging Contaminants
Susceptible populations	Selected opportunistic pathogens	Deteriorating infrastructure
Wastewater collection and treatment	Chemicals (agricultural and industrial)	Personnel/Operator training
		Source water quality
		Surveillance

[179] G.F. Craun, and Calderon, R.L., "Waterborne Disease Outbreaks Caused by Distribution System Deficiencies," *Journal of the American Water Works Association* 93(2001).

Microbial contamination in parts of distribution systems can also play a role in risks of endemic illness.[180] [181] Biofilms in distribution systems can provide a favorable environment for some bacterial pathogens such as opportunistic pathogens that cause disease primarily in people with weak or immature immune systems (usually the very young or very old). These pathogens can enter distribution systems from fecal contamination and then replicate and colonize parts of the system. Non-enteric pathogens, such as legionella, Pseudomonas aeruginosa, and Mycobacterium avium-intracellulari, can also colonize parts of the distribution systems and plumbing systems in buildings and may play a role in waterborne disease. Biofilm in the distribution system can also protect viral and protozoan pathogens from disinfection and allow them to survive longer.[182] From a water-security perspective, these issues can arise from technological or natural hazards, but manmade hazards, i.e., intentional contamination could also easily introduce such pathogens.

Compounding this problem are aging distribution systems that are particularly vulnerable. The majority of water distribution system pipes in the U.S. are reaching the end of their expected lifespan within the next 10 to 30 years. Analysis of main breaks in such older systems have documented a sharp increase in the annual number of main breaks from 1970 through 1989, totaling about 2200 breaks per year, which is increasing.[183] The only feasible course of action to decrease such scenarios is to make substantial investments in conveyance systems infrastructure. The U.S. Environmental Protection Agency (USEPA) predicted that transmission and distribution pipe replacement rates need to be about 0.3 percent per

---

[180] P. Payment, Richardson, L., Siemiatycki, J., Dewar, R., Edwards, M. and Franco, E., "A Randomized Trial to Evaluate the Risk of Gastrointestinal Disease Due to Consumption of Drinking Water Meeting Currently Accepted Microbiological Standards," *American Journal of Public Health* 81(1991).

[181] P. Payment, "Epidemiology of Endemic Gastrointestinal and Respiratory Diseases - Incidence, Fraction Acttributable to Tap Water and Costs to Society," *Water Science and Technology* 35(1997).

[182] J.D. Storey, "Statistical Significance for Genome Wide Studies," *Proceedings National Academy Science* 100(2003).

[183] Snoeyink Vernon L., V.L., Hass, C.N. and Boulos, P.F., *Drinking Water Distribution Systems - Assessing and Reducing Risks* (The National Academies Press, 2006).

year, rising to two percent by 2040 to adequately maintain water infrastructure. Currently, investment in this infrastructure is insufficient. Within the current economy trend, it will be an even greater challenge for public and private water utilities to generate the necessary excess revenue to implement water infrastructure improvements required to retain sustainability.

Problems in these areas in developing and lesser developed industrial nations seem insurmountable. These nations have inadequate resources to maintain and in many cases, even to develop such systems. Both rapid population growth and rapid urbanization is exacerbating this problem, which often overwhelm demands on existing water systems which is also coupled with illegal connection to distribution systems in poor neighborhoods. For developed nations, about 20 percent of water conveyed through distribution systems is leaked at various connections in valves. For lesser developed nations, the World Health Organization has indicated this amount generally ranges from 25 to 45 percent. Interdependent with water are associated energy problems (see chapter 4), particularly power outages that contribute to low or negative pressure in conveyance pipes and which allow contaminated water or wastewater surrounding the pipes to be drawn in through any cracks. Many of the largest documented waterborne outbreaks in the last two decades have been associated with cross-contamination in distribution systems (e.g. typhoid in Duschanbe, Tajikistan, 1997; cholera in Cape Verde, 1994-1997; Guinea Bissau, 1996; and Trajillo, Peru, 1990).[184]

Basic Information on Water, Sanitation, and Hygiene

Diseases, deaths, and related health problems due to lack of good quality water are staggering on a global scale, as illustrated below:

---

[184] V. Renkevich, Bekker, P., Muradov, B., Mirkamilova, A., Alikulov, A., Ermannatov, A., Beigemkulv, N., Mishivna, O., Zhinenko-Zhilenskaya, S., Van Gilder, T., Balluz, L. and Roberts, L., "Multi-City Water Distribution System Assessment," ed. USAID/CDC (1998).

- **An estimated 2.6 billion people (over 35 percent of the global population) lack access to improved sanitation.[185] [186]**
- **Globally, 884 million people lack access to an improved water source.[187] [188]**
- **Unsafe drinking water, inadequate availability of water for hygiene, and lack of access to sanitation contribute to about 88 percent of deaths from diarrheal diseases, mostly in developing countries. This number accounts for 18 percent of all deaths of children under the age of five; more than 5,000 children are dying every day as a result of diarrheal diseases.[189]**
- **Improved water sources reduce diarrhea morbidity by 21 percent; improved sanitation reduces diarrhea morbidity about 37 percent; and the simple act of washing hands at critical times can reduce the number of diarrhea cases by as much as 35 percent. Improvement of drinking-water quality would lead to a 45 percent reduction of diarrhea episodes.[190]**
- **The impact of clean water technologies on public health in the U.S. is estimated to have had a rate of return of 23 to 1 for investments in water filtration and chlorination during the first half of the 20th century.[191]**

---

[185] Bos Prüss-Üstün A., R., Gore, F. & Bartram, J., "Safer Water, Better Health: Costs, Benefits and Sustainability of Interventions to Protect and Promote Health," (Geneva: World Health Organization, 2008).

[186] Census Bureau, "Population Clocks," ed. International Programs Center (U.S. Census Bureau).

[187] An improved water source is water that is supplied through a household connection, borehole well, protected dug well, public standpipe, protected spring, or collected rainwater.

[188] Ibid

[189] UNICEF, "Progress for Children: A Report Card on Water and Sanitation," (UNICEF, 2006).

[190] UN, "Health, Dignity, and Development: What Will It Take? ," ed. United Nations Millennium Project (UN, 2007).

[191] D. Cutler, and Miller, G., "The Role of Public Health Improvements in Health Advances: The 20th Century United States," (Cambridge: National Bureau of Economic Research, 2004).

- **Water and sanitation interventions are cost effective across all world regions. These interventions were demonstrated to produce economic benefits ranging from $5 to $46 per dollar invested (USD).[192]**
- **Water, sanitation, and hygiene have the potential to prevent at least 9.1 percent of the global disease burden and 6.3 percent of all deaths.[193]**
- **According to the World Health Organization and UNICEF, improved sanitation could save the lives of 1.5 million children per year who would otherwise succumb to diarrheal diseases.[194]**
- **Millions of people globally are infected with neglected tropical diseases (NTDs). These diseases are most often found in places with unsafe drinking water, poor sanitation, and insufficient hygiene practices and thus are water and/or hygiene-related. Examples include Guinea Worm Disease, Buruli Ulcer, Trachoma, and Schistosomiasis.[195] [196]**
- **Worldwide, soil-transmitted helminthes (parasitic worms) infect more than one billion people because of lack of adequate sanitation.[197]**

Waterborne Diseases

There are a wide variety of waterborne diseases related to public-health issues. Tables 5.1 to 5.4 present the more common diseases, microbial agent, agent source, and general symptoms:

---

192 Haller Hutton G., L., and Bartram, J., "Global Cost-Benefit Analysis of Water Supply and Sanitation Interventions," *Journal Water Health* 5, no. 4 (2007).
193 Prüss-Üstün A., "Safer Water, Better Health: Costs, Benefits and Sustainability of Interventions to Protect and Promote Health."
194 WHO, "Progress on Drinking Water and Sanitation – Special Focus on Sanitation," ed. UNICEF (WHO, 2008).
195 — — —, "Neglected Tropical Diseases, Hidden Successes, Emerging Opportunities," ed. World Health Organization (WHO, 2006).
196 P.J. Hotez, Molyneux, D.H., Fenwick, A., Ottesen, E., Ehrlich, S., and Sachs, J.D., "Incorporating a Rapid-Impact Package for Neglected Tropical Diseases with Programs for Hiv/Aids, Tuberculosis, Malaria," *PloS Med* 3, no. 5 (2006).
197 WHO, "Soil-Transmitted Helminths," (World Health Organization, 2004).

Table 5.1: Protozoal Infections

Disease and Transmission	Microbial Agent	Sources of Agent in Water Supply	General Symptoms
Amoebiasis (hand-to-mouth)	Protozoan (Entamoeba histolytica) (Cyst-like appearance)	Sewage, non-treated drinking water, flies in water supply	Abdominal discomfort, fatigue, weight loss, diarrhea, bloating, fever
Cryptosporidiosis (oral)	Protozoan (Cryptosporidium parvum)	Collects on water filters and membranes that cannot be disinfected, animal manure, seasonal runoff of water.	Flu-like symptoms, watery diarrhea, loss of appetite, substantial loss of weight, bloating, increased gas, nausea
Cyclosporiasis	Protozoan parasite (Cyclospora cayetanensis)	Sewage, non-treated drinking water	Cramps, nausea, vomiting, muscle aches, fever, and fatigue
Giardiasis (oral-fecal) (hand-to-mouth)	Protozoan (Giardia lamblia) Most common intestinal parasite	Untreated water, poor disinfection, pipe breaks, leaks, groundwater	Diarrhea, abdominal discomfort, bloating, and flatulence

		contamination, campgrounds where humans and wildlife use same source of water. Beavers and muskrats create ponds that act as reservoirs for Giardia.	
Microspori-Diosis	Protozoan phylum (Microsporidia), but closely related to fungi	The genera of Encephalitozoon intestinalis has been detected in groundwater, the origin of drinking water [3]	Diarrhea and wasting in immunocompromised individuals

Table 5.2: Parasitic Infections (Kingdom Animalia)

Disease and Transmission	Microbial Agent	Sources of Agent in Water Supply	General Symptoms
Schistosomiasis (immersion)	Members of the genus Schistosoma	Fresh water contaminated with certain types of snails that carry schistosomes	Rash or itchy skin. Fever, chills, cough, and muscle aches
Dracunculiasis (Guinea Worm	Dracunculus medinensis	Stagnant water containing	Allergic reaction, urticaria rash,

Disease)		**larvae**	**nausea, vomiting, diarrhea, asthmatic attack.**
Taeniasis	**Tapeworms of the genus Taenia**	**Drinking water contaminated with eggs**	**Intestinal disturbances, neurologic manifestations, loss of weight, cysticercosis**
Fasciolopsiasis	**Fasciolopsis buski**	**Drinking water contaminated with encysted metacercaria**	**GIT disturbance, diarrhea, liver enlargement, cholangitis, cholecystitis, obstructive jaundice.**
Hymenolepiasis (Dwarf Tapeworm Infection)	**Hymenolepis nana**	**Drinking water contaminated with eggs**	**Abdominal pain, severe weight loss, itching around the anus, nervous manifestation**
Onchocerciasis (River blindness)	**Onchocerca volvulus and Wolbachia**	**Black fly bites (insects breed in fast-moving water)**	**Skin papules, swollen lymph nodes, itching, swelling of face, skin changes. Destruction of eye tissue leading to blindness.**
Echinococcosis (Hydatid disease)	**Echinococcus granulosus**	**Drinking water contaminated with feces (usually canid) containing eggs**	**Liver enlargement, hydatid cysts press on bile duct and blood vessels; if cysts rupture they can cause anaphylactic shock**

Coenurosis	**Multiceps**	**contaminated drinking water with eggs**	**increases intracranial tension**
Ascariasis	**Ascaris lumbricoides**	**Drinking water contaminated with feces (usually canid) containing eggs**	**Mostly, disease is asymptomatic or accompanied by inflammation, fever, and diarrhea. Severe cases involve Löffler's syndrome in lungs, nausea, vomiting, malnutrition, and underdevelopment.**
Enterobiasis	**Enterobius vermicularis**	**Drinking water contaminated with eggs**	**Peri-anal itch, nervous irritability, hyperactivity and insomnia**

Table 5.3: Bacterial Infections

Disease and Transmission	Microbial Agent	Sources of Agent in Water Supply	General Symptoms
Botulism	**Clostridium botulinum**	**Bacteria can enter an open wound from contaminated water sources. Can enter the gastrointestinal tract by consuming contaminated**	**Dry mouth, blurred and/or double vision, difficulty swallowing, muscle weakness, difficulty breathing, slurred speech,**

		drinking water or (more commonly) food	**vomiting and sometimes diarrhea. Death is usually caused by respiratory failure.**
Campylobacteriosis	**Most commonly caused by Campylobac-terjejuni**	**Drinking water contaminated with feces**	**Produces dysentery like symptoms along with a high fever. Usually lasts 2–10 days.**
Cholera	**Spread by the bacterium Vibrio cholerae**	**Drinking water contaminated with the bacterium**	**In severe forms it is known to be one of the most rapidly fatal illnesses known. Symptoms include very watery diarrhea, nausea, cramps, nosebleed, rapid pulse, vomiting, and hypovolemic shock (in severe cases), at which point death can occur in 12–18 hours.**
E. coli Infection	**Certain strains of Escherichia coli (commonly E. coli)**	**Water contaminated with the bacteria**	**Mostly diarrhea. Can cause death in immunocompromised individuals, the very young, and**

			the elderly due to dehydration from prolonged illness.
M. marinum infection	Mycobacterium marinum	Naturally occurs in water, most cases from exposure in swimming pools or more frequently aquariums; rare infection since it mostly infects immunocompromised individuals	Symptoms include lesions typically located on the elbows, knees, and feet (from swimming pools) or lesions on the hands (aquariums). Lesions may be painless or painful.
Dysentery	Caused by a number of species in the genera Shigella and Salmonella with the most common being Shigella dysenteriae	Water contaminated with the bacterium	Frequent passage of feces with blood and/or mucus and in some cases vomiting of blood.
Legionellosis (two distinct forms: Legionnaires' disease and Pontiac fever)	Caused by bacteria belonging to genus Legionella (90percent of cases caused by Legionella pneumophila)	Contaminated water: the organism thrives in warm aquatic environments.	Pontiac fever produces milder symptoms resembling acute influenza without pneumonia. Legionnaires' disease has severe symptoms such

			as fever, chills, pneumonia (with cough that sometimes produces sputum), ataxia, anorexia, muscle aches, malaise and occasionally diarrhea and vomiting
Leptospirosis	Caused by bacterium of genus Leptospira	Water contaminated by the animal urine carrying the bacteria	Begins with flu-like symptoms then resolves. The second phase then occurs involving meningitis, liver damage (causes jaundice), and renal failure
Otitis Externa (swimmer's ear)	Caused by a number of bacterial and fungal species.	Swimming in water contaminated by the responsible pathogens	Ear canal swells causing pain and tenderness to the touch
Salmonellosis	Caused by many bacteria of genus Salmonella	Drinking water contaminated with the bacteria. More common as a food borne illness.	Symptoms include diarrhea, fever, vomiting, and abdominal cramps
Typhoid fever	Salmonella typhi	Ingestion of water contaminated with feces of an infected person	Characterized by sustained fever up to 40°C (104°F), profuse sweating,

			diarrhea, less commonly a rash may occur. Symptoms progress to delirium and the spleen and liver enlarge if untreated. In this case it can last up to four weeks and cause death.
Vibrio Illness	Vibrio vulnificus, Vibrio alginolyticus, and Vibrio parahaemoly-ticus	Can enter wounds from contaminated water. Also got by drinking contaminated water or eating undercooked oysters.	Symptoms include explosive, watery diarrhea, nausea, vomiting, abdominal cramps, and occasionally fever.

Table 5.4: Viral Infections

Disease and Transmission	Microbial Agent	Sources of Agent in Water Supply	General Symptoms
Adenovirus infection	Adenovirus	Manifests itself in improperly treated water	Symptoms include common cold symptoms, pneumonia, croup, and bronchitis
Gastroenteritis	Astrovirus, Calicivirus,	Manifests itself in	Symptoms include diarrhea, nausea,

	Enteric Adenovirus, and Parvovirus	improperly treated water	vomiting, fever, malaise, and abdominal pain
SARS (Severe Acute Respiratory Syndrome)	Coronavirus	Manifests itself in improperly treated water	Symptoms include fever, myalgia, lethargy, gastrointestinal symptoms, cough, and sore throat
Hepatitis A	Hepatitis A virus (HAV)	Can manifest itself in water (and food)	Symptoms are only acute (no chronic stage to the virus) and include Fatigue, fever, abdominal pain, nausea, diarrhea, weight loss, itching, jaundice and depression.
Poliomyelitis (Polio)	Poliovirus	Enters water through the feces of infected individuals	90-95percent of patients show no symptoms, 4-8 percent have minor symptoms (comparatively) with delirium, headache, fever, and occasional seizures, and spastic paralysis, 1 percent have symptoms of non-paralytic aseptic meningitis. The rest have serious symptoms resulting in paralysis or death

Polyomavirus infection	Two of Polyomavirus: JC virus and BK virus	Very widespread, can manifest itself in water, ~80percent of the population has antibodies to Polyomavirus	BK virus produces a mild respiratory infection and can infect the kidneys of immunosuppressed transplant patients. JC virus infects the respiratory system, kidneys or can cause progressive multifocal leukoencephalopathy in the brain (which is fatal).

Water Scarcity

Water resources are finite, but also required for human physiology. Available freshwater is linked to human health in various ways such as for ingestion, food production, and hygiene — relating directly to the diseases discussed in Tables 5.1-5.4. Also, adequate water for ingestion and food preparation ranges from about 1.8 to 5 liters per capita per day.[198] However, water consumption increases in warm climates, with physical activity and during pregnancy. The World Health Organization recommends at least 7.5 liters per capita per day to meet these demands.[199]

For hygiene purposes, the amount of water use generally varies with distance from the water source and climate. When people must walk farther than one kilometer or spend more than 30 minutes for total water collection time, per capita water use drops to between five to 10 liters per capita per day. This level is insufficient to sustain adequate hygiene. When the residence is hooked to distribution systems, water use tends to be between 60 to 100 liters per day per capita. As early as 1977, it was discovered that many waterborne diseases are actually from washing due to inadequate water

[198] G. Howard, and Bartram, J., "Domestic Water Quantity: Service Level and Health," ed. World Health Organization (Geneva: WHO, 2003).
[199] Ibid

quantities available for washing food, hand, laundry, and cooking utensils. Diseases generally associated with lack of sufficient water include shigellosis, scabies, and trachoma — the best solution for decreasing these diseases is to provide more water, preferably through household connections or closer water supply stations. Sufficient water quantity and hygiene interventions have been associated with 24 to 42 percent median reduction in diarrheal disease morbidity and hygiene respectively.[200]

The greatest global demand for water is from agriculture. Within the U.S., about 34 percent of all water used is for agriculture while elsewhere over 70 percent of the world's developed water supplies are used for irrigation.[201] [202] However, water requirement for food production can vary greatly based on culture, type of diet, and need for irrigation. There is also the issue of 'virtual water' (water used in the production of a good or service). Effective management of 'virtual water' likely will become key to water sustainability and distribution. For example, ethanol produced from corn requires nearly 2,500 liters of water to produce one kilogram (300 gal per lb) of ethanol. In the U.S., corn commonly is grown in areas experiencing a 20 to 50 percent growth in population. This combination could change irrigation or crop management practices but still significantly stress water resources. Similar trends occur globally.

In the U.S., water use has, while increasing slightly, stabilized to an extent; but internationally, water use has risen dramatically in the past 50 years due to population growth, which creates greater demands on all industries including agriculture, manufacturing, and many others. Consequently, increasing water scarcity threatens agricultural production, public health, political stability, the economy and security in many parts of the world. Given its disparate and sometimes finite nature, current water-use rates are not sustainable. For example, there is serious aquifer depletion in China, India,

---

[200] L. Fewtrell, and Colford, J., "Water, Sanitation, and Hygiene: Interventions and Diarrhoea - a Systematic Review and Meta-Analysis," ed. World Bank (Washington Dc: The International Bank for Reconstruction and Development, 2004).

[201] Tindall, "Water Security-National and Global Issues."

[202] D. Seckler, Amarasinghe, D., Molden, D., deSilva, R., and Barker, R., "World Water Demand and Supply, 1990-2025: Scenarios and Issues," ed. International Water Management Institute (Sri Lanka: International Water Management Institute, 1998).

Pakistan, North Africa, and the Middle East. Also, in the western U.S. Additionally, ten major U.S. cities are facing critical water-shortage problems, which include Orlando, Atlanta, Tucson, Phoenix, Fort Worth, San Francisco, Las Vegas, Houston, and Los Angeles. Others, especially New York, are borderline, but could face grim circumstances due to non-redundant, i.e., single-source, supply systems. This non-sustainability will cause an increase in water-related health issues through increases in disease and potentially resulting famine. Ensuing water stress and shortages are discussed in chapter 1; the enormity illustrates the scope of this problem. Additionally, hygiene will play a major role, yet is greatly diminished with scarce or poor quality supplies.

Case Study: Cholera — the Importance of Hygiene

Throughout history, populations around the world have sporadically been affected by devastating outbreaks of cholera. Recorded evidence of cholera epidemics dates to as early as 1563 in India. In the nineteenth century cholera spread from its apparent ancestral site in the Orient to other parts of the world, producing pandemics in Europe. The first cholera pandemic was recorded in 1817, and we are now well into the seventh cholera pandemic, which started in Indonesia in 1961 and spread rapidly in Asia, Europe, and Africa, and reached South America in 1991. The disease then spread swiftly through Latin America, causing nearly 400,000 reported cases and over 4,000 deaths. Cholera has now become endemic in many parts of the world. According to the Pan American Health Organization (PAHO), a total of 1,076,372 cases and 10,098 deaths were reported in the region of the Americas by June 1995. In 1999, the World Health Organization was notified that a total of 254,310 cases and 9,175 deaths had occurred globally. Poor surveillance and the stigma caused by the disease likely led to under reporting by affected countries. Estimates indicate numbers closer to 120,000 deaths and many more cases each year. The increasing spread of cholera in recent years may reflect a lack of international quarantine enforcement by some countries, which also have primitive public water supplies and inadequate sanitary regulations, the international mobility of carriers in the world's population, and the quick transport of contaminated food and water by ships and aircraft.

Cholera is an infection caused by the bacteria Vibrio cholerae. Infection is caused by drinking water or eating food contaminated with the bacteria and by poor sanitation, personal, and domestic hygiene practices. The bacteria present in feces of an infected person are the main source of contamination — the principal site affected is the gastrointestinal tract. Symptoms include acute watery diarrhea (sudden diarrhea with profuse, watery stools), vomiting, suppression of urine, rapid (severe) dehydration, fall of blood pressure, cramps in legs and abdomen, subnormal temperature, and complete collapse. Death may occur within 24 hours of onset unless prompt medical treatment is given to the patient.

Healthy carriers of V. Cholerae may vary from 1.9 to 9.0 percent. These symptomless carriers excrete vibrios intermittently with the duration of pathogen discharge being relatively short, averaging 6 to 15 days with a maximum period between 30 to 40 days. Chronic convalescent carriers have been observed to shed vibrios intermittently for periods of 4 to 15 months. Survival of vibrios in the aquatic environment relates sharply to various chemical, biological, and physical characteristics of a given stream or estuarine water. The viability of V. cholerae in surface waters has been observed to vary from one hour to 13 days. Although cholera vibrios may persist for only a short time in grossly polluted aquatic environment, fecal contamination from victims of epidemics and the carriers may continue to increase their population in water. This was illustrated by the cholera epidemic that gripped Northern and Southern KwaZulu Natal beginning in August 2000, the most serious epidemic to date in South Africa. The migration of people from province to province and between southern African countries has allowed the disease to spread to seven of the nine provinces in South Africa. The Department of Water Affairs and Forestry's Community Water Supply and Sanitation Services section developed a strategy to monitor the cholera outbreak and track the emergency water supply and sanitation intervention that each province is implementing to curb the spread of the disease. By July 27, 2001, the total number of cases was over 100,000 with more than 200 fatalities. Statistics

suggest that despite the interventions the government and other stakeholders implemented, the cholera situation worsened.

Additional Risks

Cholera occurs in epidemic form when there is rapid urbanization without adequate sanitation and access to clean drinking water. Hence, the focus of epidemics/pandemics has shifted to developing countries over the last century, particularly to rapidly growing mega cities. Other risk factors include poor hygiene, overcrowded living conditions, and lack of safe food preparation and handling. Unstable political and environmental conditions such as wars, famines, and floods that lead to displaced populations and the breakdown of infrastructure are significant risk factors.

The socio-economic impacts of water and sanitation related diseases are often underestimated and appear to be among the reasons for the deplorable state of many water supply and sanitation initiatives. Cholera, like other water-related diseases, can cost governments billions of dollars to eradicate. Absenteeism by the workforce caused by cholera adversely affects industrial output; cholera outbreaks can adversely affect tourism and tax revenues (productivity losses for business and individual due to the illness decrease tax revenues); and cholera outbreaks could lead to loss of trade. Primary health-care education is a vital component in prevention of cholera. This disease is one of many, yet illustrates the need for adequate water supply and sanitation as basic requirements in public health regardless of the state of a country's development. Additionally, natural disasters of all kinds serve to exacerbate this issue. The recent 2010 earthquake in Haiti serves as an example.

Priority Areas in Water and Public Health

In lesser developed nations, hygiene and sanitation are overriding factors in public health, especially waterborne diseases. Morbidity and mortality from diseases such as cholera are high, but the overwhelming burden of diarrheal disease inevitably remains undiagnosed. A summary of priority areas for water quality in

transition economies, lesser and developing nations, and developed nations is listed in Tables 5.1-5.4.

Around the globe, the connection between hygiene, sanitation and disease has been and continues to be demonstrated through the relation between disease incidence and socioeconomic status. Many large cities around the world, particularly in Brazil and India, are divided into administrative or 'class' zones, which is typically based on socioeconomic status. In the poorer areas, which typically have less sanitation and hygiene, cholera remains the best known waterborne disease, particularly in developing nations. The disease, illustrated in the previous case study, is both epidemic and pandemic due to its ability to thrive in the environment in association with plankton and other aquatic organisms.[203] Cholera arrived in South America in 1991 due to any number of events that have not been proven, such as ship bilge water discharge, imported foods, etc. The human and health consequences of cholera spread were enormous, with over one million cases and 10,000 deaths.[204] Understanding its interdependence with water is a critical health issue. New evidence suggests the nature of this disease is changing, with new strains arising; among these are the V. cholerae, serogroup O139, which emerged in India in epidemic form. Investigation of such cases seems to suggest that the emergence of new strains could be due to both the quality of water and effects on hygiene from quantity and quality of water. It may be that E. coli, other pathogens, and virulence factors in the case of gene transfer could be transferred between species. This would make disease control and monitoring more difficult. Also, gene transfer increases the potential use-threat from terrorists. From a security perspective one might ask whether or not scarcity of water could create a regional, national, or global pandemic?

From a global perspective, E. coli infections are believed to far exceed those of cholera and other waterborne bacterial diseases — estimated morbidity and mortality from cholera are in the tens of thousands annually. In terms of research and science the key areas to

---

[203] R.R. Colwell, "Global Climate and Infectious Disease: The Cholera Paradigm," *Science* 274(1996).
[204] R. Tauxe, Seminario, L., Tapia, R., and Libel, M., "The Latin American Epidemic. ," in *Vibrio Cholerae and Cholera: Molecular to Global Perspectives* (ASM Press, 1994).

tackle would be hygiene and sanitation and emerging disease, especially the ecology of infectious disease.

Transition Economies versus Developed Nations

Problems in transition economies are not that different than in developed nations, but they appear to be more pronounced. The major cause of these water related health problems is deteriorating infrastructure. As an example, work in Russia illustrates that original infrastructure was built for much smaller populations than today. Along with a shortage of resources for watershed protection and development that lacks environmental protection controls, water quality is often poor. In industrialized areas industrial wastes cause source water quality to be poor. Coupled with equipment and infrastructure deterioration, there is often high organic loading in drinking water that is often over chlorinated, resulting in very high concentrations of disinfection byproducts.[205] When linked to limited water treatment plant capacity home storage of water (often in the bathtub) becomes necessary, especially in taller apartment buildings. Back siphonage can occur, increasing chances of disease. The work indicated a potential relation between disease and exposure for both viral (1-2 days) and protozoan (6-7 days) diseases.

In developed nations, particularly the U.S., water-related health issues are partially moderated by the ability of larger utilities to maintain sufficient pressure so that pipe leakage is outward the pipe rather than siphonage in. This causes frequent breaks and wasted water but reduced disease occurrence. Also, drinking water research in the U.S. has been driven by the Safe Drinking Water Act and the industry is heavily regulated and closely monitored by the EPA. The EPA has published the Contaminant Candidate List (CCL), now in its second iteration (CCL2) that includes 42 chemicals and nine microbiological contaminants. With the rising trend of emerging contaminants, i.e., drugs excreted by the body that have not been used by normal bodily functions, the list is growing. However,

---

[205] A.I. Egorov, Tereschenko, A., Altshul, L., Vartiainen, T., Samsonov, D., LaBrecque, B., Maki-Paakkanen, J., Drizhd, N.L., and Fort, T., "Exposures to Drinking Water Chlorination by-Products in a Russian City," *International Journal Hygiene Environmental Health* 206(2003).

microbial contaminants include viruses, bacteria, protozoa, and algae. While these are closely watched, most are not yet regulated due to lack of accurate detection methods. Persistence, survival, and proliferation of pathogens in drinking water are receiving the most research attention. Thus, the key research areas in developed nations appear to be methods of detection for CCL organisms, proteomic and genomic approaches to better understand pathogen survival, disinfection alternatives such as chlorine versus chloramines, piping materials, biofilm analyses, and health consequences from disinfection byproducts (DBPs).

An original priority list has not changed much since 2004 and includes training (many waterborne disease outbreaks have been attributed to poor operator training), surveillance (a focus of the medical community on population health rather than just individual health), health linkage and data integration (development of effective tools to link exposure pathways), risk communication (based on cultural differences), development of corrosion and biofilm resistant piping material (particularly in repair of failing infrastructure), better detection methods (currently treatment plants are not set up to detect biohazards, radiation, and other deadly chemicals), and cheaper technologies such as membrane type, including remote monitoring. Due to the role of water in life, these issues have become particularly important to the national security of many nations and to the U.S. to the Department of Homeland Security.

Various ongoing practices help provide clean quality water and promote conservation. Increasing effectiveness of irrigation practices to reduce the need for developing additional water supplies is being attempted in many areas so that water not used for irrigation can be more readily treated and used for human consumption and hygiene. Water reuse as a result of water scarcity has gained renewed interest even in the U.S. Reuse is generally defined as the use of highly treated water for irrigation and landscaping (non-potable reuse) or to supplement surface or groundwater sources used as drinking water supplies (potable reuse). Highly-treated water used for irrigation is usually sent directly to a water treatment plant. The National Research Council in 1998 concluded that planned, indirect potable reuse is a viable application of reclaimed water, but only

when there is a careful and thorough assessment that includes contaminant monitoring, health and safety testing, and system reliability evaluation.

Water conservation issues are a necessary area of improvement in relation to water and health. The primary area for attention is failing and leaking distribution systems since back siphonage at lower pressures can cause a penetration of both bacterial and virus waterborne hazards into a system.

For developing nations, implementing innovative, low-cost sanitation approaches is a necessity since both water quality and sanitation are interdependent. Poor sanitation leads to water contamination. Around the globe, the main source of water contamination is due to sewage and human waste. One practice, dry sanitation, is an attractive option due to water scarcity and the infrastructure needs and costs associated with waterborne sewage and wastewater treatment. The main challenge of using dry or ecological sanitation is achieving effective pathogen destruction so that handling or use of stored excreta for agriculture results in transmission of infectious pathogens.

These measures become extremely important in developing nations in Asia and elsewhere that are witnessing the growth of megacities (cities with a population greater than 10 million). Unlike cities such as New York and London that developed over a century and had the economic and human resources to expand water and sanitation services, newer megacities explode in population with growth rates of over six percent per year. Also, most of these new megacities are in countries with poor economies that cannot support timely and planned development of water and sanitation services. While such cities would generally offer economy of scale in development of water systems, most recent growth in megacities is unfortunately in poorer, underserved neighborhoods with limited technological solutions and financial resources.

Conclusions

Generally, solving health-related water issues, particularly in developing nations and those with disparate water supplies is a staggering challenge. The inequitable access to water and sanitation

in these areas is the product of the disparities of fresh-water resources, income, and the power and institutional capacity within country. As an example, in high-income countries access to safe water and sanitation is 98 percent while it is 79 percent and 49 percent for middle and low-income countries, respectively. As with a great many global issues, the burden falls to the poorest of the poor. Globally, these groups are six times more likely to lack improved water access and four times more likely to lack adequate sanitation.

Reducing this disparity is complicated by the need to improve both financial sustainability and provide services. Long-term viability of public water and sanitation services requires user fees and inputs from customers, which are essential toward ensuring services are valued properly (see chapter 15), scarce resources overuse is avoided, and maintenance of the system is provided. This requires limited external resources to be maximized to top efficiency, which requires use fees and funding for initial project establishment. Failure to accomplish these basic goals leads to increased health problems among the populace, can trigger civil unrest, and is therefore a security concern.

Fees for sustainability of systems in these nations are generally obstacles to the poorest communities and result in inequitable benefits with subpar sanitation and water quality. Often, this has led to subsidized water tariffs that are unsustainable long term and also limit incentives for providers to extend services to the underserved.[206] A variety of solutions exists that could be enacted to solve these issues. First, incorporate lower-cost technologies and allow users to choose their level of service; the latter is ideal, but seldom possible. Second, parallel social investments need to be made along with water and sanitation investments to ensure users benefit from reduced water collection time associated with newly improved access. Third, for larger communities, water costs or tariffs could be adjusted to ensure basic needs; but also overuse could be discouraged through block pricing that is typically subsidized initial water allotments, but raises rates as consumption increases. Finally, financing mechanisms need to be creative (an example would be

---

[206] S.M. Olmstead, "Water Supply and Poor Communities: What's Price Got to Do with It?," *Environment* 45, no. 10 (2003).

small loans) and established such that even the lowest income communities can invest in water and sanitation improvements.

Barriers that impede progress of poorer nations obtaining adequate water of sufficient quantity and quality and for sanitation are many. First, the primary barrier is financial resources that result in inadequate investment in water and sanitation infrastructure. Approximately 90 percent of water related aid from organizations such as the UN, Food and Agricultural Organization (FAO), IMF, and others goes to about a dozen countries; the remainder goes to countries in which a majority of the population has no access to improved water supplies. Thus, water aid is being used as a political tool rather than as a means to reduce disparate access. Consequently, there are many failed water and sanitation projects around the globe because financial aid was linked to specific multi-national engineering firms who installed unsustainable conventional water and wastewater treatment plants for the sake of increased profits. Second, there is lack of political will to tackle tough problems in this area, as well as a general lack of consumer awareness of the health hazards associated with poor-quality water. Third, too often, there is a failure to conduct assessments of water and sanitation interventions to determine whether they are successful and if they can remain sustainable. Fourth, there is a tendency to avoid new, low-cost technologies while applying conventional processes without community involvement, even when conventional processes are shown to be inadequate and inappropriate. During a tough global economy, these issues remain a problem despite awareness — primarily due to declining international investments in water, which is surprising given it is 'the' most important resource.

Solutions to these interdependent problems will require development of distribution systems that maintain water quality, are sustainable, that can be monitored, and that may work conjointly with home water treatment. In the latter, the treatment plant could produce medium quality water that could be further treated in the household for drinking (too much chlorination has been shown to be a problem with many more cases of diarrhea reported when using piped water from local treatment plants). This would entail a focus of resources at the home to provide point-of-use treatment for drinking water (analogous to point-of-source water-heater technology used in

such countries as El Salvador), the economic costs and benefits of point-of-use, and the health costs associated with this approach.

Additional solutions would be needed to solve water scarcity and related health problems. For most countries, improving efficiency of agricultural, industrial and domestic water use through better efficiency would make more water available for drinking and hygiene. New technologies for monitoring also are needed, especially in water reuse processes. There are a wide variety of issues that should be investigated and include but are not limited to low-cost technologies, reducing risks from wastewater irrigation in low income countries, economic policies that are effective in promoting water conservation and overall use by sector, monitoring strategies for effective elimination of microbial pathogens and chemical contaminants likely to be found in local waters, transboundary water sharing (see chapter 13), safe ecological sanitation, and many others. These need to be specifically focused on in developing megacities due to a possible pandemic from related water and health issues. All solutions should work toward improving access, affordability, and sustainability of clean drinking water and sanitation. In remote areas, these processed could be heavily coupled with solar energy since these areas generally lack necessary conveyance infrastructure.

Perhaps a way forward for improvement would be to break down water-related public health issues into broad-scope development areas that could most rapidly bring about change. These might include water sustainability and supply, water for economic improvement, water-related disaster-management processes, water pricing and financing, and so forth. This would help develop knowledge, especially in developing nations, increase capacity, ensure effective technology use, enhance investments in water-related projects such as sanitation and supply, and build improvements in other areas and infrastructure related to water.

CHAPTER 6: Water Supply Problems for Large Cities

Executive Summary

Simultaneous shortages of food, water, and power, created in large part by water shortages to cities, could dramatically destabilize mass population sustainability, security, and governance, which make water security and supply issues a matter of national stability and security. The most pressing water-supply issues facing almost all cities are increasing population and urbanization — the primary causes of water shortages. Population growth in arid regions dramatically reduces available water supplies from both ground and surface waters. In the U.S., examples include Phoenix, Las Vegas, and Denver, as well as others that are located in semi-arid to desert conditions.

U.S. cities are short of water, especially in the arid West where the Colorado River supports about 22 million people, is drawn upon by seven states, and supplies such cities as Los Angeles, San Diego, Las Vegas, Phoenix, and Denver, and also provides large volumes of water for agriculture. The story is similar for the Rio Grande River, which has intermittently failed to empty into the Gulf of Mexico since 2001. Global outlooks are similar: Lake Chad in Africa, for instance, has been depleted 95 percent over the past 40 years.

Future projections for the nation's water supplies are bleak. Scientists estimate a 50 percent chance of Lake Mead and Lake Powell, both supported by the Colorado River, falling below minimum power pool levels by 2017 which would result in no live water storage by 2021. Other groups estimate minimum power pool levels as early as late 2012.[207] The effects of these shortages are potentially catastrophic: below minimum power pool levels, water levels in the reservoir are too low to spin the hydro turbines, resulting in a cessation of hydroelectric power production. Most of the electricity generated from Hoover Dam goes to three states: Arizona

[207] TinMore Institute (www.tinmore.com)

gets about 19 percent; Nevada about 24 percent; Southern California gets about 56 percent, which is split for use with 29 percent of the total going to the Metropolitan Water District of Southern California for water conveyance and distribution. In California, some of the major cities receiving power from Hoover Dam are Burbank, Glendale, Pasadena, Los Angeles, Azusa, Anaheim, Banning, Riverside, and others with 5.5 percent going to Southern California Edison. Clearly, this hydro-electric supply is very important. Consequently, if water levels in Lake Mead drop to critical shortage levels (1075 feet), water supply would be greatly reduced due to loss of electricity and the ability to pump remaining water out of the reservoir (see chapter 4). Agricultural production would be severely impacted, as would energy production and some commodity prices due to cascading failures extending across critical infrastructure systems. The resulting shortages in food, water, and power would affect millions of U.S. citizens and could dramatically destabilize security and governance, especially if the current poor economic outlook persists. Water supply is therefore a matter of national stability and security, not only for the U.S., but for all countries.

Introduction

Two issues of water capacity are particularly critical: (1) quantity — water supply for sustainability, and (2) quality — clean water for human consumption. Improving the sustainability and security of our nation's drinking water and wastewater infrastructures has become a top priority since the terrorist attacks on 9/11. This has led to heightened interest of spatial data on water capacity and greater strategic planning for re-invention of local, state, and national policy jurisdictions concerning water ownership and use.

A variety of strategies could be used to reduce supply and sustainability related problems to enhance security. Implementation of the following water-supply issues could result in needed and substantial improvements in water efficiency, conservation, infrastructure, and water recycling. However, because city planning and development require decades to accomplish, it is advantageous to begin implementing policy in these areas as quickly as is feasible. At the center of such policy debates are issues of local ecology,

watershed management, and geology management of local interests versus state and national priorities. From a macro perspective, run off and contaminants influencing ocean health may also link to other policies where a delicate ecosystem could be placed at risk. The BP oil leak in the Gulf of Mexico in the summer of 2010 is a clear example. In such instances, municipal water practices may influence the by-products of contaminants that could affect human health on a long-term basis, with the more important being pharmaceuticals (in the category of emerging contaminants), fertilizers, oil spills, and pet waste. The issues of greatest concern and planning include

- **Residential sprawl**
- **Increasing permeability of urban lands**
- **Implementing low-water lawns**
- **Implementing urban farming**
- **Investment in infrastructure**
- **True pricing of water**
- **Ecological sanitation**
- **Urban water recycling**

Water Supply Issues for U.S. Cities

Simultaneous shortages of food, water, and power to cities could dramatically destabilize mass sustainability, security, and governance, which make water-supply issues a matter of national stability.

Water scarcity has been a serious issue throughout history. The record-setting droughts of the 1930s, which caused the 'Dust Bowl,' were so extensive they led to an exodus of nearly 2.5 million people from the Great Plains.[208] The 1950s droughts, although statistically worse than those of the 1930s Dust Bowl era, did not have a similar impact because of preventative measures, such as irrigation systems, reservoirs, and lakes instituted in the wake of the previous series of droughts.[209] In more recent times, "lake droughts" have threatened water supplies for the cities of Dallas (2006) and Atlanta

[208] Donald Worster, *Dust Bowl: The Southern Plains in the 1930's* (London: Oxford University Press, 1979).
[209] Ibid.

(2007-2008) and, particularly in the latter case, have set off a flurry of negotiations and lawsuits between neighboring states (Alabama, Florida, and Georgia) over conflicting water rights. Similar problems have occurred internationally (China, Pakistan, India, and the Middle East), where water supplies are being rapidly depleted due to distribution patterns and increasing population. For example, generally, there are many manufacturing plants and people in the north, but there are larger water supplies and fewer people in Southern China. Globally, larger problems loom: scientists note that an overall depletion of groundwater is occurring because the resource is being consumed faster than it can be replenished. As an example, a recent report estimates a 50 percent chance of live storage Lakes Mead and Powell disappearing by 2021, threatening the highly populated and economically sensitive U.S. cities of Los Angeles, San Diego, Las Vegas, and Phoenix.[210] The potential impacts of depleting these resources are staggering. The resulting food, water, and power shortages, all level 1 critical infrastructures (see figure 1.1), would have dramatic impacts to the stability of the areas affected, likely regional, and could cause immense human suffering for modern day standards of living.

Public use accounts for 11 percent of total water withdrawals in the U.S., behind thermoelectric power (48 percent), and irrigation (34 percent).[211] However, irrigation should not be viewed as a problem, but rather a significant user of water that provides needed food for a growing population. And, as population increases, agricultural water use will increase by necessity. Thermoelectric power generation uses water to cool power plants or heat water into steam to spin turbines. Though water demands for thermoelectric power are high, approximately 98 percent of this water is returned to the source after a one-time use.[212] And, although irrigation-water withdrawals are an obvious target for research and reform in water conservation, to the uninformed, the area that contains the highest

[210] T.P. Barnett, and Pierce, D.W., "When Will Lake Mead Run Dry?," *Water Resources Research* 44, no. W03201 (2008).

[211] Hutson, "Estimated Use of Water in the United States in 2000."

[212] SIU, "Water Use Benchmarks for the Thermoelectric Power Generation," ed. Southing Illinois University Department of Geography and Environmental Resources (Carbondale2006).

potential for water conservation is public use. Farmers have been enhancing water conservation measures for the past 50 years. Outlined below is a brief synopsis of some of the problems related to public water use, along with potential solutions (long term) that could reduce water scarcity.

Increasing population and urbanization

Urbanization (movement of people from rural areas to major cities) is causing significant water stress in cities and regions around the world. Because of the increased opportunities available for citizens living in cities, primarily employment, urbanization is occurring more rapidly than at any time in history. The 2007 revision of a United Nations report states that in 2008, the urban population of the world will outnumber the rural population for the first time in history. Additionally, the report states that the world rural population is projected to begin decreasing in about a ten years.[213] This process is accelerated in the U.S. Between 2005 and 2050, population in the U.S. is projected to increase from 296 million to 438 million,[214] with a majority of individuals residing in cities instead of rural areas. For the first time, urban populations in the U.S. now outnumber rural population bases. This trend will continue to shift as the economy worsens because people will continue to seek needed employment. Urbanization needs to be controlled to meet resource supply.

The implications of these trends are critical; not only does overall population growth correspond to about a 50 percent increased water demand, but also the increase in urbanization indicates that this increased demand will be disproportionately distributed between major cities and rural areas. This has significant implications on all facets of the water-supply issue: the development and maintenance of infrastructure intended for distribution of water, ongoing litigation, water-related policy/law, agricultural production, the aforementioned water-scarcity issues, and other problems.

---

[213] UN, "World Urbanization Prospects, the 2007 Revision, Executive Summary," ed. Department of Economic and Social Affairs United Nations, Population Division (New York: UN, 2008).

[214] J.S. Passel, and Cohn, D., "U.S. Population Projections: 2005–2050," (Pew Research Center, 2008).

Growth in arid regions

Complicating the urbanization problem is the fact that the greatest population growth in the U.S. is in the most arid regions. Between 1990 and 2000, the southwestern U.S. experienced a 40 percent increase in population in Arizona and a 30 percent increase in Colorado. These increases are likely to continue, yet the western and southwestern U.S. represent the driest climate regimes in the world. Population in these regions cannot be sustained without massive water infrastructure projects, including the Colorado Arizona Project (which delivers water from the Colorado River to central Arizona) and the Colorado River Aqueduct (which delivers water to cities in southern California, including Los Angeles and San Diego). These huge pipes, canals, and massive dams — the Hoover, Glen Canyon, Parker, and Davis — make urban growth and agriculture possible in the surrounding regions. Conjointly, they contribute to water scarcity problems; by diverting water from one scarce area to another, the depletion of the resource will occur much more rapidly.

Impervious Conditions of Cities

Cities cause significant water-supply problems through interruption of the hydrological cycle, i.e., replacement of permeable land with impermeable streets, roads, and structures. In a natural environment, water on the earth's surface is either evaporated, percolates deeper into the ground, or moves via runoff into streams, lakes, rivers, or other bodies of water. The presence of concrete and asphalt present in many cities short-circuits this process by preventing percolation of water through the vadose or unsaturated zone (the area between the soil surface to the top of the groundwater table) into aquifers. As a result, a greater percentage of water that would originally be available for groundwater recharge, sustenance of plants and other vegetation, and treatment for reuse as recycled water, is instead sent to storm drains and ultimately into streams, rivers, lakes or oceans.

This phenomenon is being observed on a larger scale as well. Watersheds are experiencing reduced evaporation and less precipitation — a slow drying out (dehydration). The U.S. as a whole is experiencing a net water loss. For every one percent of roofing,

paving, car parks, and highways constructed, water supplies decrease in volume by more than 100 billion cubic meters per year.[215]

Expansion of cities — suburban sprawl — into surrounding farmlands causes over competition with farmers for both land and irrigation water. The percentage of arable cropland steadily declines as fields either remain fallow (left unplowed and unplanted during the growing season) due to lack of water or they are paved under. The revenue backing of cities, whose managers have decided have an endless supply of tax-payer revenues, makes it difficult for the farmer to win the water-supply battle either personally or in court. Left unchanged, this trend will cause future food shortages. The latter could have a severe impact on civil unrest and eventually homeland and national security, as well as on global stability since over 100 countries depend on substantial grain and other food supplies from the U.S.

Lawns

Most lawns in the U.S. are Kentucky bluegrass or mixtures that include it. Kentucky bluegrass is water intensive, requiring 18 gallons of water per square foot per growing season.[216] Golf courses are especially wasteful of water, using about 312,000 gallons per day for an 18-hole course. Based on the number of U.S. golfers, this equates to roughly 3,355 gallons of water for each golfer — enough to provide water for 20 people for one day. By some estimates, lawns are the largest irrigated crop in the U.S. in terms of surface area, about 40 million acres — three times more acreage than for irrigated corn.[217] Most of the water used for lawns is potable and, has accordingly incurred significant energy expense for treatment.

Total water use by lawns and runoff from impermeable conditions of cities compounds the water-scarcity issue through shorting the hydrologic cycle and decreasing food security. Increasing populations will make this practice unsustainable in the near future.

---

[215] M. Barlow, "Blue Gold, the Global Water Crisis and the Commodification of the World's Water Supply" (paper presented at the International Forum on Globalization 2001).

[216] Staff, "Xeriscaping," (2006).

[217] C. Milesi, et al., "Mapping and Modeling the Biogeochemical Cycling of Turf Grasses in the United States," *Environmental Management* 6, no. 3 (2005).

Low water prices

In addition to exponential population growth and urbanization, low water prices are the root cause of increasing water scarcity because they do not provide incentives for conservation. Low water rates do not reflect the true value of water, which the authors refer to as "Blue Gold." Compared with other developed countries, the U.S. has the lowest water bills when calculated as a percentage of household income.[218] The low cost of water in the U.S. (1) does not encourage customers to conserve, (2) does not demonstrate the true value of water or related resources, and (3) does not fully accommodate for the rising costs of aging infrastructure and provide revenues from use for repair. As an example, one unit of water (1,000 gallons) in metro Denver costs about four dollars (USD). Considering that a pack of six bottles of water, eight ounces each, is similar in pricing, there is a significant price disparity of this precious resource. As an analogy, just as city and government officials see taxpayer revenue as limitless and free, so too do citizens view water. Both circumstances need to be acknowledged and resolved. This issue is addressed in greater detail in chapter 15.

Water-based sanitation

Almost all cities use potable water to dispense of waste. As Lester Brown notes in his book, Plan B 3.0, "The one-time use of water to disperse human and industrial wastes is an outmoded practice, made obsolete by new technologies and water shortages. Water enters a city, becomes contaminated with human and industrial wastes, and leaves the city dangerously polluted." [219] Once clean water has flushed human waste, it must be sent to expensive, energy intensive wastewater treatment facilities. Wastewater plants cannot remove all the toxins added (by manmade means), which include pharmaceuticals and many other chemicals. These are collectively called 'emerging contaminants' and include all products consumed and excreted by the human body such as caffeine from coffee, tea, and other beverages, medicines of all types, and other compounds. The

---

[218] EPA, "Water and Wastewater Pricing," ed. Office of Water (EPA, 2007).

[219] Lester Brown, *Plan B 3.0*, ed. Earth Policy Institute (New York: W. Norton and Company, 2008).

problems in this area are expanding rapidly. Enhanced and new technologies could help solve this problem.

Aging water infrastructure

Because of low water rates, cities cannot raise sufficient revenue to maintain water delivery, wastewater, and treatment systems. These conveyance and waste infrastructures are nearing the end of their life spans and are beginning to fail, causing significant wastes of potable water. In February 2008, four million gallons of water gushed from a 30-year-old ruptured water main in Denver, Colorado. Three lanes of Interstate 25 had to be shut down for two weeks to repair the leak and resulting sinkhole. The 85-mile-long Delaware Aqueduct in New York leaks one billion gallons of potable water a month, enough to change the ecology of the area.[220] It also is enough to supply 5.4 million people with an average daily supply (rate is based on 185 gallons per person per day).

Thousands of miles of pipes, many buried over 100 years ago, need to be replaced in the next 30 years.[221] These deteriorating delivery and conveyance systems, responsible for significant amounts of leakage,[222] along with collapsed storm sewers and old storm water systems that commingle, overflow with wastewater,[223] and will likely require the largest replacement of infrastructure since these systems were installed. The American Water Works Association stated, "We stand at the dawn of the replacement era."[224] Water pricing will need to be adjusted upward to solve this problem and then the increase must be applied to the cause, not distributed for other projects or for political self interest (see chapter 15).

---

[220] Ibid.

[221] AWWA, "Reinvesting in Drinking Water Infrastructure, Dawn of the Replacement Era," (2001).

[222] CBO, "Future Investment in Drinking Water and Wastewater Infrastructure," ed. Congress of the United States (Congressional Budget Office, 2002).

[223] Ibid.

[224] Ibid.

Declining investment

Federal and municipal investment in water distribution, delivery, and wastewater systems is declining.[225] However, other basic infrastructure systems such as highways, airports, transit systems, harbors, and waterways continue to receive substantial federal funding.[226] Given the short- and long-term implications of ignoring the growing water problems in the U.S. and around the world, it is critical that water-based policy decisions be given more attention and also coupled with energy policy. From a policy perspective, the funding disparity between water infrastructure and other infrastructure systems is illogical.

There are a variety of estimates concerning the cost to repair to water infrastructure:

- **The Water Infrastructure Network estimates that the U.S. will need to invest nearly one trillion dollars into water delivery and wastewater infrastructure systems over the next 20 years.[227]**
- **The American Water Works Association projects $250 billion over 30 years to replace deteriorated delivery systems only, not including the cost of wastewater infrastructure.[228]**
- **The U.S. Congressional Budget Office, in 2002, estimated that from 2000 to 2019, annual costs for investment will average between $11.6 billion and $20.1 billion for drinking water systems and between $13.0 billion and $20.9 billion for wastewater systems.[229]**
- **The U.S. EPA projects that investments of $276.8 billion will be needed over the next 20 years for delivery, treatment, storage, and supply projects.[230]**

---

[225] WIN, "Water Infrastructure Now, Recommendations for a Clean and Safe Water in the 21st Century," (Water Infrastructure Network, 2001).
[226] Ibid.
[227] Ibid.
[228] AWWA, "Reinvesting in Drinking Water Infrastructure, Dawn of the Replacement Era."
[229] CBO, "Future Investment in Drinking Water and Wastewater Infrastructure."
[230] EPA, "Drinking Water Infrastructure Needs Survey and Assessment, Third Report to Congress," ed. Office of Water (Washington DC: USEPA, 2005).

Because of the differences in parts of the systems that need to be replaced or repaired, the numbers vary widely. However, a conservative estimate between all sources would suggest an amount of about $650 billion (USD) during the next 30 years for potable and wastewater distribution, delivery, and treatment plants alone. Accounting for inflation and increasing prices, the necessary amount would be about one trillion dollars for 30 years. In approximate terms, this would account for $3,000 per person. As an example, the city of Denver (population 598,707 in July 2008) would need to expend $1.796 billion on water infrastructure to bring it to 100 percent efficiency. This is an enormous cost. Given the average price of water in Denver proper of $5.28 per unit (unit = 1,000 gallons), with an average water bill of $390 per year per person, rates would need to be quadrupled to pay for the required maintenance and upgrade or depreciated over a 10-20 year term. However, due to the dreadful mismanagement exhibited at all levels of government (local, state, and national) for the past 50 years, even if rates increased by this amount, it is entirely likely the money collected would be diverted to other, 'deemed necessary,' self-interest projects and water infrastructure would continue a declining state of disrepair, even as residents pay for the upgrade.

Cities in conflict with agriculture

Growing population centers have three main problems that threaten sustainability: (1) they remove cropland during expansion; (2) they waste vast amounts of water (about 20 percent of all water conveyed) through leaking distribution systems; and (3) they use large amounts of water for non-food crops such as lawns and golf courses. Uncontrolled growth in the face of limited resources will eventually lead to calamitous failure. The old mining towns in the arid West, for example, disappeared as gold and other precious ores disappeared. Current cities such as Phoenix and especially smaller towns, will meet the same fate if water sustainability fails — water is as necessary for economic development as gold was to the old mining towns.

Cities and agriculture depend on the same water, either surface reservoirs or groundwater. However, cities have large tax bases and enough money to outspend agricultural interests by

considerable margins. In legal and political battles related to water resources, larger cities with greater political power and resources, usually win over both individuals and even larger farming cooperatives. As a case in point, the High Plains Ogallala aquifer could become so overdrawn that pumping costs will prohibit profitable agriculture. With good policy and planning, the Ogallala could last for centuries, but under current usage policy and with the burden of an increasing population, the timeframe for effective depletion of the Ogallala may be less than 60 years, depending on the area.[231] If the U.S. and surrounding region move into a cooling climate shift as various hydrologic and climate models suggest, it could be much sooner since in cooler climates there is less precipitation. As Marc Reisner noted in his classic, Cadillac Desert, "the overdraft of the groundwater on the high plains is the greatest in the nation, in the world, and in all of human history." [232] Agriculture and municipal water use must become collaborative — policies should be developed that ensure this (see chapter 16).

Without adequate policies, agriculture will inevitably end in the U.S. West, forcing crops to be grown elsewhere or even in other countries — a shift that has already begun. This stretches the logical supply line, already 1,500 miles, increasing risk and vulnerability and potentially disastrous consequences; this shift also affects political interdependencies, over which there is little control. Consequently, the U.S. could become ever more dependent on international resources, especially energy and food, heightens risk for domestic sustainability and security if the countries relied upon for these resources are not allies or if there is major disruption of commodity supply lines.

Proposals for Comprehensive Reform

As cities grow, they generally become more efficient at sustaining their populations than suburbs or rural settings. For example, a thousand city dwellers in an apartment building will have a smaller water, energy, and carbon footprint than a thousand people

231 Marc Reisner, *Cadillac Desert* (New York: Peguin Books, 1993).

232 Ibid.

living in single-family homes in a rural area. However, cities depend on resources like food and water that may need to be transported long distances. A lofty goal would be for U.S. cities to become autonomous and self-sustaining by producing rather than importing most of their own food. With current food supplies being shipped an average of 1,500 miles from source to user, vulnerability arises with hidden, yet significant risks. However, achieving such a goal would require a massive push toward the self reliance America achieved in the past, but which through increased agricultural mechanization, technological advancements, and political maneuvering has drifted far from.

Viable solutions for the following could increase water supply and food and energy security. Vast improvements in water efficiency, conservation, and recycling can be made in all U.S. cities, but city planning and development take decades to accomplish and can change substantially with each city administration, often with no continuance of well developed policies. Thus, a continuation policy between administrations would be most favorable.

Halt sprawl

Sprawl can be halted by increasing population density in cities so that water and other resources do not need to be transported as far. By decreasing the distance that water, power, and other resources need to be conveyed and transported, costs used for building new infrastructure (i.e. pipes, pumping stations, etc.) could be redirected to maintain and improve existing infrastructure. In addition, water loss due to conveyance pipes leaks are lessened because of fewer sources for leakage to occur. This is a key factor for conservation — less energy necessary for conveyance by pumping water over shorter rather than longer distances. Efficiency of operations would improve for almost all critical infrastructures and yield significant savings. Savings would also be gleaned across city departments such as police, fire, public health, etc.

Halting sprawl requires vertical expansion (building upward) such as has been accomplished in Hong Kong and other mega cities in lieu of lateral expansion with one story businesses, single family homes, and other structures that use significantly more space. For example, some single apartment buildings in Hong Kong have a

5,000 unit capacity. Where possible, cities could grow downward as well, as in Atlanta, Georgia. Subterranean cites are less resource-intensive to build, and more water and energy efficient. This is especially true in arid areas, where groundwater resources are much farther underground than in wetter regions. Additionally, city utilities should not be obligated to build water infrastructure to new sprawling suburban developments and golf courses far from the urban core. Realistically, dilapidated and inefficient suburbs should be altogether abandoned for efficiency projects that could be used for energy and agricultural production purposes or as infrastructure overhauls for urban centers. Detroit, due to its broadly deteriorating state and mass exodus with many projects, suburban areas, and failed factories would make an interesting case study to implement this theory.

U.S. cities should obtain control of as much arable land as possible around their urban perimeters, in addition to gaining control of source watersheds where possible. This will help slow or halt sprawl while allowing cities the ability to effectively manage their own watershed and food supply through what is referred to as localization. This process is especially important since water, energy, and transportation costs will likely increase dramatically in the near future, even as gas prices currently soar. Every city in the U.S. should have as much control of their water and food supply as possible to reduce risk and vulnerability and lessen reliance on the federal government in time of disaster. However, this would rely heavily on personal and group self reliance.

Increase permeable urban land

The large water-impervious areas present in cities present a major hydrologic problem for local ecosystems. Paved, compacted, and denuded surfaces convey water away from aquifer recharge zones to drains and rivers, shorting the hydrologic cycle and enhancing watershed dehydration.

U.S. cities can dramatically increase the amount of water permeable surfaces to reduce run off and encourage aquifer recharge through practically road-less, car-free patchworks of continuous gardens and parks, meandering for miles, forming neighborhoods, business districts, mini-ecosystems, and other methods. Although

careful long-term planning is required, the benefits of "greening-up" cities and making them more water-permeable are potentially significant. For example,

- **Cities that contain more gardens and parks could produce their own food, making them more economically independent and help ameliorate regional climate and grow jobs;**
- **Cities could become more aesthetically pleasing, which would improve morale and encourage citizens to care for their land;**
- **Aquifer recharge would be much more efficient and would improve the availability of groundwater; and**
- **Reduction of the "heat island effect" due to pavement in cities would decrease, leading to cooler, more energy efficient inner cities that do not need as much energy for cooling homes.**

Whether there is a desire to pursue these processes or not, it is entirely likely that resource shortages will force cities along this path.

Encourage low water lawns

Cities should encourage low water lawns and Xeriscaping, landscaping and gardening in ways that reduce or eliminate the need for supplemental irrigation; this is generally accomplished by using native plants that are adapted to the climate and require minimal or no irrigation. Local governments could encourage this by offering incentives to residents who replace their lawns with less water-intensive landscaping. Each lawn replaced would save 2,500 gallons of water per week, which would increase water supplies, reduce pumping and distribution costs, and make more water available for urban farming and other uses. Increasing energy and treatment costs could force these issues despite the beauty of a well tended lawn. Policy should not be impeded to allow this when possible, especially in water scarce areas. For example, the city of Phoenix has long encouraged native grasses and Xeriscaping to significantly reduce water loss.

Implement Urban Farming

Cities often out-compete farmers for water resources as they sprawl into surrounding farmland — covering fields once used for agriculture with water-intensive lawns and impervious pavement. The unrestricted sprawl of urban areas along with the associated inefficient use of water resources and declining agricultural production is becoming unsustainable due to population growth.

Many countries have well developed urban farming. Shanghai has found a way to halt sprawl and help feed citizens with nutrient recycling farms throughout the city. The city manages 300,000 hectares of farmland to recycle the city's human waste. Half of Shanghai's pork and poultry, 60 percent of its vegetables, and 90 percent of its milk and eggs come from farms surrounding the city.[233]

In U.S. cities, every unused patch of urban earth could potentially be turned into an urban farm or made permeable with native plants. Hundreds of thousands of vacant lots in cities across the U.S. could be transformed, creating "a regenerative effect . . . when vacant lots are transformed from eyesores — weedy, trash-ridden dangerous gathering places — into bountiful, beautiful, and safe gardens that feed people's bodies and souls."[234] This concept is not new and is common in various large cities in the U.S. In Milwaukee, an urban farm operation called Growing Power grows greens, herbs, vegetables, and raises goats, ducks, turkeys, chickens, bees, and tilapia and perch. They also operate gardens throughout Milwaukee, and have several other urban farms in Chicago. They sell food to local retail stores, co-ops and restaurants in the Milwaukee and Chicago areas.[235] The program has been fairly successful and is a potential model for other large urban areas. Further, those who receive city benefits but are not employed are enlisted for labor and rebuild their self esteem, obtain skills training and other personal growth opportunities — people helping people.

---

[233] Jac Smit, "Urban Agriculture's Contribution to Sustainable Urbanisation," *Urban Agriculture* 2002.

[234] Katherine H. Brown, and Carter, Anne, "Urban Agriculture and Community Food Security in the United States: Farming from the City Center to the Urban Fringe," ed. World Urbaization Prospects United Nations Population Division (New York2003).

[235]Barbara Miner, "An Urban Farmer Is Rewarded for His Dream," *New York Times*(2008), http://www.nytimes.com/2008/10/01/dining/01geniUS.html.

Invest in infrastructure

Cities and the federal government should reinvest in water infrastructure. The costs to repair existing infrastructure are high, perhaps as much as a trillion dollars over the next 20 years.[236] However, the case for federal investment is quite compelling. Because of the extraordinary cost and the wide-ranging nature of the problem, no individual municipality could bear the full cost of repairs alone. The costs cannot be simply passed on to individual consumers either: the estimated doubling of rates required to repair infrastructure across the nation would put increased pressure on consumers and could push up to one third of the U.S. population into economic hardship.[237] [238]

Adjusting water prices to the suggested levels in the current economic climate could well lead to severe recession on a localized and regionalized basis. The federal government, along with private firms, could provide opportunity to finance new investments and competitive markets. Improvements to infrastructure, in conjunction with water-conservation methods, could reduce the impact of necessary tax hikes. As a case study, the Delaware Aqueduct that provides about one-half of New York City's drinking water is in serious need of repair. It could fail at any time, and there is no redundancy to this system. Put in perspective, although improving the aqueduct would be expensive, the cost of doing nothing will be much, much greater. Additionally, security and sustainability risks from allowing these systems to continue to degrade could have serious consequences on the people, our public health, and the economy and homeland security.

Fair water pricing

Increasing the price of water to consumers will raise enough revenue to maintain the distribution and delivery systems and will encourage conservation (see chapter 15). Ultimately, the citizen will pay to upgrade the water infrastructure through increased water

---

[236] WIN, "Water Infrastructure Now, Recommendations for a Clean and Safe Water in the 21st Century."

[237] Ibid.

[238] Ibid.

rates and/or taxes. The true cost of water is far below its current value. For example, the average unit price (one unit is 1,000 gallons) nationwide is only $1.50 — far too cheap. This is about the same cost for an eight-ounce bottle of water in a convenience store or a two liter bottle of soda pop. This suggestion does not infer that city mayors should immediately increase prices. Increasing the price of water is a healthy way to shift the culture from wasteful consumption practices to healthier conservation practices needed in the future. The sooner such a strategy is implemented the sooner the added benefit of an investment in a lasting water infrastructure will be achieved. And, the current 20 percent loss in volume of water leaking from distribution systems will be stopped and recovered, saving both water and energy. The economics of water is more fully discussed in chapter 15.

Implement ecological sanitation

Cities can separate water delivery systems from sanitation systems by abandoning water-based sanitation and adopting dry ecological sanitation instead. Water-based sanitation systems pollute valuable freshwater supplies. As an example, water supply is generally derived from sources that have minimal pollution, is purified and then that same purified water is used for drinking, washing clothes, and flushing toilets. The waste is then drained to a common treatment facility. Pure water could be delivered for consumption, while protecting potable water from being flushed into sewers. Dry sanitation would allow for human waste to be reused in urban agricultural projects the composting toilet is one possibility. These relatively inexpensive systems are aerobic composters. The urine is collected separately from fecal matter. Dry composting converts human excrement into humus, which is largely odorless, and comprises about 10 percent of the original volume.[239] The humus can be used to enrich soils, while the urine is a nitrogen rich fertilizer. This reduces the need for energy intensive chemical fertilizers.[240] Composting human waste is especially convenient for urban farming and more sensible than disposing of waste in rivers. Composting is

---

[239] Brown, *Plan B 3.0.*

[240] Peter Rogers, "Facing the Freshwater Crisis," *Scientific American Online* 229, no. 2 (2008).

widely used in Asia and the Pacific Rim, but has been slow to catch on in the U.S. despite low health risks.

Ecological sanitation (Ecosan) can decrease urban water use, reduce water bills, lower energy needed to pump and purify water, eliminate sewage water disposal problems, and restore the nutrient cycle. China is a world leader in ecological sanitation and has more than 100,000 urine diverting, dry composting toilets in use in Beijing. Other countries with these toilets in the demonstration stage or further are India, Uganda, South Africa, Mexico, Bolivia, and seven countries in West Africa.[241] Awarding incentives to homeowners after effecting sound practices would be a good way to initiate this methodology.

Recycle Urban Water

Recycling the same water continuously is effective and cost efficient. Once water delivery is separated from sanitation, recycling urban water becomes a simpler process.[242] Consider that the implementation of the aforementioned ecological sanitation systems on a massive scale combined with an upgrade of water delivery and waste systems could result in only a small amount of water lost to leakage or evaporation through each cycle. Wastewater systems would continue to be necessary, but waste treatment plants could be reengineered and retrofitted into water recycling plants.

Through proper urban planning, investment in infrastructure, equitable water pricing, ecological sanitation, and other existing treatment technologies, large cities could potentially cut overall water use by 35 percent or more (based on U.S. per capita water use of 185 gallons per day).

Water Supply Issues Associated with Dams

Many cities obtain water from aquifers or from surface water; however, more cities are dependent upon surface water than groundwater.[243] Thus, water-supply issues associated with reservoirs

---

[241] Brown, *Plan B 3.0.*

[242] Ibid, pg 204.

[243] Hutson, "Estimated Use of Water in the United States in 2000."

and dams greatly affect many cities. Cities of the western U.S., such as Phoenix, Houston, Las Vegas, Los Angeles, and Denver are artificial oases in the desert and would not exist without subsidized water from dams, large reservoirs, and water projects. Under the auspices of the Bureau of Reclamation, more than 5,000 dams were built between 1930 and 1970. The Hoover Dam was completed in 1931, Parker Dam in 1938, Grand Coulee Dam in 1942, and Glen Canyon Dam in 1963. These dams were built to develop agriculture and urbanize the West.

Arguments in favor of dams are difficult to refute. Dams provide for irrigation; about 16 percent of U.S. food production relies on Dam water.[244] Hydropower provides clean, cheap electricity. There can be no cheap reliable energy without water or reliable water without a consistent energy supply.[245] The two resources are interdependent. Dams provide water for industry and urban consumption and also provide flood control. However, there are numerous problems with dams.

Dams Lose Water to Evaporation

The annual, substantial loss of water from a reservoir in arid regions of the West is typically equal to 10 percent of its storage capacity.[246] Lake Mead, for example, loses about 2.85 million acre feet of water when at maximum capacity — one trillion gallons annually. This water loss increases the salinity of the remaining water, which threatens aquatic life and soils, destroys wetlands, and makes irrigation for agriculture difficult.[247] There is currently no cost efficient way to reduce evaporative loss from dams.

Dams and Sediments

Storage of water in dams is reduced by sediment build up. An estimated one-half to one percent total storage is lost each year to

---

[244] Martin W. Doyle, et al., "Stream Ecosystem Response to Small Dam Removal: Lessons from the Heartland," *Geomorphology* 71(2005).

[245] Tindall, "Water Security-National and Global Issues."

[246] Brown, *Plan B 3.0.*

[247] Barlow, "Blue Gold, the Global Water Crisis and the Commodification of the World's Water Supply."

sedimentation in reservoirs worldwide.[248] At one percent per year, a dam would only have a 100-year lifespan. Since most of the Dams in the U.S. were built in the last 50 years, excepting Hoover Dam and other very large dams, many of these dams will end their usefulness around the same time. Meanwhile, the billions of tons of sediment that replenished soils in river basins and farmlands and added to estuaries and coastlines remains trapped upstream, robbing downstream agricultural soils of nourishment and in some cases accelerate rates of coastal erosion.[249] However, current knowledge and technologies can somewhat mitigate these effects.

The Mississippi-Atchafalaya Delta slowly expanded into the Gulf of Mexico in the past, fed by sediments entirely from the West and Midwest states. Today, dams located in the basins that feed the Mississippi block sediment flow to the delta by roughly half.[250] This may result in one-third to one-half of the delta disappearing in the next few decades.[251] Loss of the delta will have deleterious economic consequences, as well as environmental degradation problems. Additionally, a lack of offshore sediments leaves coastlines vulnerable to erosion from storms. This was tragically demonstrated by Hurricane Katrina in Louisiana in 2005. Reduced offshore sediments, exacerbated by dredging for ship traffic, greatly increased flooding damage in coastal and wetland areas south of New Orleans.

Dams Dehydrate Watersheds and Damage River Ecosystems

River basins are important recharge zones for groundwater and aquifers, but every dam deprives a river of some of its flow. Ordinarily this water would recharge groundwater or nourish the river ecosystem, but behind a dam, water is subject to increased evaporation. Water that escapes evaporation is consumed by cities or used by agriculture and is therefore less likely to flow downstream or

---

248 M. Falkenmark, et al., "Human Modification of Global Water Vapour Flows from the Land Surface" (paper presented at the Proceedings of the National Academy of Sciences of the United States America, 2005).

249 Phil Dickie, "Rich Countries, Poor Water," ed. WWF Global Freshwater Programme (Netherlands: WWF Global Freshwater Programme, 2006).

250 Reisner, *Cadillac Desert*.

251 Ibid.

into another ecosystem, despite current management practices. Comparative to water impervious cities, dams deprive watersheds of the water that previously contributed to the hydrologic cycle. Nevertheless, the benefits generally outweigh the costs.

After dam construction, flooded vegetation decomposes, creating anoxic (oxygen-deficient) conditions at the reservoir bottom. Anaerobic bacteria (those which thrive in oxygen-deficient environments) consume the dead vegetation and can liberate mercury from the soil into the water in a form that fish ingest, allowing mercury to enter the food chain and threaten the food supply.[252] However, this is not a widely occurring circumstance. The bacteria also emit methane and carbon dioxide (both greenhouse gases) and hydrogen sulfide. In some cases, a reservoir producing hydroelectricity can emit as much carbon as a coal-fired electrical generation plant.[253] This can occur for years after the area has been flooded.[254]

Dams also threaten fish stocks by fragmenting river ecosystems. The Grand Coulee Dam blocks salmon from returning to the high tributaries of the Columbia, their historical spawning grounds. Other dams on the Columbia have fish ladders, but the Northwest salmon population is now less than half its original size since the Grand Coulee was completed.[255] The health of ecosystems versus continued survival of a larger population has resulted in heated controversies regarding dams and their possible removal.

Dam Hydroelectricity May Fail

Proponents of hydroelectricity claim dams do not take water from the river, only its energy, which is untrue since dams assist in shorting the hydrologic cycle. If the estimates that Lake Mead and Lake Powell will reach minimum power pool levels by 2012 to 2017 are accurate, there will be no hydropower to pump remaining reservoir water.[256] Assuming hydroelectric generation from Hoover

---

[252] Barlow, M., and Clarke, T. "Blue Gold, The Fight to Stop the Corporate Theft of the Worlds Water." The New York Press, New York, 2002. Pg. 49.
[253] Ibid.
[254] Ibid.
[255] Ibid, pg 50.
[256] Barnett, "When Will Lake Mead Run Dry?."

Dam stopped, what alternative energy source could be used to make up the deficit for seven million people? This could become an important issue affecting more than 22 million people dependent on the energy and water from Lake Mead. Also, according to the FBI, prior to the 9/11 terrorist attacks, Mohammed Atta scouted Hoover Dam as a potential target.[257] It likely remains a high priority target of terrorist groups; however, failure could result due to technological or natural hazards, e.g., earthquakes.

Proposals for Dams

If the U.S. can implement the following proposals, we could potentially protect our water supply and river ecosystems.

Reengineer Some Dams

U.S. river ecosystems should be allowed to recover where possible and be managed more effectively. Reengineering a dam could assist this process by restoring wetlands and tributaries; however, this process must be carefully studied to determine long-term effects of reengineering, and to ensure that benefits can be realized. Even though dismantling or reengineering of dams may result in a more secure water supply and healthier U.S. Rivers, significant problems may arise that hamper these efforts. First, a river ecosystem might only partially recover from the negative effects of the dam, after many decades and even with careful planning and study.[258] The U.S. Army Corp of Engineers encountered this problem in Florida when they straightened the flow of the Kissimmee River and later was forced to restore the river to its original course for ecosystem health and water supply sustainability. Second, sediments in a dam's reservoir could be contaminated with industrial or mining related toxins, a nearly insurmountable problem. Public concerns, environmental problems, economic hurdles, research studies, and legal impediments slow this improvement process. Only a few of 500

---

[257] Tamm, "Hoover Dam, Boulder City, Nevada, Mileage Review: Las Vegas, Nevada."
[258] Doyle, "Stream Ecosystem Response to Small Dam Removal: Lessons from the Heartland."

proposed dam removals in the U.S. have been initiated to meet specific ecological goals.[259]

In November 2008, the Bush administration announced an agreement between the U.S. Department of Interior, Dam owner PacifiCorp utilities, and the governors of Oregon and California to remove four dams along the Klamath River. The agreement proposes to restore salmon habitat along the Klamath and its tributaries, but allows time to implement alternate sources of water and power. This agreement was made possible because it is cheaper to remove the dams than to build fish ladders.[260] Time will be needed to assess the overall scope and impact of dam removal.

Dismantling or reengineering a dam is not always possible. Whenever this is the case, floodgates could be opened, depending on water needs, to allow natural-river flows and unrestricted fish passage during critical times of the year.[261] However, there is no easy answer for dam removal problems and, more than likely, it will be a trial and error approach that delivers solutions, even after careful study.

Halt Construction of New Dams?

Cheaper options for water supply may exist as alternatives to building new dams. Conservation, efficiency gains, better management, recycling, and reuse could free up as much water as a new reservoir holds; however, substantial studies would need to be completed to determine sustainability compared to a building a dam and would need to be regionally specific. Since 1998, the decommissioning rate for large dams has overtaken the construction rate in the US.[262] One of the reasons for this is because the best sites for dam construction have already been used.

---

[259] D.D. Hart, et al., "Dam Removal: Challenges and Opportunities for Ecological Research and River Restoration," *BioScience* 42(2002).

[260] Jeff Barnard, "Deal Paves Way for Dams' Removal on Western River," *Klamath Bucket Brigade*(2008), http://hosted.ap.org/dynamic/stories/k/klamath_dams?site=txhar&section=home&template=default.

[261] Commission, "Dams and Development, a New Framework," (World Commission on Dams, 2000).

[262] Dickie, "Rich Countries, Poor Water."

Store Water Underground

A better way to store water is underground (known as water banking), through artificially recharging aquifers, which minimizes river ecosystem damage and eliminates water loss due to evaporation. Water banking diverts water to giant porous basins, where it percolates through the soil into a natural aquifer. California is the national leader in this practice, storing at least three billion cubic meters of water per year in water banks.[263] Phoenix also has impressive water banking projects, such as the New River-Agua Fria River Underground Storage Project and Granite Reef Underground Storage Project that divert water from the Colorado River via the Central Arizona Canal Project to store in aquifers for future use.[264] However, this is an energy intensive process.

Interstate water banking is an interesting development among states in the Colorado River basin. Nevada pays Arizona to store excess Colorado River water if it is available. When Nevada needs more water, they can take it from Lake Mead. Arizona then recovers an equivalent amount from their water banks to restore the lake.[265] Unfortunately, population growth diminishes potential sustainability of this process so that in the future it will be one of several water-supply projects.

Another method of underground water storage, termed aquifer storage recovery, stores drinking (treated) water underground through dual purpose wells that can inject water into the aquifer or pump it out.[266] This method was first used in Florida, which now has at least 30 such sites.[267] [268] Resulting aquifer draw down, sink holes, and other issues may terminate this process. Other states with aquifer storage recovery projects include California,

---

[263]Andres Sahuquillo, ed. *Strategies for the Conjunctive Use of Surface and Groundwater*, Drought Management and Planning for Water Resource (Boca Raton: CRS,2006).

[264] SRP, "Srp Stores Water for Tomorrow," (SRP Water Services, 2008).

[265] Arizona Water Banking Authority, "Interstate Water Banking Rule Issued,"(1999), http://www.azwaterbank.gov/annc/interstate_water.pdf.

[266]Sahuquillo, ed. *Strategies for the Conjunctive Use of Surface and Groundwater*.

[267] Ibid, pg 55.

[268] USGS, "Review of Aquifer Storage and Recovery in the Floridan Aquifer System of Southern Florida," ed. Water Resources Division (Reston: Government Printing Office, 2004).

Colorado, Kansas, Texas, Nevada, Washington, New Jersey, and West Virginia.[269] Simply removing dams is not the answer to water-supply problems. Dams, as part of the entire water supply, require infrastructure upgrades, better management, and enhanced technologies to cope with continued needs due to population growth.

Conclusions

Water is a critical resource; large cities consume vast quantities of it, food production is totally dependent upon water, and nearly all U.S. energy production requires it — from oil extraction to hydroelectric power. Thus, water scarcity is a matter of national security and stability, especially in the face of serious shortages. Cities use large volumes of water on non-food crops, waste potable water through sewers, and lose at least 20 percent of supply through leaks in the conveyance system because of deteriorating distribution components. For various reasons, cities and government fail to invest financial resources for basic maintenance and upgrades to water infrastructure. Both cities and agriculture are threatened with water scarcity from dehydrating watersheds and overdrawn aquifers because of an increasing population — scarcity is particularly acute in arid areas. Concurrently, falling water levels in reservoirs such as Lake Mead could soon drop below power-pool levels, cutting hydroelectric power. The near future for large cities could witness simultaneous shortages of water, food, and power, possibly resulting in mass civil unrest, decreased economic stability, and diminished continuity of local government. This does not include possible terrorist acts that could cause greater and more rapid cascading failure of these processes. Continued adequate governance and prevention of a dramatic destabilization of large cities, especially in the western U.S. will require that city and federal governments implement more efficient water-supply policies that focus on both sustainability and security.

---

[269] R. Pyne, and David, G., *Groundwater Recharge and Wells: A Guide to Aquifer Storage Recovery* (Boca Raton: CRC Press, 1995).

CHAPTER 7: Water Sustainability, Distribution and Protection —Dams to Reservoirs

Executive Summary

Construction of Hoover Dam was one of the greatest undertakings in human history considering its scale and scope, manpower necessary to achieve the project, and economic and social impacts. The waters impounded behind Hoover Dam have played an integral role in the burgeoning of agriculture and urban development in the American Southwest — providing water to about 22 million people and hydro power to about seven million. The Colorado River is the lifeblood of this region and Hoover Dam is, quite literally, the heart of the system. All of the major cities and the majority of the agricultural lands in this region would not exist without the security of water reserved in Lake Mead. The management and mitigation of this stored water will become increasingly significant as a function of rapidly increasing population and increasing demand.

The centralized nature of Hoover Dam coupled with substantially increasing resource needs in the American Southwest — that greatly depend on Hoover Dam to facilitate a viable and renewable source of water and power — pose a liability to the future security and sustainability of the region. Total reliance on the entrapment of water in a hot and arid climate regime utilized by millions of people and large agricultural investments is not a sustainable endeavor. Additionally, these issues pose a significant threat to the security of critical resources (access to water, food, and power) due to a centralized, non-redundant water supply.

The critical water resources provided by Hoover Dam are distributed to populated and agricultural areas in Nevada, Arizona, and California. The areas immediately at risk from a failure of Hoover Dam are those areas directly dependent on it for critical resources, which include southern Nevada (Las Vegas and surrounding area – 2 million people; Central and Southern Arizona (primarily Phoenix and Tucson – approximately four million people); and Southern California (from Los Angeles to San Diego – 22 million people). A number of smaller communities located downriver from the Hoover Dam are also highly dependent on these resources. In addition to populated areas at risk, large agricultural establishments in the Imperial and Coachella Valleys' in southern California as well as in the Yuma and Blythe areas in southwest Arizona are largely dependent on waters regulated by Hoover Dam.

The combination of these agricultural areas use nearly 85 percent of the water distributed from Hoover Dam and reservoirs downstream. A total production yield of approximately three billion dollars was achieved in 2006. Hydroelectric power generated at Hoover Dam and other hydroelectric downstream generators provides approximately 2080 megawatts annually (over four billion kilowatt-hours of power). The majority of this electric power is supplied to California (56 percent); however, Arizona and Nevada receive a significant share as well.

Failure of Hoover Dam would present simultaneous security risks to our basic needs as a society — water, food, and energy.

1. Municipal and industrial water needs — Nearly four million acre-feet of industrial and municipal water needs would not be met, leading to an instantaneous water shortage to more than 22 million people, notwithstanding the loss of 30 million stored acre-feet throughout the Lower Basin system.
2. Agricultural water needs — Over 1.5 million acres of land would not receive irrigation water, resulting in a loss of industrial and food-stuff valued over three billion dollars in failed crops. The loss of this reliable supply of resources would have both local and national impacts.
3. Clean Electrical Power — Southern California, Arizona, and Nevada would have large populations (approximately seven million people) without power, and diversion of power could lead to rolling blackouts. Redundant power sources may be ineffectual.
4. Economic Losses — Loss of the Hoover Dam would cause a significant downturn in production and loss of jobs with cascading failures in the supply chain and other critical infrastructure that would have a severe rippling effect through the nation. Failure would affect

energy, commodity, and food prices extensively, as well as have other unseen effects that will not be discussed here due to sensitivity and security issues.

The security risks to critical resources are overly relevant because of the number of people and agricultural lands that are directly and solely dependent on resources provided either directly or indirectly from Hoover Dam. Additionally, any clear and present resource security risks are likely to occur simultaneously to a large population, causing deprivation of critical resources with almost no alternatives available for substitution, consequently posing a significant security risk to the entire population of the American Southwest and that could affect the entire U.S. The availability of resources is growing ever scarcer due to increasing population. As more people compete for finite resources, sustainability will likely fail at some juncture and many people will not be able to meet basic resource needs. A failure of Hoover Dam would exacerbate this situation many fold, likely catalyzing the American Southwest into a society-wide downward spiral, perhaps of chaotic proportions. Hoover Dam's designation as critical infrastructure will grow in magnitude as the population dependent on water and energy resources provided by Hoover Dam grows.

A catastrophic breech or failure of Hoover Dam would initially release 10 trillion gallons of water impounded in Lake Mead, which would flow downstream in a massive torrent overflowing and destroying Davis Dam (adding the volume of the Mojave Reservoir to the torrent) and the Parker Dam (also adding the volume of Lake Havasu to the torrent). After the massive flood and without the security of reserve water, the arid, dry, and harsh climate that encompasses the American Southwest would cause total failure in cropping systems and result in non sustainability of the population at large. Entire economic sectors, such as the multi-billion dollar gaming industry of Las Vegas and the multi-billion dollar agricultural industry in southern California, would fail. Major negative economic and environmental residual effects would follow this catastrophic event. It is difficult to predict the exact effects of such an event to the local and national environmental and economic landscape because an event of this magnitude and scope has never been experienced.

However, it could be assumed that this event would cause large-scale disruption, both locally and nationally — the duration of the residual effects of this event would not be short lived.

The major mechanisms of failure would include earthquakes and terrorist attacks. The likelihood of a terrorist attack remains the highest probability of dam inoperability and would likely occur due to contamination of Lake Mead with biological agents such as Anthrax, Botulism, or others; through chemical agents, such as Nerve (G and V agents); or with Biotoxins such as Ricin, Digitalis, etc. Bio-agents would cause the most immediate damage through poisoning the water supply. Other terrorist threats could potentially rely on explosives of various types, including semi-tractor mounted artillery with armor piercing-rounds. As an example, high explosive armor-piercing rounds (105mm or larger capable of striking targets 3-6 km away) could potentially be truck mounted. The new bypass that prevents traffic from driving directly across Hoover Dam, but is adjacent to the dam's face, makes such a scenario enticing, i.e., mounting the artillery inside the back of a semi and utilizing a frontal attack with multiple shells.

The role and significance of Hoover Dam has increased in scope and scale with increased population and agricultural production dependent on the resources provided by the dam and its auxiliary downstream projects. Hoover Dam now more than ever, serves as the sole lifeline for millions of people in the American Southwest. It is therefore crucial to continue the incident avoidance measures and improve upon them since implementation after the 9/11 attacks.

The shadow cast by the limited resources and the growing population of the American Southwest pose a dire and urgent dilemma to the future security of the American Southwest and could have a profound effect on national security.

Introduction

This chapter focuses on a case study of the potential national security risk subsequent to failure of Hoover Dam. The purpose and design of the infrastructure projects undertaken by the Bureau of Reclamation in the upper and lower Colorado Basins were to help

develop the West through steady control and mitigation of the waters of the Colorado River. This goal was achieved through cooperation with state and local entities to aid in the planning, construction, and implementation of large-scale water diversion, storage, and delivery infrastructure along with the generation, management, and distribution of clean electricity generated from hydro-power. These diversion projects were intended to stimulate economic growth, improve living conditions, and generally enhance the quality of life in the West through the cultivation and provision of the waters of the Colorado River.[270] The greatest achievement in this process was construction of the Hoover Dam. To understand the risks and vulnerabilities of this invaluable system, it is necessary to understand the purpose of its construction, the history behind it, and the general construction process.

As the bulk of these projects have been complete for some time, the Bureau of Reclamation currently provides safe and dependable water supplies for agricultural, municipal, and industrial use to large portions of land and a great number of people in the American Southwest including Los Angeles, Phoenix, Las Vegas and other major cities. Additionally, clean, renewable electricity is produced and distributed from many of the Bureau's project sites such as Hoover Dam, and in many cases the water quality is protected or improved. Additional benefits of these projects include increased area for recreational activities, controlled nature of flooding events (previously unpredictable and detrimental), and the introduction of new habitat for fish and wildlife. The management and mitigation of water stored in many of the Bureau's projects in the American Southwest will likely become increasingly significant as a function of rapidly increasing population, and subsequent increasing demand for water for agricultural purposes.[271]

The Colorado River runs through seven states in the American Southwest and currently more than 20 major dams impede natural flow along the course of the river system. The combined volume of water impeded at any one time is equal to approximately 60 million

---

[270] J.E. Evens, et al., "Lessons from a Dam Failure," *Ohio Journal of Science* 100, no. 5 (2000).

[271] J.V. DeLong, "Dam Fools," *Reason Online*(1998), http://www.reason.com/news/show/30592.html.

acre-feet, or about 4 years of natural annual river flow. The Bureau of Reclamation operates all of the major dams in the system, including Glen Canyon Dam and Hoover Dam. In accordance with the 1922 Colorado River Compact, the Colorado River Basin was divided into an upper and a lower basin; it was determined that Lee Ferry, located 16 miles downriver from Glen Canyon Dam, would serve as the boundary between the two basins. The Upper Basin resources facilitate parts of the states of Utah, Wyoming, Colorado, and New Mexico. The Lower Basin resources facilitate most of Arizona, southern California, and southern Nevada, as well as small sections of New Mexico and southwestern Utah. The majority of these resources are stored at one of two locations: Glen Canyon Dam, located in the Upper Basin on the Utah-Arizona border and storing Lake Powel Reservoir: and Hoover Dam, located in the Lower Basin on the Nevada-Arizona border and storing Lake Mead Reservoir. Glen Canyon Dam and Hoover Dam are considered very critical infrastructure features within the Colorado River System — of vital importance in the effort to maintain successful implementation of the Bureau of Reclamation mission.

History of the Bureau of Reclamation and Hoover Dam

The history of the projects undertaken by the Bureau of Reclamation in the American Southwest, particularly the within the Colorado Plateau, began with the westward migration of homesteaders. In the mid-1800s the American Southwest had been fitted with a network of railroads through the interests of influential railroad companies, which were heavily indebted to the federal government at the time. A large campaign was initiated by the Federal Government that targeted people in the east as well as European citizens to migrate to the American Southwest. The claims of this campaign (considered false by many) offered promises of favorable farming conditions, clement weather conditions, and untapped resources waiting for exploitation. A number of settlers had staked claims in the Colorado Plateau area during the 1849 California gold rush, and by the 1880s all of the suitable sites (those near divertible water sources) had been claimed, leaving the vast number of remaining settlers in calamitous conditions — most without a source of clean water. Understanding the need for

mitigation of water resources in the area, several private water irrigation companies, funded by eastern capital, as well as several states agencies, including those in Colorado and California, attempted to take on the task of irrigating large portions of the vast, dry American Southwest. All of these efforts failed and it was determined that the only feasible way to sustain agriculture and urban growth and development in the area was for the Federal Government to intervene.

The Reclamation Act was passed on June 17, 1902 and the Reclamation Service (designated the Bureau of Reclamation in 1923) was initiated. The new agency gained most of its irrigation and arid land use practices from the Mormons (the Church of Jesus Christ of Latter-day Saints), who had developed effective irrigation processes in Utah, California, and Arizona. Eventually, the Mormon influence was deeply imbedded within the practices of the agency; Mormon or 'Church' law was adopted to deal with irrigation mitigation and the majority of the members of the fledgling agency were also of the Mormon faith. No one had ever attempted to tame the dry, arid American Southwest, which resulted in inexperienced, brash, and idealistic, farmers, engineers, and politicians hastily proposing and initiating projects with little understanding of weather and precipitation patterns, growing seasons, and soil fertility. Consequently, during the early years of the Reclamation Service, these outside influences resulted in few projects being satisfactorily completed and often with economic marginality.

The lack of population — only 11 million populated the entire western United States in 1930 — and the lack of political clout combined with (eastern) public indifference toward the area — made it difficult to authorize, plan, and implement well organized and socially beneficial projects. This changed when Franklin D. Roosevelt passed several bills that authorized the construction of dozens of dams throughout the American West. The Bureau of Reclamation's past and present practices of impeding the rivers of the west in order to irrigate land, provide water for growing populations and industry, produce hydroelectricity, control flood events, and construct recreational areas transformed the American West (particularly the arid southwest) from a hostile, unpredictable region into habitable land by providing valuable water for millions of people.

The Salton Sea

The need for controlled irrigation in the American Southwest was most severe in the fertile Imperial Valley in southern California. Agricultural activity began in this region in earnest after 1900 when the first water diversion projects proved successful on a small scale. Growth in the region's agricultural output resulted in the construction of the Imperial Canal, which accessed water from a manufactured diversion in the Colorado River that then flowed into the low-lying Imperial Valley. Within two years of construction the poorly planned Imperial Canal was impeded with silt and sediment deposited from the Colorado River; a new diversion was ordered by the Bureau of Reclamation. The California Development Company, responsible for the irrigation project, built another diversion canal, this time on Mexican Territory and out of the jurisdiction of the Bureau of Reclamation. In 1905, the fickle nature of the Colorado River displayed its fury in a massive flood with a discharge measuring an estimated 150,000 cubic feet per second. This flood event was initiated by heavy rainfall and snow melt in the Upper Colorado Basin and subsequently caused the overflow and eventual breach of an Imperial Valley dike. This breach diverted a large portion of Colorado River into the Salton Basin and continued to submerge the basin for over two years. The rapid influx of water and the lack of any substantial drainage from the basin caused the formation of the Salton Sea, south-southeast of Los Angeles.[272]

In addition to the fledgling agricultural endeavors and salt mining operations that occupied the area, the town of Salton, as well as Torres-Martinez Indian lands and Southern Pacific Railroad interests and equipment were all present in the basin — now inundated by the Salton Sea. An effort was made to halt the flow of water into the Salton Basin, but only after intense federal demands. Three million dollars (1905 dollars) were spent by the Southern Pacific Railroad to remedy the failed dike infrastructure and divert flow through a more reliable canal system. By 1907 this effort was complete; however, by this time the creation of the Salton Sea,

[272] Tony Herrera, "Unintended Consequences of a River," June 27 2007.

California's largest body of water, had inundated more than 376 square miles of potential agricultural land. The Salton Sea has remained more or less in its current state due to influx of agricultural irrigation runoff of more than one million acre feet per year. More importantly, the flooding event of 1905 was the underlying catalyst mandating control of future flood events caused by the Colorado River, which spurred the creation of myriad construction projects in the Upper and Lower Colorado Basin; most notable of these is Hoover Dam.

By 1920, southern California held most of the human population of the western United States and encompassed the largest and most productive agricultural regions in the west, including the Imperial and Coachella Valleys, and was quickly expending existing water supplies (California Groundwater Bulletin 118, 2004).[273] Delegates from California, Arizona, Nevada, New Mexico, Utah, Colorado, and Wyoming met in 1922 and negotiated for eleven months — the result was the Colorado River Compact. Based on the Bureau of Reclamation's estimated average annual flow of 17.5 million acre-feet (maf) through the entire Colorado River Basin, 8.5 maf were allotted to the Lower Basin, 7.5 maf to the Upper Basin, and 1.5 maf were reserved for Mexico.

Unfortunately, the determination of 17.5 maf as the average annual flow of the Colorado was based on 18 years of above-average flows; the longer-term average appears to be considerably less. Decades of drawn-out, contentious courtroom and Congressional battles were to come before today's water rights were eventually established.

Lower Basin

The Lower Colorado Basin is comprised of approximately 138,000 square miles; however, 90 percent of the water supplied to this area is from snowmelt and precipitation in the upper basin, the remaining 10 percent flows into the main channel of the Colorado River via tributaries located below Lee Ferry.[274] The three major

---

[273] Staff, "Coachella Valley Groundwater Basin, Indio Subbasin," (California Groundwater, 2004).
[274] T. Piechota, et al., "The Western U.S. Drought: How Bad Is It?," *EOS* 85, no. 32

storage units in the lower basin include Hoover, Parker, and Davis Dams. Hoover Dam is the northernmost (furthest upstream); it is unequivocally the most pronounced of these units, the most integral feature of the lower basin. Lake Mead helps supply the annual needs of about 22 million people and is a dependable supply of water for over two million acres of agricultural crops.[275] The three aforementioned dams produce a combined 2,500 megawatts of electricity every day, with Hoover Dam producing the bulk (2,080 megawatts.

Hoover Dam

The flooding of the Salton Basin and formation of the Salton Sea led to the Fall-Davis report, an extensive study on the possibilities of damming the Colorado River for the benefits of irrigation and electrical power. Based on the report, Congress passed the Boulder Canyon Project Act in 1928, authorizing the construction of a high dam at or near Boulder Canyon and the All-American Canal to bring water to the Imperial Valley. The All-American Canal was the first of several canal projects that eventually brought irrigation water to other agricultural regions of California and southern Arizona.

Construction of Hoover Dam was one of the greatest undertakings in human history considering its scale and scope, manpower necessary to achieve the project, and economic and social impacts. Hoover Dam stands 726.4 ft high (second only to the Oroville Dam near Oroville, California), and is 1,244 ft long at its crest. The dam is 660 ft at its base and 45 ft thick at its crest. Hoover Dam utilized approximately 4.36 million cubic yards of concrete and required over 21,000 men working day and night to complete; 112 of these men died during the construction process; 96 of them at the construction site. The waters impounded behind Hoover Dam have played an integral role in the burgeoning of agriculture and urban development in the American Southwest; the Colorado River is the lifeblood of this region and Hoover Dam is, quite literally, the heart of the system. Without doubt, all of the major cities and the majority of the agricultural lands in this region would not exist without the

---

(2004).

[275] D. Gardner, et al., "Agriculture and Salinity Control in the Colorado River Basin," *Natural Resources Journal* 15, no. 63 (1975).

security of water reserved in Lake Mead, which has a volume of over 28.5 million acre-feet when full (one acre foot of water equals 325,851 gallons — the approximate amount used by a family of four in one year). Figure 7.1 depicts a schematic of Hoover Dam.

Figure 7.1: Hoover Dam schematic (Source: Bureau of Reclamation).

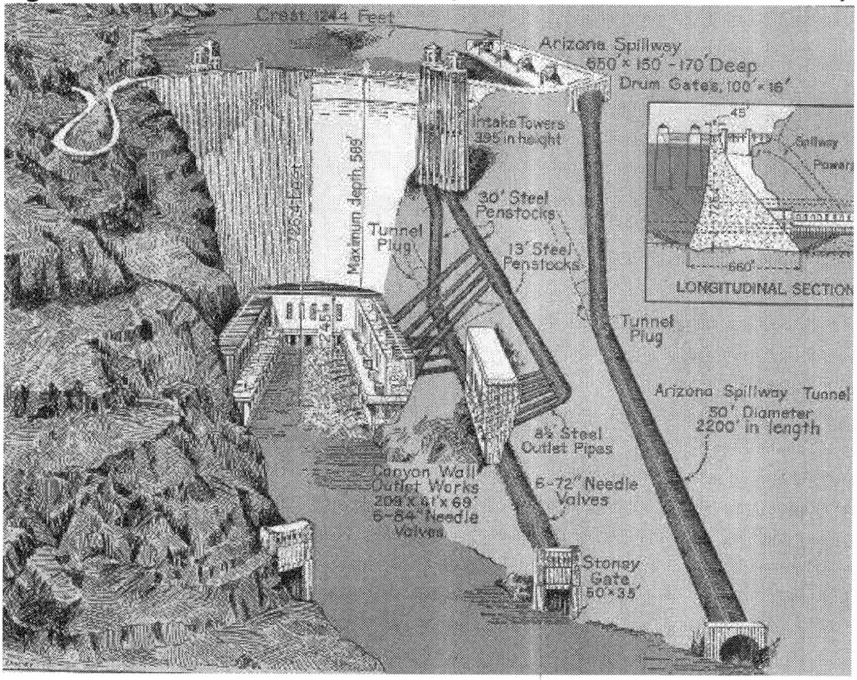

Currently, the Colorado River water impeded at Lake Mead provides resources to irrigate over two million acres in the United States and 500,000 acres in Mexico. Hoover Dam is the core of a water conservation and conveyance system that provides municipal water to over 22 million people in Arizona, California, and Nevada.[276] Furthermore, electrical power generated at Hoover Dam is provided to some seven million people across three states, but is providing less people with energy as power pool levels diminish due to less water in Lake Mead.

The large populations that rely on these critical resources are rapidly increasing, as are the agricultural lands in the area. Agriculture

[276] Endeco, "Monitoring and Protecting the Water Quality in Lake Mead, Nevada," (YSI Environmental, 2006).

in the area is expanding to a lesser degree, due to geographic and climatic constraints.[277] The centralized nature of Hoover Dam coupled with substantially increasing resource needs in the American Southwest, which greatly depends on Hoover Dam to facilitate a viable and renewable source of water and power — pose a liability to the future security and sustainability of this area.[278] Total reliance on the entrapment of water in a hot and arid climate regime utilized by millions of people and large agricultural investments is not a sustainable endeavor. Additionally, these issues pose a significant threat to the security of critical resources (access to water, food, and power) due to a centralized water supply, especially in context of the extreme precipitation and temperature conditions of the region.

Construction of Hoover Dam

It required more than three years of meticulous surveying to identify a suitable location for Hoover Dam. It was initially determined that Boulder Canyon would provide a suitable location for the dam (hence the alternate name of Boulder Canyon Dam often referred to in historical texts); however, after some deliberation it was determined that the dam would be build in Black Canyon, approximately 5 miles downriver from Boulder Canyon. This decision was made because Black Canyon could capture more water and, geologically, had a denser rock structure in its canyon walls that would aid in compensating for the high pressures produced by large volumes of water. Construction of Hoover Dam began on 1931 by Six Companies, Inc., a conglomeration of six domestic firms that specialized in large-scale construction and concrete projects, and Union Carbide Corporation (contracted to manufacture immense blocks of ice that were used to cool water which was circulated through the massive concrete structure of Hoover Dam). The dam was completed in 1936.

The initial stages of the project included the construction of two coffer dams, built to maintain the worksite and prevent flooding. Even though the river had not yet been diverted, construction of the upper coffer dam began in September 1932. After the diversion

[277] S.L. Postel, et al., "Human Appropriation of Renewable Fresh Water," *Science* 271, no. 5250 (1996).

[278] Tindall, "Water Security - Nation State and International Security Implications."

tunnels on the Arizona and Nevada sides of the dam were completed, the river could be diverted, and the work completed much more efficiently. Four diversion tunnels were blasted through the canyon walls: two on the Nevada side and two on the Arizona side. These tunnels were 56 feet in diameter with a combined length of about 16,000 feet.

Once the coffer dams were erected and the construction site deemed safe from water inundation, excavation for the dam foundation began. It was determined that the dam would need to rest on solid rock to achieve maximum stability for many years into the future. Consequently, it was necessary to remove all accumulated erosion soils and other loose material from the riverbed until sound bedrock was reached. This effort was conducted to avoid liquefaction of the ground beneath the dam in case of a moderate to severe earthquake, which is much less likely within bedrock. Work on the foundation excavation was completed in June 1933. During excavations of the riverbed for the foundation, approximately 1.5 million cubic yards of material was removed. Also, a great effort was expended on the walls of the canyon that would trap impounded waters behind the dam — hundreds of miles of canyon walls were prepared by scrubbing or blasting until unweathered parent material was exposed. This effort was performed to avoid water seepage into cracks and fissures that had accumulated over time due to unrelenting heat and cold of the harsh Arizona-Nevada desert and to avoid severe landslide events.

The first batch of concrete was poured on June 6, 1933. No structure of the magnitude or scale of the Hoover Dam had previously been constructed; accordingly, many of the engineering and architectural practices used in construction of the dam were attempted for the first time. Concrete heats up and contracts as it cures (an exothermic process). This resulted in differential cooling and localized contraction of the concrete which posed a grave concern to engineers. It was determined that if the dam were built in a single continuous pour (an almost impossible feat), the concrete would require about 120 years to cool to ambient temperature. The resulting stresses within the dam would have caused detrimental cracking and inevitable collapse of the entire structure. To remedy this problem, Hoover Dam was built in a series of interlocking trapezoidal columns with interconnecting joints between columns. The chemical heat generated by concrete setting was dissipated by imbedding over 582 miles of one-inch steel pipe through the interconnecting concrete blocks. River water was circulated through these pipes to help dissipate the heat from the curing concrete. After this, chilled water from a refrigeration plant on the lower coffer dam was circulated through the coils to further cool the concrete. Hoover Dam was constructed for a service life of about 1,500 years. Because other dams have been built upstream, the silt accumulating under the Hoover Dam has decreased significantly; this effect has doubled the expected lifetime of Hoover Dam to 3,000 years, although this may be a bit liberal.

Areas at Risk of Critical Resource Security

The critical water resources provided by Hoover Dam are distributed to populated and agricultural areas in Nevada, Arizona, and California; these areas would be most directly impacted by a failure of Hoover Dam. According to the Colorado River Compact, Lower Colorado River Basin water allocation is 7.5 million acre-feet and is distributed as follows: California receives 4.4 million acre-feet (58.7 percent), Arizona receives 2.8 million acre-feet (37.3percent), and Nevada receives 300,000 acre-feet (four percent). The locations most at risk within these states include the heavily populated areas that are primarily or partially dependent on resources provided by Hoover Dam; these include Los Angeles and surrounding areas (which depend on Hoover Dam for 50 percent of water supplies), the Phoenix Metropolitan area, large portions of Tucson and greater Las Vegas. A number of smaller communities located downriver from the Hoover Dam are also highly dependent on these resources. In total, approximately 22 million inhabitants in these three states are wholly dependent on water provided by Hoover Dam for municipal purposes.

In addition to populated areas at risk, large agricultural establishments in the Imperial and Coachella Valleys' in southern California as well as in the Yuma and Blythe areas in southwest Arizona are largely dependent on waters regulated by Hoover

Dam.[279] The total agricultural land area that is impacted by water regulated through Hoover Dam is approximately two million acres; the combined agricultural output of these area exceeded three billion dollars in 2007.

Water resources are delivered to the various population centers or agricultural areas via a series of aqueducts and canals. The water delivery systems are managed at central locations and distributed through other Bureau of Reclamation projects such as Lake Havasu for more remote population centers and agricultural areas. The major water conveyance and delivery systems are depicted on the map below and described in the following sections. Figure 7.2 depicts the various water delivery systems in the Upper and Lower Colorado River Basin; note the canals and aqueducts in the American Southwest.

Figure 7.2: Lower Colorado River Basin Water Delivery Infrastructure Systems - Colorado River Aqueduct (Source: U.S. Bureau of Reclamation).

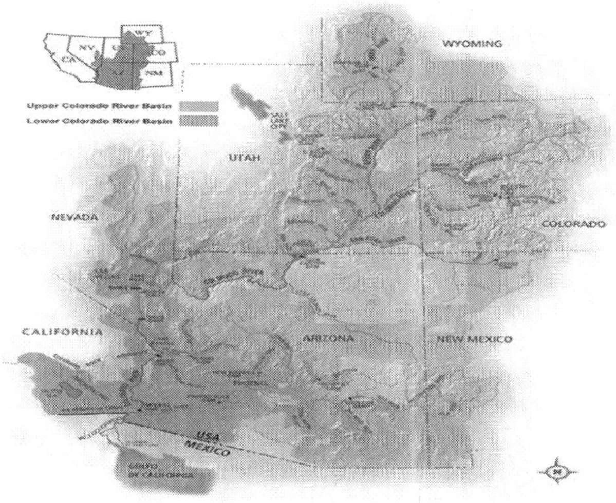

This water conveyance project spans 242 miles and delivers water from Lake Havasu across the Mojave Desert to the greater Las Angeles area (Figure 7.3). The aqueduct was constructed from 1933 to1941 by the Metropolitan Water District of Southern California to

[279] Gardner, "Agriculture and Salinity Control in the Colorado River Basin."

ensure a steady supply of drinking water to Los Angeles and now serves southern California communities from Ventura County to San Diego County. The maximum delivery capacity is approximately 1.3 million acre-feet a year, or enough municipal water for about five million people annually. This water delivery system is gaining in significance due to the growing population in the Los Angeles area (about 17 million people). Also, water litigation and allocation tie-ups, as well as historic contamination in reservoirs leading to remediation measures and groundwater pollution have further stressed the area and placed a greater demand on the Colorado River Aqueduct.[280]

Figure 7.3: Colorado River Aqueduct (CRA) delivery system for Central Arizona Project (Source: California Metro Water District).

This project was initiated in 1973 and final installation of infrastructure took place in 1993 with the addition piping for water delivery to the Tucson area. This project diverts water a distance of 336 miles from Lake Havasu across the central Arizona desert and into central and southern Arizona (Figure 7.4). The Central Arizona Project is managed and operated by the Central Arizona Water Conservation District. The project was designed to provide water to agricultural lands in the Yuma and Blythe areas in southwestern

---

[280] Antonio R. Villaraigoso, "Securing L.A.'S Water Supply," (Los Angeles: City of Los Angeles Department of Water and Power, 2008).

Arizona, as well as municipal water for several Arizona communities, including the metropolitan areas of Phoenix and Tucson. At maximum capacity this aqueduct delivers 2.2 million acre-feet of water a year, enough municipal water for nearly ten million people.[281] However, unlike the Colorado River Aqueduct, the Central Arizona Project is a mixed use delivery system and devotes the majority of its water (about 80 percent) to agricultural needs rather than municipal needs. The agricultural lands that are provided water from this project total about one million acres and have a production value of $1.4 billion annually.[282]

Figure 7.4: Central Arizona Project (CAP) deliver system (source: U.S. Bureau of Reclamation).

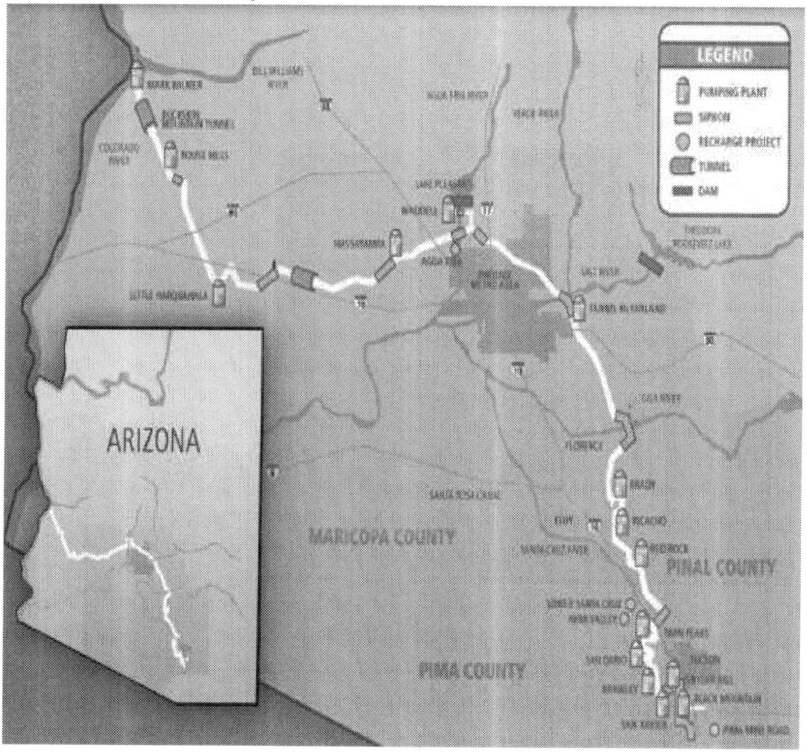

[281] Staff, "Balancing Water Need on the Lower Colorado River," (Yuma Desalting Plant/Cienega de Santa Clara Workgroup, 2005).

[282] — — —, "Securing Arizona's Water Future," ed. Arizona Department of Water Resources (2004).

All American, Coachella Canals, etc.

The All American Canal delivery system brings water to the Imperial Valley in southern California. The canal spans 80 miles across the southern California desert and delivers water from the reservoir created by the Imperial Diversion Dam on the California-Arizona border. It is the largest irrigation canal in the world, carrying up to 26,155 cubic feet per second of water. The canal was built by the United States Bureau of Reclamation in the 1930s and was completed in 1942. The canal is the valley's only source of water and as such serves as the lifeline for those dependent on it for municipal and agricultural purposes.[283] The Bureau of Reclamation owns the canal and its offshoots; however, the Imperial Irrigation District operates it. The All American Canal feeds, from east to west, the Coachella Canal, East Highline Canal, Central Canal and the Westside Main Canal (Figure 7.5). The total capacity of this canal is 1.3 million acre-feet annually (or, enough for about five million people).[284] The majority of the water channeled through this canal is used for agricultural purposes; approximately one million acres are irrigated by this system with a total production value of $1.6 billion annually.[285]

The combination of these agricultural areas uses nearly 85 percent of the water distributed from Hoover Dam and reservoirs downstream. A total production yield of approximately $3 billion was achieved in 2006. Most of the crops produced include heavily water-consumptive crops such as cotton, which is used primarily in the textile industry, and alfalfa to provide feed for livestock in the area. About 1.3 million acres of agricultural land area are used for this purpose. Other crops include dates, lettuce, cotton, carrots, citrus fruits, cantaloupes, watermelons, barley, tomatoes, sugar beets, grapes, sweet corn, and bell peppers. Livestock grown in the area include robust cattle and diary industries, sheep, goats, chickens and

---

283 Kevin Rafferty, "Aquaculture in the Imperial Valley - a Geothermal Success Story," (GHC Bulletin, 1999).

284 Staff, "California's Colorado River Water Allocation," (The Metropolitan Water District of southern California, 2007).

285 Refugio Gonzalez, et al., "Agriculture and Livestock in the Imperial Valley, Mexicali, and San Lui Rio Colorado," (San Diego State University, 2000).

other foul, swine, and fish.[286] This area produces a large percentage of the winter vegetables that are consumed nationally.

Figure 7.5: All American Canal and ancillary delivery systems (Source: U.S. Bureau of Reclamation).

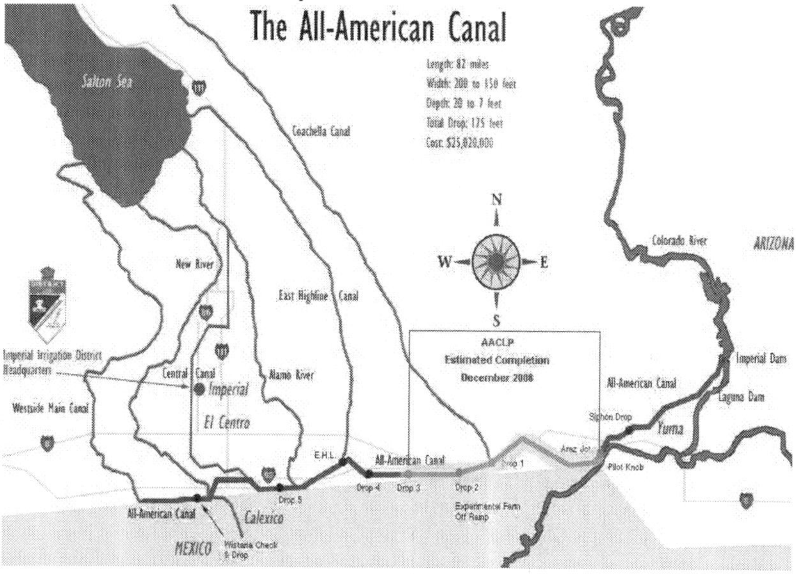

Power Generation and Distribution

Hydroelectric power generated at Hoover Dam and other hydroelectric downstream generators provide a small but effective renewable source of clean electricity to over 2.5 million people in southern California, Arizona, and southern Nevada.[287] The centerpiece of the hydroelectricity generation infrastructure is emplaced at Hoover Dam; the maximum electrical output of the 17 Francis and two Pelton turbines located at Hoover Dam is approximately 2080 megawatts annually (over four billion kilowatt-hours of power).[288] The majority of this electric power is supplied to California (56 percent); however, Arizona and Nevada receive a significant share as well — 19

---

[286] Ibid.

[287] J.G. Edwards, "Hoover Dam's Reduced Output Haaving Little Impact on Nevada Power," *Review Journal*, no. July (2004).

[288] B.A. Mork, "The Big and the Small: Victoria Hydro Versus Hoover Dam," (Michigan: Michigan Technical University Power Engineering Society, 2003).

and 25 percent, respectively. Table 7.1 details the percentage of power distribution from Hoover Dam to the various power delivery locations.

Table 7.1: Distribution of power generated at the Hoover Dam hydroelectric plant

Location	Power Allocation (percent)
Arizona	18.9 percent
Nevada	23.4 percent
Metropolitan Water Dist of Southern California	28.5 percent
Burbank, CA	0.6 percent
Glendale, CA	1.6 percent
Pasadena, CA	1.4 percent
Los Angeles, CA	15.4 percent
Southern California Edison Co.	5.5 percent
Azusa, CA	0.1 percent
Anaheim, CA	1.1 percent
Banning, CA	0.04 percent
Colton, CA	0.1 percent

Additionally, Davis and Parker Dams are located downriver from Hoover Dam and serve integral roles in the distribution of water resources to population centers in southern California and Arizona. These Reclamation projects were also outfitted with hydroelectric power generation equipment to meet the demands of a growing population. The Davis Dam has a maximum output capacity of 251 megawatts and Parker Dam has a maximum output capacity of 120 megawatts.[289] Thus, Hoover Dam (classed as both critical infrastructure and a national monument) is one of the United States' most valuable resources. Its continued sustainability and security are imperative.

[289] Staff, "Parker and Davis Dams," ed. Parker and Davis Dams Field Division (DesertUSA, 2006).

Security Risks Presented by a Failure of Hoover Dam

Failure of Hoover Dam would present simultaneous security risks to our basic needs as a society – water, food, and energy.

Municipal and industrial water needs – nearly four million acre-feet of industrial and municipal water needs would fail to be met, leading to an instantaneous water shortage to more than 22 million people, notwithstanding the loss of 30 million stored acre-feet throughout the Lower Basin system.

Agricultural water needs – Over 1.5 million acres or land would not receive irrigation water, resulting in a loss of industrial and food-stuff valued over three billion dollars in failed crops. The loss of this reliable supply of resources would have both local and national impacts.

Clean Electrical Power – Southern California, Arizona, and Nevada would have large populations (approximately two million people) without power, and diversion of power could lead to rolling blackouts. Additionally, compensatory power generated from other power plants would likely be produced from coal and not from a clean source.

Economic Losses – loss of the Hoover Dam would mean electricity loss not just to homes, but also to businesses and industry, causing a significant downturn in production and loss of jobs with cascading failures in the supply chain and other critical infrastructure that would have a severe rippling effect through the nation. Failure would affect energy, commodity, and food prices extensively, as well as have other unseen effects that will not be discussed here due to sensitivity and security issues.

The security risks to critical resources are especially relevant because of the number of people and agricultural lands that are directly and solely dependent on resources provided either directly

or indirectly from Hoover Dam.[290] In addition, any clear and present resource security risks are likely to occur simultaneously to a large population and not at some steady rate over time due to non-redundancy (no back-up supply). This simultaneous deprivation of critical resources to a large population with almost no alternatives available for substitution of these resources poses a significant security risk to the entire population of the American Southwest and that could affect the entire U.S. — additional to present security risks to critical resources. The availability of resources is growing ever scarcer due to increasing population. As more people compete for finite resources, sustainability will likely fail at some juncture and many people will not be able to meet basic resource needs. A failure of Hoover Dam would exacerbate this situation many fold, likely catalyzing the American Southwest into a society-wide downward spiral, perhaps of chaotic proportions. Hoover Dam's designation as critical infrastructure will grow in magnitude as the population dependent on water and energy resources provided by Hoover Dam grows.

Areas Most at Risk

The areas most directly at risk from a failure of Hoover Dam are those areas directly dependent on it for critical resources:
Southern Nevada (Las Vegas and surrounding area – two million people) receives 90 percent of its municipal and industrial water and 25 percent of the power generated by Hoover Dam turbines;
Central and Southern Arizona use about 40 percent Colorado River water (primarily Phoenix and Tucson – total population approximately four million people) and receives 19 percent of Hoover Dam's power generation; and

Southern California is about 35 percent dependent on Colorado River water (from LA to San Diego – 22 million people) and receives 56 percent of Hoover Dam's power generation.

---

[290] Jesse Allen, "Drough Lowers Lake Mead," ed. Earth Observatory (NASA Earth Observatory, 2003).

If Hoover Dam catastrophically failed or breeched, initially the ten trillion of gallons of water impounded by Hoover Dam would flow downstream in a massive torrent overflowing and destroying Davis Dam (adding the volume of the Mojave Reservoir to the torrent) and Parker Dam (also adding the volume of Lake Havasu to the torrent). After the massive flood and without the security of reserve water, the arid, dry, and harsh climate that encompasses the American Southwest would cause total failure in cropping systems and result in non sustainability of the population at large. Over a million acres of agricultural lands would dry up in a matter of weeks. Twenty-two million people in various populated centers would be without municipal water for an undisclosed amount of time, likely resulting in mass migration eastward and northward.

Entire economic sectors, such as the multi-billion dollar gaming industry of Las Vegas and the multi-billion dollar agricultural industry in southern California and Southwestern Arizona would cease to operate. Major negative economic and environmental residual effects would follow this catastrophic event. It is difficult to predict and gauge the exact effects of such an event to the local and national environmental and economic landscape because an event of this magnitude and scope has never been experienced. However, it could be assumed that this event would cause large-scale disruption, both locally and nationally — the duration of the residual effects of this event would not be short lived.

Mechanisms of Failure

Many different types of dams have failed throughout the U.S. and the world, in most cases causing loss of lives and high costs of damage.[291] Dams are likely to fail for a variety of reasons:

- **Inadequate design**
- **Poor construction**
- **Poor geotechnical analysis**
- **Landslide induced waves in the reservoir**
- **Military strike**

---

[291] Staff, "An Incomplete History of Dam Failures and near Failures in the U.S.," (Association of State Dam Safety Officials, 2007).

- **Earthquakes**
- **Terrorist attack**

The first five scenarios from the list above are unlikely to affect Hoover Dam due to the diligent and comprehensive expertise in geotechnical analysis, design, and construction utilized during construction. Tedious efforts were made to strip the canyon walls of any areas prone to exfoliation of rock face into the reservoir. Also, the shape of the reservoir (Lake Mead) impounded behind Hoover Dam is not conducive to wave action directly onto the dam. Also, a military strike is unlikely due to active security and surveillance.

Earthquakes

The threat of an earthquake occurring in the vicinity of Hoover Dam is high; in fact, at least four earthquakes of magnitude five or greater have occurred in the vicinity of the dam since construction. Although earthquakes often cause liquefaction of the ground beneath a dam, causing structural instability due to the sheer mass of a dam on liquefied ground, this type of failure is generally associated with dams that are built on unstable ground and usually excludes bedrock.[292] Hoover Dam is not likely to be susceptible to earthquake derived damage or structural failure due to liquefaction.[293] Recent data seems to suggest that earthquakes in the Nevada and Arizona in proximity to Hoover are increasing.[294] However, the sound structural nature of Hoover Dam is reinforced by the test of earthquakes over time; to date, no ill effects to the structural integrity of Hoover Dam have resulted (including quite significant events in close proximity to the dam).[295] Likely, earthquake damage would result in fractures of rock surrounding the dam.

---

[292] Leslie Harder, F., et al., "Failure of Tapo Canyon Tailings Dam," (University of Californai: University of California, 1996).

[293] Larry Nuss, K., "Seismic Analysis of Hoover Dam," ed. Bureau of Reclamation Structural Analysis Unit (Bureau of Reclamation, 1998).

[294] M. Hutch, "Nevada?Arizona Earthquaks Increasing Recently," *Hutch Report*(2008), http://mhutch.blogspot.com/2008/02/nevadaarizona-earthquakes-increasing.html.

[295] Steven Nelson, A., "Earthquake Prediction and Control," (Tulane University, 2003).

Acts of Terrorism

The likelihood of a terrorist attack remains the highest probability of dam inoperability. This scenario was low priority prior to terrorists' attacks on September 11, 2001. Afterward, regulating bodies involved with national security adopted an 'Anything is Possible" philosophy. Consequently, Hoover Dam has been on higher security alert and listed as a featured critical Infrastructure of high priority by the Department of Homeland Security and other national security agencies.[296] Four potential attack scenarios are listed below.

Contamination of Lake Mead — Generally, various experts have concluded the likelihood of reservoir contamination is low given that several freighter cars of toxin would need to be dumped into the water supply for any effect. However, this threat reduction is likely too sanguine because the relevant characteristics of a biological agent's potential as a weapon include its stability in a drinking water systems, virulence, culturability in the quantity required, and resistance to detection and treatment. Depending on the chemical or biologic agent used, this benign assessment of logistics is naïve.[297] Bioterrorism or chemical threats could deliver massive contamination by small amount of microbiological agents or toxic chemicals and could endanger the public health of thousands, particularly children and the elderly. Factually, Al Qaeda and other terrorist groups are known to possess specific chemicals that could indeed bring such a threat to fruition, and they have even boasted about possessing such capabilities. Also, large systems such as Lake Mead are nearly impossible to completely physically secure, leaving them vulnerable to attack. A few examples of highly toxic biological and chemical agents include—

Category A Biological Agents — Anthrax, Botulism, Plague, Smallpox, Tularemia, Viral Hemmorraghagic Fevers (filoviruses [e.g., Ebola, Marburg] and arena viruses [e.g., Lassa, Machupo])

---

[296] Michael Chertoff, "Testimony by Secretary Michael Chertoff before the House Homeland Security Committee," *Homeland Security Committee Testimonies*(2005), http://www.dhs.gov/xnews/testiony/testimony_0034.shtm.

[297] Tindall, "Water Security - Nation State and International Security Implications."

Chemical Agents — Nerve (G and V) agents, Biotoxins (Ricin, Digitalis), etc.

Precision guided marine munitions device — Torpedo or C4 delivery device (to take out one 8-inch square steel beam, for example, would require 8 to 10 pounds of C4). Also, steel-plate force induction explosive methodology has the potential to cause substantial damage.

Long-range artillery munitions — High explosive armor piercing rounds (105mm, 120mm, and 155mm projectiles capable of striking targets 3-6 km away). These could potentially be truck mounted and utilized from atop the new bypass.

The likelihood of success each of the above scenarios decreases from the top of the list to the bottom. The potential of a precision guided marine munitions delivery device such as a torpedo or C4 delivery system, while questionable, is possible; however, a large quantity of explosive material would be needed to counteract the dissipation of energy due to the device being detonated under water. Plate detonation processes could overcome this problem to some extent and perhaps achieve success. Hopefully, this type of activity would be detected by the myriad of security measures implemented around Lake Mead.

The probability of a long range artillery munitions being deployed toward the dam is significantly higher than the aforementioned scenarios because of the distance at which these devices can be effectively deployed (3-6 km), well outside of the surveillance or patrol area associated with Hoover Dam. However, a semi-trailer truck mount is not out of the question and could be easily hidden. Additionally, because there is no water to dissipate the force of impact (which would presumably occur on the western face of the dam), the amount of damage to the dam could be considerably greater.

Fortunately, the new bypass no longer allows traffic over the dam face and negates such strategies as truck bombs. Unfortunately, it makes a truck mounted, concealed artillery munitions possible because of parallel alignment of the bypass with the dam face. The

complete lack of border security along the southern U.S. border with Mexico does not negate this scenario as it is entirely likely terrorists may already have this capability within the U.S. And, engineering calculations indicate a nominal size, armor piercing munitions could achieve some level of success with this scenario — not discussed due to security issues.

Hoover Dam is an arch gravity dam, meaning that it relies on its arch design and its massive weight to maintain structural integrity. The sheer mass of the water pressing on the arched (eastern) portion of the dam actually reinforces the strength of the dam by adding to its compression strength against the canyon walls. Any breach in the arch design would compromise the compression strength of the concrete in that area and increase the reliance on the tensile strength of the concrete of areas adjacent to the failure. Also, the immense pressure imposed by the mass of the water behind the failed area would greatly aid in further failure and, perhaps, total failure of Hoover Dam.

Incident Avoidance Measures

Since the attacks of September 11, 2001, a number of increased security measures have been emplaced. These include but are not limited to:

- Installation of vehicle checkpoints, one on the Nevada side and one on the Arizona side (prior to new bypass)
- Modification to visitor tour routes – no more "interior tours"
- Greater difficulty in acquiring permits for contractors – permit holders and drivers of vehicles are subject to background checks and other security measures if necessary
- Use of magnetometers and X-ray screening for all visitors and contractors
- Increased patrol and surveillance in and around Lake Mead, especially in the vicinity of Hoover Dam, to include extensive aerial monitoring.

Approximately $5.5 million per year is allocated to security, including law enforcement in the Hoover Dam and Lake Mead area.[298] The construction of a $240 million by-pass project diverting traffic from traversing the dam has been completed and greatly reduces vulnerability from truck-bomb scenarios such as the one similar to the Oklahoma City bombing of the Murray Federal Building.

Conclusions

The role and significance of Hoover Dam has increased in scope and scale with increased population and agricultural production dependent on the resources provided by the dam and its auxiliary downstream projects. Hoover Dam now more than ever serves as the sole lifeline for millions of people in the American Southwest. Over 22 million people are dependent on municipal waters regulated through the dam and nearly two million acres of agricultural land irrigated by waters provided directly or indirectly, as well two to seven million people reliant on clean electrical power provided by Hoover, Davis, and Parker Dams. A failure of Hoover Dam would have a significant impact on the American Southwest, primarily in the greater Los Angeles area, the metropolitan Phoenix area, and Las Vegas and the surrounding area, and the large agricultural areas in southern California and southwestern Arizona. Recognition of these implications and the realization of terrorism directed at critical infrastructure features have catalyzed increased security measures, including completion of a bypass project to remediate security risks posed by over-dam vehicular traffic.

It is unlikely Hoover Dam will fail in the near future (approximately 500 years), either by natural or anthropogenic causes. The greater issue is that a growing population in the American Southwest coupled with limited critical resources increases the imperative nature and value of resources provided by Hoover Dam and its auxiliary components. Although failure of Hoover Dam is not of imminent concern, the issues surrounding the lack of critical resources available to a growing population in the American Southwest should be. The shadow cast by the limited resources and

---

[298] Staff, "Symmetry Synchronized Technology to Help Secure Hoover Dam," in *Case Study* (AMAG Technology, 2007).

the growing population of the American Southwest pose an urgent dilemma to the future security of the American Southwest and could have a profound effect on national security.

PART II: THREATS-SUPPLY AND INFRASTRUCTURE ISSUES

CHAPTER 8: Water Interdependence with Critical Infrastructure

Executive Summary

In 1998, the President's Commission on Critical Infrastructure highlighted the importance of interdependencies among infrastructures and recognized that the economic sustainability and prosperity, security, and social well being of the U.S. depend on infrastructure reliability. Although, the surface interdependencies are more easily understood, only a few comprehend the complex underlying interdependencies. Failure to understand the complexities and the cascading failures and resulting disruptions among infrastructures will decrease the effectiveness of response and recovery efforts during man-made, natural, or technological hazards, or may result in common cause failures that leave planners and emergency response personnel unprepared to effectively deal with operational continuity and the impacts of these disruptions. Understanding and sustaining resiliency of water and wastewater and interdependent infrastructures requires individuals who understand more than the surface components of these systems, but also the ability to simulate through modeling-type scenarios possible hazards scenarios to be able to assess economic, technical, and national-security implications of technology and policy decisions designed to ensure water infrastructure reliability.

Increased use of technology and development of automated monitoring systems due to a growing population in order to achieve better efficiency of scale has increased vulnerability to many infrastructure systems. This occurs due to the use of Supervisory Control and Data Acquisition (SCADA) systems and the almost complete reliance on these systems by the industry sector and their respective open marketplace for purchasing and selling infrastructure services such as electricity and related commodities. SCADA systems have linked infrastructure in unique ways, creating new complexities and greater vulnerability.

Interdependencies among infrastructure can generally be categorized into four components: (1) cyber; (2) physical; (3) logical; and (4) geographical. Water and wastewater systems have interdependencies with other infrastructure that are unique and that must be understood when developing and conducting vulnerability assessments, response and recovery plans, and security and sustainability. The dimensions of interdependency within an infrastructure need to be considered since interdependencies transcend individual sectors as well as companies and organizations that work within them. The scale; complexity; range of linkages, such as water supply to emergency services; and regional interdependence such as electrical power coordinating councils and others to the national scale as a whole, which include interstate transportation and other systems, all may be overlain internationally with banking and financial, telecommunications, and Internet systems, as well as other critical infrastructures.

Gaps in understanding the analytic capability of infrastructure and related systems are apparent in the context of analyzing multiple scenarios of possible events that involve interdependence between one or multiple infrastructure and related components within even one system. Each linkage between systems is important. The more common will be discussed.

The types of failure that can occur within infrastructure include (1) cascading; (2) escalating; and (3) common cause. Infrastructures are also linked to varying degrees, which influences vulnerability and response requirements, resiliency, and operational considerations. SCADA systems, deregulation, business mergers, and related components can dramatically affect both the economic and business aspects of the infrastructure environment and have become an important part of infrastructure that is rarely discussed. These are particularly important since 85 percent of all infrastructures are owned by the private sector and are run as 'for profit' businesses. Increasing operational efficiency as a result of adding IT components (although a boon to business) has alternatively led to the proliferation of cyber interdependencies between systems. Unfortunately, this has also led to the introduction of new vulnerabilities, particularly from cyber attack from both the terrorist and criminal elements. Deregulation has resulted in shedding excess

capacity that previously served as a buffer against system failure and has reduced redundancy in some systems; business mergers have also further eliminated redundancy. These and other issues have caused more interdependency between infrastructures, with little cushion against failure and almost no redundancy in terms of alternative supply or source.

Along with these factors has been the increase of legal and regulatory issues, increased environmental regulations, government investment decisions, and public health and safety concerns. All have served to influence infrastructure operations and interdependence. The crucial role of water is profound. Water infrastructure and shortages have a cascading detrimental effect on all facets of economic, public health, social areas, the political arena, transportation, trade, and interdependencies between various industries — these are the complexities that are not surficial and which scant few understand.

Introduction

In 1998, the President's Commission on Critical Infrastructure highlighted the importance of interdependencies among infrastructures and recognized that the economic sustainability and prosperity, security, and social well being of the U.S. depend on infrastructure reliability. These infrastructures include telecommunications, power and energy (electricity, natural gas, and oil), water (water supply and wastewater systems), transportation (air, rail, road, and water), banking and finance, emergency and government services, and others (see chapter 1, specifically figure 1.1). Additionally, the commission recognized the mutual dependencies, especially the vulnerability due to interconnectedness of information and communications with almost all infrastructures. Because of these interdependencies, infrastructure is vulnerable in ways never imagined.

Understanding and sustaining resiliency of water and wastewater and interdependent infrastructures requires individuals who understand more than the surface components of these systems, but also the ability to simulate through modeling-type

scenarios possible hazards scenarios to be able to assess economic, technical, and national-security implications of technology and policy decisions designed to ensure water infrastructure reliability.

Types of Interdependencies

Generally, interdependencies have been considered as either geographical or physical. As an example, a physical relation is represented by the dependence of water on electricity for pumping and the interdependence of energy to require water to make steam and cool its equipment (see chapter 4). Geographic interdependencies arise from sharing common corridors with other infrastructure such as water pipelines, electrical transmission lines, gas pipelines, and so forth, which increases the vulnerability of each system and the consequences due to failure from a hazard.

Increased use of technology and development of automated monitoring systems due to a growing population and to achieve better efficiency of scale has increased vulnerability to many infrastructure systems. This occurs due to the use of Supervisory Control and Data Acquisition (SCADA) systems (discussed in detail, along with solutions in chapter 12) and the almost complete reliance on these systems by the industry sector and their respective open marketplace for purchasing and selling infrastructure services such as electricity and related commodities. SCADA systems have linked infrastructure in unique ways, creating new complexities and greater vulnerability. Examples include the dependence of the stock market on the Internet and the energy market on the Internet and other E-commerce systems which have resulted in complex links to financial markets and which illustrate the scope and scale of cyber and logical interdependence among these systems.

Interdependencies among infrastructure can generally be categorized into four components: (1) cyber; (2) physical; (3) logical; and (4) geographical. Cyber interdependence is when an infrastructure depends on IT systems, telecommunications, and information transmitted through the infrastructure. Physical interdependence is where the output of one infrastructure is used by another; water and energy are good examples. Logical interdependence is when the resilience and operations of one

infrastructure depend on the state of another infrastructure in a non-physical, cyber, or logical way such as the linkages of and through financial markets. Geographical interdependence is when two or more infrastructures are co-located in the same area, such as the sharing of a transportation corridor between a water pipelines adjacent to energy transmission lines, which can be affected by one of the three primary hazards. Regardless of the categorization, the links between infrastructures can vary in scale and complexity, yet all scenarios must be weighed to effectively analyze risk and vulnerability and related response actions.

Water Infrastructure Interdependencies

Water and wastewater systems have interdependencies with other infrastructure that are unique and that must be understood when developing and conducting vulnerability assessments, response and recovery plans, and security and sustainability. The primary interdependency of water with other infrastructure is listed in Table 8.1. The table illustrates interdependencies in the grade of high (H), medium (M), or low (L). However, it does not include subcomponents within interdependence such as SCADA systems, co-location, operations centers, delivery, energy supply, back-up systems, maintenance, and others. These need to be accounted for within the vulnerability assessment framework. Additionally, the dimensions of interdependency within an infrastructure need to be considered since interdependencies transcend individual sectors as well as companies and organizations that work within them.

Gaps in understanding the analytic capability of infrastructure and related systems are apparent in the context of analyzing multiple scenarios of possible events that involve interdependence between one or multiple infrastructure and related components within even one system. Each linkage between systems is important. The more common will be discussed.

Table 8.1: Infrastructure Interdependencies (high=H; medium=M; and low=L) with Water (surficial only).

Infrastructure Dependency	Agri-culture	Food	Water	Public Health	Emer. Services	Govt.	Defense Industrial Base	Information & Telecom	Energy & Power	Trans-portation	Banking & Finance	Chemical Industry	Postal & Shipping
Agriculture	----	H	L	H	L	L	L	L	L	L	L	L	L
Food	L	----	L	H	L	L	L	L	L	L	L	M	L
Water	H	H	----	H	M	M	M	L	M	L	L	H	L
Public Health	M	M	M	----	H	M	M	L	L	M	L	L	L
Emergency Services	L	L	L	H	----	H	L	L	L	M	M	M	L
Government	L	L	L	M	H	----	H	M	L	M	H	L	M
Defense Industrial Base	L	L	L	L	M	H	----	L	L	L	L	L	L
Information and Telecom	L	M	M	H	H	H	H	----	H	H	H	M	H
Energy and Power	H	H	H	H	H	H	H	H	----	H	H	H	H
Transportation	H	H	M	M	H	H	H	L	H	----	L	H	H
Banking and Finance	M	M	L	L	L	H	L	M	M	M	----	M	L
Chemical Industry	L	L	L	M	M	L	H	L	M	L	L	----	L
Postal and Shipping	L	L	L	L	L	M	M	L	L	L	M	L	----

Let us first begin by describing the types of failure that can occur within infrastructure, which include (1) cascading; (2) escalating; and (3) common cause. Cascading failure is the most commonly mentioned in literature and lay articles and is referred to as a disruption in which one infrastructure causes a disruption in a second. As an example, power is cut off, but then, in addition to power being disconnected, water conveyance is halted, and communications in the form of television in the home are also cut. Thus, the power failure cascaded into other systems. Escalating failures are the disruption in one infrastructure that intensifies, affecting independent disruption of a second infrastructure. As an example, mudslides clog a roadway that prevents utility workers from reaching and repairing a ruptured water main. In this way, repair of the ruptured main is delayed due to the transportation failure and the water main failure increases in intensity and effect. Common cause failures are the disruption of two or more infrastructures at the same time as a result of a common cause such as a natural hazard. Hurricane Katrina and the disruptions it caused in New Orleans among all infrastructures is an excellent case study.

Varied other conditions affect how failures occur, the damages that occur due to failure, as well as response, recovery, and other processes in reaction to failure. Some of these include the organizational structure(s) of interconnected infrastructures, operational relations, and spatial variability and makeup of the system in question. The resiliency of a system (or organization), commonly referred to as operational resiliency, should also be considered. The water infrastructure and energy infrastructures are both excellent examples because of daily peak demands and seasonal variations (summer, winter, etc.) in regard to load, maintenance schedules, weather, reserve capacity, outages, and other operational factors that can change the interdependence within systems.

Infrastructures are also linked to varying degrees, and these connections influence vulnerability and response requirements, resiliency, and operational considerations. The flexibility between these linkages, such as transportation and delivery of supplies for water treatment, could be short term and induce little or no vulnerability, whereas treatment of water requiring electricity for

pumps, etc., would be immediately affected and are therefore much more vulnerable. Unseen factors become another part of the failure scenario. These could include IT and ICS, deregulation, business mergers, and related components that can dramatically affect both the economic and business aspects of the infrastructure environment. These are particularly important since 85 percent of all infrastructures are owned by the private sector and are run as 'for profit' businesses. Increasing operational efficiency as a result of adding IT components (although a boon to business) has alternatively led to the proliferation of cyber interdependencies between systems. Unfortunately, it has also led to the introduction of new vulnerabilities, particularly from cyber attack from both the terrorist and criminal elements. Deregulation has resulted in shedding excess capacity that previously served as a buffer against system failure and has reduced redundancy in some systems; business mergers have also further eliminated redundancy. These and other issues have caused more interdependency between infrastructures, with little cushion against failure and almost no redundancy in terms of alternative supply or source.

Along with these factors has been the increase of legal and regulatory issues, increased environmental regulations, government investment decisions, and public health and safety concerns. All have served to influence infrastructure operations and interdependence. Consequently, interdependencies are not what they seem. For example, Figure 8.1 illustrates interdependencies between water infrastructure and all other infrastructures and whether that interdependency is high, medium, or low as a result. Figure 8.1 illustrates infrastructures by level and the dependency of one on another related to various hazards.

From table 8.1, the interdependence of water related to transportation infrastructure is low. Figure 8.1 illustrates a similar relation. However, the interdependency relates to the type of failure — cascading, escalating, or common — and the particular component of infrastructure. For example, the scenario of low consequence holds true as long as the transportation effect is very short term or in this case affects roadways. However, if the transportation infrastructure is a waterway, such as the Mississippi River, and is extremely flooded, as in the spring of 2011, the

consequence of interdependence between water and transportation being low, no longer has validity. In fact, the consequence is now very high. These types of considerations must be analyzed to determine true failure effects. Also, consider a scenario in which water is involved in a transboundary issue, is a large part of economic sustainability, or could reflect and cause significant foreign policy shifts. Neither Table 8.1 nor Figure 8.1 address these issues and so, are surficial in scope, serving only to introduce a base understanding of interdependencies.

Figure 8.1: Relation of anthropogenic, natural, and technological hazards to critical infrastructure (Source: Author, used by permission).

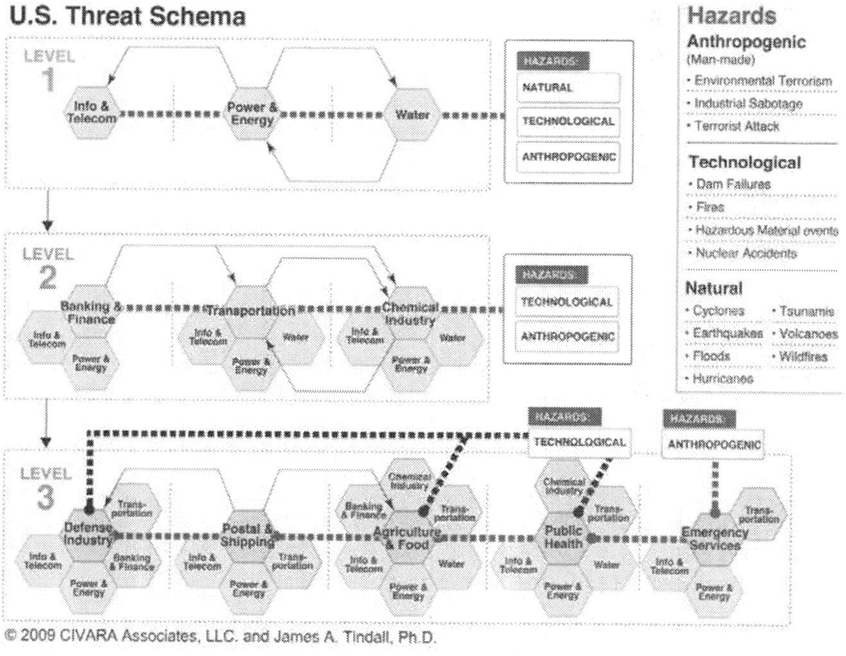

Case Study:

Water Security in China — A Comparison of Interdependence with Infrastructure

Many countries are dealing with water stress issues, but perhaps none more so than China. This is important to the U.S. for at least two reasons: (1) China is the world leader in manufacturing; and (2) China is the largest holder of U.S. debt.[299] China's unexpected water shortages pose a rising threat to world food and water security. Water security is important to maintain delivery of vital human services through critical infrastructure systems and to maintain public health and the environment globally. The threat, interdependent with water security, is also economic in nature since China is expected to be the global economic engine. To maintain a projected eight percent annual growth,[300] which economists feel is necessary to keep the global economy from floundering, China needs adequate water supplies for the industrial and population bases in the north. Water shortages will prevent this from occurring, especially as they affect critical infrastructure. Examples include power and energy, water, food and agriculture, public health, and so forth.

Critical Infrastructure

Critical infrastructure is the systems and/or assets, which are indispensable for the functioning and sustainability of both the society and economy, and therefore the security of a nation and its people for public health and safety. Key losses of water can cripple a region, state, province, or nation.[301] But, perhaps more importantly, critical water issues will have a profound impact on the geographic region of concern and likely be transnational in scope in terms of

---

[299] Government, "Holders of U.S. Debt/Treasuries,"(2010), http://www.treasury.gov/resource-center/data-chart-center/tic/Documents/mfh.txt.

[300] Z. Hu, and Khan, M.S., *Why Is China Growing So Fast?* (International Monetary Fund, 1997).

[301] James A. Tindall and Andrew A. Campbell, "Water Security - Nation State and International Security Implications," *Disaster Advances* 2, no. 2 (April 2009): 10, https://maroon.cudenver.edu/webmail/imp/view.php?popup_view=1&index=4091&mailbox=INBOX&actionID=view_attach&id=2&mimecache=232e177755aa175ed319 40e6d5234312.

effects on adjoining regions and countries and foreign policy issues. The crucial role of water is profound. Water shortages have a cascading detrimental effect on all facets of economic, health, social areas, and the political arena. With proper interpretation, China and other countries can use water interdependence as an indicator to predict future effects of water shortages and impacts on related areas of concern such as transportation, trade, economics, and interdependencies between various industries.

Water Shortages

In some water-stressed areas within China, there is an increasing population and manufacturing base; in other areas, water is plentiful, but population, economy, and industry remain stable.[302] Overall, China suffers greatly from physical water scarcity combined with economic water scarcity. Water shortages in China are driven by three main factors:

1. Water resources distribution patterns
2. Pollution caused by natural and anthropogenic effects
3. Increases in manufacturing and population that are interdependent with water distribution.

China contains 25 percent (2.8 trillion cubic meters) of the world's total water resources and about 20 percent of the world's population. Intensified water shortages could decrease world water and food security, threatening global economic prosperity and increasing potential conflicts from myriad sources, mostly related to resources. This is particularly troublesome when coupled with an already declining global economy with most of the world entering a deepening recession and some countries on the verge of depression.

Water Distribution and Population Patterns

Water shortages in China occur because of the countries' water and population distributions. China has a diverse geography with a wide spectrum of climates, creating severe flooding in the

[302] David Seckler, "An Overview of Climate Change,"(2008), http://ase.tufts.edu/gdae/Pubs/wp/08-01OverviewOfClimateChange.pdf.

south but severe droughts in the north. In May 2006, southern China had three rainstorms with 400 mm (15.75 inches) or more rainfall from each storm, resulting in flooding, destruction of crops, deaths, and an economic loss of nearly $1.6 billion (USD). Concurrently, northern China experienced a severe drought — receiving 17.8 mm (0.7 inches) of rain in four months.[303] Inadequacy of water distribution cascades into water conveyance, distribution, and supply problems, affecting agriculture and industry and the overall economy. Climate change is predicted to impact China's water availability and distribution as well. Northern China has 14 percent of the nation's water, while southern China contains 86 percent of China's water supply. The natural climate fluctuates seasonally and regionally. For example, climate change is expected to increase the number of heavy precipitation days, which will increase flood frequencies in southern China, as well as drought frequency and scarcity in northern China. China's population distribution pattern is also a factor in creating serious water deficits.

Natural climate and water distribution variations are a challenge to resource management, which make sustainability difficult.[304] Natural variations make it challenging to separate climate-change issues from water-distribution problems and to obtain accurate hydrologic cycle time series data that will aid in better management. These challenges should become part of the decision-making support tools for water managers and planners when constructing water infrastructure projects such as a dams; they also represent an area the U.S. is well suited technologically for providing assistance to China. Climate change is not constant but cyclic in nature, especially drought cycles; therefore, water projects such as dams could be designed in a way that would enhance supplies and that can be efficiently updated even though there is no current economic incentive to invest in flexible structures.[305]

---

[303] Ibid.

[304] N. Arnell, and Hulme, M., "Implications of Climate Change for Large Dams and Their Management,"(2007), http://www.wca-infonet.org/servlet/CDSServlet?status=nd0xmjm2ljexntu3nsy2pwvujjmzpwrvy3vtzw50cyyznz1pbmzv.

[305] Ibid.

Pollution

Compounded with distribution issues is pollution, which is a major threat to water security due to effects on water quality. It affects downstream, urban to country, and surface to subsurface water supplies — deteriorating supplies with time. From the Chinese Civil War (1927-1950) to the Great Leap (1957-1959) there has been a dramatic increase in the total number of China's factories, which has led to increasing pollution, deforestation, and soil erosion. Factories were relocated from coastal areas because they were considered to be militarily vulnerable until economic reform began in 1978.[306] The economic reform actually became a driver of environmental degradation because of continuous industrialization. The multiplication of factories has created a significant shortage of water-treatment plants. Approximately 20 percent of wastewater is treated — leaving 80 percent of industrial wastewater untreated and discharged back into rivers.[307] China's water laws are outdated and weak, and the responsibilities for enforcing regulations for water resources appear weak as well; it remains unclear what entity is accountable for this process. A study performed in 2005 investigated 509 China cities; the study demonstrated that only 23 percent of factories properly treated sewage before disposal. The water quality in the north (due to population and manufacturing base increase) is uniformly worse than in the south, resulting in an estimated cost of pollution-induced water scarcity of 1 to 3 percent local GDP in water-scarce areas of China.[308]

The pollution problems in China are so severe that they are spilling over into neighboring countries, creating acid rain, dust storms, and increased levels of trace metals. China leads the world in total emission of organic pollutants, accounting for 70 percent of China's river and lake pollution as well as half of China's underground water sources pollution.[309] China also leads the world in illegal

---

[306] Staff, "State Environmental Policy Act (Sepa):Report on China's Ecological Issues," (ECY, 1999).

[307] — — — , "2006 Statistic Bulletin on China Water Activities," ed. Ministry of Water Resources (Beijing: People's Republic of China, 2006).

[308] F. Kahrl, and Roland-Holst, D., "China's Water- Energy Nexus," *Water Policy*(2007), http://are.berkeley.edu/~dwrh/CERES_Web/Docs/Cn_H2O_Erg_KRH080109.pdf.

[309] Sekiguchi, *Water Issues in China*.

importation of timber, creating significant deforestation rates. Meanwhile, the U.S. and other countries question the potential negative impact China's pollution and water problems could have globally and when that impact may be expected. Other related issues that are affected by this pollution include human health, sustainability of supply, and water treatment, as well as others.

Manufacturing and Population Growth

China has the world's largest population (1.3 billion; 20 percent of world total) and is the current leader in manufacturing with a $177 billion in trade surplus in 2008.[310] Continual improvements in China's economic system and increases in population (expected to peak in 2030) have intensified the demand for clean water. China consumes 72.8 billion gallons per day (GPD) of water while the U.S. population of 305 million, consumes 55.8 billion GPD.[311] The population of China has doubled over the past 10 years with an expected one percent drop in recent years because of factors such as the one-child policy China implemented in 1979. China's per capita environmental impact is below the level of developed countries; however, the proportionate increase in total human impact on the global environment will be extraordinary if China's per capita environmental impacts reach levels of developed countries.[312] Given population and manufacturing trends, this is likely to occur within the next decade. Also, urbanization (the trend of moving from farming communities to new industrial zones that use much more water, especially big cities) is increasing within China. Industry (farming, mining, and manufacturing) uses large amounts of water. Continual population increases also augment per capita water use.

Population migration is one solution for avoiding water shortages, but due to continuous industrialization, urbanization, and population growth, people will likely be forced to live in the disaster and hazard prone areas of China. Consequently, solutions to China's

---

[310] Mark Sircus, "Water: The World Is Facing a Dire Shortage of This Essential Element," *Natural Health, Natural Living, Natural News*(2008), http://www.naturalnews.com/023267.html.
[311] Hutson, "Estimated Use of Water in the United States in 2000."
[312] Jianguo Liu, and Diamond, Jared, "China's Place in the World: Environmental Impact of a Giant," *Nature* 435, no. 30 (2005).

water problems will require successful water diversion schemes with strategies that account for these processes by utilizing improved infrastructure. The need to change agricultural land use (e.g. from extensive pasture land) also may be required.[313] China's lead position in global manufacturing has allowed "a comparative advantage and relocated its resources away from capital, land and energy intensive dirty industries to labor intensive cleaner industries"[314] making it 30 percent cleaner than in the past two decades. However, it has also resulted in environmental trade deficits, overwhelmed with other sources of pollution, changing and offsetting other environmental gains.

Other Issues

China's poor environmental hygiene is magnified and is the brunt of blame as the world is confronted with global water-security issues through its effects on other countries. As an example, Japan suffers acid rain problems caused by China's coal-fired power plants, in addition to a toxic yellow dust problem from the Gobi Desert. The U.S. is finding various pollutants in both water and air that have traveled across the Pacific Ocean from China. Many countries outsource manufacturing to China. The goods produced result in creating a significant portion of pollution that travels around the world. So, in a roundabout way, we are contributing to the problem most of the global community is complaining about.

China's water shortages and security threaten economic development, political stability, and human health as the problem advances beyond environmental issues. Insufficient water resources are beginning to limit industrial and agricultural outputs potentially curbing China's economic growth rate and food production, which could negatively impact the United States' foreign policy due to a declining world economy as it faces rising unemployment. "The international financial crisis ... is equally a challenge and an opportunity," China's energy czar, Zhang Guobao, wrote recently in the official newspaper People's Daily, also saying: "The [economic] slowdown ... has reduced the price of international energy resources

---

[313] Ibid.

[314] J.C.H. Chai, "Trade and Environment: Evidence from China's Manufacturing Sector," *Sustainable Development* 10, no. 1 (2002).

and assets and favors our search for overseas resources."[315] The Chinese are also taking advantage of the global financial crisis in other ways. As an example, Weichai Power is expected to buy the French plant that General Motors is selling because of debt. And, although the Chinese economy has been also been negatively impacted by the global crisis, according to Ericka Downs, a China energy specialist in the Brookings Institution in Washington, "what sets China apart is that Chinese banks have not been so badly hurt, and the policy banks still seem ready to lend in support of key government objectives."[316]

U.S. — China relations are complexly intertwined; if China is not successful, it could be potentially devastating to both countries. This creates an imperative need for the U.S. to cooperate with China to ameliorate their water-shortage crisis as well as protecting it from a series of cascading failures of systems that could threaten U.S. national security. A progressive and aggressive China foreign policy could help protect U.S. national security, encourage the emergence of a China that meets its responsibilities both to the international community and to its own people, and ensure that Americans as well as Chinese are able to enjoy a rising standard of living.

Conclusions

The economic sustainability and prosperity, security, and social well being of any country depend on infrastructure reliability. The mutual dependencies due to interconnectedness of information and communications with almost all infrastructures have increased infrastructure vulnerability in ways never imagined, which is particularly true of water due to SCADA systems. Failure to understand the complexities and the cascading failures and resulting disruptions among infrastructures will decrease the effectiveness of response and recovery efforts during man-made, natural, or technological hazards, and could result in failures that leave nations unprepared to effectively deal with operational continuity and their impacts.

---

[315] Peter Ford, "China's Buying Spree in Global Fire Sale," *The Christian Science Monitor* (2009), http://www.csmonitor.com/2009/0223/p01s03-wosc.html.
[316] Ibid.

Infrastructure interdependencies comprise four types: (1) cyber; (2) physical; (3) logical; and (4) geographical. Because of this, interdependencies can transcend individual sectors as well as companies and organizations that work within them. Regardless of infrastructure failure type — cascading, escalating, or common cause — a variety of conditions affect how each failure occurs, resulting damages, response, recovery, and other processes. Some of these include the organizational structure(s) of interconnected infrastructures, operational relations, and spatial variability and makeup of the system in question.

In addition to infrastructures being linked to varying degrees, it is no longer only national infrastructure issues that are a primary concern. As the China case study indicates, critical water issues have profound impacts on geographic regions and can be transnational and even international in scope. These can affect adjoining regions and countries and foreign policy issues, as well as supply and sustainability, total infrastructure, economic and trade and transboundary issues, human health and possible conflicts. The issues of China are not unlike those of the U.S. or other countries and relate directly to critical infrastructures that drive sustainability of a country.

The crucial role of water is profound. Water infrastructure and shortages have a cascading detrimental effect on all facets of economic, public health, social areas, the political arena, transportation, trade, and interdependencies between various industries — these are the complexities that are not surficial and which scant few understand.

Tribal Water Symbol

CHAPTER 9: Agricultural Water Security & Bioterrorism

Executive Summary

Attacks against agriculture are not new, and have been conducted both by nation-states and by sub-state organizations throughout history. At least nine countries (Canada, France, Germany, Iraq, Japan, South Africa, United Kingdom, United States and former USSR) had documented agricultural bioweapons programs during some part of the 20th century. Four other countries (Egypt, North Korea, Rhodesia and Syria) are believed to have or have had agricultural bioweapons programs.[317]

Although individuals or sub-state groups have used bioweapons against agricultural or food targets, only a few can be considered terrorist in nature. In 1952, the Mau Mau (an insurgent organization in Kenya) killed 33 head of cattle at a mission station using African milk bush (a local plant toxin). In 1984, the Rajneesh cult spread salmonella in salad bars at Oregon restaurants to influence a local election.[318]

Millions of Americans receive high quality drinking water every day from their public water systems, (which may be publicly or privately owned). Nonetheless, drinking water safety cannot be taken for granted. There are a number of threats to drinking water: improperly disposed chemicals; animal wastes; pesticides; human wastes; wastes injected deep underground; and naturally-occurring substances can all contaminate drinking water. Likewise, drinking water that is poorly treated or disinfected, or which travels through an improperly maintained distribution system, may also pose a health risk.

---

[317] Jim Monke, "Agroterrorism: Threats and Preparedeness," ed. Congressional Research Service (Washington DC: Library of Congress, 2004).

[318] Ibid

Groundwater is used as a drinking-water supply by about one-half of the U.S. population, including almost all people residing in rural areas. Domestic wells provide drinking water to about 43.5 million people, representing 15 percent of the total U.S. population.[319]

Drinking water supply systems, especially treatment and distribution/storage facilities, may present targets of opportunity from physical destruction, intentional contamination, or cyber attack by terrorists.

As the population and demand for safe drinking water from domestic wells increase, the occurrence of individual and multiple VOCs and related human-health problems have also increased. [320] Frequently detected VOCs included chloroform, toluene, 1,2,4-trimethylbenzene, and perchloroethene.

According to a 1998 National Research Council report, an effective food safety system protects and improves the public health by ensuring that foods meet science-based safety standards through the integrated activities of the public and private sectors.[321] The experiences of the seven countries that had to overcome challenges show that reforming and streamlining food safety systems are possible when a consensus exists among government agencies, the food industry, and consumer organizations.[322]

Although the U.S. food supply is generally safe, each year, according to a Center for Disease Control and Prevention (CDC) estimate, tens of millions of Americans become ill and thousands die from eating unsafe food. Furthermore, USDA's Economic Research Service has estimated that the costs associated with food-borne illnesses are about seven billion dollars, including medical costs and productivity losses from missed work.[323]

---

[319] Hutson, "Estimated Use of Water in the United States in 2000."

[320] B. Rowe, Toccalino, P., Moran, M., and Price, C., "Occurrence and Potential Human Health Relevance of Volatile Organic Compounds in Drinking Water from Domestic Wells in the United States," *Environmental Health Perspectives* 115, no. 11 (2007).

[321] GAO, "Oversight of Food Safety Activities," (Washington DC: Government Accountability Office, 2005).

[322] Ibid.

[323] Ibid.

The safety and quality of U.S. food supply is governed by a complex system that is administered by 15 agencies. The principal federal agencies with food safety responsibilities operate under numerous statutes underpinning the federal framework for ensuring the safety and quality of the food supply in the United States. These laws give the agencies different regulatory and enforcement authorities, and about 70 interagency agreements aim to coordinate the combined food safety oversight responsibilities of the various agencies. The federal system is supplemented by the states, all of which have their own statues, regulations, and agencies for regulating and inspecting the safety and quality of food products.

Canada, Denmark, Germany, Ireland, the Netherlands, New Zealand and United Kingdom established a single agency within each country to lead food safety management or enforcement of food safety legislation and modified existing food safety laws. These countries had two primary reasons for consolidating their food safety systems: public concern about safety of the food supply and the need to improve program effectiveness and efficiency. As a result, significant qualitative improvements of their food systems and in some cases financial savings may be achieved.[324] The seven countries are in the World Bank's high-income category, where consumers have very high expectations for food safety. None of the countries has conducted an analysis to measure the effectiveness and efficiency of its consolidated food safety system relative to that of the previous system.

Naturally occurring outbreaks of diseases signal the devastation that could result from a carefully choreographed intentional release. Thus the recent Foot and Mouth disease epidemics in Taiwan and Great Britain, or hog cholera in the Netherlands, or the infection of Florida citrus trees with citrus canker, aptly demonstrate the vulnerability of living targets to biological pathogens and the economic chaos that can result from an outbreak — intentional or otherwise.

The most effective biological weapon agents would be highly infectious, communicable, and lethal; efficiently dispersible; easily produced in large quantities; stable in storage; resistant to environmental degradation; and lacking vaccines or effective

[324] Ibid.

treatments. Biological agents may be targeted directly against humans through injection or topical application; deployed against agricultural crops, livestock, poultry, and fish; applied as a contaminant of food or drinking water; disseminated as an aerosol; or introduced through a natural vector such as an insect.[325]

Authorities may be persuaded that a disease outbreak is natural, providing cover or plausible deniability to biological terrorists. An example is the recent E-coli outbreak in Europe that has spread to the U.S., which has thus far managed to control it. According to European scientists, the source of the outbreaks is unknown and causes have ranged from Spanish cucumbers to vegetables from other countries. At the time of this writing more than 2,400 people have become ill and 23 are dead.[326]

Only two biological attacks attempted by terrorist organizations have been documented. The first example is widespread food poisoning carried out by the Baghwan Shree Rajneesh cult in Oregon in 1984. The other includes a number of unsuccessful attempts by the Japanese-based Aum Shinrikyo organization, in the early 1990s, to spread anthrax and botulinum toxin.

Nationally representative Canadian and U.S. surveys, using the same set of questions to assess food security, indicated that seven percent of Canadians lived in food insecure households in 2004, compared with an average of 12.6 percent of U.S. residents in 2003-05. Younger adults, single parents, unemployed adults looking for work, adults out of the labor force because of disability, and people in households where no adult had completed a two- or four-year college degree were more likely to live in food insecure households. Food insecurity was also strongly associated with low income in both countries.

In light of the September 11, 2001, attacks on the World Trade Center and the Pentagon and the subsequent anthrax attacks on the U.S. Capitol, there is an increasing awareness that a potential exists for a terrorist attack against agriculture in the United States. In fact,

---

[325] H. Parker, "Agricultural Bioterrorism: A Federal Strategy to Meet the Threat," ed. Institute for National Strategic Studies (Washington DC: National Defense University, 2003).

[326] Baertlein, "Major E.Coli Outbreaks Decline, Salmonella Up."

most experts agree that it is not a matter of "if" but "when" a microbe will be used against the American public through agriculture.

GAO's expert panel cited distribution systems as among the most vulnerable physical components of a drinking water utility, a conclusion also reached by key research organizations. Also cited were the computer systems that manage critical utility functions; treatment chemicals stored on-site; and source water supplies. Experts further identified two key factors that constitute overarching vulnerabilities: (1) a lack of the information individual utilities need to identify their most serious threats and (2) a lack of redundancy in vital system components, which increases the likelihood an attack could render an entire utility inoperable. Nearly 75 percent of the experts (32 of 43) identified the distribution system or its components as among the top vulnerabilities of drinking water systems.

Introduction

As global population continues to increase, there is a growing demand for safe, reliable sources of water to meet the food production needs of that population. Farmers, ranchers, and rural communities are particularly susceptible to the mounting pressures to provide more water to urban areas at the expense of water supplies for rural and agricultural communities. Urbanization (the expansion of a city when its country's population migrates from rural to urban areas, primarily in search of employment and security) is a primary driver of competition between industry, urban, and agricultural competition for water supplies. This process, along with potential bioterrorism of water and food supplies, as well as drought related disaster and other hazards may be pushing us to the brink of a global crisis of food production problems and related public-health failures. The security of water for agriculture from myriad threats is paramount to the sustained well being of the population. Agricultural water security describes the need to maintain adequate water supplies to meet the food and fiber needs of an expanding population while maximizing the efficiency of water use in agriculture.

Humans depend on water in many ways, well beyond the few liters needed daily for drinking and, it is the most critical resource for the production of food. Various forms of agriculture, practiced on

about half of Earth's land surface, provide the vast majority of food that over six billion people in the global community eat. Agriculture also provides much of the fiber for cotton, wool, and linen for clothing.

In every irrigated global region, water supplies are a limitation to further expansion of irrigated agriculture. In many regions, renewable supplies have already been exhausted, resulting in falling groundwater levels and greatly reduced river flow. In some regions, the depletion of water resources due to irrigation has reached crisis proportions. Within the U.S., the Colorado River rarely reaches the Sea of Cortez (often called the Gulf of California), and even the Yellow River of China is sometimes drained completely. The Aral Sea in central Asia has lost half its surface area, and most of its volume and its once enormous fishing industry. In the United States, especially California, attempts have been made to divert water away from irrigation in favor of urban, industrial, and environmental purposes. Farmers can now "rent" annual water allocations without losing their permanent water rights. Irrigation efficiency is improving with drip irrigation systems such as those pioneered in water-short Israel. In the southern Great Plains, some farmers are simply reverting back to dry-land agriculture as groundwater levels fall so low that they cannot afford to pump water to the surface. Thus, agriculture is constantly faced with two primary issues, although there are many others, to maintain stability in food production: water supply and water quality. In regard to water quality, which is a part of agricultural water security, agriculture uses vast quantities of water and also causes varying levels of pollution through what is termed nonpoint-source contaminants. Runoff from agricultural fields often contains eroded soil, fertilizers, animal manure, or pesticides that together form a major source of water pollution.

This form of nonpoint-source pollution remains remarkably unregulated by government. Recent initiatives include Total Maximum Daily Load requirements that are imposed on whole watersheds. Moreover, the U.S. Department of Agriculture now utilizes two methods to induce farmers to decrease polluted runoff:

- **Cross-compliance, in which farmers are required to adopt soil conservation measures to control erosion if they are to remain eligible for public subsidies; and**

- **Conservation payments to farmers, such as the Conservation Reserve Program, to take highly erodible or streamside land out of crop production.**

Despite good intentions, these policies have not been successful in addressing the environmental issue, which will not be discussed herein.

Constant climate change processes and disparate distribution of both precipitation and water supplies are beginning to cause greater problems in the food supply chain. As an example, drought and the reliability of water supplies for agriculture and rural communities historically have been linked to Western states within the U.S. However, issues surrounding agricultural water security have expanded well beyond U.S. Western states and now represent not only a national crisis, but an international one as well. Water supplies for irrigated agriculture in many areas within the U.S., Europe, China, India, Pakistan, and other countries are being consumed through the urbanization process. Shifts in the allocation of water resources will have dramatic impacts on the long-term supply of food and fiber on a global scale.

Just how important is agricultural water security and what effects would it have on the population at large? An example is the 1996 U.S. drought that clearly illustrates the risks and impacts of agricultural water security. In 1995, a severe drought developed in parts of western Texas and New Mexico. The drought persisted into 1996 in both states. As the persistence continued, the drought expanded into Arizona, the central and eastern parts of Texas, as well as parts of California, Colorado, Kansas, Nevada, Oklahoma, and Utah. The drought area intensified during the late winter and spring months, reaching its severest level in May through July for various parts of the affected region.

The first impacts of drought began to appear in February 1996, when the incidence of range fires increased dramatically in Texas, Oklahoma, and Kansas, causing injuries and significant damage.[327] By March, depleting groundwater supplies became a serious problem in parts of Texas, especially the Barton

---

[327] K. O'Hanlon, "Texas Grass Fire Burns out of Control, Dozens of Homes Destroyed," *AP Online*(1996).

Springs/Edwards Aquifer Conservation District; residents were asked to cut water usage by 20 percent.[328] By April, the U.S. Department of Agriculture (USDA) reported that winter-wheat conditions in 19 states ranged from poor to very poor condition; the most severe problems were in Kansas, Oklahoma, Missouri, and Illinois.[329]

In May, the USDA reported that prices for gasoline, diesel, and liquefied petroleum were 15 percent above 1995 levels. Ski resorts in New Mexico reported reduced revenues of more than 20 percent.[330] Central Arizona, California, and New Mexico experienced an increase in fires.[331] In June, estimates of agricultural losses for cotton, wheat, feed grains, cattle, and corn were reported at $2.4 billion in Texas alone, with an additional $4.1 billion in losses for agriculturally related industries such as harvesting, trucking, and food processing.[332] Cascading failures caused reduced availability of irrigation water, which led to a reduction in vegetable crop production in Texas; this resulted in concomitant losses in both jobs and income.[333] Estimates of drought-caused losses in Texas were revised to about five billion dollars, reflecting lower commodity prices than originally estimated.[334] National Agricultural Statistics Service data shows that Colorado's winter wheat crop was down 31 percent.

Water restrictions continued to increase in many cities across the region. Houston residents were forced to cut back on nonessential use[335] and Santa Fe residents were forced to reduce water usage by 25 percent. Water levels in the Edwards Aquifer, the primary source of water for 1.5 million people in San Antonio and five counties in south Texas, were the lowest ever recorded.[336] Fires

---

[328] Staff, "Drought Alert Sounded in Edwards Aquifer Region of Texas,"(1996).
[329] C. Edwards, "Wheat Futures Soar as Kansas Crop Written Off,"(1996).
[330] Reuters, "Southwest Drought Threatens Broad Economic Damage,"(1996b).
[331] Associated Press, "Dry Weather Raises Threat as Fires Burn in Western States,"(1996b).
[332] UPI, "Southwest Farmers Battle Record Drought,"(1996).
[333] N. Antosh, "Water Shortages in Texas Result in Crop Cutbacks," *Houston Chronicle*, August 18 1996.
[334] J. Fohn, "Agriculture Column," *San Antonio Express*, August 21 1996.
[335] Staff, "Dow Chemical Institutes Drought Plan to Reduce Houston Area Water Use. June 2," *Houston Chronicle*, June 2 1996.
[336] W. Smith, "Southwestern Drought Takes Toll on Farmers, Businesses," *Chicago*

continued to be a major problem throughout the drought, particularly in New Mexico, Arizona, Nevada, Colorado, and Utah. In Colorado, fires burned more than two million acres (810,000 ha).[337] Reduced forested and plant coverage led to Colorado and New Mexico reporting wind and insect damage to crops, causing greater losses.[338] [339] As plants succumbed to lack of water, livestock began to take a toll on range lands by overgrazing, which worsened existing erosion problems in Arizona. A shortage of hay throughout the region reached disastrous proportions in June, forcing ranchers to sell cattle at the lowest prices in ten years.[340] Environmental damages began to emerge as endangered species were affected, landscapes were eroded, and fires damaged countless areas.[341] Due to reduced water for irrigation and through rainfall, nitrate levels in hay rose dramatically in Oklahoma, reaching toxic or near-toxic levels for livestock.[342]

Food prices responded to the lower production levels for milk, meat, produce, and other foodstuffs.[343] [344] As an example, the price of fruit increased more than 22 percent in June.[345] Fires continued to burn throughout the region and expanded into the Pacific Northwest and the northern Rocky Mountain states.[346] [347]

There are no official estimates of the total losses and damages from the 1996 drought. However, given the five billion dollars in impacts that occurred in Texas, total regional impacts can be safely estimated at about $15 billion in physical and resource losses. No

---

Tribune, June 27 1996.

337 C. Hillard, "Wildfire Threat," *AP Online*(1996).

338 Reuters, "Drought-Hit Texas Asks Mexico to Enforce Water Pact,"(1996a).

339 — — —, "Southwest Drought Threatens Broad Economic Damage."

340 Smith, "Southwestern Drought Takes Toll on Farmers, Businesses."

341 M. Holmes, "Battling Drought, Texas Biologists Try to Save Endangered Species," *Southwest Sunday*, June 27 1996.

342 S. Schafer, "Toxic Hay Threatens Cattle in Oklahoma," *Tulsa World*, July 29 1996.

343 S.H. Lee, "Dairy Industry Cites Drought as Cause of Rising Milk Prices," *Dallas Morning News*, July 8 1996.

344 L. Carrillo, "Labor Department Confirms What Consumers Know: Food Prices Increasing," *Sun Sentinel*, July 14 1996.

345 Ibid

346 T. Laceky, "Rain, Snow, Frost Helping Calm Western Fires, but Winds Still Threaten," *AP Online*(1996).

347 Associated Press, "Emergency Declared as Arizona Fires Rage,"(1996a).

effort has been made to quantify social and environmental impacts. Perhaps the most remarkable effects were the significant level of regional vulnerability, the diversity of impacts through cascading failures, and the lack of preparedness in response to many of these impacts. What could have happened if the drought had lasted another six months or longer?

As such events have continued around the globe, governments, agencies, corporations and others have attempted to implement policy to mitigate the effects of such disasters. As an example, in 2003, USDA and the Interior Department signed a Memorandum of Understanding (MOU) aimed at promoting improved water management and rapid response to emerging water-supply shortages in the West. This MOU highlighted the need for expanding the research and education programs focused on better management of water resources, which are described below.

Research Needs in Agricultural Water Security

Scientific information abounds regarding the efficient use of water for agricultural irrigation. Similarly, much is known about the impacts of drought on plant growth and productivity. Research should focus on expanding the knowledge base of agricultural water security through programs aimed at

- Risk assessment associated with drought — links to global change,
- Risk management for farmers and ranchers facing impacts of drought,
- Economics of water supply and water conservation,
- The role of water banks — environmental credit trading opportunities,
- Development of drought-tolerant or water-conserving plant species for agriculture and landscaping, and
- Impacts of water reuse on downstream water supplies — whether upstream efficiency leads to decreased supply downstream.

Educational Needs in Agricultural Water Security

Ample educational materials exist for improving water conservation and water management. Unfortunately, much of this information has not been adapted to local watershed conditions. Moreover, citizens often fail to recognize their role in advancing or threatening agricultural water security. The focus should be to provide outreach and educational programs aimed at

- Understanding the limits of water supply in western watersheds;
- Improved/expanded application of known/existing science for irrigation and water management through educational programs;
- Place-based education — eliminating sub-tropical lifestyles in desert climates;
- Educating water managers — impacts of water supply will be disproportionately felt by lower income families;
- Educating landscapers — use of drought-tolerant trees, reduce/eliminate turf and lawns, use of drip irrigation (instead of sprinklers), reuse of irrigation water;
- Educating the public (adults) — public service ads, include water supply as part of the local television/radio weather reports, campaigns to convert toilets and showers to water-conserving models; and
- Educating the public (youth) — building water conservation as part of the basic curriculum, i.e., "water wise" school programs.

Other needs for agricultural water security and protection of food supply revolve around a great many issues that include such topics as bioterrorism preparedness, security for biological agents and toxins, homeland security role in agriculture, agricultural border inspections, clean water acts and other water related acts, and many others. However, there is insufficient room to discuss them within this text. Thus, our focus will be primarily on agriculture as a target from both disruptions of water supply and bio-terrorism attacks on

agriculture. The relation between the two is complex and interdependent.

Agriculture as a Target

The agricultural and food infrastructure of the United States is potentially susceptible to terrorist attack, whether through attacking dams, levees, and water supply pipelines and aqueducts, poisoning agricultural water supplies during critical agronomic phases, or using biological pathogens on crops and animals. The impact of such an attack on the economy is complex, but could be substantial. In the case of bioterrorism, some animal diseases could potentially be transmitted to humans. Scientific and medical research on plant and animal diseases may lead to the discovery and development of new diagnostics and countermeasures, reducing the risk and impact of a successful terrorist attack.[348]

Within the water-supply community, focus has been on physical security and safeguarding infrastructure hubs. Within the bioterrorism component, the goal of the U.S. animal and plant health safeguarding system is to prevent the introduction and establishment of exotic pests and diseases, to mitigate their effects when present, and to eradicate them when feasible. In the past, introductions of pests and pathogens were presumed to be unintentional and occurred through natural migration across borders or accidental movement by international commerce (passengers, conveyance, or cargo). However, a system designed for accidental or natural outbreaks is not sufficient for defending against intentional attack. Although the U.S. system is being upgraded to address the reality of agro-terrorism in terms of bioterrorism, both components (i.e., water security measures and bioterrorism countermeasures) appear insufficient to prevent an attack.

The National Research Council outlines a three-pronged strategy for countering the threat of agro-terrorism: deterrence and prevention, detection and response, and recovery and management. Agricultural water security attacks could occur against any water

---

[348] D. Monke Shea, J., and Gottron, F., "The Natinoal Bio- and Agro-Defense Facility: Issues for Congress," ed. Congressional Research Service (Washington DC: Library of Congress, 2007).

supply in the form of conventional explosives to disrupt water supply or a bioterrorism attack to poison critical water resources. Singular and multiple bioterrorism attacks could be directed at many different targets in the farm-to-table food continuum, including crops, livestock, food products in the processing and distribution chain, wholesale and retail facilities, storage facilities, transportation, and food and agriculture research laboratories.

Given that Usama Bin Laden's primary goal was to attack U.S. and western interests for maximum economic affect, it is likely that terrorists would choose to attack livestock and crops to cause severe economic dislocation. Over the past decade, the U.S. has endeavored to increase its ability to detect, prevent, and respond to terrorist threats and incidents. This focus on protecting the country from attacks, which has involved considerable financial outlays, has contributed to an increasingly well-protected public infrastructure. However, that infrastructure is still very weak in preventive abilities. Critical to this endeavor has been the development of vulnerability-threat analyses that are designed to maximize both antiterrorist efforts and consequence management procedures. In contrast to other critical infrastructure, agriculture, has received little attention with respect to protection against terrorist and other incidents, excepting natural hazards which the sector is all too accustomed to dealing with. In terms of accurate threat assessments and consequence management procedures, the agriculture sector, and the food industry in general, have not been a part of the wide ranging emphasis that has been given to critical infrastructure protection in the United States.[349]

Fortunately, the potential of terrorist attacks against agricultural targets (agroterrorism) is increasingly recognized as a national security threat, especially after the events of September 11, 2001. Agroterrorism is a subset of bioterrorism — defined as the deliberate introduction of an animal or plant disease with the goal of generating fear, causing economic losses, and /or undermining stability. Attacks against agriculture are not new, and have been conducted or considered by both nation-states and substate organizations

---

[349] P. Chalk, "Hitting America's Soft Underbelly: The Potential Threat of Deliberate Biological Attacks against the U.S. Agricultural and Food Industry," (Washington DC: Rand Corporation, 2004).

throughout history. [350] **The results of an agroterrorism attack could include major economic crises in the agricultural and food industries, loss of confidence in government, and possibly human casualties. Humans could be at risk in terms of food safety or public health, especially if the chosen disease is transmissible to humans (zoonotic). Also, public opinion could be particularly sensitive to a deliberate outbreak of disease affecting the food supply and confidence in government could be eroded if authorities appear unable to prevent such an attack or to protect the nation's food supply.**

Importance of the World's Agricultural Industry

The critical issue with agroterrorism is the low level of technical knowledge required to use it. Agriculture, as well as all activities included in the production cycle of the entire food industry, and the food industry in general is extremely important to the social, economic, and political stability of the world — the U.S. provides grains and other food supplies to over 100 countries around the world. Within the U.S., farming directly employs less than three percent of the population — one in eight people work in an occupation that is directly supported by food production.[351]

Unfortunately, the agriculture and food industries are vulnerable to deliberate and accidental disruption including man-made, natural, and technological hazards. An example of accidental versus deliberate disruption could be the recent (May 2011) E-coli outbreak in Europe that has spread to the U.S., which has thus far managed to control it. According to European scientists, the source of the outbreaks is unknown; suspected causes have ranged from Spanish cucumbers to vegetables from other countries. At the time of this writing more than 2,400 people have become ill and 23 are dead.[352] **The German outbreak was caused by the rare strain of Shiga toxin-producing E-coli known as STEC O104:H4. It appears to be the deadliest outbreak of E-coli ever seen, with a third of patients developing the severe complication called hemolytic uremic**

---

[350] Monke, "Agroterrorism: Threats and Preparedeness."

[351] Chalk, "Hitting America's Soft Underbelly: The Potential Threat of Deliberate Biological Attacks against the U.S. Agricultural and Food Industry."

[352] Baertlein, "Major E.Coli Outbreaks Decline, Salmonella Up."

syndrome (HUS), which frequently leads to kidney failure and can result in death.[353] Public health officials in the United States focus on the deadly Shiga toxin-producing E-coli infection known as O157:H7, which is best known for causing the 1993 outbreak that killed four people who had consumed tainted hamburgers from Jack in the Box. Since the origin in Europe cannot be found, is the outbreak natural or, is it accidental?

Critical concerns in this area include the increased susceptibility of livestock to disease, a general lack of farm/food related security and surveillance, vulnerability of water infrastructure, the concentrated and intensive nature of farming practices (both crop and animal), an inefficient, passive disease-reporting system that is further hampered by a lack of trust between regulators and producers, veterinarian training that tends not to emphasize foreign animal diseases or large scale husbandry, and a prevailing focus on aggregate, rather than individual, livestock statistics.[354]

Food supplies are not only vital for feeding our own population and others around the world, and important for the nation's economic health, but American agriculture is also a vivid example of the capabilities of modern scientific farming made possible by fossil fuels and high-tech agronomy, plant genetics, healthy soil, and abundant water. Water supplies and food supplies are susceptible to attack from myriad sources.

Bio-agents that could be employed as biological weapons include living organisms (micro-organisms and macro-organisms), chemical products of living organisms (including biological toxins), manufactured substances that mimic the action of biological substances, and genetically modified organisms. Among biological agents, anthrax and smallpox have the greatest potential for mass human casualties and disruption.

Although many 'experts' gloss over the potential deadly aspects of anthrax (Bacillus anthracis) and other biologicals as bio-weapons, special laboratory and defense-grade equipments are not needed for its production. These experts generally follow the principle of normalization, whereby behaviors and ideas are made to seem "normal" through repetition or ideology, i.e., that terrorists'

[353] Ibid
[354] Ibid

could never carry out such an attack with anthrax because they are not smart enough. Unfortunately, such expert bias has been stated so often that most Americans no longer believe such an attack is likely. The normalization of expert opinions has essentially constructed a terrorists' norm of conduct — the brain power of a terrorist is minimal, they are rag-tag peasants with no education, the way they would act and think is predictable, they have an specific inability to grasp complex weapon construction, and so forth; then, the 'expert' rewards or punishes those who do not conform to their expert opinion or who deviate from it, despite the overwhelming facts available that refute the experts' claims. So, anthrax spores can be produced in vitro and used as a biological weapon without special skills or equipment; although not a weapons grade bio-hazard, it is still deadly. Anthrax does not spread directly from one infected animal or person to another; it is spread by spores which can be transported by clothing or shoes.

Anthrax easily tolerates general water treatment methods that use 1-2 parts per million of chlorine to kill most waterborne pathogens; anthrax can attach to pipes or biofilms within the pipes and can pass through conveyance systems to reach agricultural irrigation systems or the consumer tap. Holding anthrax at a specific concentration of chlorine for a specific time period will kill it — the specific concentration and time period are not listed due to security issues.

Anthrax was among the first animal diseases for which a vaccine was developed. In 1881, Louis Pasteur developed a vaccine consisting of two different preparations given two weeks apart. This procedure gained widespread use and was only slightly modified over the next 50 years. In the late 1930s a vaccine using a weakened, non-disease causing strain of B. anthracis was developed (the "Sterne" strain) and it is in fact the strain used in today's vaccines. Diseased animals can spread anthrax to humans, either by direct contact (e.g., inoculation of infected blood to broken skin) or by consumption of a diseased animal's flesh. The body of an animal that had active anthrax at the time of death is and remains a source of anthrax spores for decades.

Anthrax is naturally occurring, generally in alkaline soils with high nitrogen levels caused by decaying vegetation, alternating

periods of rain and drought, and temperatures in excess of 60 degrees Fahrenheit. Spores (bacterial in nature) are soil-borne, and, because of their long lifetime, are still present globally and at animal burial sites of anthrax-killed animals for many decades; spores have been known to have reinfected animals over 70 years after burial sites of anthrax-infected animals were disturbed.[355] Thus, locations of outbreaks in the U.S. where animals were buried in the 1930s, 1970s, 1990s, and more recently, very likely contain viable anthrax that can be produced and spread.

Both anthrax and smallpox are highly lethal; stable enough to be applied as an aerosol; capable of large scale production; and have already been weaponized by hostile nations — anthrax by Iraq and both anthrax and smallpox by Russia, as well as other countries. Other agents of significant human concern include plague, tularemia, botulinum toxins, and viral hemorrhagic fevers, such as Ebola. Scientists have recently expressed concern that terrorists could exploit the potential for the creation of life forms using new knowledge about the gene sequences of living organisms. This technology could result in the manufacture of genetically engineered pathogens, toxins, or synthetic superbugs, which could be employed as biological weapons or even programmed to target specific ethnic groups. Terrorists could also develop and deploy a mix or 'cocktail' involving multiple biological agents or a combination of biological and chemical agents, severely impeding efforts to identify the cause of illness and to provide effective treatment. As an example, Saddam Hussein employed a chemical cocktail involving multiple agents in his attack on the predominantly Kurdish Iraquitwon of Halajba in March 1988.[356]

Agriculture and the food industry are very important to the social, economic, and political stability of the U.S. and most other countries. There is considerable vulnerability for a conventional attack on water supply systems, but more importantly, a significant threat to both agricultural water supply, and crop and animal components from a bio attack. The U.S. produces and exports a large

---

[355] Jeanne Guillemin, *Anthrax* (University of California Press, 2001).

[356] H. Parker, "Agricultural Bioterrorism: A Federal Strategy to Meet the Threat," ed. Institute for National Strategic Studies (Washington DC: National Defense University, 2003).

share the world's grain — $53 billion of agricultural products in 2002 — making it an important food source for other countries. If export markets were to decline following an agroterrorism event, U.S. and global markets could be severely disrupted.

Agricultural Bio-warfare & Bioterrorism

Anti-agricultural bio-warfare and bioterrorism differ significantly from similar activities directed against humans. A variety of possibilities for economic gain abound for perpetrators — possible perpetrators include corporations (which may have state-of-the-art technical expertise), terrorists, criminals, organized crime, and others. Agriculture has several characteristics that pose unique problems for managing the threat: attacks are much easier to initiate, the agents are not hazardous to humans, delivery systems are readily available and unsophisticated, maximum effect can be obtained from obscure and less secure locations, delivery from outside the target country is possible, and an effective attack can be constructed to appear natural. These characteristics make biological attack(s) on the agricultural sector a potentially serious threat. What are the characteristics and motivations of terrorists?

Terrorists that May Resort to Agroterrorism

There are likely three types of terrorists who would resort to this type of terrorism: (1) terrorists with political goals; (2) religiously motivated terrorists; (3) radical ecosystem terrorists and animal rights activists; and (4) criminals.

Terrorists with political goals cannot afford to antagonize the population since they need support of the populace to achieve desired goals. Because of this, this type terrorist would pretend to be nonviolent since, although high death numbers are possible, economic chaos would likely be the end result of agroterrorism. Whether this group wants a change in what they view as an inept or oppressive government or has some other goal, agroterrorism would be a form of indiscriminate violence due to lack of bloodshed and open violence as has been witnessed in Iraq, Afghanistan, and other countries. These types of terrorists most often rely on individuals

sympathetic to their cause; therefore, causing economic damage with limited violence would be a better means to achieving those goals. Also, the strategy of terrorists is changing to focus more on economic damage rather than destruction. Usama Bin Laden was the main driver of this thrust, which appears to now be more adaptable, especially since the goal can be achieved without using suicide bombers and the consequences if caught are much less severe. Targets that are less protected; in addition, command and control facilities can cause more economic damage than blowing up buildings indiscriminately. A good example of this type of terrorist dates to 1979, when Palestinian terrorists poisoned Israeli crops to sabotage the Israeli economy.[357] Cyber terrorism and many other tools are at their disposal and, even if poisoning agricultural products did little harm, the psychological effects due to extensive media coverage could dominate the headlines for weeks. And, as a bioweapon, such an attack would likely be considered use of a weapon of mass destruction, with potential long-term lingering psychological effects. Depending on what crop was attacked, commodity prices could soar. Also, ease of such an attack, including possible state sponsorship or domestic terrorist cooperation, through a covert delivery, would undoubtedly panic a populace.

Terrorists with religious motivations are not as constrained as those who are politically motivated. They do not fear public backlash and would not hesitate to carry out an agroterrorism attack that would cause mass death and casualties. Whether through infecting people via animals, poisoning water supplies that irrigate crops, destroying water pipelines, infecting cattle yards with anthrax, or any other scenario, these types of terrorists would be merciless. Although the U.S. food supply is very diverse, the most likely attack would damage a crop sufficiently to cause food shortages, trade embargoes on grain or cattle, and so forth; therefore, anti-agricultural weapons may better suit their purpose, at least as part of a strategy that is of larger scale than tactical scenarios. Additionally, fear and hunger are common human emotions and sufferings that could help build a psychological alliance with local militia hostile to the nation's government and/or domestic terrorists for economy of scale and greater chances of success.

---

[357] Bruce Hoffman, *Inside Terrorism* (New York: Columbia University Press, 1998).

Radical ecosystem terrorists and animal rights activists have long voiced opposition to deforestation, animal fur, and many other issues. Some of these groups even believe that agriculture itself is not natural in regard to modern monoculture crops such as wheat, rice, corn, and soybeans. They target a variety of facilities such as laboratories, ski lodges, nuclear power and other electrical plants, genetically engineered crops and so forth. These terrorists could target any particular crop, most likely genetically engineered ones, to cripple its production or spread disease. Because agroterrorism is considered by them to be nonviolent, this method of attack allows economic destruction without loss of human life. From their ideological perspective, this is preferable and acceptable. While they are not considered dangerous, they can be quite destructive. One such group (the Breeders) spread the Mediterranean fruit fly in California in 1989 to protest agricultural practices in the state.[358]

Criminals are the last potential group that may use agroterrorism as a weapon. While many believe that such an attack would be organized criminal groups, it is entirely likely that a few individuals would utilize this method as a small faction. However, both groups' motives would likely be the same, which would be to influence price in the commodities markets. Additionally, since many of these bio-organisms are pathogens that can be extremely effective in targeting only one type of organism, there is a high likelihood of extortion or blackmail by threatening to infect a target company's crops or livestock. Pests such as the Mediterranean fruit fly could also be used to gain a competitive edge since any fruit crops such as oranges infected by this pest would be quarantined and no exports or imports would be allowed. Thus, agroterrorism attacks as a form of economic warfare could be considerable. Disgruntled employees and others could easily use such bioweapons to 'get back' at their boss or former company. As an example, perhaps a loved one died from smoking; this could cause a backlash against tobacco companies with the natural target being the tobacco crops, which could be easily infected. And, without the likelihood of human death or injury, a moral line is more easily rationalized, justified, and crossed. Another example is the drug war. In 2000, a fungus was developed that could

[358] Reuters, "Officials Advertise to Contact Mystery Group Claiming Medfly Release," *Los Angeles Times*(1990).

potentially kill crops used in Latin America for drug harvesting.[359] Apparently never put in place due to potential and severe retaliation from the drug cartels, such an attack is possible, but the drug cartels have the financing and development means to mount a counter attack of similar nature on agricultural crops in the U.S.

Other potential users of agroterrorism include countries for military, political, ideological, or economic reasons. Due to likely severe consequences, such efforts would be covert so that the attack looked natural, such as a point-source outbreak, or multiple outbreaks with an apparently natural common source. In the 1980s, for example, Iraq used chemical weapons extensively against Iran, as well as internally against civilian minorities, with virtually no political consequences.

Corporations may also be likely to use this form of attack. Agricultural corporations, including producers, processors, and shippers could benefit significantly from the economic impacts, market share changes, and financial market effects of a successful biological attack. Unfortunately, many of these corporations employ expert plant pathologists or veterinarians and have large collections of pathogens. The combination of motivation, expertise, and materials within a single, closed organization is worrisome. As with a country, due to risk of reprisal, implementation would likely mimic a natural outbreak. Individuals known as bio-criminals or another category and could include past and disgruntled employees, ideologically motivated individuals, speculators on the commodities market (particularly traders), or individuals with a profit motive.

Potential Goals of an Attack on Agricultural

Regardless of what group may utilize agroterrorism as a method of attack, there could be many reasons for implementing an agroterrorism attack. Examples include destabilizing government, altering supply and demand, disrupting the food supply, or bio-control of plants or animals; these are briefly discussed below.

---

359 Jim Robbins, "Drug War Awaits Attack of Killer Fungus," *New York Times*, July 18 2000.

Disruption of the agricultural sector can cause societal dislocation. More importantly, direct losses of plants or animals on a larger scale could cause food shortages, increases in food prices, and unemployment. Depending on severity, all of these could have serious destabilizing effects on social and political structures. And, the more detrimental the economic state, the more rapid and severe such destabilization would be. Most developed countries, although vulnerable to disruption of the agricultural sector, have robust social and political institutions. This would likely lessen any discontent and would not result in government or institutional collapse. Less developed nations would be much more vulnerable. However, the potential for substantial economic damage is high for a well-planned attack, and the consequences for the food supply, export trade, and financial markets could be serious. It would be beneficial not to underestimate the potential of an agroterrorism attack.

In the occurrence of a widespread-epidemic or outbreak of an agricultural pathogen or disease that imposed or relaxed trade restrictions, rapid and significant changes of supply and demand of the affected crop or animal materials on domestic and international markets could occur. This would influence commodity markets and result in shifting and possibly out-of-control prices. Note that this is one of the possible motives for criminal elements. A biological attack could also be used to manipulate futures markets and of course financial markets.

This is the classic rationale for the inclusion of anti-plant programs in national biological weapons (BW) programs. Every major state BW program has generally included an anti-agricultural component, from the WWI German use of anthrax and glanders (a rare and contagious disease that primarily affects horses) against animals to the Iraqi program using wheat cover smut. For most agroterrorism agents, effective use would require large stockpiles and extensive delivery efforts; however, more likely is potential for delivery by covert agents to initiate point-source epidemics of highly contagious agents. BW proliferator states are likely to include anti-animal and anti-plant agents in their developing arsenal, and if they also support terrorist groups, such groups might be allowed to engage in bioterrorism.

The use of legitimate bio-control provides an unfortunate body of knowledge and range of ready-made delivery technologies for the interested agricultural bioterrorist or biowarfare program. Two recent programs have helped develop pathogens of drug crops as bio-control agents. Both were conducted under UNDCP auspices; one was funded and performed by the U.S. (fungal pathogens of coca), and the other was funded by the U.S. and UK and performed by Uzbekistan (fungal pathogens of poppy). Both programs involved the development of biological agents and delivery devices and are presumably intended for use principally in other countries. Crucially, none of the potential target states has agreed to allow use of these bio-control agents and, permission for implementation will probably never be given. Both individuals and terrorists will likely be interested in bio-control agents. The deliberate and illegal 1997 importation of Rabbit Hemorrhagic Disease Virus (RHDV) into New Zealand to control exploding rabbit populations that were devastating agricultural crops is an example. And extreme activist groups opposed to such technology might consider biological attack on genetically engineered plants, a form of bio-control.

Impacts of a Major Agricultural/food Related Disaster

The impact of a major agricultural/food related disaster in the U.S. would be significant and could extend beyond the agricultural community to affect other segments of society. An immediate effect of a major act of biological agroterrorism would be economic disruption, generating costs on at least three different levels, including economic loss due to containment measures and the destruction of disease ridden crops or livestock, an indirect multiplier effect from compensation costs paid to farmers for the destruction of agricultural commodities and losses suffered by directly and indirectly related industries, and international costs due to protective trade embargoes imposed by major external trading partners. Similar instances would occur in other countries and, the less developed the country's economy and less robust the agricultural sector, the more drastic the effects would be.

A successful act of agroterrorism could undermine confidence in government, potentially resulting in loss of continuity of

government. The release of contagious pathogens against livestock, crops, or water — the contamination of farm to table continuum through the introduction of toxic or bacterial agents — could cause public panic about food sources and potentially lead to speculation about the effectiveness of contingency planning against weapons of mass destruction in general. A major act of agroterrorism would almost certainly be a catalyst for widespread public condemnation. Mass eradication and disposal of livestock in particular could be controversial, possibly eliciting protests from affected farmers and animal rights and ecosystem and environmental groups. Additionally, such an attack would have the secondary effect of creating psychological fear, possibly widespread panic. If human deaths also occurred in this attack, fear and panic would soar. This is the modus operandi of well-known terrorist tactics, i.e., eliciting a psychological response, thereby using fear and panic to create an overall atmosphere of anxiety.

Imagine a small agroterrorist attack — a large cattle feedlot holding about 2,500 cows in Florida is spiked with two pathogens, anthrax and foot and mouth disease (Aphtae epizooticae), both readily available. The lot is constantly wet and drains downhill into a storage pond which, unnoticed, leaks into an irrigation ditch. After an incubation period, cattle begin showing symptoms of both diseases and are quarantined. News of the outbreak spreads quickly through the media and people stop buying beef products because of psychological effects even though the beef is determined to be safe. A USDA and DHS investigation ensue, but already export, trade, reporting, and quarantine policies are enacted; beef from Florida cannot be exported or shipped out of state. During this frenzy, people who have eaten at several local restaurants become ill. The fresh vegetables they consumed, although thoroughly washed, had anthrax adhered to the leaves. The restaurants were temporarily closed, but only after the patrons had been diagnosed with anthrax poisoning. The concurrent episodes are not linked for about two weeks and then, a heightened anxiety ensued as fear gripped the city of Miami. It appeared from investigations that the outbreak was natural, analogous to the recent E-coli outbreak in Europe. How far would the economic and fear factors progress? Although not a real attack, an accidental contamination of this nature did occur with less

lethal pathogens; it was localized and news never made it to the general public. Imagine the consequences!

Whether terrorists target food products, water that irrigates them, or animals and crops for deliberate contamination, serious public health and economic consequences will result. Psychologically, consumer confidence would be undermined. As an example, consider the Tylenol scare in the U.S. in 1982; the Chicago-area poisonings killed seven people and led to massive panic, prompting Tylenol maker Johnson & Johnson to halt advertising and issue an immediate nationwide recall. The incident resulted in improved industry-wide product safety standards, including tamper-proof seals and increased security at manufacturing plants. Johnson & Johnson's numerous efforts, which adhered to the company's creed, to put the needs of others first, were widely applauded by the public and PR industry. The recall, a first of its kind, resulted in more than $100 million in losses for the company. This instance remains a model crisis case study. It is now believed by some that Unabomber Ted Kaczynski could be the person responsible for this crime.[360] Thus, the mere threat of such an attack would seriously undermine consumer confidence in the safety of our food supply and potentially destabilize export markets.

Financial losses would accrue from a number of interrelated consequences, including direct losses of agriculture commodities to diseases, costs of diagnosis and surveillance, required destruction of contaminated crops and animals to contain disease, cost of disposal of mortalities and carcasses, damage to consumer and public confidence, need for long term quarantine of infected areas, losses due to export and trade restrictions, disruption of commodity markets, job losses, possible restaurant and other business closures, and many others.

A devastating outbreak of foot and mouth disease (FMD), a highly contagious viral disease of cloven hoofed animals, was reported in Taiwan in March 1997. FMD is an infectious virus capable of spreading as a wind-driven aerosol over 170 miles from its source. Within six weeks, FMD had spread throughout Taiwan, necessitating

---

[360] Ryan Whalen, "Fbi Investigates Unabomber in '82 Tylenol Scare," *BeartoothNBC.com*(2011), http://www.beartoothnbc.com/news/montana/6460-fbi-investigates-unabomber-in-82-tylenol-scare.html.

the slaughter of more than eight million pigs and shutting down the nation's valuable pork exports. The origin of the disease was reportedly traced to a single pig from Hong Kong, and China was suspected of deliberately introducing the disease into Taiwan.[361]

While the economic impact of bioterrorism against farm animals would be substantial, experts have concluded that an attack against American crops would have greater consequences since crops comprise a larger percentage (54 percent) of the $202 billion farm value of American commodities; crop products contribute more to exports. More importantly, crops comprise the major components of prepared feeds for livestock, poultry, and farm raised fish. Also, a deliberate contamination of processed foods by terrorists could have devastating consequences, not only in terms of human health, but also in terms of economic impact and loss of consumer confidence in the safety of U.S. food supplies, not to mention potential human casualties, especially if the chosen disease is transmissible to humans (zoonotic).

The production agriculture sector would suffer economically in terms of plant and animal health, and the supply of food and fiber could be reduced in certain regions based on which products are targeted in the attack (e.g., dairy, beef, pork, poultry, grains, fruit, or vegetables), while demand for other types of food may rise due to food substitutions.

Depending on the disease and means of transmission, the potential for economic damage would depend on a number of factors, such as the disease agent, location of attack, rate of transmission, geographical dispersion, how long the disease remains undetected, availability of countermeasures or quarantines, and incident response plans. Potential costs are difficult to estimate and can vary widely based on cascading interdependencies.

Direct financial loss due to mortality or morbidity of domestic animals or crop plants can vary from insignificant to catastrophic. One of the major determinants of the magnitude of the direct losses will be the rapidity with which the disease is detected and diagnosed. In developed countries most of the foreign diseases of greatest concern would likely be identified fairly early, reducing direct disease losses.

---

[361] Parker, "Agricultural Bioterrorism: A Federal Strategy to Meet the Threat."

The control of an outbreak of an imported, highly contagious animal or plant disease is routinely controlled by destruction of all potentially exposed healthy host organisms. With animal diseases, this normally means the slaughter of all host animals in the immediate vicinity. With plants, thousands of acres of crop plants may need to be destroyed to contain an outbreak. Thus, the losses attendant on outbreak control can exceed, often by several orders of magnitude, the direct losses due to the disease itself. Destruction of exposed hosts is often the only option when the agent is bacterial or viral. For fungal agents, on the other hand, destruction of exposed crops may be reduced by the use of fungicides. However, this is an expensive process and adds significantly to the cost of the outbreak; it also may cause environmental damage.

A number of important threats to crop plants are from insect pests, rather than microbial pathogens. These outbreaks are usually controlled by use of pesticides rather than destruction of exposed plants, which, as with control of fungal disease, can be costly. Widespread broadcast of insecticide may also cause environmental or human health damage as well.

Importing countries free of a particular disease are generally quick to block imports from countries in which a disease breaks out. This happens frequently, as these diseases periodically resurface in areas from which the disease has been absent; trade restrictions typically last a month or two when control of the outbreak is rapid, or they may be in force much longer if disease control is slow and difficult. An example is the EU restriction on the import of UK beef due to the Bovine Spongiform Encephalopathy (BSE) outbreak; BSE is commonly known as mad-cow disease. Major agricultural exporters are particularly vulnerable. For instance, the Taiwan FMD outbreak in swine in 1997 cost about $1 to 2 million (USD) in direct losses, but cost four billion dollars in eradication and disinfection costs, and a cumulative $15 billion in lost export revenues. An FMD outbreak in Italy in 1993 again had trivial direct costs, but nearly $12 million in eradication and disinfection costs and $120 million in lost trade revenues. A potential outbreak of FMD in California could cost $6 billion or more even if the outbreak were confined to California and eradicated within a few months.

The substantial market effects of a widespread outbreak, or one that has major impacts on international trade, could have secondary effects, such as share-holder losses, revenue losses to processors and shippers, and other effects. If losses are very large and if future losses are perceived as likely, significant levels of investor panic could lead to market destabilization.

A widespread outbreak of exotic animal disease is likely to be controlled by slaughter of exposed animals. Similar to the 2001 outbreak of FMD in the UK, this could result in the slaughter of millions of animals; the disposal of such a large number of carcasses can have significant effects on air quality (if carcasses are incinerated) or water quality (if carcasses are buried and adequate care to protect the water table is not taken). Also, if an exotic disease were established in wild animal populations, it will be much more difficult to eradicate, and could have negative effects on biodiversity if eradication were attempted. As an example, FMD infects virtually all cloven-hoofed animals and could easily spread from domestic animals to wild deer, sheep, elk, or bison populations.

Vulnerabilities of Agricultural to Deliberate Bio-terrorism

Agriculture has several characteristics that pose unique threat management problems. Agricultural production is geographically disbursed in unsecured environments. Livestock are frequently concentrated in confined locations then transported and commingled with other herds. Pest and disease outbreaks can result in rapid export or import embargos. Additionally, many veterinarians lack experience with foreign animal diseases that are resilient and endemic in foreign countries. More importantly, agriculture and food production generally have received less attention in counter-terrorism and homeland security efforts, although recently agriculture has garnered attention in the expanding field of terrorism studies such as laboratory and response systems that are being upgraded to address the reality of agroterrorism.

Although there are a few recorded instances of terrorists actually using disease against agriculture, a realistic potential for disruption exists. What makes the vulnerabilities of agriculture so worrisome is that the capability requirements for exploiting

agricultural sector weaknesses are not significant and are considerably less than those needed for a human-directed bio-attack. A bio attack on an agricultural water supply could be as effective as infecting a herd of animals at a feed lot, perhaps more, since produce field-to-table timelines are so rapid, generally within 3-7 days. Several author examples include squash production in Virginia which was harvested on Monday and on store shelves by Wednesday in Washington, DC; sugar-pod peas that were in myriad Asian restaurants the day after harvest; sugar-pod peas were also in restaurants the day after harvest in Washington DC, Baltimore, and Fairfax. Another example includes green peppers harvested on Monday and in restaurants and produce sections in Miami by Wednesday and New York restaurants by Thursday. Obviously, depending on the crop product, the timeline can be very rapid. Also, by the time contamination is detected, the infected produce is long gone from store shelves due to sale, freshness concerns, and spoilage.

Other unique vulnerabilities to the agricultural sector include the large number of pathogenic and bio-agents to choose from. The Office International des Epizooties (OIE) in the U.S. has identified 15 pathogens with the potential to severely affect agricultural populations and/or trade. Most of these diseases are environmentally hardy, having the ability to exist for extended periods of time on organic or inorganic matter, and typically are not the focus of concerted livestock vaccination programs. Many foreign animal diseases are non–zoonotic (cannot jump the animal-human species barrier); therefore, minimal risk of latent or accidental (human) infection is associated with these pathogens. A perpetrator is not required to have an advanced understanding of animal disease epidemiology and transmission modes, nor is there any need for elaborate containment procedures, personal protective equipment, and/or prophylaxis antibiotics in the preparation of the disease agent. Animal diseases can be quickly spread to affect large numbers of herds over wide geographic areas. This factor reflects the intensive and concentrated nature of modern farming activities in the U.S. and abroad and the increased susceptibility of livestock to viral and bacterial infections. Consequently, weaponization in agroterrorism is a non-issue since the animals themselves are the primary vector for

pathogenic transmission. If the objective is human deaths, the food chain (crops, animals, and water) offers a low-tech mechanism that is conducive to disseminating both toxins and bacteria. Additionally, developments in the farm to table food continuum have greatly increased the number of entry points for these agents. These openings for contaminants combined with the lack of security and surveillance at processing and packing plants have helped substantially augment the technical ease of orchestrating a food-borne attack.[362]

The volume of imported items entering the United States has also made it impossible for border inspectors to physically inspect every incoming cargo container or each and every international passenger's luggage, which can be key pathways through which FMD and other pathogens could enter the country, and for the smuggling of insects such as the Mediterranean fruit fly to intentionally infect crops.[363]

Although the U.S. agriculture sector and food supply have been largely secure from deliberate contamination, the potential exists for relatively easy infection — accidentally or deliberate. As an example, in 1984, in the U.S., a cult group poisoned salad bars at several Oregon restaurants with Salmonella bacteria. As a result, 750 people became ill.[364] The United Kingdom estimated that its outbreak of FMD resulted in over $10 billion (USD) in losses to tourism and the food and agriculture sectors and the slaughter of over four million animals. The latter case illustrates that accidental infection can be a significant as deliberate infection. This does not imply that mitigation processes should not be sought. To obtain a pathogen, a terrorist group could try to isolate the organism from the environment, order it from a biological collection or laboratory, or be given it by a state sponsor. However, to isolate a human pathogen from the environment would require a terrorist group to have access to someone with, at minimum, expertise in microbiology. As an example, Aum Shinrikyo, a well-funded and organized cult that

---

[362] Chalk, "Hitting America's Soft Underbelly: The Potential Threat of Deliberate Biological Attacks against the U.S. Agricultural and Food Industry."
[363] GAO, "Freshwater Supply: States' Views of How Federal Agencies Could Help Them Meet the Challenges of Expected Shortages."
[364] Ibid.

released nerve gas on the subways of Tokyo, attempted to culture Ebola virus and Bacillus anthracis (the causative agent of anthrax) by collecting these agents from infected individuals and the environment, but failed to produce a lethal weapon. In contrast, culturing of many animal and plant diseases from the environment is far easier. The former Soviet bioweapons scientist noted that the Soviets found anti-agricultural weapons far easier to produce.[365] It is also rumored that agents of Aum Shinrikyo has Russian connections. The New Zealand farmers who wanted to eradicate rabbits eating their crops has rabbit calcicivirus smuggled through one of the tightest airport/port bio-security regimes in the world and, without using any special equipment, the farmers cultured the virus and disseminated it by contaminating vegetable left out for the foraging rabbits.[366]

Many potential sites for release of an animal or water agent, such as auction houses and reservoirs, have very low security. Access to large numbers of animals with destinations all over a country or region is simple and easy. Seeds, fertilizers, and pesticides provide routes for infection of crop plants, although with somewhat higher (but still not robust) security. And of course pastures and fields themselves have essentially no security at all. The moral barrier, i.e., directly taking human life, is less an issue. It is often argued that there is an innate human revulsion to the use of biowarfare; however, it is unlikely that this sentiment extends to biological attack on plants or animals. Furthermore, the response after a biological attack on plants or animals would be less substantial than if the attack involved human victims, and the penalties of being identified as the perpetrator would be lighter.

An additional issue unique to the agricultural sector is that an attack may not require multiple dispersal/infection locations for maximum effectiveness if the goal is to disrupt trade by introducing a highly contagious disease. Also, it is likely the majority of such attacks could be made to look natural due to the high background of naturally-occurring disease. A deliberately instigated outbreak could possibly be mistaken for a natural one. If avoiding detection were

---

[365] Kenneth Alibek, "The Soviet Union's Anti-Agricultural Biological Weapons," *Annals of the New York Academy of Sciences* 894(1999).

[366] et al. Wilson, "A Review of Agroterrorism."

important, the attack likely would be constructed to take advantage of the ensuing confusion, especially if the goal is disruption of international trade, where few cases are necessary.

Additionally, multiple point source outbreaks can be initiated by contaminating imported feed or fertilizer, without even entering the country since many countries import materials such as straw, animal feed, or fertilizer. This provides an opportunity for introducing serious pathogens without even having to enter the target country. It also allows the possibility of initiating multiple outbreaks over a large geographic area in a way that mimics a natural event (such as the recent outbreak of foot and mouth disease in Japanese cattle in two widely separated prefectures, thought to have been introduced by straw imported from China).

Abundant, affordable, and safe food supplies in the U.S. and other developed countries are largely taken for granted, and agricultural products are not viewed as vulnerable to significant disruption. These attitudes and preconceptions prove that cognitive dissonance theory is at work in the agricultural sector. Factually, it is difficult for Americans to imagine a world where the availability of food radically changes for the worse — a dysfunctional attitude.

Other issues in this area include genomics, which is transforming the sciences that underlie the development of chemical and biological weapons, as well as protection against them. Genomics will facilitate protection of plants and animals against biological attack through development of new vaccines, new pesticides, new diagnostic reagents, and new genetic varieties easier and more rapidly, which should facilitate a coordinated defense of agriculture against biological attack, at least for countries willing to make this a priority and spend the necessary funds. However, genomics also demonstrates the possibility of constructing genotype-specific biological control or weapons agents, i.e., those targeting specific agricultural varieties; it is a very real possibility. And, agriculture is highly vulnerable to these type weapons given the large mono-culture crop practices and genetic seed production technology used throughout the U.S. These type systems utilize large acreages with genetically identical cultivars and high-density husbandry of genetically inbred animal strains. Such practices reduce diversity among crops and animals and the genetic variability that makes populations resistant to genotype-specific weapons, and instead creates conditions (large, dense populations) that facilitate disease spread.

Countries Most at Risk

The countries or U.S. states that are most vulnerable to economic attack dependent on the agricultural sector are those with the following attributes:

- High-density, large acreage agriculture;
- Heavy reliance on mono-culture agriculture that restricts the range of genotypes,
- Location free of specific serious animal or plant pathogens or pests;
- Major agricultural exporters or heavy dependence on a limited number of domestic agricultural products;
- Substantial domestic unrest, target(s) of international terrorism, or unfriendly neighbor of states likely to be developing bio-weapons programs;
- Weak plant and animal epidemiological infrastructure; and
- Heavy reliance on large reservoirs for irrigation of agriculture crops with no redundancy of water supply.

For those locations that demonstrate the above risk factors, the threat of biological attack against its agricultural sector should be taken seriously. Note that six of the listed risk factors characterize U.S., European, and Russian agriculture.

Due to the openness and thus the vulnerabilities inherent within agricultural systems, deterring bio-attacks is not easy. Several primary measures include enacting appropriate legislation, especially at the state level. While legislation can be a significant deterrent to biological attack it is not always easy to enforce at the farm level. The legislation should provide for substantial criminal penalties for the hostile use of biological agents against plants or animals as well as people, and it should provide for extradition for anyone charged with using such agents against the agricultural sector of another state.

States that already have enacted such legislation should review its provisions to ensure that it adequately covers biological attack on plants and animals. Also, ensuring the identification of early outbreak is a critical factor since it could make the difference between an easy to control outbreak and one that escapes control and assumes disastrous proportions. For example, the UK FMD outbreak of 2001 was likely so severe because it was not noticed for almost a week after the initial introduction. Educational efforts to ensure rapid and proper identification of disease would be helpful. The latter would also require new diagnostics, particularly for animals, which would allow the ability to diagnose infection prior to the onset of symptoms and could allow control measures implementation prior to additional spread, thus facilitating control.

For plants, early detection is particularly problematic. Very large numbers of individual plants may be present in a given area and a very small proportion of these are closely observed by farmers; consequently, plant diseases can spread significantly before detection. Better techniques of detection of plant diseases are needed — remote sensing could be a key factor in this identification process. Once detected, outbreak should have effective control response and processes; otherwise, plants become enticing targets. A biological attack on the agricultural sector is likely to be covert. Such attacks will be options for perpetrators only to the extent that they maintain plausibility as natural events. Therefore, increased epidemiological capacity, especially in strain identification from molecular sequence data, makes it increasingly difficult to escape detection, and would act as a substantial deterrent.

Finally, it is ironic that so much has been written and so many policies developed regarding diversity in the work force, i.e., that diversity results in stronger, more economically competitive firms and yet within the agricultural sector, non-diversity has become the norm, especially regarding cropping culture which makes crops more disease susceptible. States that engage in high intensity agriculture of a limited range of varieties could reduce their vulnerability to both deliberate and natural disease outbreaks by increasing the use of intercropping, expanding the diversity of genotypes utilized, reducing the size of acreage, and a variety of other agricultural changes designed to reduce susceptibility to disease outbreaks.

However, the current conditions developed as a result of increasing mechanization in an attempt to maintain stability of food supply for a growing global population. Reversing this trend will not be easy, and potential solutions must be carefully considered. Various other measures could be introduced, but there is insufficient space to discuss herein.

Agricultural Bioterrorism Agents

To understand the threat of agroterrorism, it is necessary to recognize the pathogens, disease, and other sources and their characteristics from which the threat can occur. From the hundreds of animal and plant pathogens and pests available to an agroterrorist, fewer than two dozen likely represent significant economic threats. Determinants of this level of threat are the bio-agent contagiousness and potential for rapid spread, and its international status as a "reportable" pest or disease (i.e., subject to international quarantine) under rules of the World Organization of Animal Health (also commonly known as the OIE, the Office International des Epizooties).

Animal Pathogens

The Agricultural Bioterrorism Protection Act of 2002 (subtitle B of P.L 107- 188, the Public Health Security and Bioterrorism Preparedness and Response Act) created the current official list of potential animal pathogens. The list is specified in the select agent rules implemented by USDA-APHIS (Animal and Plant Health Inspection Service) and the Centers for Disease Control and Prevention (CDC) of the Department of Health and Human Services (HHS). The Act requires that these lists be reviewed at least every two years.

OIE Lists A and B.

The OIE's List 'A' diseases is transmissible animal diseases with the potential for serious and rapid spread, irrespective of national borders. List A diseases have serious socioeconomic or public health consequences and are critically important in international trade. List B diseases are transmissible diseases considered to be of socioeconomic or public health importance contained within countries, but also significant in international trade.

Select Agents list

The regulations establishing the select agent list for animals (9CFR 121.3) set forth the requirements for possession, use and transfer of these biological agents or toxins to ensure safe handling and protection from use in domestic or international terrorism. APHIS determined that the biological agents and toxins on the list have the potential to pose a severe threat to agricultural production or food products.

Plant pathogens

The agricultural Bioterrorism Protection Act of 2002 (subtitle B of P.L. 107-188) also instructed APHIS and CDC to create the current official list of potential plant pathogens. The Federal government lists biological agents and toxins for plants in 7 CFR 331.3. The number of micro and macro organisms that could be employed in agroterrorism is diverse. These include microscopic pathogens, insects, weeds, and other organisms or biological substances. Agent categories and potential uses are listed in Table 9.1.

List 'A' diseases (Table 9.2) are considered to be highly infectious and capable of being widely and rapidly spread across international borders but also to have the potential to inflict catastrophic economic losses and social disruption. List 'A' diseases are rigorously monitored worldwide by OIE whose member countries are required to report outbreak within 24 hours of laboratory confirmation. Reports of List 'A' outbreaks trigger immediate and severe trade restrictions on affected products. A number of existing or potential bioweapons pathogens are not included among the disease agents list.

Tables 9.1 to 9.3 are only a partial list of potential agroterrorism pathogens; many others, more recently updated, could potentially be adapted to cause severe economic damage and possibly death. Only 222 bioterrorism-related incidents have occurred in a 100 year period, about one every four years. Only one attack resulted in mass human casualties — the Salmonella contamination of food by the Rajneesh cult in Oregon in 1984.

Fourteen of 24 confirmed cases of bioterrorism, i.e., bio-crimes, are food or agriculture related. Only three incidents targeted commercial animals or plants (next table) and, of all cases, only six appear to be clearly linked to attacks on commercial plants and animals. A selected timeline is given in Table 9.3.

Table 9.1: Summary of Categories of Biological potentially useful in agroterrorism (Source: Parker, 2003).

Category/Agent	Potential target	Examples
Micro-organisms		
Bacteria, rickettsia	Commercial animals, plants, fish, food borne pathogens	Bacillys anthracis (anthrax), Xanthomonas spp., botulinum toxin; Salmonella spp.
Viruses	Commercial animals, plants, fish, food-borne viruses	Foot and mouth disease; Avian influenza virus; African swine fever virus; Newcastle disease virus; banana bunch top virus
Fungi	Commerical plants, fish	South American wheat blight; corn seed blight; wheat smut; soybean rust; rice blast
Protozoans	Commercial animals, fish, food-borne protozoans	MSX disease of oysters; Whirling disease of fish; protozoan parasites
Microalgae	Commercial fish, shellfish	Red Tide, Pfisteria piscicida
Macro-organisms		
Insects, worms	Commercial plants, animals	Boll weevil; screw worm; whitefly; wheat aphid; grapelouse; Asian longhorn beetles; nematodes
Weeds	Commercial plants	
Aquatic vertebrates and invertebrates	Commercial fish and shellfish	Lamprey eel; zebra musse; sea lice
Biologically derived active substances	Comercial animals, plants, fish	
Artificial designed biological-mimicking	Commercial animals, plants, fish	Biological toxins

substances		
Genetically modified organisms	**Commercial animals, plants, fish**	**Superweeds and superbugs**

Table 9.2: List 'A' Diseases (Source: Parker, 2003).

Animal and plant pathogens with potential bioweapons application	
Pathogens weaponized or pursued for weaponization potential	**Additional pathogen with weaponization potential**
Animal Pathogens	
African swine fever **Anthrax** **Foot and mouth disease** **Hog cholera/classical swine fever** **Ornithosis/Psittacocis** **Rinderpest** **Trypanosomiasis** **Poxvirus**	**African horse sickness** **Avian influenza** **Bluetongue** **Bovine spongiform encephalopathy** **Contagious bovine pleuropneumonia** **Lumpy skin disease** **Newcastle disease** **Paratuberculosis/Johne's disease** **Peste des petites ruminants** **Pseudorabies virus** **Rift valley Fever** **Sheep and goat pox** **Swine vesicular disease** **Vesicular stomatitis**
Plant Pathogens	
Rice blast (Magnoporthe grisea) **Wheat stem rust (Puccinia graminis)** **Wheat smut(Fusarium graminearum)**	**Wheat Pathogens** **Wheat dwarf geminivirus** **Barley yellow dwarf virus** **Pseudomonas fascovaginaei** **Clavibacter tritic** **Corn Pathogens** **Barley yellow dwarf virus** **Pseudomonas fascovaginaei** **Sclleropthora rayssiae (Brown stripe mildew)** **Peronoschlerospora sacchari (Sugarcane downy mildew)** **P. Philippinensis (Philippine downy mildew)** **P. Maydis (Java downy mildew)** **Soybeans** **Phakospora sachyrhizi (soybean rust)**

	Soybean dwarf virus **Pyrenochaeta glycines (Red leaf blothc)** **Cotton** **Fusarium oxysporum f. sp. Vasinfectum (Australian)** **Xanthomonas campestris pv. Maloacearium (Africa); Geminivirus**

Table 9.3: Selected agricultural of food bioterrorism incidents in the 20th century (Source: Parker 2003).

Year	Nature of incident	Alleged perpetrators
1997	Spreading rabbit hemorrhagic virus among wild rabbit population in New Zealand	New Zealand farmers
1996	Food poisoning in Texas hospitals using Shigella	Hospital lab worker
1995	Food poisoning of estranged husband using Ricin	Kansas physician
1984	Food poisoning of residents of The Dallas, Oregon, using Salmonella in restaurant food	Rajneesh religious cult
1970	Food poisoning of Canadian college students	Estranged roommate
1970	Food poisoning with typhoid and dysentery agents	Japanese physician
1952	Use of plant toxin to kill livestock	Mau Mau (Kenya, Africa)
1939	Food poisoning via Salmonella-contaminated pastry	Japanese physician
1936	Food poisoning via Salmonella (typhoid)	Japanese physician
1932	Attempted food poisoning of Lytton Commission members investigating Manchuria takeover via fruit contaminated with Cholera	Japanese military
1916	Food poisoning involving numerous	New York dentist

	pathogens	
1915	**Infection of U.S. and allied draft animals and livestock with glanders and anthrax**	**German intelligence**
1913	**Food poisoning of family members with cholera and typhus organisms (Germany)**	**Former employee of chemist's shop**
1912	**Food poisoning using poisonous mushrooms**	**Frenchman trained as a druggist**
Threatened use (not related to food poisoning)		
1989	**Threat to release "Medflies" (fertile Mediterranean fruit flies) in California to infect crops in protest against pesticide spraying**	**The "Breeders", an extremist environmental group**
1984	**Attempt to kill a race horse with pathogens (insurance scam, confirmed possession)**	**Two Canadians**
1984	**Threat to spread Foot and mouth disease to wild pigs, which would then spread disease to livestock (no confirmed possession)**	**Australian prison inmate**
1980	**Threat to use biological agents against crops (no confirmed possession)**	**Tamil guerrillas, Sri Lanka**
1970	**Epidemic of African hog fever virus in Cuba alleged to have been deliberately inflicted by the United States (false case, no evidence)**	**U.S. Government (CIA)**

Conclusions

The consequences of a biological attack against U.S. food and agriculture could be devastating — in terms of both economic impact and the undermining of public confidence in the nation's food supply. The scope and scale of the agricultural industry, combined with the simplicity of obtaining, weaponizing, and using

anti-agricultural agents and the diversity of transnational and domestic terrorist groups who would be interested in employing these agents, make any implementation of deterrence and prevention unlikely to be fail safe. Additional prevention, mitigation, security, and educational measures need to be employed to limit the damage incurred if terrorists successfully deploy a biological attack against the agricultural sector via crop, animal, or water measures.

Any proposal for potential solutions will probably require a significant investment, particularly at the federal level. A variety of proposals could include many areas and may involve the following:

1. Enhanced surveillance of the agricultural diseases that could cause prolific economic and public health problems. This surveillance should begin at the farm level to detect diseases before symptoms become visible or before diseases are communicable to other animals and plants, which may include providing samples from farms, feedlots, and reservoirs on a regular basis to local or regional laboratories. The CDC has been fairly successful with this methodology against human diseases,
2. Development of better computer models that can predict both the geographical range of spread of a specific disease and rate of that spread. These could be coupled with climate change and transportation models for human travel issues. This would be effective for concentrating testing in the most likely areas for spreading to occur,
3. Most countries have long stockpiled vaccines for humans in event of disease such as Smallpox, SARS, and so forth. This same strategy could be used for animals and crops in regard to insecticides, anti-fungals, antibiotics, and related components that would be useful in stopping spread of a disease or pathogen to uninfected sectors of agriculture. Likely, this would be led by the private sector since it is unlikely the federal government could or would stockpile sufficient supplies,

4. **Other areas may include more funding for directed research in this area for genome sequencing and development of new vaccines and antibiotics, such as for additional vaccines for FMD viruses; creation of a network of professionals from various industries who can be mobilized in case of massive outbreak; and development of skills that can immediately determine the extent of disease spread and boundaries to reduce economic loss due to trade sanctions.**

A great many issues could be investigated and best potential solutions determined for each. Education would go a long way in quick recognition of a disease at the farm level and simple methods for monitoring, which may prevent rapid spread out of a localized area. The list is virtually endless, but also policy related from the local to national level.

Despite prevention and mitigation measures, terrorists have the motivation and technology to cripple a vital sector of an economy — agriculture. And, given the goal of Usama Bin Laden, e.g., to destroy the U.S. and developed nations economically, agroterrorism has the potential to be a primary key to assist in that specific goal. The underlying complexities and relation of agriculture to other key sectors of critical infrastructure and the economy are currently insufficiently understood to strictly limit the damage done and to reduce the usefulness of this powerful and often overlooked class of weapons of mass destruction. Ultimately, destroying the food supply destroys the people.

CHAPTER 10: Manmade Hazard: The Terrorist' Water Weapon

Executive Summary

The most serious terrorist threat to U.S. water supplies is the flight or sudden emergence of simultaneous and coordinated black-swan. A coordinated 'black swan' terrorist attack on the U.S. water supply, dependent on severity, could involve a reordering of defense priorities to the maintenance of civil order within the continental United States. A paradigm case of a terrorist 'black swan attack' was the three day terror attack on Mumbai from 26-28 November 2008. In 1993, Bin Laden declared war on America and stressed his commitment to "the defeat of the U.S. economy." By 14 September 2003, Bin Laden claimed the success of the 9/11 attacks. Not surprising, Al Qaeda psychological warfare strategists have an impressive sociological understanding of the vulnerabilities of western target societies, including the importance of the relationship between consent and legitimacy of government.

Since the 2001 terrorist attacks, the FBI has identified and interviewed Al Qaeda supporters who planned attacks against U.S. water supplies and plans. The potential attacks against Hoover and TVA Dams, as scouted by Mohammed Atta, if successful, would potentially be catastrophic. A cascading attack on water infrastructure would disrupt and in some cases destroy key storage and distribution nodes. The chaotic consequences would ensure that the U.S. would not immediately respond to a spectacular Al Qaeda attack as government priorities would be diverted to terrorist induced socio-economic dislocation, a form of Al Qaeda induced Hurricane Katrina. Simultaneous co-coordinated attacks on targets across the U.S. would complicate the attack picture.

There are over 5,700 facilities and structures vital to American national security and economic well being. A terrorist attack against a single vulnerable high-value infrastructure target of over five and a half thousand key nodes of U.S. vital infrastructure would exhibit

many of the characteristics and consequences of a natural disaster, including social dislocation, disorientation and panic, widespread anomie and social disorganization, threats to public order, public health crises and possible epidemics. Shortly after the 9/11 attacks, captured Al Qaeda documents from Al Qaeda camps in Afghanistan and suspected terrorists in the U.S. revealed that Al Qaeda and jihadists have the intention and the capability to conduct terrorist attacks on water supplies and infrastructure. The goal to attack U.S. water infrastructure is unlikely to change, despite Usama Bin Laden's death; instead, his demise will, rather than be a significant loss to Al Qaeda's operations, be a boon for recruitment, and there is also a real possibility of attack from other terrorist groups.

A water infrastructure attack would likely be executed in four stages: (1) intelligence collection; (2) distraction and diversion of security forces; (3) attack by U.S. indigenous person(s); (4) use of bio-agents as weapon of choice to poison large supplies.

The threat profile to U.S. water infrastructure is reconfigured, as empirical and sociological investigations have verified that talented engineers are embedded in the senior ranks of Al Qaeda and other jihadist groups. As an example, the founder of Al Qaeda and 9/11 attacks mastermind, Usama Bin Laden, earned a degree in civil engineering from King Abdul-Aziz University, and Khalid Sheikh Mohammed, the planner of the 9/11 attacks, was a graduate of North Carolina Agricultural and Technical State University in North Carolina. The adversary is far from being the young angry jihadist typified in the past. For example, in 2006, jihadists issued a new form of terrorist counterintelligence, intended to neutralize monitoring and detection of jihadists and jihadist web sites by Western security services. The first edition of the 64-page electronic magazine Technical Mujahidin, published by al-Fagr Information Center, was forwarded to password protected jihadist forums on 28 November 2006. The Technical Mujahidin contains articles of file concealment and protection and describes methods and software to ensure IT security. Links are provided to VMware virtual machine and key generators to unlock features. The second issue of Technical Mujahidin contains 72 pages focusing on psychological operations, weapon systems, and concealment techniques. New communications also describes

steganography — the art of hidden messages and, steganalysis — the art of detecting hidden messages.

Terrorists have demonstrated operational interest in the TVA Dams — the Douglas and Norris TVA Dams' area. The best tool to defeat them is likely counterintelligence. Internal counterintelligence (CI) programs are essential to counter a wide spectrum of insider threats ranging from targeted terrorist moles within the target infrastructure to employees, contractors, and sub-contractors who may have direct or indirect affiliations to foreign intelligence services, or terrorist patron states, and individuals with untraceable or unverifiable familial tribal ethnic connections to pro-terrorist groups, organizations, or regimes. A paradigm CI failure occurred in May 2009; a California Water Service Company (CWSC) employed Abdirahman Ismael Abdi, who was not a U.S. citizen. He was holding a British passport and working on a fraudulent H1B visa. Employed as an auditor at CWSC in San Jose, California and using his electronic key card, he gained access to the secure electronic gate at the CWSC parking lot; then, he used the computers of two CWSC employees to send over $9 million dollars to three separate accounts in Qatar.

Terrorists are the primary counterintelligence threat to the United States, often boasting of their intention to destroy the U.S. As early as 1996 Usama bin Laden referred to the relation between Al Qaeda's concept of asymmetric warfare and the need for conspiracy. "Due to the imbalance of power between our armed forces and the enemy forces, a suitable means of fighting must be adopted, i.e., using fast-moving light forces that work under complete secrecy."

Although many threats are a form of nerve warfare and taqiyya (deception), Al Qaeda has four operational advantages: (1) technical and human assets in the form of "home grown" jihadists; (2) secure human and technical clandestine communications; (3) clandestine assets in Islamic Diasporas; and (4) the ability of its engineering elite to inflict a single spectacular attack on water infrastructure, which could wreak massive damage to U.S. social cohesion and the economy.

The history of successful terrorist attacks can be summarized in two words "too late." After the 9/11 attacks and Al Qaeda's history of attempts to obtain WMD, the issuing of fatwas, which provide religious sanction for the use of WMDs against the U.S., the sophistication of Al Qaeda technology and the critical role of its engineering operatives and the emergence of home grown jihadism, the U.S. cannot afford to be too late — again.

Jihadist adversaries have a clear and stated strategic objective — the destruction of the U.S. economy and infrastructure, particularly water, which is the foundation of life and the engine that creates economic sustainability. There may be too many victims of such an attack or attacks to look back in hindsight — the recognition of defeat and the flight of the black swan of terrorist planned devastation.

Introduction

'Black Swan' Terrorist Attacks on the U.S. economy and water security

The most serious terrorist threat to U.S. water supplies is the flight or sudden emergence of simultaneous and coordinated black-swan attacks', a disruptive break from a trend line or an undervalued threat to deauthorize U.S. government and economic security. Most likely, such an attack would come from a transnational terrorist group. A recent list of terrorist groups (not all of them) is given in Table 10.1. Terrorist groups' attack methodology inverts all modes of warfare. Counter terrorist analysts have traditionally been preoccupied with the concept of 'surprise'. A black swan terror attack is an 'outlier' — an event that lies beyond normal expectations; they are not repeated, cannot be predicted, and have high impact. In the aftershock, a black swan attack seems as if it were inevitable. The 9/11 attacks and the recent Mumbai India attacks indicate a new threat syntax — the 'shock attack' characterized by high impact and high disruption of symbolic national infrastructure and icons.

Al Qaeda's concept of strategic 'shock' is integrated into their psychological warfare objective — the erosion of consent and crisis of authority within the U.S. This concept is also likely mirrored by other terrorist groups despite Bin Laden's death. Also, it should be noted that it was Mohammed Atta who masterminded the 9/11 attacks. Bin Laden was the thought catalyst and for the past five years has been only a figure head of Al Qaeda. Therefore, to believe that threat of terrorist attacks will terminate due to Bin Laden's death

would be a defective assumption and would follow the cognitive dissonance principle. A coordinated 'black swan' terrorist attack on the U.S. water supply, dependent on severity, could involve a reordering of defense priorities to the maintenance of civil order within the continental United States.[367] Al Qaeda's and other terrorist groups' concept of jihad is therefore the greatest existential threat to the United States and its critical infrastructure which defines the U.S. as the world's dominant power.

Al Qaeda's highly skilled elite, many with engineering and IT qualifications, constantly research U.S. vulnerabilities. The strategic objective of these continuous efforts is to destroy the U.S. economy and the collateral destruction of critical infrastructure. Al Qaeda strategy is dynamic. No other terrorist organization dedicates more research to the operational advantage of 'black swan' attacks than Al Qaeda.

Table 10.1: Recent list of international terrorist groups — list does not include domestic terrorists of any countries or other potential terrorist groups. (Source: U.S. Department of State; accessed online: http://www.state.gov/s/ct/rls/other/des/123085.htm).

Current List of Designated Foreign Terrorist Organizations – May 11, 2011
1. Abu Nidal Organization (ANO)
2. Abu Sayyaf Group (ASG)
3. Al-Aqsa Martyrs Brigade (AAMS)
4. Al-Shabaab
5. Ansar al-Islam (AAI)
6. Asbat al-Ansar
7. Aum Shinrikyo (AUM)
8. Basque Fatherland and Liberty (ETA)
9. Communist Party of the Philippines/New People's Army (CPP/NPA)
10. Continuity Irish Republican Army (CIRA)
11. Gama'a al-Islamiyya (Islamic Group)
12. HAMAS (Islamic Resistance Movement)
13. Harakat ul-Jihad-i-Islami/Bangladesh (HUJI-B)
14. Harakat ul-Mujahidin (HUM)
15. Hizballah (Party of God)
16. Islamic Jihad Union (IJU)
17. Islamic Movement of Uzbekistan (IMU)
18. Jaish-e-Mohammed (JEM) (Army of Mohammed)

[367] N. Freier, ed. *Known Unknowns: Unconventional Strategic Shocks*, Defense Strategy Development (2008).

19. **Jemaah Islamiya organization (JI)**
20. **Kahane Chai (Kach)**
21. **Kata'ib Hizballah (KH)**
22. **Kongra-Gel (KGK, formerly Kurdistan Workers' Party, PKK, KADEK)**
23. **Lashkar-e Tayyiba (LT) (Army of the Righteous)**
24. **Lashkar i Jhangvi (LJ)**
25. **Liberation Tigers of Tamil Eelam (LTTE)**
26. **Libyan Islamic Fighting Group (LIFG)**
27. **Moroccan Islamic Combatant Group (GICM)**
28. **Mujahedin-e Khalq Organization (MEK)**
29. **National Liberation Army (ELN)**
30. **Palestine Liberation Front (PLF)**
31. **Palestinian Islamic Jihad (PIJ)**
32. **Popular Front for the Liberation of Palestine (PFLP)**
33. **PFLP-General Command (PFLP-GC)**
34. **al-Qaida in Iraq (AQI)**
35. **al-Qa'ida (AQ)**
36. **al-Qa'ida in the Arabian Peninsula (AQAP)**
37. **al-Qaida in the Islamic Maghreb (formerly GSPC)**
38. **Real IRA (RIRA)**
39. **Revolutionary Armed Forces of Colombia (FARC)**
40. **Revolutionary Organization 17 November (17N)**
41. **Revolutionary People's Liberation Party/Front (DHKP/C)**
42. **Revolutionary Struggle (RS)**
43. **Shining Path (Sendero Luminoso, SL)**
44. **United Self-Defense Forces of Colombia (AUC)**
45. **Harakat-ul Jihad Islami (HUJI)**
46. **Tehrik-e Taliban Pakistan (TTP)**
47. **Jundallah**
48. **Army of Islam (AOI)**

The Black Swan Attack on Mumbai

A paradigm case of a terrorist 'black swan attack' was the three-day terror attack on Mumbai, the economic capital and largest city in India. At least 264 people were killed, including 28 nationals from 10 countries from 26-28 November 2008.[368]

The jihadist magazine 'Sada Al-Jihad' claimed the attack was based on surprise, as commentators did not believe that such an attack would occur on the Asian continent. The attack was also

[368]Staff, "The Attack Was Coordinated from Pakistan by Phone .The Terrorists Were Instructed Not" to Saddle Yourself with the Burden of the Hostages. Immediately Kill Them." The Terrorist Replied: Yes, We Shall Do Accordingly, God Willing'," *New York Times* 2009.

unique in that the terrorists arrived from Pakistan by sea. The strategic objective was to restore tension between Pakistan and India and therefore weaken the fight against the Mujahedeen. It is conceivable that tensions were heightened due to the attack, especially with pressing transboundary water issues that keep both countries in a heightened state of stress.

The jihadist monthly 'Qadaya Jihadiya' Magazine (Discussions on Matters of Jihad), published on behalf of the "Al-Yaqin Media Center", released a 24-page document dedicated to the analysis of the terrorist attack in Mumbai and described the attack as "September 11th no. 2," referring to the precise execution, multiple targets, number of casualties, and the implications for local, regional, and international arenas.

The writer noted the amazement and confusion among Western intelligence services, since the attack was wide scale with a high level of planning and execution — a high standard of fighting skills and suicide bombers were not involved.

The 'black swan' dimension included simultaneous attacks against multiple targets — law enforcement officials, population centers, and areas where foreigners stayed — and it involved taking hostages. The two unique elements were entry to the city by sea, and the attack power of a small group of terrorists frightening an entire city. The Mumbai attack was also an example of economic jihad (following Bin Laden's objectives), and damage to India's financial capital and to tourism. Most significantly the world's intelligence services received a 'strategic shock'.

The jihadist online forum, 'Al-Faloga' illustrates Al Qaeda research capabilities and attack methodology. The most disturbing extract is two accurate and detailed target maps of the continental United States. Map one depicts 23 critical U.S. Department of Energy facilities; map two depicts airport bases and U.S. air force and naval facilities.[369]

---

[369]ICT, (ICT's Jihadi Websites Monitoring Group, 2009).

Bin Laden's D4 terrorist Concept

D1: Destabilizing the U.S. Economy

In 1993, Bin Laden declared war on America and stressed his commitment to 'the defeat of the U.S. economy."[370] By 14 September 2003, Bin Laden claimed the success of the 9/11 attacks as attacking the "very heart of the America's economy."

....On September 11...believing nothing could harm it –...disaster struck them....they struck the very heart of America's economy "Americas is a superpower...but all this is built on foundations of straw. So it is possible to target those foundations and focus on their weakest points, which even if you strike only one-tenth of them, the whole edifice will totter and sway.....I also counsel them [young jihadists] to manage their affairs in secrecy, especially the military affairs of the jihad..."[371]

D2: De-authorizing the U.S. Government at All Levels[372]

Al Qaeda psychological warfare strategists have an impressive sociological understanding of the vulnerabilities of western target societies, including the importance of the relationship between consent and legitimacy of government. Bin Laden noted:

"All of this is built upon an unstable foundation, which can be targeted, with special attention to its obvious weak spots." If it is hit in one hundredth of these of those spots, God Willing, it will stumble, wither away..."

Modern states derive legitimacy from consent. De-authorization of

---

[370] Usama Bin Laden, (2009).

[371] Usama Bin Laden's sermon "Among a Band of Knights" Cited B. Lawrence (Ed) Messages to the World-the Statements of Usama Bin Laden Verso, N.Y. 2005, p195. Delivered February 14, the holiest day of the Islamic calendar. A thirty minute audiotape was circulated on websites and republished in the Arabic language international morning newspaper Al Hayat (Arabic: "life"), which has a circulation of almost 300,000 and is distributed in most Arab countries. Bin Laden's Sermon for the Feast of the Sacrifice MEMRI No. 476, March 2003.

the government refers to the withdrawal of consent by citizens. The themes of Al Qaeda propaganda depict the U.S. and Western governments as lacking political legitimacy. Al Qaeda plans to create a terrorist induced 'crisis of consent', a 'legitimacy crisis' or crisis of 'provoked authority' due to the U.S. government's perceived inability to fulfill its first duty — the physical security of citizens.

D3: Destroying Vital Infrastructure — Notably Water Infrastructure

Since the 2001 terrorist attacks, the FBI has identified and interviewed Al Qaeda supporters who planned attacks against U.S. water supplies and plans. The potential attacks against Hoover and TVA Dams, as scouted by Mohammed Atta, if successful, would potentially be catastrophic.

D4: Deterring Retaliation against Planned Attacks

Retaliation, if possible, against a 'shock attack' would be complicated by the problem of identifying the location due to Al Qaeda's and other terrorist groups mastery of technological deception.

The "Katrina Effect"

The cascading attack on water infrastructure would disrupt and in some cases destroy key storage and distribution nodes. The chaotic consequences would ensure that the U.S. would not immediately respond to a spectacular Al Qaeda attack as government priorities would be diverted to terrorist induced socio-economic dislocation, a form of Al Qaeda induced Hurricane Katrina. Simultaneous co-coordinated attacks on targets across the U.S. would complicate the attack picture.

There are over 5,700 facilities and structures vital to American national security and economic well being. A terrorist attack against a single vulnerable high-value infrastructure target of over five and a half thousand key nodes of U.S. vital infrastructure would exhibit many of the characteristics and consequences of a natural disaster, including social dislocation, disorientation and panic, widespread

anomie[373] and social disorganization, threats to public order, public health crises and possible epidemics.[374]

Complex societies are dependent on the water infrastructure to ensure the availability of clean water for day-to- day living, the provision of essential public health services and, above all, social order and government continuity under attack — a vulnerability that Al Qaeda has studied and combined within the context of psychological and economic warfare. A 'black swan' terrorist attack would be amplified by celebratory video footage and audio clips on the estimated 5000 — 7000 identified global jihadist web sites as was observed with the 9/11 attacks.[375]

Bin Laden's targets: The U.S. Economy and Psychological Warfare

In 2004, Bin laden boasted of the economic cost of the 9/11 attacks:

"Psychological shock 'depression' and psychological trauma ...Al Qaeda spent $500,000 on the September 11 attacks, while America lost more than $500 billion at the lowest estimate, in the event, and its aftermath. That makes a million American dollars for every Al-Qaeda dollar, by the grace of God Almighty. ..The mujahidin forced Bush to resort to an emergency budget...this shows the success of our plan to bleed America to the point of bankruptcy."[376]

On 21 October 2001, Usama bin laden boasted of the economic costs to the U.S.:

"The amount reaches no less than $1 trillion by the lowest estimate, due to these successful and blessed attacks. American studies and analysis and have mentioned that 70 percent of the American people are still suffering from depression and psychological trauma as a result of the

---

[373] Anonmie refers to the lack of the usual social or ethical standards in an individual or group; lack of norms.

[374] Ibid

[375] Ibid

[376] Y. Fouda, and Fielding, N., *Masterminds of Terror* (London: Penguin Books, 2003).

incident of the two towers and on the attack on the defence Ministry, the Pentagon."

Although Bin Laden's claim is overstated, it demonstrates that he was aware of the psychological effects of terrorist 'spectaculars'.[377]

AL Qaeda strategists

Al Qaeda strategists follow Bin Laden's strategic objective of economic warfare (jihad bil-mal) which dictates Al Qaeda targeting doctrine, especially in relation to targeting critical infrastructure. In the Al Qaeda magazine Mu Askar Battar claimed: "The goal is hitting more targets than one to create disruption in the stability needed for the moving the economic sector..."[378]

The terrorist Abu Mus'ab noted in 2003, ..."the destruction of its economy will cause the U.S. to disintegrate, collapse, and disappear ...therefore studying the America's economy is [even more crucial] than examining its military forces'.[379]

In 2005, an Islamic commentator noted in an article entitled "Al Qaeda's battle is an Economic battle] not a Military One." ....the primary goal of Al Qaeda's war against America is to defeat it economically. Anything that causes losses to its economy we regard as a victory. The 9/11 attacks was successful by every standard — the U.S. is still reeling from the economic impact...those who take interest in our battle against America ...will embrace this strategy without reservation..The important question is not how many infidels died in the attacks...but the effect they had on the American economy. [We can] shorten the duration of the battle by ...by focusing all our strength on military targets.'[380] Although economic defeat of the U.S. was a call forwarded by the late Usama Bin Laden, it now appears a rallying cry among all terrorist groups.

---

[377] Ibid

[378] G. Wolam, "War by Other Means," (Yale Global, 2009).

[379] E. Alshech, "The Battle Is Economic Rather Than Military-an Economically Oriented Concept of Jihad Emerges in Islamist Discourse, September 11 2007 (387," *An Economically Oriented Concept of Jihad Emerges in Islamist Discourse* 387(2007).

[380] Ibid

At the trial of former Canadian computer software developer, Momin Khawaja, it was revealed that he referred in a series of emails in 2003 specifically to economic [J]ihad:" We [need] [constant] economic [jihad] blow after blow until they cripple and never raise gain... Because of Sept. 11, the Airline industry is dead, travel and tourism is dead, [and] the U.S. dollar is dead. Trillions of dollars in lost revenue, thousands of businesses bankrupt and the negative impact continues till this day."[381] Would you say that the actions of the 19 men on September 11 are the most accurate, effective, and honorable way of conducting economic jihad? Imagine if there were 10 September 11's.

Al Qaeda Operational Interest in Water Terrorism

Shortly after the 9/11 attacks, the FBI assessed: ..."due to the vital importance of water to all life forms...the FBI considers all threats to attack the water as serious threats."[382] Captured Al Qaeda documents from Al Qaeda camps in Afghanistan and suspected terrorists in the U.S. reveal that Al Qaeda and jihadists have the intention and the capability to conduct terrorist attacks on water supplies and infrastructure.[383] In 2002, former U.S. President George Bush in his State of the Union address noted that captured Al Qaeda documents included detailed maps of several U.S. municipal drinking systems.[384] It is likely the goal to attack U.S. water infrastructure will not change despite Usama Bin Laden's death; instead, his demise will, rather than be a significant loss to Al Qaeda's operations, be a boon for recruitment. Ayman Muhammad Rabaie al-Zawahiri has already been

---

[381]Staff, "Emails Criticize 'West's Dominance," *Toronto Star*, September 1 2009.

[382] Terrorism: Are American Water Resources and Environment at Risk? Testimony R.L. Dick, Deputy Assistant Director Counter-terrorism Division NIPTC, October 2001.

[383] In 1996, an individual used a simple explosive device to destroy the master terminal of a hydroelectric Dam in Oregon. The structure was unaffected but the attack described by the FBI as 'simple' disabled the power generating turbines and forced a switch to manual control. the FBI summarized: A coordinated attack on a regions infrastructure systesm (e.g. the SCADA systems that control Washington DC electric power, natural gas and water supply, would have a profound effect in the nation's sense of security. This incident demonstrated how minimal sophistication and material can destroy a SCADA system. Testimoy of K. Lourdeau, Assistant Director, Cyber Division, FBI Congressional Testimony, February 2004.

[384] President George Bush, 2002 State of the Union Address.

named as the likely replacement for Bin Laden and, according to various sources, is far more dangerous than Bin Laden, having a long sinister history and joining the Muslim Brotherhood as early as age 14.[385] It would be foolish for security and intelligence officials to assume terrorist goals and potential attacks have receded.

U.S. Targets

Plot 1:

In 2002, Federal officials arrested two Al Qaeda terror suspects who carried documents relating to methods of poisoning American water supplies. Documents related to water poisoning were found at the residence of one of the suspects. The second arrest involved an individual who was accused of carrying documents concerned with the poisoning of water supplies. Both men were linked to a prominent London-based cleric, Sheikh Abu Hamza al-Masri, who was suspected of supplying the brothers with information concerning poisoning of water supplies.[386]

Plot 2:

In 2002, conceited terrorist Lyman Faris informed government investigators he was angered by the U.S. invasion of Afghanistan and proposed to two-co-conspirators (later sentenced) that they fly a plane into the Hoover Dam. The plot was terminated because the preferred operation was destruction of the New York City Suspension Bridge and derailment of trains in Washington D.C.

Plot 3:

From May-June 2001, an unidentified individual (later identified as having to ties to Al Qaeda) frequently attempted to obtain maps of the water-supply systems in Canton, Ohio. The FBI

---

[385] Assad Elepty, "Bin Laden's Replacement: Ayman Al-Zawahiri," *Pakistan Christian Post*(2011), http://www.pakistanchristianpost.com/viewarticles.php?editorialid=1272.

[386] Staff, "Terrorists Considered Poisoning Water Supplies,"(2004), http://www.uswaternews.com/archives/arcquality/4repoterr8.html.

was contacted after the 9/11 attacks and was informed that the individual often visited the library and requested detailed maps of Canton's water system and books relating to micro-biology and animal-borne diseases. He also sought maps of water lines running under Highway 77 to the Canton Mercy Medical center. The individual claimed he had been able to identify parasites in people that could not be identified by others.

The individual informed the librarian that his workplace was Case farms, a large Chicken poultry processing plant. Two of his co-workers, Karem Koubriti and Ahmned Hannan were arrested in Detroit on 17 September 2001 after false identification papers were found in their apartment. The apartment was previously occupied by senior Al Qaeda operative, Nabil Al-Marabh.

Plot 4:

In May 2009, a senior Al Qaeda member and the AQ training chief discussed the possibility of poisoning U.S. water supplies. The London-based weekly Arabic language newspaper Al-Majalla reported email correspondence between an Al Qaeda member and abu Mohammed al-Ablaj, reportedly a senior member of Al Qaeda.[387]

The Al Qaeda strategist Al-Ablaj did not rule out "the use of Sarin gas and the poisoning of drinking water in American and Western cities:[388] Also the forum member Al-Khilfalater posted links to a file-hosting website, mergaupload.com, which contained material on explosives and poison production manuals. Al-Khalahs offered a wide spectrum of chemical substances for attacks including cyanide, hydrochloric acid, anthrax, potassium cyanide, aniline hydrochloride, sodium nitrite, cobalt chloride, cobalt nitrate, and the most sinister, the most toxic compound — thallium.

Another forum member suggested a number of other poisonous gases that could be used in an attack, including chlorine gas, mustard gas, hydrogen cyanide, and nerve gas. He did not discuss delivery methods but claimed that poisonous gases were easy to prepare and requested other participants to speculate on developing distribution aerosol systems. Other participants posted

---

[387] ExpressIndia, "Qaeda Threatens to Poison Us Water Supplies,"(2003), http://www.expressindia.com/news/fullstory.php?newsid=21749.
[388] Ibid

photos of water pipelines, water towers, and diagrams demonstrating methods of inserting chemical substances into the target water system. A mechanical engineer suggested attacks were possible through valves or ventilation openings. A contributor, perhaps for taqiyya/deception purposes, claimed the attacks were forbidden by Islamic fiqh (jurisprudence), but the majority of the forums members dismissed his concerns and claimed such attacks were religiously sanctioned.

In 2002, the FBI's National Infrastructure Protection center issued a bulletin indicating that Al Qaeda were attempting to gain remote control of American water supplies and wastewater plants. The Bulletin read: "U.S. law enforcement and intelligence agencies have received indications that Al Qaeda members have sought information on multiple SCADA-related Web sites. They specifically sought information on water supply and water management [in the U.S.] and abroad."[389]

In September 2008, a jihadist internet forum posted details of plots to use chemical and biological agents to contaminate water resources in Europe, Great Britain, and Denmark. The most prolific contributor, Baghdad al-Khilafa (a pseudonym), was responsible for over a thousand postings (mainly on weapons and explosives) and claimed the attacks were motivated by Denmark's mockery of the Prophet Mohamed, and the 'infidels' attack on Muslims in Iraq, Afghanistan, Morocco, Somalia, Eastern Turkistan, and Chechnya. The plan was to kill as many civilians as possible by contaminating the main water supplies of European capitals with chemical substances.[390]

Outline of the Proposed Water Attack Plot

The plot consisted of four stages:

---

[389] Kevin Poulsen, "Fbi Issues Water Supply Cyberterror Warning," *Security Focus*(2002), http://www.securityfocus.com/news/319.

[390] Staff, "Back Breaking Blow to Denmark, the Uk and the European Union,"(2008), www.al-ekhlasas.net.

Stage one:

Intelligence collection involving reconnaissance, casing facilities, and area familiarization and assessment of most suitable time for attack.

Stage two:

Distraction and diversion of security forces at the target facility with a "mock' or diversionary operation.

Stage three:

"A fair skinned blonde" would execute the attack and exit the country immediately after the operations.[391]

Stage four:

Terrorists would use highly poisonous chemicals to contaminate the target water supply.[392]

A forum member questioned the religious authorization of an attack, which would kill innocent men, women, and children, including Muslims living in Europe. This opposition infuriated the majority of forum members, who provided their interpretations of Quranic verses and various Hadiths to justify the killings, and continued to exchange information relating to the terrorist plan.

---

[391]"A fair skinned blonde" refers to Al Qaeda's increasing preference for indigenous radicalized westerners who have the natural cover provided by being a citizen of the target country. they are often converts to Islam and are attracted to spectacular attacks to prove their successful conversion to Islam, i.e., Al Qaeda. And, although many believe the death of Usama Bin Laden will bring a fairly quick end to this specific terrorist group, it should be noted that most terrorist groups share information and operational methods thus, this practice will likely continue.

[392]Abdul Hameed Bakier, "Jihadis Discuss Means of Poisoning the Water Supply of Denmark and Great Britain," *Terrorism Focus* 5, no. 32 (2008), http://www.jamestown.org/single/?no_cache=1&tx_ttnews[tt_news]=5147.

Al Qaeda's arsenal

1: Terrorists and Engineers

The threat profile to the U.S. water infrastructure is reconfigured as empirical and sociological investigations have verified that engineers are embedded in the senior ranks of Al Qaeda and other jihadist groups.[393]

The 9/11 terrorist attacks were the first case of coordinate attacks on iconic infrastructure, the White House, and a civilian population by members of the engineering profession using engineering methods and project management techniques. Engineers are central to Al Qaida's mission and are its key leaders, planners, conceptualizers, and strategists. A study conducted in 2009 by Oxford researchers found that engineers are three to four more times as likely to be present among violent Islamic groups in the Muslim world.[394]

The researchers ascertained that in 78 of 196 cases, engineers played key roles. This over representation of engineers applied to the 13 militant groups in the sample and to all 17 nationalities. Of 259 Islamic students in Western countries who had garnered attention for carrying or plotting attacks, mainly in European countries, nearly 60 percent were engineers. The probability of a Muslim engineer becoming a violent Islamist was calculated to be three to four times higher than among other graduates.[395]

2: Al Qaeda's Engineers

The founder of Al Qaeda and 9/11 attacks mastermind, Usama Bin Laden, earned a degree in civil engineering from King Abdul-Aziz University in 1979. Twenty five individuals were involved in the 9/11 attacks on Washington and New York. From those 25 individuals, eight were engineers; 15 of the remaining 25 were Saudis. There was one Saudi engineer. The lead hijacker, Mohammad Atta, was an

---

[393] D. Gambetta, and Hertog, S., "Can University Subjects Reveal Terrorists " *Making New Scientists* (2009).

[394] — — —, "Engineers of Jihad," *Sociology Working Papers*(2008), http://www.nuff.ox.ac.uk/users/gambetta/engineerspercent20ofpercent20jihad.pdf.

[395] Ibid.

architectural engineer and a member of the Engineers Syndicate, controlled by the Muslim Brotherhood at Cairo University.[396]

Khalid Sheikh Mohammed, advocate and planner of the 9/11 attacks, was a graduate of North Carolina Agricultural and Technical State University in North Carolina. Thirty per cent of the university's mechanical engineering students came from Middle Eastern countries, namely Saudi Arabia and Kuwait. In Mohammed's graduation class, nine of the 28 students were of Middle East descent.[397]

Ramzi Yousef, described as "the world's most dangerous terrorist" studied electrical engineering. In 1987, he travelled to Al Qaeda camps in Afghanistan and returned to the Glamorgan Institute of Higher Education in England and studied computer aided electrical engineering. He obtained a Higher Diploma in Electrical Engineering, and he was the lead conspirator in the first attack against the World Trade center in 1993. His accomplice was Nidalk Ayayd, a chemical engineer. Yousef is now serving a life sentence.

Abu Musab al-Sur, the leading Al Qaeda strategist until his capture by U.S. authorities in 2005, studied engineering at the University of Aleppo in Syria. In his publications, Al Sur openly advocated the use of WMDs against Western targets and conceptualized "leaderless resistance" — small decentralized jihadist cells or groups that operated independently of each other. He described Westerners as "bacteria epidemics and locusts which like bacteria could only be killed by insecticides and medicines."[398] Additionally, Al Takfir Wal Hijra was founded in 1969 by Shukri Mustafa, an agricultural engineer and former member of the Muslim brotherhood. Additionally, Muhammad Abd al-Salaam Faraj, a member of Al-Jihad, played a critical role in the assassination of Egyptian President Sadat.[399]

---

[396] Ibid

[397] Ibid

[398] Jim Lacey, *A Terrorist's Call to Global Jihad: Deciphering Abu Musab Al-Suri's Islamic Jihad Manifesto* (Tower Books, 2008).

[399] PWHCE, "Muhammad Abd-Al-Salam Faraj," (PWHCE, 2009).

Pakistan

Two of the three founders of Lashkar-e-Taiba (Army of the Pure), the world's most dangerous terrorist group, a Sunni group based in Pakistan, included Zafar Iqbal and Hafiz Mohamed Saeed. They were professors of engineering and technology at Lahore University of Engineering and Technology.[400]

India

In August 2008, the terrorists involved in serial bomb attacks in Ahmadabad included a mechanical engineer, an ITI diploma in electrical engineering, and an IT diploma in radio technology. [401]

Hamas

Yahya Abd-al-Latif Ayyash, the notorious bomb builder for the terrorist organization Hamas, is credited for developing suicide bombings and was trained in electrical engineering. He was given the nickname Al-Muhandis — "the Engineer." Ayyash graduated from Bir Zeit University in 1987 and received a Bachelor of Science in electrical engineering in 1991.[402] Also, the central leader of Hizb ut–Tahrir, Abu Rishtar, is a Jordan-based engineer.

South East Asia Terrorist engineers

Jemaah Islamiyah (JI), the bomb maker of the Al Qaeda linked Indonesian terrorist group, is assessed by regional security services as the most dangerous terrorist in South East Asia and has evaded detection for ten years. He became a jihadist while studying for his master's degree after joining a religious study [recruiting] group at the home of Wan Min bin Mat, a lecturer in project management in

---

[400] Reuters, "Let Founder Leads Prayers for Usama in Pakistan," *IBN Live World*(2011), http://ibnlive.in.com/news/let-founder-leads-prayers-for-Usama-in-pakistan/151134-2.html.

[401] Robin David, "They Are Engineering Jihad," *Times of India*(2008), http://articles.timesofindia.indiatimes.com/2008-08-22/ahmedabad/27891289_1_engineering-taufique-abdul-subhan-qureshi-alias.

[402] Ayyash was assinated January 5, 1996 by a bomb laden cell phone containing 15 grams (about 1/2 ounce) of RDX explosives.

the faculty of science and engineering at the University of Technology, Malaysia, in Johor.

The Master bomb maker of the 2004 and 2005 Bali bombings, Azahari Husin, was also trained as an engineer.[403] JI has actively recruited from Indonesia's leading institutes, including the University of Technology of Malaysia, Universities Semarang, and Bandung University of Technology.[404] Zulkifli bib-Hir, Malaysian born, was trained in engineering in the United States; he was involved in multiple bomb attacks in the Philippines.[405]

The personality traits of engineers make them 'excellent planners and field operatives'; they also think in terms of systems, risk management, and networks and as a result, are thorough and meticulous. Many engineers are discrete concerning their professional work and can quickly develop skills in clandestine communications. They have specialized knowledge for accurate targeting based on engineering criteria (structural weakness and vulnerabilities) to inflict maximum damage.

In 2005, a British intelligence assessment claimed 'a network of extremist recruiters' was circulating on British university campuses targeting people with technical and professional qualifications, particularly engineering and IT degrees.[406]

Computer and IT specialists

Computer and IT specialists figure prominently in Islamic terrorist organizations. The vulnerability and centrality of computer systems in the U.S. water infrastructure raises the threat of embedded terrorists or moles in key water infrastructure, notably major dams.

---

[403] Raymond Bonner, "The Choreography of a Terrorist Strike - Asia - Pacific - International Herald Tribune," *Asia - Pacific - International Herald Tribune, Global Edition of the New York Times*(2006), http://www.nytimes.com/2006/07/03/world/asia/03iht-bali.2105058.html?scp=8&sq=azaharipercent20husinpercent20bomber&st=cse.

[404] Zachary Abuza, *Political Islam and Violence in Indonesia*, ed. Summit Ganguly, Asian Security Studies (New York: Routledge, 2007).

[405] Staff, "Us Offers $5m for Terror Suspect " *BBC News Online*(2007), http://news.bbc.co.uk/2/hi/asia-pacific/6500783.stm.

[406] R. Winnett, and Leppard, D., "Leaked No 10 Dossier Reveals Al-Qaeda's British Recruits," *Times Online*(2005).

The Emergence of Technical Mujahidin

In 2006, jihadists issued a new form of terrorist counterintelligence, intended to neutralize monitoring and detection of jihadists and jihadist web sites by Western security services. The first edition of the 64 page electronic magazine Technical Mujahidin, published by al-Fagr Information Center, was forwarded to password protected jihadist forums on 28 November 2006. The edition was written under the direction of the Emir of Al Qaeda, Abu Hamza al-Muhajir. The Technical Mujahid contains articles of file concealment and protection and describes methods and software to ensure IT security. Links are provided to VMware virtual machine and key generators to unlock features.

Pretty Good Privacy (PGP) software is rejected as inadequate for security needs of the Mujahedeen. Jihad in the information sector is described as "a main pillar in the battle of Islam against the Crusaders and the polytheist belief." Advertisements for the Juba sniper video from the Islamic army in Iraq and promotion of its release on DVDs in Iraq are used as an example of electronic jihad.

For future issues the authors write, "My kind technical Mujahid brother, the magnitude of responsibility which is placed upon you is equal to what you know in the regard of information. Do not underestimate anything that you know: perhaps a small article that you write and publish can benefit one Mujahid in the Cause of Allah or can protect a brother of yours in Allah. This way you will gain the great reward with permission of Allah.[407]"

Second Issue-Technical Jihad

The second issue of Technical Mujahid published in Arabic contains 72 pages focusing on psychological operations, weapon systems, and concealment techniques. The magazine is organized into six sections of technical training.

---

[407] A parallel Arabic-English translation was published on 29 November 2006. WorldAnalysis.net Aug 24, 2009. See also Dancho Danchev – Analysis of the Technical Mujahid, Issue One, December 11 2006. 'Mind Streams of Information Security Knowledge'. See also MEMRI, Special Dispatch – No 1375, December 1, 2006, 'Islamist Websites Monitor No. 29'

The first section is a brief history of encryption from secret ink and Morse code, to binary symmetrical encryption keys (256 bit and Ultra strong Symmetric Encryption) and encryption algorithms using the best five in cryptography (AES finalist algorithms) software. Great detail is provided about symmetrical encryption keys of 256-bit (Ultra Strong Symmetric Encryption), encryption keys for symmetric length of 2048-bit RSA [(leader in public/private key encryption)], Pressure data ROM (the highest levels of pressure), keys and encryption algorithms [for converting ciphertext into passable human text] (Stealthy Cipher), and automatic [encryption algorithmic identification] during decoding (Cipher Auto-detection).

Additional components covered in the newsletter include multicast encrypted via text messages supporting the immediate use [of] forums (Secure Messaging), transfer files of all kinds to be shared across text forums (Files to Text Encoding), production of digital signature files and ensuring correctness, and digital signature of messages and files [to guarantee the authenticity of messages and files]. The chase for technology among these groups to gain the necessary knowledge to defeat cyber systems and gain access or control of SCADA and other operational systems, such as ICS, may only be surpassed by that of the U.S. Department of Defense. Some security experts have implied that the efficacy of this [information] among Islamists and Arabic-speaking hackers could prove significant. These groups are determined, persistent, and relentless in their efforts — they should not be readily dismissed.

Concealment Science

The author notes perceptively..." the thing that scares the FBI the most is the use of secret communication techniques, by jihadists, known as "concealment science." The article describes steganography — the art of hidden messages and, steganalysis — the art of detecting hidden messages.

The merits of concealing data in "innocent images" is discussed, and includes image pixels, mathematical equations to prevent distortions in pictures which conceal data, and the disadvantages of openly available encryption which can be deciphered using hexadecimal editors.

The Mujahideen software application is a dual system that conceals encrypted data in a picture and compresses the files to counter steganalysis. The author advises jihadists to use multiple concealment techniques such as compression, encoding, concealment or communication — engineering techniques such as Spread Spectra

The second section deals with 'designing Jihad websites' and uploading websites to the internet via foreign web site host companies. Website development is important to the jihadists as the internet is used for communication across the "area of war" conflict and recruitment for jihad.

The third section, entitled 'Smart Weapons, Short Range Shoulder-Fired Missiles,' discusses and recommends two short-range shoulder-fired missiles for anti-aircraft attacks. Technical and operational specifications are authoritatively discussed and include illustrative examples. Counter measures against missiles are also included, as is a glossary of English- Arabic terms.

Mujahidin Secrets or Secrets of the Mujahedeen

Section 4 is called 'The Secrets of the Mujahedeen, an Inside Perspective'. Mujahidin Secrets is a computer program written by the security section of the Global Islamic media front and is described as the first Islamic encryption software. The section recommends creating Islamic encryption tools and covers five topics: encryption and correspondence through the Internet; encrypting personal emails; the degree of encryption (128 bit and asymmetric 1024 bit); encryption keys and public encryption keys; and passwords and private encryption and decryption keys.

The author claims the program provides the highest level of encryption in asymmetric encoding that provides secure transfer of public encryption keys. The keys that use "key prints" which identify the recipient can be safely advertised in jihadist forums. The encryption training program is reportedly highly technical and claims to be superior to all international encryption systems.

Sections 5 and 6, 'Video Technology and Subtitling Video Clips,' illustrates Al Qaeda use of video recording of target sites and has been well documented, notably prior to the 9/11 attacks. The section refers to signal reception, sample rates and vertical video

samples, and how to dub video clips with subtitles and background voiceovers. The writer of the section stresses the importance of translating jihadist propaganda into as many foreign languages as possible.

The editor concludes with the exhortation: "My technical jihad brother, this magazine gives you the opportunity to share whatever scientific knowledge you have with thousands of jihadis frequenting the Islamic forums..."

In brief summary, the mastery of technical detail and more significantly, the operational use of clandestine sophisticated cyber warfare evident in the web sites could be used with great effectiveness against key water infrastructure, which is dependent on computer aided systems (SCADA) and against water infrastructure and dams (see chapter 12 for more details regarding SCADA and other computer aided issues).

On January 1, 2007, the Global Islamic Media Front (GIMF) announced the imminent release of new computer software called "Mujahedeen Secrets." It is "the first Islamic computer program for secure exchange [of information] on the Internet," and provides users with "the five best encryption algorithms, and with the symmetrical encryption keys (256 bit), asymmetrical encryption keys (2048 bit) and data compression [tools]." This will further extend jihadist Internet deception capabilities.

Mujahedeen Secrets is free, password protected, written in Arabic, and does not use cookies. The program runs from either Flash drive or PC and is robust. The press announcement claims Mujahedeen Secrets "Is the first program of the Islamic multicast security across networks. It represents the highest level of technical multicast encrypted but far superior. All communications software, which are manufactured by major companies in the world so that it integrates all services communications encrypted in a small-sized portable. Release 1 of the 'secrets of the mujahedeen' the bulletin brothers in the International Islamic Front and the media have registered qualitatively in the field of information and jihadist exploit the opportunity to thank them for their "wonderful and distinctive ...And the continuing support of a media jihadist group loyalty in the technical development of a network of Islamic loyalty program and the

issuance of this version, in support of the mujahedeen general and the Islamic State of Iraq in particular."

Mujahedeen Secrets is described as "the first Islamic program for secure communications through networks with the highest technical level of encoding."[408] Mujahedeen Secrets 2 was released in February 2008 with the added ability to encrypt chat communications. The encryption software is based on open source RSA code and can encrypt binary files which can be posted on ASCII-text-based bulletin boards and Web sites.

The TVA Dams

Al Qaeda has demonstrated operational interest in the TVA Dams as well as the Douglas and Norris TVA Dams area. An IED placed on a recognized "vulnerability line" would cause both structures to collapse and sweep away smaller dams. Approximately 2.1 million acre-feet of water would cascade into the Tennessee valley. Two other dams and two nuclear plants would be flooded and debris pours from reservoirs would flood and devastate surrounding areas with mass morbidity and mortality.[409] Researchers have also investigated the travel of 9/11 lead terrorist Mohammad Atta from Las Vegas to the Hoover Dam, Boulder City, when he was in the Las Vegas area between 06/28/2001 to 07/01/2001 and 07/01 to 02/24/2001.[410]

The social and public health disorientation caused by the contamination crises in Milwaukee (1993) and Ohio (2000) would be multiplied by a spectacular and successful terrorist contamination attack, conceived clandestinely. The terrorist could use steganography and encrypted communications to evade counter measures and neutralize SCADA systems.

Some experts could argue that these techniques and tactics of evading law enforcement and intelligence did not work for Usama Bin Laden. However, he was on the run for over a decade and

---

[408] Reuters January 18, 2008 'Jihadi software promises secure Web contacts'

[409] Congressional Staff, *9/11 and Terrorist Travel: A Staff Report of the National Commission on Terrorist Attacks Upon the United States* (Franklin: Hillsboro Press, 2004).

[410] Tamm, "Hoover Dam, Boulder City, Nevada, Mileage Review: Las Vegas, Nevada."

although he finally met his end, what was the cost? In his own words, his goal was to "Bleed America to the point of bankruptcy." The hunt for OBL led the U.S. along this path despite OBL's later years of being tactically and strategically irrelevant to the terrorist movement other than as a figure head. Others have already taken up the mantle of leadership.

The Critical Role of Counterintelligence (CI)

Internal counterintelligence programs are essential to counter a wide spectrum of insider threats ranging from targeted terrorist moles within the target infrastructure to employees, contractors, and sub-contractors who may have direct or indirect affiliations to foreign intelligence services or terrorist patron states, and individuals with untraceable or unverifiable familial tribal ethnic connections to pro-terrorist groups, organizations, or regimes. Key personnel with access to critical sensitive and compartmentalized information should be subject to background vetting, dependant on their access to critical facilities.

The Insider C/I Threat

The Abdi Case

A paradigm CI failure occurred in May 2009; a California Water Service Company (CWSC) employed Abdirahman Ismael Abdi who was not a US citizen. He had been ordered in absentia to be deported to Somalia on 15 May 2005. He was holding a British passport and working on a fraudulent H1B visa. He was subsequently employed as an auditor at CWSC in San Jose, California.[411]

On 27 April 2009 he resigned from the CWSC and on that evening he used his electronic key card to gain access to the secure electronic gate at the CWSC parking lot then used the computers of two CWSC employees to send over $9 million dollars to three separate accounts in Qatar and fled. On April 28 he arranged for his

[411] Staff, "California Water Company Insider Steals $9 Million, Flees Country," *SC Magazine*(2009), http://www.zimbio.com/SC+Magazine/articles/594/California+water+company+insider+steals+9.

wife and two children to travel to Frankfurt, Germany. Abdi attempted to book a flight to London on 1 May 2009. [412] He then attempted to deposit a stolen check from CWSC (approximately $25,000) into his personal account at the bank of America. On 6 May, a no bail arrest warrant was authorized by the Superior Court of the Santa Clara, California. Abdi fled to Canada on May 5; he was later arrested in England.[413]

Terrorists and Counterintelligence

Al Qaeda is the primary counterintelligence threat to the United States. "...We should not underestimate the skill of our enemies and their determination to conceal their activities and deceive us. They understand how we collect intelligence, how we are organized, and how we analyze information. Just like them, our intelligence services must constantly adapt and innovate. Thus, we have aggressive efforts underway to find new ways to discern terrorist "signals" from the background "noise" of society, but we must also recognize that enemies will deliberately create "noise" in the system in order to conceal the real signals."[414]

Al Qaeda, as most other terrorist groups, is a secret organization; still, its adherents boast openly of their intention to destroy the United States. Khalid Sheikh Mohammed, the architect of the 9/11 attacks, bragged, "This is what we do for a living." If terrorism is to throw terror into the heart of your enemy and the enemy of Allah then we thank Him, the most merciful, and the most compassionate for enabling us to be terrorists. It is in the Quran.

The five key 9/11 terrorists rejected the U.S. government's accusation of conspiracy.

"...Were you expecting us to inform you about our secret attack plans? Your intelligence apparatus, with all its abilities, human and logistical, had failed to discover our military attack plans before the blessed 11 September operation. They were unable to foil our attack. We ask, why

---

[412] Ibid

[413] Ibid

[414] Paul Wolfowitz, "Prepared Testimony of Deputy Secretary of Defense Paul Wolfowitz for the Senate Select Committee on Intelligence and the House Permanent Select committee on Intelligence: Joint Inquiry Hearing on Counterterrorist Center Customer Perspective," September 2002.

then should you blame us, holding us accountable and putting us on trial? Blame yourselves and your failed intelligence apparatus and hold them accountable, not us."

."... We were exercising caution and secrecy in our war against you. This is a natural matter, where God has taught us in his book, verse 71 from An-Nisa: ((O you believers! Take your precautions, and either go forth (on an expedition) in parties, or go forth together.)) Also, as the prophet has stated: "War is to deceive.""'

"Our prophet was victorious because of fear. At a month distant, the enemy did not hear from him. So, our religion is a religion of fear and terror to the enemies of God: the Jews, Christians, and pagans. With God's willing, we are terrorists to the bone. So, many thanks to God. The Arab poet, Abu-Ubaydah Al-Hadrami, has stated, "We will terrorize you, as long as we live with swords, fire, and airplanes."

Conclusions

As early as 1996, Usama bin Laden referred to the relation between Al Qaeda's concept of asymmetric warfare and the need for conspiracy. "Due to the imbalance of power between our armed forces and the enemy forces, a suitable means of fighting must be adopted, i.e. using fast-moving light forces that work under complete secrecy."[415]

The formation of the DHS counterintelligence unit in September 2003 was a significant counter measure.[416] As the Director pointed out, "America is vulnerable to adversaries who seek information about our nation's Homeland Defense programs, classified or unclassified. Counterintelligence can neutralize the communications of adversaries, monitor intensions and capabilities, monitor foreign travel, and report 'any real or possible contacts with foreign intelligence services

[415] Usama Bin Laden, "A Declaration of War against the Americans occupying the Land of the Two Holy Places": A message from Osame Bin Laden to his Muslim brethren all over the world generally, and toward the Muslims of the Arabian Peninsula in particular.
[416] Government Security, "New Dhs Counterintelligence Unit Fights Foreign Threats,"(2008), http://business.highbeam.com/437480/article-1G1-184460545/new-dhs-counterintelligence-unit-fights-foreign-threats.

or terrorists. Criteria have been established to alert sensitive employees to requests for classified and sensitive information or access to systems, responding to request to bring back an envelope or packages sent from foreign countries.[417]

However, a successful pro-active aggressive counterintelligence program against Al Qaeda and other terrorist group's threats to U.S. water and related infrastructure requires a coordinated collection platform between government agencies. The FBI manages background investigations for persons who apply for positions in the Department of Energy and the Nuclear Regulatory Agency. The FBI is the lead counterintelligence agency and is involved in international terrorism threats and attacks on the national critical infrastructures. FBI background checks are essential to ensure the U.S. water infrastructure has a defensive counterintelligence shield.

Friendly and liaison agencies should be tasked to identify, neutralize, interdict, and capture Al Qaeda operatives who demonstrate any degree of operational interest in attacks on U.S. infrastructure targets. Collection platforms and programs should prioritize attacks on U.S. water and related infrastructure and offer reward programs for vital information concerning prospective threats.

Al Qaeda is dedicated to counterintelligence which is essential to its survival and operational objectives. In June 2009, a Jihadist website posted a lengthy treatise, "Guidance on the Ruling of the Muslim Spy." The book included a forward by Ayman Al-Zawahiri, Al Qaeda's second in command, who described it as "valuable, serious, scientific and practical research on the Islamic judgment of spying."[418] Al Qaeda documents underscore that Al Qaeda agents and assets (witting and unwitting) will perform a vital operational role in its threatened spectacular attacks against the continental United States and its water infrastructure.

Although many threats are a form of nerve warfare and taqiyya (deception), Al Qaeda has four operational advantages: (1) technical and human assets in the form of "home grown" jihadists; (2) secure human and technical clandestine communications; (3)

---

[417] Ibid

[418] Ayman Al-Zawahiri, "Guidance on the Ruling of the Muslim Spy," (2009).

clandestine assets in Islamic Diasporas; and (4) the ability of its engineering elite to inflict a single spectacular attack on water infrastructure, which could wreak massive damage to U.S. social cohesion and economy.

The history of successful terrorist attacks can be summarized in two words — "too late." After the 9/11 attacks and Al Qaeda's history of attempts to obtain WMDs, the issuing of fatwas, which provide religious sanction for the U.S. of WMDs against the U.S., the sophistication of Al Qaeda technology and the critical role of its engineering operatives and the emergence of home grown jihadism, the U.S. cannot afford to be too late — again.

Jihadist adversaries have a clear and stated strategic objective — the destruction of the U.S. economy and infrastructure, particularly water, which is the foundation of life and the engine that creates economic sustainability. There may be too many victims of such an attack or attacks to look back in hindsight — hindsight is not 'wonderful'; it is recognition of defeat and the flight of the black swan of terrorist planned devastation.[419]

[419] Nassim Taleb, *The Black Swan: The Impact of the Highly Improbable* (New York: Random House, 2007).

CHAPTER 11: Environmental Terrorism: Jihad and Eco-Forest Fires

Executive Summary

Wildfires can cause major disruptions of the water supply to a city due to debris flow and other processes and therefore play a major role in water security. The major post-fire pathways for the transport of various constituents are mudslides and erosion — often termed debris flow. This flow carries nutrients down slope into streams and reservoirs to varying degree. The effects of wildfires should not be underestimated. In recent years a large number of fires have been anthropogenic (manmade), either intentionally or accidentally. Also, terrorists consider fire a strategy to achieve operational and economic objectives against their enemies. In early February 2009, the Victorian Bushfire disaster, now known as "Black Saturday," killed 210 people and was called "murder on a grand scale."

Approximately half of Australia's 20-30,000 annual bush fires are deliberately lit. Arson estimates for States vary, but the overall rate is high; the same is true in the U.S. and other countries. Few bushfire arsonists are identified due to destruction of evidence, lack of witnesses, and secrecy. They are 'loners'. Fewer are arrested, fewer convicted, and the most common sentence is generally less than two years; it is difficult to determine whether those who set fires and are caught are terrorists. Additionally, few arsonists confess unless confronted by incontrovertible evidence; they also lack remorse and rarely admit guilt.

Among the variety of arsonist types are urban arsonists, a homogenous group who act with a specific objective and rarely engage in 'expressive' or 'impulse driven' fires; terrorist arsonists, with generally ideological, religious, or political motivations; bushfire sociopaths, who do not have a concept of civil society and lack any concept of the social or the 'other'; and other types. Regardless of their type, these arsonists represent significant security risks to water supplies and security and to other critical infrastructure through wildfire arson. The effects of these type attacks are not just

immediate, but can continue long-term because of early spring debris-flow issues which further damage the environment and decrease water quality as reservoirs and streams fill with ash and other fire deposits. Additionally, timber exports can be affected as can pharmaceutical supplies since this industry relies on certain species of plants and trees for drug ingredients.

Large forest fires can retard air traffic and cause manpower shortages since even the military could be called upon to help extinguish a fire that is quick moving and large in scope — the latter is more likely in a war zone. The mere mention of fire increases stress in most people's psychological makeup; consequently, the mention of terrorist-caused fires could induce fear and panic dependent on fire size. And, it is very likely that arsonists, especially jihadists, are honing their techniques and capabilities for arson as a weapon. As engineers and chemists, terrorist arsonists are well aware of accelerants (not listed here due to security concerns) that can cause fire by absorbing oxygen from the air after a few minutes or, more conventional means such as road flares; tennis balls filled with home-made napalm, gasoline, kerosene, diesel fuel, other chemicals such as acids (sulfuric and others); and electronic devices for delayed ignition.

The effects of large wildfires can be catastrophic, costing millions of dollars in damage, destroying thousands of acres of land and the environment, and leaving lasting effects on the economy, agriculture, the environment, and other sectors. Wildfires can significantly affect water security through destruction and disruption of infrastructure, supply and distribution, rail and truck transportation, air traffic, power supply and transmission, and can cause public health and environmental hazards resulting in severe economic damage, loss of life, and loss of species. Additionally, timber exports and pharmaceutical supplies can be affected.

Although arson is easily detected, the arsonist is not. The terrorist arsonist acts upon inspiration, ideology, and revenge. They consider the setting of forest fires legal under extremist Islamic law as part of an "eye for an eye"; additionally, the act can produce "amazing results." The destruction of resources — water, infrastructure, forests, food supplies, etc. — has been practiced in war throughout world history. The psychological traits of terrorist arsonists — ease of escape, minimal penalties for the crime, and generally causing

minimal loss of life — make wildfire arson a weapon of choice, even though patience is required for the proper environmental conditions conducive to large fires. However, the cyclical nature of climate change would generally result in opportune time frames of only one to three years. Therefore, terrorist arsonists pose a particularly egregious threat since these groups prolifically study methods of destruction to the smallest detail. This could make wildfire arson a weapon of choice, especially for causing extensive economic damage and spreading fear and panic. It is much easier to start a fire than to build and IED, and panic from fire is much higher that threat from a bomb. To test the theory, simply yell 'fire' in a theatre — chaos and panic will immediately ensue.

Introduction

Wildfires can cause major disruptions of the water supply to a city due to debris flow and other processes and therefore play a major role in water security. This chapter will describe those basic processes, the terrorist arsonist, and related issues. The major post-fire pathways for the transport of various constituents are mudslides and erosion — often termed debris flow. This flow carries nutrients down slope into streams and reservoirs to varying degree. The flow can be small and fairly localized, causing mere turbidity and an increase in treatment costs such as more chlorine, or the flow can be substantial, clogging streams and reservoirs and resulting in huge economic and environmental loss and consequences. Temporary changes in water quality within a fire management area will very likely occur during watershed runoff events after a fire. In response, the water supply will incur additional near-term water treatment costs due to post-fire inputs of sediment, ash, and nutrients. Long-term, the nutrients previously locked in the vegetation will continue to enter the reservoir and streams as ash and sediment after storm events. Depending on the severity of the storms in the few years following a fire, the affected management area or watershed may be able to recover sufficiently to prevent nutrient loading to the reservoir. Increased algae blooms including odor and taste concerns may also be an issue for at least five to ten years following a fire. The effects of wildfires, whether on grasslands, steep slopes, or

mountainous terrains on water quality and supply should not be underestimated. In recent years a large number of fires have been anthropogenic, either intentionally or accidentally. Also, terrorists now consider fire as a strategy to achieve operational and economic objectives against their enemies.

'The reality of the bushfire arsonist is the normal person's nightmare; the normal person's reality is the nightmare of the bush arsonists'.

In early February 2009, Prime Minister Kevin Rudd addressed parliament on the Victorian Bushfire disaster now known as "Black Saturday", in which 210 people died. He concluded: "the nation now must attend to, as a matter of grave urgency, the problem of arson." This is simply murder on a grand scale."[420]

This chapter examines the psychological dimensions of the bushfire arsonist and the effects of fire on water supply.

Bushfire arsonists

Australia is an arsonist's playground. Approximately half of Australia's 20-30,000 bush fires are deliberately lit. Arson estimates for States are varying but the overall rate is high.[421] [422] Few bushfire arsonists are identified due to destruction of evidence, lack of witnesses, and secrecy. They are 'loners'. Few are arrested, fewer convicted, and the most common sentence is usually less than two years, and it is difficult to determine whether those who set fires and are caught are terrorists. Additionally, few arsonists confess unless confronted by incontrovertible evidence; they also lack remorse and rarely admit guilt.

Psychologists, criminologists, and a spectrum of experts propose a mosaic of theories. The judicial system struggles with the question of mens rea (intention) and motive: "Why do they do it? And why do they continue?" Rebekah Doley, Australia's leading arson fire

---

[420] Transcript of speech in House of Representatives, 11 February 2009.

[421] C. Bryant, "Deliberately Lit Vegetation Fires in Australia," *Trends & issues in crime and criminal justice no. 350* 350(2008).

[422] D. Muller, "Patterns in Bushfire Arson," *Bushfire Arson Bulletin*, no. 58 (2009), http://www.aic.gov.au/documents/E/9/3/percent7be93e0523-a159-4ba9-9109-6fd579d9d4bbpercent7dbfab058.pdf.

researcher, pioneered the study of bushfire arsonists: 'we are beginning to find out more about bushfire arsonists ...we have a long way to go towards understanding exactly who they are.'[423]

Urban arsonists

Urban arsonists form a group distinct from bushfire arsonists. They are a homogenous group who act with a specific objective and rarely engage in 'expressive' or 'impulse driven' fires. Juvenile arsonists may be thrill seeking or reacting to peer-group pressure. They have specific targets, which are predominantly instrumental — the destruction of a specific object for a specific purpose such as destruction of a school, insurance fraud, or revenge against authority figures and institutions. Many are motivated by financial gain and targeted or diffuse revenge. The incidence of severe psychopathology is low; they do not seek to inflict massive or catastrophic damage on entire communities. Urban arsonists are more easily detected by forensic evidence. Generalizations derived from urban arson studies cannot be applied to bushfire arsonists.

Terrorist Arsonists

This group of arsonists is difficult to categorize because their motives are much different than those of other arsonists. Generally, they are ideological, religious, or politically motivated; included in this group would be ecosystem or environmental and animal rights activists. They are belief-driven, with specific objectives such as economic damage, media attention, and so forth, using arson, specifically wildfires, as a means to an end. They can be revenge motivated against non-Muslim/Islamic groups or countries, especially the U.S. and its allies, have a committed mind set, and engage in wildfire arson to inflict maximum damage on a target to increase psychological fear among a populace and government. They have specific targets with a desire to cause not only immediate damage, but a series of cascading events and disruption to supply and

[423] C. Johnston, "Inside the Mind of a Firebug," *The Age*(2009), http://www.theage.com.au/news/in-depth/inside-the-mind-of-a-firebug/2006/12/15/1166162313927.html.

distribution that will be ongoing for the short term and cause even more damage while spreading fear and panic. The terrorist arsonist is not motivated by financial gain, but rather committed to their belief in Islam — radical Islam. Their goal is to inflict maximum damage with minimal effort. They are also the group or individual less likely to be caught. If they are caught, the penalties for wildfire arson are minimal compared to IEDs and other type attacks. These minimal penalties are acceptable.

The bush fire arsonist: psychological characteristics

The bushfire arsonist has a 'will to power' and pervasive sense of inexpressible resentment against all others. Lacking power, authority, status, social acceptance, and self esteem their compensatory will to power is expressed by arson. Psychological classification and diagnostic criteria include:[424]

DSM IV classifications[425]

Cluster A:

- **Paranoid and schizotypal personality disorders.**

Cluster B:

- **Primarily anti-social personality disorder (malignant narcissism) and borderline personality disorders.**

Diagnostic criteria:

1. **Chronic sense of emptiness.**
2. **Alexthymic - unable to communicate feelings through language. The phenomenological world of the bushfire**

[424] et al. Cameron, "Black Saturday: The Immediate Impact of the February 2009 Bushfires in Victoria, Australia," *Medical Journal of Australia* 191, no. 6 (2009).

[425] The Diagnostic and Statistical Manual of Mental Disorders (DSM) is the standard classification of mental disorders used by mental health professionals in the U.S. It is intended to be applicable in a wide array of contexts and used by clinicians and researchers of many different orientations (e.g., biological, psychodynamic, cognitive, behavioral, interpersonal, family/systems). Disorders follow an axis scale of I to V-referring to clinical disorders, personality disorders, general medical conditions, psychosocial and environmental problems, and global assessment of functioning scale respectively.

arsonist is rarely revealed as they lack communication and language skills.

3. Anhedonic - pleasure is not derived from loving relationships with family, partners, friends and asocial affiliations but with fire-related sensations.
4. Disorganized attachment patterns in childhood, lack of parental containment and boundary setting.
5. Failures of personal and identity integration, notably in relation to shyness, perceived inferiority accompanied by aggressive feelings.
6. Feelings of abandonment, real and imagined.
7. Inability to cope with frustration and aggression.
8. A spectrum of disabilities, including low cognitive skills, poor locus of control, poor impulse control, super ego pathology, lack of remorse or guilt.
9. A history of abuse, paternal or maternal loss, limited parental care and monitoring; parental disorders including depression, alcohol and drug abuse.
10. Poor psycho sexual integration and history of failed or disruptive relationships which may trigger fire setting as 'acting out' or revenge fantasies against loss of real or imagined significant other.
11. History of peer rejection and subsequent suppressed aggression; abreaction concerning feelings of inadequacy, relationship loss, or separation.

Generally, excepting terrorist arsonists, these are the types of people most likely to fall through societal cracks unnoticed, but who can cause catastrophic events and damage that can be long term. The Hayman fire and additional case studies discussed below and threats to water security discussed previously serve as examples. Setting a wildfire could exact an inexorable amount of revenge.

The Bushfire Sociopath

Bushfire sociopaths are the most potent type of arsonists as they do not have a concept of civil society and lack any concept of the social or the 'other'. They symbolize rejection of the 'civilizing

processes — the domestication of fire for the purpose of creating and maintaining civilization.'[426] [427] They are most commonly recidivists and specialize in setting catastrophic bushfires. They are power seekers who define social relations in terms of power gradients. Their power seeking through arson is a function of their psychopathology.[428] Communal and affective ties are paths to power and lighting catastrophic fires gives them the feeling of omnipotence over others; total power over life and death. General characteristics for this type arsonist are detailed in Table 11.1. Could the bushfire sociopaths be considered terrorists? Certainly terrorists will use wildfire arson to achieve their objectives. U.S. officials monitoring terrorist web sites discovered a call for using forest fires as weapons against "crusader" nations, which may explain some recent wildfires in places like southern California and Greece.[429]

The Malignant Narcissistic Arsonist

The term 'malignant narcissist' refers to a syndrome of narcissistic personality, paranoid and anti social tendencies and ego syntonic aggression (aggression consistent or harmonious with the total personality).[430] [431] The malignant narcissist is a rare type of arsonist with a more complex psychopathology — a triad of disorders. Their narcissism is reflected in a sense of pathological entitlement and the belief they are not subject to conventional restraints on behavior. They tend to be pathologically grandiose with

---

[426] J. Goldsbloom, "The Domestication of Fire as a Civilising Process, Theory Culture and Society," *SAGE* 4(1987).
[427] — — —, "The Civilising Process and the Domestication of Fire " *Journal of World History* 3, no. 1 (1992).
[428] J. The Psychology of Wickedness: Psychopathy and Sadism (Reid Meloy, Psychiatric Annals 27:9 September 1997 630-633), "The Psychology of Wickedness: Psychopathy and Sadism," *Psychiatric Annals* 27, no. 9 (1997).
[429] Staff, "U.S. Intel Alerted to Threat of 'Forest Fire Jihad'," *World Tribune*(2008), http://www.nationalterroralert.com/2008/01/15/forest-fire-jihad-being-threatened-on-terrorist-websites/.
[430] O. Kernberg, *Severe Personality Disorders: Psychotherapeutic Strategies* (London: Yale University Press, 1984).
[431] — — —, *Borderline Conditions and Pathological Narcissism* (New York: Aronson, 1975).

marked super ego pathology (lack of conscience), poor locus of internal (self control), and characteristic demonstrations of joyful cruelty and sadism.[432]

Table 11.1: Psychological Characteristics of the Bushfire Sociopath.

Deceitfulness, reckless disregard for safety of others.
Consistent irresponsibility in occupational roles.
Lack of remorse and indifference to or rationalization for hurting mistreating others; inability to 'metalize' to conceive of others acting as a separate individual; with a separate mind; chronic emotional detachment and absence of consequential thinking.
Dominated by primary process thinking and the pleasure principle at an infantile and regressed level but capable of manipulation and deception to avoid detection.
Alexthymia, a condition of impaired cognition and affect and inability to express their feelings and thoughts in language is evident in their 'confessions'. Poverty of affect and thought and concrete thinking reflect their incapacity to symbolize or emphasize with human suffering.
Emotional life is dominated by negative feelings: boredom, contempt and devaluation of others, exhilaration and pleasure through dominance.
Framed by early manifestations of psychopathology, including cruelty to animals and fascination with fire.
Early signs of conduct disorder, persistent oppositional disorder, poor task completion, and in teenage years, illicit drug use and anti social conduct and contact with law enforcement.
May have obsession with fetishized sexual objects and collect pornography; fire setting maybe part of a paraphilia; sexual dysfunction and impotence. Fantasized mastery achieved by fire-setting.
Inability to maintain relationships involving trust, love, reciprocity. Tends to be misogynist with unresolved Oedipal conflict and enmeshment with mother.
Fears and resents dependence and loss of an imagined loved object can initiate explosive rage in terms of fire setting.
Recognized in local community as 'loners' and 'weirdo's, with no web of social affiliations.
Fire is the compensatory and primary interest in their life.

[432] G.H. (Pollock, "Process and Affect," *International Journal of Psychoanalysis* 59(1978).

The malignant narcissists, rage, as expressed in fire setting, may be a reaction to a narcissistic injury. Compensatory revenge fantasies against imaginary persecutors, past, present, and future may erupt into narcissistic rage, which finds expression in arson. They may engage in fire setting in multiple locations to challenge and 'outwit' police and bushfire authorities and play a deadly 'game' in which each fire is regarded as a 'victory'. If arrested, they present as insouciant and indifferent as they believe that they are wrongly accused and misunderstood and that the authorities do not have the necessary knowledge or skills to charge them. They rarely confess and feel no remorse or guilt; their psychological characteristics are listed in Table 11.2. This clearly reflects psychology, which Usama Bin Laden was well aware of and practiced. Based on intelligence reports, it must be assumed that wildfire arson has been added to the terrorist groups' techniques and methodologies list.[433]

They enjoy the 'high' of risk-taking and fire-setting and in some cases, their fire- setting is a paradoxical form of paranoia — a form of preemptive attack on fantasized persecutors. Many seek to neutralize their aggressive drives by using fire setting as a form of ego-syntonic behavior to deflect or neutralize potentially overwhelming aggressive feelings. They often hoard 'souvenirs' of fires and maintain media records, videos or press cuttings, which are a form of narcissistic supply and assist them in revisiting their victims' suffering. Their grandiosity extends to the delusional belief that they will never be identified.

The 'Pseudo Volunteer Firefighter' Arsonist

Pseudo volunteer firefighter arsonists are inadequate across many domains: employment, education, status, relationships and, above all, self esteem. They tend to be serial offenders and set fires in multiple areas. They are subject to compensatory fantasies that they are 'model firefighters. The theme of rejection, in all of its manifestations, sets the frame for revenge.

Their record of fire spotting, early warnings, revelry in fire, and over commitment arouses their colleagues' suspicion and they may

---

[433] Staff, "U.S. Intel Alerted to Threat of 'Forest Fire Jihad'."

move to another location where they join another volunteer fire service and set multiple fires. The only way they can achieve the heroic status they desperately seek is by setting fires. They are often the first on the fire scene, where they play their favored role — the hero. Their unique psychological characteristics are listed in Table 11.3.

Table 11.2: Psychological Characteristics of the Narcissistic Arsonist.

Derives ecstatic and euphoric feelings observing the effects of the fire and its destabilizing effects and induce feelings of 'liveliness' from fire setting, observing and attending fire scenes.
Sets fires during days of declared fire danger due to high winds, low humidity, high air temperatures and tinder box conditions, which ensure spread of fires and extend the scope of the fire.
Fire setting is a means of relief from overwhelming affect or 'flooding'.
Low educational standards and levels of literacy.
Few hobbies and prone to chronic levels of 'boredom'; low frustration tolerance.
Motivation is affective and rarely for financial gain.
Inability to symbolize and 'concrete thinking'.
Displacement of affect in which fire setting can be used as a substitute 'punishment 'against a target which is unrelated to the fire but may act as a 'trigger' and weaken impulse control.

A single volunteer arsonist can set many fires, as they have 'natural cover' for their activities. The high incidence of volunteer firefighters arrested on suspicion of arson throughout 2009 and the number of arrests of fire fighting arsonists over the past decade is disturbing, as it de-authorizes the volunteer fire fighters, who are intrinsically motivated and genuinely heroic. The volunteer arsonist is also motivated by envy — the volunteer brigade has local community acceptance and status, which the volunteer arsonist lacks, and is the 'good object', which the arsonist cannot tolerate. The pseudo volunteer firefighter must destroy the goodness he fears is located in the volunteer brigade and which he lacks, by arson.

Table 11.3: Psychological Characteristics of the 'Pseudo volunteer Firefighter' Arsonist.

Craves hero status.
Closer identification with father than mother; father may be a firefighter regarded as a 'hero'.
Driven by personal and professional underachievement and feelings of entitlement.
Predominantly male.
Lacks stable interpersonal relationships.
Interested in fire service to the extent that it serves need for excitement, average to above average intelligence but poor academic performance.
Does not have a defined career path or interests other than 'being a firefighter' and using volunteer status to become a community or public hero.
Poor occupational record, menial or unskilled labor.
Uses sophisticated fire setting techniques and materials and prepared to travel to join volunteer services.
Derives power from assuming lead role in fire setting, warning authorities and investigating fires.
Engages in high risk fire setting and engenders a suspicion by accurate forecasting of fires, claiming pin point accuracy of fires and guiding officers to the fire scene, which leads to their exposure as arsonists.
Appears over-committed and assume the role of professional rather than volunteer firefighters. (Firefighter Arson Special Report, FEMA USFA –TR-141 January 2003)

The Terrorist Arsonist

The terrorist arsonist acts upon inspiration, ideology, and revenge. They consider the setting of forest fires legal under extremist Islamic law as part of an "eye for an eye"; additionally, the act can produce "amazing results."[434] Fires have been deliberately set in many states and countries, including California, Greece, and

[434] Ibid.

Australia. No one person or group has been caught or claimed responsibility for such actions; however, terrorists believe that burning trees to carry out jihad is permissible. Why would terrorists not believe this? The destruction of resources — water, infrastructure, forests, food supplies, etc., — has been practiced in war throughout world history. The psychological traits of terrorist arsonists proposed by the authors are listed in Table 11.4.

Terrorists have likely targeted forests in nations they consider at war with Muslims, which would minimally include the U.S., Australia, Russia, and Europe, as well as Israel. For example, in June 2009, initial investigations by fire fighter squads in fire locations in Israel found a likelihood of arson for numerous fires that had broken out in one general area. "This is man-made terror," a fire commander said. "Fires don't just break out on their own."[435] Targeting the enemy with wildfire arson is a plausible scenario for any terrorist group, transnational or domestic, since the short-term damage can be extensive, disrupting power and water supplies and then can continue long-term through continued early spring debris flow issues, further damaging the environment and decreasing water quality as reservoirs and streams fill with ash and other fire deposits. Additionally, timber exports can be affected, as can the pharmaceutical industry, since it relies on certain species of plants and trees for drug ingredients.

Large forest fires can retard air traffic and cause manpower shortages since even the military could be called upon to help extinguish a fire that is quick moving and large in scope. The mere mention of fire increases stress in most people's psychological makeup; consequently, the mention of terrorist-caused fires could induce fear and panic dependent on fire size. And, it is very likely that jihadists are honing their techniques and capabilities in arson as a weapon. As engineers and chemists they are well aware of accelerants (not listed here due to security concerns) that can cause fire by absorbing oxygen from the air after a few minutes; or more conventional means such as road flares; tennis balls filled with home-made napalm, gasoline, kerosene, diesel fuel, other chemicals such as acids (sulfuric and others); and electronic devices for delayed ignition.

---

[435] Gil Ronen, "Tens of Simultaneous Fires in Northern Israel Are 'Terror Arson'," *Arutz Sheva*(2009), http://www.israelnationalnews.com/News/News.aspx/132162.

Table 11.4: Psychological Characteristics of the Terrorist Arsonist (as proposed by Tindall & Campbell).

Absolute support for beliefs and values — willing to die for them
Avoids attention — isolationist tendencies — few interpersonal relationships
Committed mind set with specific terrorist objective(s); capable of manipulation and deception to avoid detection
Deceitfulness, art of taqiyya acceptable, disregard for safety of others to achieve mission
Willing take revenge against all crusader nations, especially U.S. as instrument of Allah
Displacement of affect in which fire setting is used as a punishment against a target — unrelated to fire — serves mission objectives
Engages in high risk fire setting for maximum damage to target(s)
Generally unrecognized in local community or groups
Intolerant of non-Muslims
Knowledge of sophisticated fire setting techniques and materials
Lack of remorse and indifference to hurting others to achieve objective
May suffer from low self esteem — exploitable by the terrorist group
Motivation is generally religious, political, or radical — rarely for financial gain
Not adverse to risk taking — willing to constantly test boundaries
Predominantly male — can be domestic, activist, or transnational terrorist
Extreme resentment of U.S., allied, and crusader nations
Untrusting, particularly of westerners
Willing to act out of revenge for relative or friend lost in conflict in Middle East

Case Study

Jason's schooling ended in year ten and involved in juvenile crime. He worked menial jobs but was often dismissed. He received a twelve-month suspended sentence for setting fires. He failed test for fire service, then joined a volunteer brigade in New South Wales in the hope he would later be accepted into the fire service. He

subsequently joined a number of volunteer brigades in different locations. He spotted fires and telephoned emergency services to ensure his brigade arrived to the fire scene. He nominated himself as the caller and described multiple ignition points and reported arsonists in the bush areas. He lit 25 bushfires from January 2001 during the NSW bushfire danger period.

During police interviews, he denied knowledge of fire setting, but overwhelmed by the evidence, he confessed. He admitted he knew the "right conditions to set bushfires," and said, "I didn't even think I had a problem." He fully understood his actions could cause injury or death to people and destroy homes and property. He was aware that prevailing weather conditions would cause large scale damage to the bush and residential areas.

He exhibited grandiose behaviors and group identification with the depiction of fire heroes at the scene of the 9/11 terrorist attacks in New York. He "wanted to look good ...and be a hero." He craved the hero status of a firefighter by setting, identifying, and extinguishing the fires.

He "never actually thought about the general public" and "didn't think about anything." He agreed that bush fires were terrifying and "could scare the living ....out of anyone." He was willing to inflict terror on people "without a second thought. I certainly was." He dismissed concern for people who lost their homes and loved ones and agreed they would be horrified at his attitude. "Yes. I realize that, but you know I could make out I had no idea of what I was doing... But I did. I knew exactly what I was doing the whole time. If I was out fighting a fire you knew that's my day fulfilled. I wasn't sitting at home. I wasn't bored... There was definitely some sort of excitement there. There was definitely the thrill."[436]

'Pure Arsonists': The Pyromaniac

According to DSM IV, pyromania is a rare impulse disorder, characterized by multiple episodes of deliberate and purposeful fire setting by individuals who experience tension or affective arousal prior to fire setting and have a fascination or attraction to fire and its

436 — — —, "Media Reports: Sixty Minutes Transcript, Nine Network," (2008).

situational contexts.[437] Pyromaniacs are often regular 'watchers' at fires, set off false alarms, and derive pleasure from watching firefighting activity. They may visit and familiarize themselves at the local fire station, or in rare cases become firefighters.

Pyromaniacs exhibit gratification, pleasure, or tension release in setting the fire, observing its effects, and becoming involved in the aftermath. Pyromaniacs are more likely to plan fire setting, have a history of alcohol dependence, generally have poor social skills and learning difficulties, and have a global obsession with fire in all its myriad forms, which is central to the existence of the individual.

Pyromania is a controversial classification, and some researchers deny its validity.[438] DSM IV criteria can be found in all types of arsonists. It appears that the severity and spectrum of personality disorders is a more significant factor than impulse-driven behavior.

Bushfire Arsonists: The Phenomenological Perspective

What psychic processes are occurring before, during, and after arsonists light fires? Published self-reports reveal their inner world is analogous to self reports by intravenous drug users and criminals who engage in high risk crime. A 'high' and an 'adrenaline rush' are commonly reported which comes from feelings of power over all others, proximal and distal, as they move from the periphery of their community to the symbolic center. In sequential terms: irresistible impulse, psycho motor agitation, restlessness, conversion symptoms (increased heart rate, voices ringing in ears), and merging of the fragmented self identity into a state of unreality leading to discharge of tension and narcissistic satisfaction. The magical thinking of childhood is restored, and fire is literally an all consuming good and they are the controlling omnipotent identity.

---

[437] DSM, "Dsm Iv 312.3 Pyromania Diagnostic Criteria "(2008), http://allpsych.com/disorders/dsm.html.

[438] R. Doley, "Pyromania Fact or Fiction?," *British Journal of Criminology* 43, no. 4 (2003).

Vignette 1

A serial arsonist volunteer fire fighter claimed: "After I lit a fire it became more of an obsession. It was like an addiction. It was like an urge, a necessity. After lighting a fire I felt 'high' and after, 'down'. There was definitely something exciting...there was definitely the thrill...there was a lot more adrenaline on the back of the truck ..."[439]

Vignette 2

'I may set several small fires or one big fire depending on my needs at the time. It is at the time of lighting the fire that I experience an intense emotional release like tension release, excitement or even panic...After the fire is extinguished, I feel sadness and anguish and a desire to set another fire. Overall it seems the fire has created a temporary solution to a permanent problem'.[440]

Vignette 3

An undetected serial arsonist is believed to have set over 100 fires in Victoria since 2000. He has forwarded letters to the police and media and some have been found at fire scenes between Wallan and Seymour (Victoria) dating from 1998. The subject writes, 'Keep up the good articles on my fires. It's good reading and it's even better nobody got (sic) hurt. All the best for you and your job… that he is beyond help...I try to stop arson but the voices in my heads won't stop until I have done some fires... If CFA volunteers are hurt, I'm very sorry but I'm giving them training each time I arson." (Letters reveal arsonist bizarre thinking, Sun Herald, 14 November 2008)

To identify himself to police he provided a detailed account of his methodology and distinguished differences in techniques. He expresses his 'marvel' at the police and fire officers' rapid response. The 'voices in his head' may refer to 'command instructions' consistent with signs of a schizotypal disorder. The letter also reveals rapidly oscillating affect and contradictory self concepts - he is admiring, helpful and an arsonist.

---

[439] R. Jackson, ed. *Peter Burgess Arsonist*, Inside Their Minds: Australian Criminals (Sydney: 2008).
[440] S. Wheaton, "Personal Accounts: Memoirs of a Compulsive Fire Setter," *Psychiatric Services* 52.

Vignette 4
The arsonist claimed a fascination with fires since childhood and that later work and marriage problems turned him into an arsonist: 'I felt like I needed to do something as destructive as I could. I cared if I hurt people but I didn't care what I was doing. I wanted everybody to feel my pain... Deep down I didn't want anyone to get hurt. But I took that chance when I set the fires, knowing that somebody could get hurt or killed'. (Telegraph UK 14 February 2009)

Vignette 5
A volunteer firefighter was allegedly suffering from severe depression due to unemployment and relationship problems. Arrested for starting fires he created, he exclaimed: 'I have got a problem. I did. I lit the fire. I don't know why. I just did'. (Sydney Morning Herald 29 June 2009)

Immersed in the immediate gratifications of their own drives and needs, they regress to primitive primary process thinking devoid of rational content. If 'aware' of the consequences of their fire setting, it is a formal or abstract recognition and devoid of affect. The lack of reflection on the consequences is a marker of their psychopathology. If they are revenge seekers and subject to abandonment or rejection fantasies, they will enjoy the sadistic attack of arson and feel all powerful and omnipotent.

Lacking an 'observable self' and an internal locus of control, they are in the 'here and now'. Overwhelmed with rage and revenge, their affect storms may create real firestorms. They may not be aware of their destructive drives and sadistic urges until they abreact in arson.

Many psychological characteristics link arsonists and pedophiles and serial killers – they have no connection or linkage with the trauma they create. The do not see living people as even part-objects. Humans are redefined as 'objects' and targets for their disordered drives and impulses, which are released in the destructive return of the repressed — which many refer to self referentially as 'my problem.' A variety of clinical psychology and psychotherapy methods are available for treatment of arsonists, but that discussion is beyond the scope of this text.

Effects of Forest Fires on Water Supply: Case Studies

The Hayman Fire-Colorado

The Hayman forest fire occurred 95 miles (153 km) southwest of Denver, Colorado, on 8 June 2002 — the largest fire in the state's recorded history — 138,000 acres (560 km^2) burned. Hundreds of forestry officials and firefighters fought the fast-moving inferno, which caused nearly $40 million in damages, burned 133 homes, and forced the evacuation of 5,340 people. The fire was not contained until 2 July 2002 and it was not brought under control until 18 July 2002. The cause of the wildfire was found to be arson. Six people died as a result of the fire — one resident and five fire fighters.

Although the fire was considered arson, it apparently was not intentional. A federal forestry officer, Terry Barton, claimed she was attempting to burn a letter from her estranged husband and set the fire inside a campfire ring within an area designated for no fires due to a severe drought. The fire quickly spread out of control and burned across four different counties. A federal grand jury indicted Barton on four felony counts of arson; she eventually pled guilty and was given a six-year sentence in a federal prison.

The fire seriously degraded the water quality of Cheeseman and Strontia Springs Reservoirs — primary water sources for metropolitan Denver — requiring eight million dollars over four years to remove debris, replace culverts, build sediment dams, and seed slopes for restoration.[441] Water supplies for the Denver area needed to be rerouted from other sources as the above reservoirs were inoperable for several months. Further, deforestation of hillsides by fire promotes flooding and debris flow during wet periods that affect water quality. What would happen to the water supply of metropolitan Denver if this fire had been intentionally set, with other reservoirs and water supply sources sabotaged conjointly? The effects could have been much more long-term and catastrophic.

---

[441] P. Robichaud, MacDonald, L., Freeouf, J., Neary, D., Martin, D., and Ashmun, L., "Postfire Rehabilitation of the Hayman Fire," ed. U.S. Department of Agriculture Forest Service (USDA, 2003).

The Cedar Fire-California

As with the Hayman fire, the Cedar Fire was human-caused but it is not known whether it was by a terrorist arsonist or another type. The fire burned out of control through a large area of San Diego County, in Southern California, in October 2003. The Cedar Fire was one of 15 wildfires throughout Southern California that month, which became known as the "2003 Firestorm" and the "Fire Siege of 2003."[442] Driven by Santa Ana Winds, the Cedar Fire burned 280,278 acres (1,134 km^2), 2,820 buildings (including 2,232 homes), and killed 15 people, including one firefighter, before being contained on November 3, making it the largest fire in recorded California history.[443]

The Cedar Fire began in the Cleveland National Forest on October 25, 2003, south of Ramona in central San Diego County. Within ten minutes of the initial report of the fire, the U.S. Forest Service had deployed ten fire engines, two water tenders, two hand crews, and two chief officers. Within 30 minutes, 320 firefighters and six fire chiefs were en route. Between the time the fire started and midnight, the predicted strong easterly (Santa Ana) winds surfaced and the fire burned 5,319 acres. By noon on October 26, the fire was burning hundreds of homes in the Scripps Ranch community of San Diego and was threatening many others.

The fire forced the evacuation of the main air traffic control facility for San Diego and Los Angeles, shutting down all commercial and general aviation in the area and disrupting air traffic across the United States. Firefighters achieved full containment on November 3 and complete control on December 5.

The Cedar Fire was started by Sergio Martinez of West Covina, California, who started the fire to signal rescuers. Martinez was charged on October 7, 2004, in federal court with setting the fire and lying about it. He was sentenced to six months in minimum-security confinement, which allowed him to leave for work and other commitments, 960 hours of community service, and five years'

---

[442] USDA, "The Story One Year Later 2004: After Action Review,"(2004), http://www.fs.fed.us/r5/fire/information/story/2004/part_1.pdf.

[443] This synopsis was extracted from the aforementioned USDA report and the California Department of Forestry and Fire Protection: Review Report of Serious CDF Injuries, Illnesses, Accidents, and Near-miss Incidents.

probation. He was also ordered to pay $9,000 in restitution. Such a small repercussion as penalty could make wildfire arson a tool of choice for jihadists.

In addition to affecting U.S. air traffic, the Cedar fire also affected municipal water supplies, namely the San Diego River Watershed (SDRW), the second largest watershed (440 square miles) in San Diego County, with a population base of about 500,000. Water resources in the watershed include the San Diego River main stem, numerous tributaries, 22 steams, five water supply reservoirs (El Capitan, San Vicente, Lake Jennings, Lake Murray, and Cuyamaca Reservoirs), a large groundwater aquifer, extensive riparian habitat, coastal wetlands, and tide pools.

General watershed threats to water resources include water quality degradation by toxic chemicals, bacteria, and total dissolved solids (TDS); excessive extraction of groundwater; proliferation of invasive species; runoff containing excessive levels of nutrients and sediments; flooding; aggregate mining operations; and habitat loss and modification. Many human activities generate the majority of these threats. Generally, the water quality in the upper watershed is of much higher quality than the lower watershed. The upper watershed's water quality is high due to the undeveloped nature of that area. The lower watershed's surface water quality tends to be poor; this is due to over 50 years of development and hydro-modifications that have adversely impacted surface water quality.

Post-fire Impacts on the El Capitan Management Area of the Watershed showed the primary COC were turbidity, nutrients, bacterial indicators, and TDS. The soils in this management area are moderate to very high in erosion hazard ratings and rapid runoff, and they are vulnerable to increased mud flows after the fire removed vegetation. The major effects of the Cedar Fire on El Capitan Reservoir include increased sedimentation with some loss of storage and turbidity during peak runoff events.

The major post-fire pathways for the transport of various constituents are mudslides and erosion, which carry nutrients and increase turbidity. Temporary changes in water quality within this management area occur for about three years after the fire. Long-term, the nutrients previously locked in the vegetation continued to enter the reservoir as ash and sediment after storm events.

Fortunately, the severity of the storms in the few years following the fire allowed system recovery sufficient to prevent nutrient loading to the reservoir. Several other management areas within the SDRW also suffered from fire damage. An exact monetary amount was not determined and, while not as costly economically as the Hayman fire in Colorado, the Cedar fire illustrates the causative effects of the consequences on water security and sustainability, the environment, energy supply, and economic issues.

The Black Saturday Bush Fires-Australia

This synopsis of the Black Saturday bushfires, a series of bushfires that ignited or were burning across the Australian state of Victoria on Saturday 7 February 2009, was developed from the final report by the Royal Commission.[444] The fires occurred during extreme dry-weather conditions and resulted in Australia's highest ever loss of life from a bushfire — 173 people died and 414 were injured as a result of the fires. As many as 400 individual fires were recorded burning simultaneously. Following about two months of little or no rain and development of an intense heat wave, temperatures were high (mid- to high 40 degrees Celsius; 110–120°F), and wind speeds were in excess of 100 km/h (62 mph). Resulting fires spread rapidly and appeared manmade. Overall conditions created several large firestorms and pyro-cumulus systems, particularly northeast of Melbourne, where a single firestorm accounted for 120 of the 173 deaths.

The fires destroyed over 2,000 houses and more than 3,500 structures in total and damaged thousands more, affecting 78 individual townships and displacing about 7,500 people. The majority of the fires was ignited by fallen or clashing power lines or deliberately lit. The catalyst was major drought that had persisted for more than a decade.

Numerous major fires erupted and were given names, including Kinglake, Kilmore East, Murrindindi Mill, Beechworth, and many others. The central Gippsland fires threatened the Loy Yang Power Station, particularly the station's open-cut coal mine.

---

[444] Royal Commission, "2009 Victorian Bushfires Royal Commission: Final Report," ed. Government Printer (Cranberra: State of Victoria, 2010).

Investigators revealed that they strongly believed arson was the most likely cause of the Churchill fire. The Dandenong Ranges fire damaged the rail track and caused the closure of the Belgrave railway line as well as all major roads. The Weerite fire also damaged the rail line between Geelong and Warrnambool. Approximately 3,000 sleepers were burnt across a four km (2.5 mi) section of track. The rail line was re-opened about ten days later. The fire caused non-quantified losses of stock and was thought to have been started by sparking from felled power lines along the Princes Highway. In some fire areas, looting was reported.

Extensive environmental impacts are associated with the fires. For example, over a million animals are estimated to have perished in the bushfires. Additionally, many of the surviving wildlife suffered from severe burns. For example, large numbers of kangaroos were afflicted with burned feet due to territorial instincts that drew them back to their recently burned and smoldering home ranges. The affected area, particularly around Marysville, contains the only known habitat of Leadbeater's Possum, Victoria's faunal emblem, putting the species under further threat.

Forested catchment areas supplying five of Melbourne's nine major dams were affected by the fires, with the worst affected being the Maroondah Reservoir and O'Shannassy Reservoir. As of 17 February 2009, over ten billion liters (2.64 billion gallons) of water had been shifted out of affected dams into others. A Melbourne Water spokesperson said that affected dams may need to be decommissioned if the contamination from ash and other material were serious enough; the spokesperson also said that forest re-growth in the burnt-out catchment areas could reduce runoff yields by up to 30percent over the next three decades. In early March 2009, smoke from the fires was discovered in the atmosphere over Antarctica at record altitudes.

The economic impacts from the Black Saturday fires were extensive. The Bushfires Royal Commission gave a "conservative" estimate of the total cost of the Black Saturday bushfires of $4.4 billion. The largest contributor to the total cost was insurance claims, which the Insurance Council of Australia reported as $1.2 billion as of August 2010. Omitted from the $4.4 billion figure were the agricultural losses sustained in the fires and the ongoing impacts on

agriculture in following seasons. The Victorian Department of Primary Industries estimated losses shortly after the fires as 11,800 head of livestock, 62,000 hectares (150,000 acres) of grazing pasture, and 32,000 tons (31,000 LT; 35,000 ST) of hay and silage.

Additional issues included changes in fire policy, home construction restriction in highest risk areas, changes to building codes (new regulations), and others.

Conclusions

Wildfires can cause major disruptions of the water supply due to debris flowing down slope and other processes and thus, can play a major role in water security. The primary post-fire pathways for the transport of various constituents are mudslides and erosion — often termed debris flow — which carry nutrients down slope into streams and reservoirs to varying degrees. The flow can be small and fairly localized, causing mere turbidity and an increase in treatment costs, and requires the addition of more chlorine or, the flow can be substantial, which clogs streams and reservoirs and results in huge economic and environmental loss and other significant consequences. Post-fire processes can be significant in terms of sediment, ash, and nutrients flow, depending on the severity of storms. This can result in temporary changes in water quality within a fire management area during watershed runoff events after a fire. In response, the water supply will incur additional near-term water treatment costs due to post-fire inputs of sediment, ash, and nutrients. Long-term, the nutrients previously locked in the vegetation can continue to enter the reservoir and streams as ash and sediment after storm events.

Wildfires can significantly affect water security through destruction and disruption of infrastructure, supply and distribution, rail and truck transportation, air traffic, power supply and transmission, and can cause public health and environmental hazards resulting in severe economic damage, loss of life, and loss of species. Additionally, timber exports can be affected, as can pharmaceutical supplies.

Wildfires are generally caused by man or naturally through lighting strikes and other scenarios. Occasionally, they can be caused

by power disruption and related issues. As discussed in this chapter, most of the fires that have caused significant damage were deliberately or accidentally set by people. With the number of arsonist characteristic type individuals, as well as the new threat of wildfire arson from terrorist groups, this threat to water security is growing. Although arson is easily detected, the arsonist is not.

The terrorist arsonist acts upon inspiration, ideology, and revenge. They consider the setting of forest fires legal under extremist Islamic law as part of an "eye for an eye" and an act that can produce "amazing results." The destruction of resources — water, infrastructure, forests, food supplies, etc., has been practiced in war throughout world history. The psychological traits of terrorist arsonists the ease of escape for the arsonist, the minimal penalties for the crime, and the general minimal loss of life make wildfire arson a weapon of choice, even though patience is required for the proper environmental conditions conducive to large fires. However, the cyclical nature of climate change would generally result in opportune time frames of only one to three years. Therefore, terrorist arsonists pose a particularly egregious hazard since these groups prolifically study methods of destruction to the smallest detail. This could make wildfire arson a weapon of choice, especially for causing extensive economic damage and spreading fear and panic. It is much easier to start a fire than to build an IED and, panic from fire is much higher that threat from a bomb. To test the theory, simply yell 'fire' in a theatre — chaos and panic will immediately ensue.

Targeting the enemy with wildfire arson is a plausible scenario for any terrorist group, transnational or domestic, since the short-term damage can be extensive, disrupting power and water supplies, and then can continue long-term through continued early spring debris flow issues, further damaging the environment and decreasing water quality as reservoirs and streams fill with ash and other fire deposits.

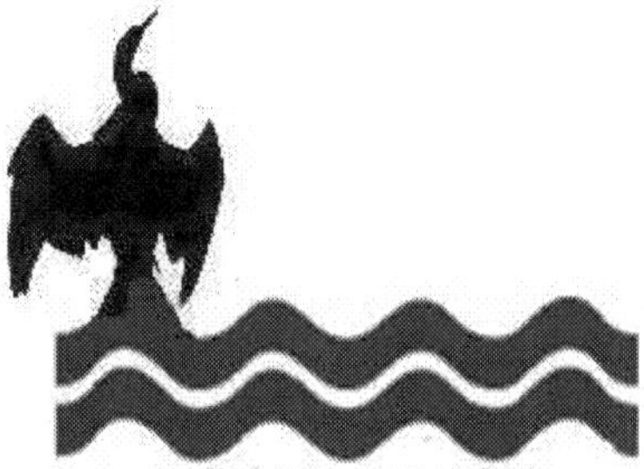

Tribal Water Symbol

CHAPTER 12: Industrial Control Systems Recommendations for Movement onto General Purpose Computer Hardware

Steven Steckel

Executive Summary

Industrial control systems (ICS) that control critical infrastructure such as flow of water, energy transmission, communications and so forth are moving to general-purpose computer hardware and software in ever-increasing numbers for cost efficiency and centralization of control. Yet best practices for information technology which shares many of the same components do not always work for industrial control systems and in some cases can be harmful. Common products and practices such as the Java programming language, virtualization, desktop security tools, remote access, standard network topology, commercial off-the-shelf operating systems, and lax password policy have the capability to cause more damage than good. Industrial control systems must go against information technology and embrace read-only operating systems, network segmentation, security through simplicity, and higher standards for employees who manage and maintain computer systems.

Industrial control systems must have their own policies and procedures, patch procedures, security software, and employees who understand the differences between information technology and industrial control systems while working on the same general-purpose computer hardware. The information technology and industrial control system worlds can never come together. Their objectives, consequences, and fates are too far apart.

ICS hardware and software is used by companies to control and monitor processes at industrial plants, flow through pipelines, transmission of electrical energy, and many other processes that keep societies advancing. ICS has been a source of particular interest for security researchers and a target for evildoers. Unfortunately, there has been little movement forward for improved security. And

unfortunately, almost all of the vulnerabilities require only basic skills to exploit — some require no skills at all.[445]

ICS exploits come in many types; some have graphical user interfaces for one click access and can be purchased on the "Internet" at a low cost. ICS also should work in isolated segregated networks. The trend in information technology (IT) of large networks that are easy to maintain should not be passed on to ICS. If an outsider can touch an ICS then company security is already compromised.

An array of methods and policies can be used to improve security; however, using current IT-type products will reduce risk and improve security for ICS only somewhat. And, both systems, particularly ICS, require a vulnerability assessment, which is one of the first steps in any security process. The assessments allow companies to understand the risk and rewards in effectively securing these systems. Risks and rewards such as testing and applying patches as they become available, properly isolating these systems within highly protected network zones, and closely monitoring them for any signs of anomalies or suspicious activity. ICS are designed to enjoy extremely long life-cycles; unfortunately, security is not always a top design consideration. Thus, it is logical to assume that other vulnerabilities exist that have not yet been discovered or disclosed — another reason why proper design, isolation and monitoring of these systems is so crucial.

Introduction

A fundamental weakness of critical infrastructures is the electronic and computer systems that control them. In hot debate regarding this issue is the role of IT versus operations personnel about system vulnerability. The procedures generally used by IT do not work well for operational control of these systems. Therefore, this chapter is geared toward the ICS executive; these are individuals with responsibility for management or oversight, development, implementation, operation, and/or security assessment and

[445] M. Abrams, and Weiss, J., "Malicious Control System Cyber Security Attack Case Study - Marooch Water Services Australia,"(2008), http://csrc.nist.gov/groups/SMA/fisma/ics/documents/Maroochy-Water-Services-Case-Study_report.pdf.

monitoring of ICS. A recent article on the local and national news web sites discussed a nuclear power plant moving from analog controls to digital controls. The article trumpeted the fact that the nuclear power plant was finally coming into the digital age. However, the article caused an attack of paranoia; a first thought was, "Hopefully the plant understands all the problems and baggage that comes along with the digital age."

This chapter is based on thirty-five years of experience in information technology and focuses on potential solutions to the vulnerability of ICS. A very real problem exists not only in the U.S., but also in developing nations with older technology which have little capital to invest in the newest systems and which therefore remain ineffective from a security perspective — to hackers and others who would access critical ICS.

Background

Industrial Control Systems are an integral part of a country's infrastructure. As such, ICS can itself be labeled as "critical infrastructure." Although comparable to IT systems, ICS systems can be both more primitive and more complex than IT systems. A solenoid that controls flow in a pipeline is a very simple device compared to a desktop personal computer. In contrast, a nuclear power plant is more complex than a desktop personal computer and incredibly more dangerous. An example is the recent radioactive release from the Fukushima Dai-ichi nuclear plant in Japan due to a tsunami caused rupture.[446] Unfortunately, this failure will be an environmental problem for the next 100 years.

To discuss this critical issue requires at least a basic knowledge of the terminology used in combined ICS processes as follows:

For description, the term "ICS" will refer to:

1. **Distributed control systems (DCS)447**

---

[446] Staff, "Japan Investigation into Nuclear Plant Radiation Leak," *BBC News Online*(2011), http://www.bbc.co.uk/news/world-asia-pacific-12859684.
447 "Distributed Control System," Wikipedia, http://en.wikipedia.org/wiki/Distributed_Control_System; http://en.wikipedia.org/wiki/Distributed_Control_System.

2. **Programmable logic controller (PLC)448**
3. **Supervisory Control And Data Acquisition (SCADA)449**
4. **Remote Terminal Unit (RTU)450**
5. **Human Machine Interface (HMI)451**
6. **A wide variety of pumps, values, sensors, controls and motors**
7. **General purpose computers doing ICS type functions**

The term "IT" will refer to:

1. **Servers**
2. **Desktops**
3. **Routers, switches, hubs, firewalls**
4. **Application software**
5. **Security software**
6. **Operating systems**

The term "cyber attacks" will refer to:

1. **Targeted attacks**
2. **Drive by attacks**
3. **Consequences from virus, worms, Trojans, root kits, bot-nets**
4. **Impacts from bad policies, techniques, design, technologies**
5. **Weapons such as electromagnetic plus (EMP) or electromagnetic interface (EMI)**
6. **Disgruntled and stupid employees**
7. **Nation states attacking targets through networks**

Crud-ware will refer to:

1. **Virus, worms, Trojans, root kits, bot-nets, hijacks, cross**

---

448 "Programmable Logic Controller," Wikipedia, http://en.wikipedia.org/wiki/Programmable_logic_controller; http://en.wikipedia.org/wiki/Programmable_logic_controller.

449 "Scada," Wikipedia, http://en.wikipedia.org/wiki/SCADA; http://en.wikipedia.org/wiki/SCADA.

450 "Remote Terminal Unit," Wikipedia, http://en.wikipedia.org/wiki/Remote_Terminal_Unit; http://en.wikipedia.org/wiki/Remote_Terminal_Unit.

451 "User Interface," Wikipedia, http://en.wikipedia.org/wiki/User_interface; http://en.wikipedia.org/wiki/User_interface.

scripting attacks, buffer overflows, SQL injection attacks, denial of service, spoofing, ping flood and any other software purposely designed to expose, alter, disable, steal, acquire unauthorized access, acquire unauthorized use of an asset, or destroy the hardware, software and information of a computer system

Crud-ware writers comprise three basic types: (1) government-sponsored, (2) organized crime-sponsored, and (3) independents. Each day, the numbers of government-sponsored crud-ware writers increases. The HB Gary Federal problem and the United States military recently stated that a retaliatory attack could occur if U.S. cyber or control systems were hacked; the response could be in kind with a retribution cyber attack or a conventional military strike.[452] The primary enemy for the U.S. appears to be China, which has been accused of planting digital bombs in the U.S. electrical grid.[453] Generally, the independents and the organized crime writers are motivated by money or for public relations. The government writers seek control over groups and individuals. However, government writers are not necessarily nation states. Al-Qaeda could theoretically be considered a nation state because of its size, reach, and follower loyalty, as well as state sponsorship by Iran and other Middle East countries. Independent groups such as 'Anonymous', while not nation state operatives, have a disproportional large capability compared to their size.[454]

In the past, ICS systems were closed and isolated analog systems that were proprietary to a vendor. System restarts were years apart and updates happened only when major component(s) sustained a critical failure. Security was never designed into these systems, and logging of events was unthinkable. Today, ICS systems are moving towards network interconnected digital systems on

---

[452] Staff, "Hbgary,"(2010), http://en.wikipedia.org/wiki/HBGary_Federal.

[453] C. Dillow, "Richard Clarke: China Is Planting Digital Bombs Throughout the U.S. Power Grid,"(2011), http://www.popsci.com/technology/article/2011-06/richard-clarke-china-laying-digital-bombs-across-us.

[454] Staff, "Alleged Anonymous Members Arrested in Turkey," *Los Angeles Times* Technology(2011), http://latimesblogs.latimes.com/technology/2011/06/anonymous-members-released-after-32-arrested-by-turkey-.html.

general purpose computer hardware. Also, some systems are connected to the "Internet" to allow long distance remote control of an ICS system. Yet "ICS best practices" lags far behind IT for its computer hardware, especially in cyber security and computer system design.

An ICS system's primary goals are reliability, efficiency, and scalability. If a critical system fails and service is not delivered or people are injured or killed, management and political fallout can be intense. Lawsuits due to liability issues, layers of government, and the public usually become involved. Thus, making cyber security and computer-system design a primary goal seems counterproductive. Yet, in the Internet-enabled connected world, cyber security and computer-system design need to gain prominence as 'the' priority for large critical infrastructure security. Failing to secure ICS safely could result in catastrophe. For example, a terrorist group could blow up a natural gas pipeline through sabotage of a control system, release raw sewage, stop the flow of water, cause power-station overload and disrupt electricity transmission, blow up liquefied natural gas terminals, or myriad other things. Organized crime could hold parts of the electrical "smart grid" ransom to extort money as they have with companies around the globe through various attacks, including denial of service (DOS). A very real problem with these systems is that failure can be deliberate or accidental and it is difficult to determine which.

Mainstream IT is more aware of cyber security and computer-system design. Information security standards are being developed worldwide by public, private, and governmental organizations. The SANS Institute[455] is a worldwide organization that exists for cyber security. The SANS Infosec Reading Room contains vast reading to assist IT specialists and others to gain additional skills in information security. Also, most major computer hardware and software vendors teach classes on computer-system design. There are also dozens of anti-crud-ware vendors worldwide, but caution must be taken to verify actual vendor status, else the download could originate from distributors of crud-ware. These issues have led to parts of the same organization having different views on cyber security and computer-

---

[455] "Computer Security Training, Network Research & Resources," SANS, http://www.sans.org/; http://www.sans.org.

system design and there is often internal conflict about the best way to secure systems. However, the general purpose of IT security is to protect the integrity of a network, the servers, and the data. This is in contrast to the purpose of ICS security, which is to protect the ability of ICS's extended facility to safely operate, despite other issues.

Chronologically, ICS is much older than IT. Yet, IT has a much better understanding of computers, networks, data and the critical security issues regarding risk, vulnerability, and mitigation. In today's world, the interface between IT and ICS is unclear at best. Too much finger pointing and too many "not done here" attitude problems abound. For ICS to progress to network interconnected digital systems, both ICS and IT must change.

Purpose and Audience

The goal of this chapter is to compile and present many of the principals necessary to adequately merge ICS and IT. In contrast to other organizational-level publications, this document will be presented as a list of ideas and 'what to do.' It will be most beneficial to ICS practitioners.

The principals presented herein can be used by:

1. ICS managers and executives
2. ICS specialists
3. Information security officers from both the IT and ICS worlds

From a generalized perspective, IT will gain little from this paper even though IT will bear the brunt of the recommendations.

Thoughts to remember for IT include:

1. IT must help ICS progress to network interconnected digital systems.
2. IT must protect ICS from IT.
3. Best practices for IT do not always work for ICS.
4. IT has an incredible amount of baggage that must stay with IT and not be transferred to ICS — transferring the

baggage will only force ICS into a further weakened state.

Case Study: Failure due to Hacker Attack-Maroochy Water Services

The potential problems of ICS are best represented by an actual circumstance that occurred which demonstrates the weakness of IT and related systems in relation to ICS. An employee, Vitek Boden, for an Australian firm (Hunter Watertech) that installed SCADA radio-controlled sewage equipment for the Maroochy Water Services in Queensland, Australia, quit the firm after a strained relationship. He applied for a job with the Maroochy Shire Council; however, the Council decided not to hire him. Consequently, Boden opted for revenge against his former employer and the Council. After packing his car with a laptop computer and stolen radio equipment, he drove around the Maroochy area on at least 46 occasions from February 28 to April 23, 2000, issuing radio commands to the sewage equipment (it is likely he helped to install this equipment). Boden caused 800,000 liters (211,000 gallons) of raw sewage to spill into local parks, rivers and the grounds of a Hyatt Regency hotel. The spill resulted in dead marine life, black-colored water, and an unbearable odor for local residents. Although captured relatively quickly, Boden's attack became the first widely known example of a malicious hack into ICS.

A More Appropriate Setup

Wastewater treatment systems are one sector of ICS systems that needs enhanced security (ICS for other critical infrastructure systems are also at risk), particularly due to the age of these systems. Not only are these systems vulnerable to failure due to age, as the Maroochy case demonstrates, they are also very vulnerable to hackers. Some wastewater treatment systems are operating on equipment as old as one hundred years and badly need upgrades. One hundred year old pipe systems for water distribution are common. A search on a popular search engine revealed several accidental discharges of raw sewage into nearby water systems. Reasons for the discharges ranged from the alarm speaker being turned off to sewer pipes being pushed beyond capacity. IT system port scans and other IT processes also make these systems vulnerable. And, as in the case of the Maroochy Water Services system, which was an insider attack, even ICS systems are not hacker proof.

The use of a fictitious wastewater treatment plant can help explain some basic ICS concepts and will highlight changes that should occur in both the IT and the ICS worlds. A wastewater treatment plant in City of Leaping Fish needs help. Their existing wastewater treatment system is 60 years old and the federal government has ordered them to replace it. The town council has decided that due to Internet vulnerability, security must be second only to the physical plant itself. The council would like to reuse as much equipment as possible to reduce costs, but maintain secure control. The federal government will assist with the cost of the new plant, but the town will need to increase taxes to completely fund it — the council is, naturally, worried about being reelected.

Physical Plant

The Leaping Fish plant is a mixture of values and solenoids using the Modbus[456] serial communication protocol, relays, cam timers, a few early-models network capable programmable logic controllers (PLC), and two HMI consoles for command and control. Most of the PLCs will be replaced with modern versions. The network of relays and cam timers has had maintenance problems for many years and will be replaced. Command and control will move from a distributed system to a centralized system. Also, the Modbus network could be reused if it is hooked up to a network connected general-purpose computer. A back-end controller server sends commands to the general purpose computer using Ethernet. The commands are translated into Modbus and sent to the plant.

The old programmable logic controllers (PLC) could be hooked up to a modern network as long as there is a router between the programmable logic controller and the network. The PLCs do not

[456] "Modbus," Wikipedia, http://en.wikipedia.org/wiki/Modbus; http://en.wikipedia.org/wiki/Modbus.

have enough clock speed to survive the noise that modern Ethernet networks produce. Generally, a standard IT system administrator function called a "port scan" will overwhelm the PLC and either crash it or cause random actions in the controlling hardware. The older the PLC is, the more it needs a router mate. The same rule can be applied to most Ethernet connected devices in an ICS network. The older a device is the more it needs a router mate protecting it from the noise on modern Ethernet networks.

Pipes and Pumps

Sixty years ago, the pipes were made cheaply from cast iron. A visual inspection using a fiber optic camera shows that the pipes are rusted out and leaking; likely they have been passing metal contamination downstream for some time. Most pumps leak and the staff has been performing manual clean up. All pumps will need to be replaced. The concrete walls and tanks are stable and usable, despite years of use. Thus, a thorough cleaning is recommended. However, the physical rejuvenation of a wastewater system is only one component; computer security also needs to be taken into account from the first stages of design and implementation.

Defense in Depth

Securing information systems against the full breadth of exploits requires the use of multiple and overlapping procedures directed against people and technology. This is due to the interactive nature of attacks against information systems and the fact that a single system cannot be fully protected unless all other systems that attach to it are protected. The current technical term is called "Defense in Depth." The theory states that if enough protection is in place against an attacker the attack will fail. The French Maginot Line of World War II used this same theory — it failed rather quickly through marginalization. Therefore, three additional security procedures should be added:

- Security through simplicity
- Security through isolation
- Security through obscurity

Security through Obscurity

In security through obscurity systems may have theoretical or actual security vulnerabilities. But these vulnerabilities may not be known, perceived to be too dangerous to the attacker, or the payoff from the attack is not worth the effort to initiate the attack. As an example, in an operating system such as IBM i, the vulnerabilities are not known and the payoff is not worth the risk. Contrasted with a Microsoft operating system where some vulnerability is known and exploited daily and more exploits are found monthly, there is low danger to the attacker and the payoff is high.

Security through Isolation

Classified systems have practiced security through isolation for many years. It works and is better than security by obscurity. This is not the 3Gs (guards, gates, and guns) security, although that is the public perception.

Security through Simplicity

The more simple a device is, generally the harder it is to access or destroy. While anything can be destroyed, is the price worth it? Cell phones that are 6-10 years old can still make calls, but they cannot perform text messaging. Thus, for such an old phone, when the next great smart phone crud-ware is released and begins attacking systems, this old phone will not be vulnerable to the new crud-ware. The latest and greatest smart phone will be very vulnerable, likely hacked and will become useless — like carrying a brick.

Computer network Topology

The current trend is to combine the ICS network with the IT network and manage both systems using IT processes. Is this the wrong way? Yes! Although IT and ICS can use the same computer hardware, the networks must be split apart — a different network for each. However, each network can have many subnets, which should

be created to separate functions and access privileges. Each subnet should have a router programmed for data movement with only the needed ports opened. A PLC with its router mate is a subnet on the ICS network. Network data moves from the ICS network into the IT network — never in the opposite direction. A router at the border of each network enforces this rule. Generally, the farther away an ICS subnet is from the ICS/IT border router, the fewer number of ports are opened and the more one way the network traffic flow should be — this type of network segmentation is part of security through isolation. This will help prevent unauthorized access.

Vendor access provides a direct access method into the ICS network without passing through defense in depth protocols. If a vendor wants Internet access to the ICS network, then a vendor must be found who has a clue about what security is. If access must be given, use a VPN connection or a dial-up modem. A trusted employee should escort the vendor at all times. Once the vendor has completed work, physically unplug the connection.

If using a dial up modem for vendor access, ensure that the phone call goes through the phone switch for the ICS network. A phone switch hooked up to the public telephone system can be compromised and allow easy access into the ICS network. The idea of controlling a wastewater plant remotely from a fishing boat while on vacation sounds wonderful, but it creates a significant vulnerability. Much like what the Germans did to the French when they flanked the Maginot Line, attackers will eventually find the network port used for remote control and use it to gain quick and easy access, bypassing defense in depth protocols. The Federal Bureau of Investigation (FBI) recently claimed that members of Al-Qaeda scoured the Internet searching for methods of gaining control of water-supply facilities and water treatment plants through their computer networks.[457] Remote control systems make it easy for hackers to gain access.

Between the IT network and the Internet is the corporate firewall. Since the IT network is attached to the Internet, this connection has the greatest potential for unauthorized access to the IT network. This connection exists to provide ICS data to the outside world, not to surf the web. A well-configured corporate firewall is

---

[457] Fox, "Fbi Warns of Potential Poison Attacks," *U.S. & World Breaking News*(2003), http://www.foxnews.com/story/0,2933,96416,00.html.

critical to the security of this network. A rule set should be developed and monitored that allows only necessary access. While most administrators are good at creating rule sets for incoming traffic, a common oversight is rules for outbound traffic. The same logic applies to outbound traffic as inbound traffic. Only the necessary ports should be opened and a network monitoring package should be run. A good network monitoring package (open source) is Snort[458]. It is used worldwide and has an enormous user community to direct operations questions to. The Snort rule set should be updated daily for best protection. Also, management should assign a trained and trusted user to read the data logs on a frequent basis. Other intrusion detection systems exist as well, but Snort is a good place to begin.

As part of the IT network there should be a network for the businesses desktop computers. This network should be considered a "dirty network." It should be isolated and compartmentalized to restrict unneeded traffic. The desktop network is usually the first network to be infected by crud-ware and has the worse repeat offenders. Since desktops are the perfect place to launch attacks against other systems, isolation of corporate desktops is one of the better ways to protect other networks.

Moving data into the ICS network must be done using portable media such as compact disks or flash drives. All portable media must go through a current security-scanning station. All media must be logged for employee name, purpose of media, and type of media. The inbound gate between the IT and the ICS networks should never be open because some types of crud-ware are constantly looking for new networks to attack. Although this does not afford the current technology ease-of-use many are accustomed to, this process is secure, effective, and efficient.

An on-site audit should be performed on a random schedule looking for illegal communication links. Any links found should justify the termination of the employee due to the critical nature of such systems and current liability issues. At the Leaping Fish plant, the installation of a new 100BaseT Ethernet network was recommended using Category 6 cable.[459] The network segmentation at the Leaping

---

[458] Staff, "What Is Snort?," SNORT, http://www.snort.org; http://www.snort.org.

[459] "Category 6 Cable," Wikipedia, http://en.wikipedia.org/wiki/Category_6_cable; http://en.wikipedia.org/wiki/Category_6_cable).

Fish plant is illustrated in Figure 12.1. A wireless network was not recommended for the reasons discussed. All but one form of wireless encryption have been broken and the remaining form was broken under a special condition. Wireless networks are precariously vulnerable. Recently, the author proved to the manager of a 300 room hotel that his wireless network was being used by the first block of houses in a housing project behind his hotel. A google.com search for "wireless network jammers" returned hundreds of hits. Many detailed procedures on the Internet explain how to build wireless jammers using off the shelf parts, including microwave ovens. ICS and IT systems should not be subjected to this vulnerability.

Figure 12.1: Leaping Fish Network

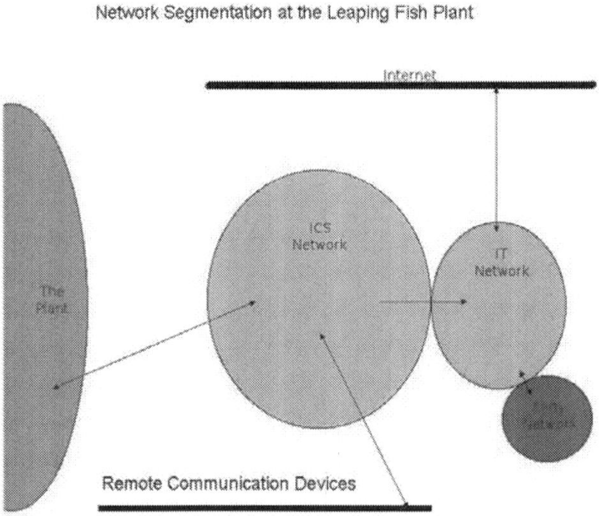

Operating systems

A "Live" version of an operating system is a bootable version that exists on a compact disk or DVD. No hard drive is actually needed to run the operating system. An advantage of this type of operating system is that it allows the user to return the computer to its previous state when the computer is rebooted. The operating system is stored completely in system memory. Even if crud-ware

manages to change the operating system in system memory, a reboot of the system removes the crud-ware. The system hard disk can be used to store data and applications, which is a very effective security methodology.

All operating systems with a "Live" version have a method to create a custom version of the operating system. This chapter was written using a custom version of a "Live" operating system on a desktop with no hard disk. Storage of data was done using a flash drive. Although initially time consuming to create a "Live" operating system, with practice, updated versions become easier and are written much more quickly; updated versions should be created often.

In the ICS network, a general purpose computer needs to have the traits of stability and sameness. Thus, the complexity of current operating systems is not needed for ICS. The best recommendation is using a "Live" or read-only operating system for all general-purpose computer systems in the ICS network. A "Live" version will satisfy the sameness requirement. Each computer then has just the needed application software stored on the hard disk.

Stability is another matter. The popular commercial operating systems are massively complex, using kernels that are very large and "clunky." All have processes running for services that will not be used. Starter or helper processes that start up large applications faster or processes that are waiting for the operator to do something are common. The more processes that are running, the less stable the operating system. For best security, an operating system should be kept as simple as possible. On the ICS network, an operating system with a multimedia player or solitaire game is not simple. This is an example of security through simplicity. As an example, a better operating system is one where parts can be removed without damaging the operating system. Large clunky applications like graphical user interfaces and web browsers should be the first to be removed.

Vulnerabilities are found weekly in applications and services. The operating system is always a favorite target. Generally, vulnerabilities are published shortly after discovery, allowing for quick profit by crud-ware writers. Other vulnerabilities become secret, allowing a select group of attackers to exploit systems for long-term profits or for other groups to monitor the system unbeknown to the operator. An operating system with large parts removed has less vulnerability, making it more secure.

At the Leaping Fish plant the Linux operating system was chosen over the Microsoft operating system because of no up-front cost, a "Live" version was available, and the majority of the operating system could be deleted without harming the ability to run ICS applications. The operating system was reduced to the kernel, a command line interface and the needed ICS applications.

Password Policy

Passwords are necessary for good security. They will be around for a long time despite the fact that biometrics was supposed to rid us of passwords; it is beginning, but the devices are not failsafe. Also, because the lifespan of some wastewater HMI consoles are another twenty plus years, passwords will remain a continued requirement.

The SANS Institute has an excellent password policy[460] which provides guidance on creating, changing, and protecting passwords. The policy is free and has strong security implications. A simple editing of the policy can convert it into a legal document for use as a corporate password policy. Password remembrance is a constant problem for most employees. Passwords on the bottom of keyboards, on the back of monitors, and in the corner of white boards should be discouraged. A popular place is on the back of badges. If a password is too complex or changes too often, employees will undermine the purpose of the password to remember it. Passwords that are 30 characters of random letters are wonderful passwords but almost impossible to remember due to complexity. Also, auto-generated passwords should be avoided and the employee should make passwords from pass phrases. An example password would be "ILoveCh0clateC00kies!" or "BigFishPr33tyWater$." Every IT department has policies on password design, which is critical because of ever increasing capabilities of modern graphics

[460] Staff, "Password Policy,"(2011), http://www.sans.org/resources/policies/Password_Policy.pdf.

processing units (GPU); they enhance the ability for cracking four character passwords within a few minutes.[461] The recommendation is for password phrases of at least 16 characters.

In some IT operations, the user IDs and passwords are shared among the operators of continuously manned operating consoles. Examples are a network operations center or the HMI consoles of wastewater treatment. This sharing must exist because these are critical systems. The damage caused by a locked user ID or a forgotten password is unacceptable and could be significant. Typically, the continuous manning of the consoles provides an additional layer of security. Other than this special case, user-level authentication should be installed. No computer hardware or software should be left with the default manufacturer password. A default password results in easy access to the equipment or application. Default passwords should be changed to robust unpublished passwords. At the very least, default passwords should follow the same rules as user-level passwords.

Virtualization

A current trend in IT is "Virtualization." Using Virtualization a guest operating system can run atop a host operating system. Guest applications then run inside of the guest operating system. Dim managers love Virtualization. It packs more applications onto fewer pieces of hardware, usually resulting in larger bonuses for the manager. In a wastewater treatment plant where one discharge of raw sewage can sicken thousands of people, Virtualization should never be used. Virtualization is a violation of security through simplicity.

Hardware control does not need the current generation of multiple processors and large, many-core servers running multiple operating systems. Small simple servers using low electrical power processors are sufficient. The servers should be smart enough to monitor each other and take over if a server fails.

---

[461] Timothy, "Cheap Gpus Rendering Strong Passwords Useless,"(2011), http://it.slashdot.org/story/11/06/05/2028256/Cheap-GPUs-Rendering-Strong-Passwords-Useless.

Clustering

Major software vendors will attempt to sell software to perform High-availability (HA) clusters. In a HA cluster, the servers watch each other; if one server fails the others take over its functions. In a load balancing cluster, multiple servers are all performing the same function. Generally, only very large web sites have load balanced clusters. Lastly, there are computer clusters more commonly referred to as "supercomputers." In the ICS world, an HA cluster is what is desired — servers that watch over each other and guarantee that a water pump or transfer valve will initiate on schedule. At the Leaping Fish plant, the Linux-HA (High-Availability Linux) software was chosen for its low cost and scalability.

Programming Languages

Making recommendations for the choice of a programming language generally causes conflicts within IT. Everyone has a favorite language and dislikes hearing that it could be marginally efficient or ineffective when addressing a problem. Despite this, a programming language that has the fewest layers of software between the code and the processor is likely the best choice. The more layers of software there are between the code and the processor, the more software there is that can break. Choose a programming language that runs across different operating systems. A popular language such as Java[462] that needs the Java Virtual Machine between the code and the processor is not usable. Likewise, heavy object oriented programming (OO) should also be avoided. While OO[463] programming is usually faster than older types of methodologies, it also hides more from the programmer than older types of programming methodologies. In a business where millionths of a second can be critical, a programming methodology such as OO, which can hide large amounts of code form the human programmer, can be dangerous. Unlike IT, an ICS human programmer should be as close to the processor as possible. At the Leaping Fish plant, the

---

[462] Staff, "Java," Oracle, http://www.java.com; http://www.java.com.

[463]"Object-Oriented Programming," Wikipedia, http://en.wikipedia.org/wiki/Object-oriented_programming; http://en.wikipedia.org/wiki/Object-oriented_programming.

decision was made to use the Perl and C programming languages. Perl has a module that allows communications with the Modbus devices, making it the first choice. Although not the author's favorite languages, they are efficient.

Web Services

A web server is the computer that answers when an operator accesses the World Wide Web. Web servers come in two types, external and internal. Web-server software is usually either the free Apache[464] server or the Microsoft Internet Information Services[465] server. Web-server software accepts requests for data and returns data depending on what the server has been programmed to return. Web servers send out data in a highly structured format so that all devices from a desktop to a smart phone can understand the data. The organization that controls the structure of the data is the World Wide Web Consortium (W3C).[466]

The external web server handles requests from the world for information on the treatment plant, party dates, telephone numbers, etc. This type of data is usually very static and simple — there is no need for databases and complex software. Since an external web server is handling worldwide requests, it needs to be on the outside of the corporate firewall — a "Live" operating system is a must for this server. Since the external web server is exposed to the trash, i.e., risks, on the Internet, it should run on simple, cheap, disposable hardware. In contrast, the internal web server hosts various web applications. This web server should have no access to the Internet — it should be blocked by the corporate firewall. The type of web server software is usually dictated by the application and is almost always installed on a multi-core server.

---

464 "Http Server Project," APACHE, http://httpd.apache.org; http://httpd.apache.org/.

465 "How to Obtain Versions of Internet Information Server (Iis)," Microsoft, http://support.microsoft.com/kb/224609; http://support.microsoft.com/kb/224609.

466 Staff, "World Wide Web Consortium," World Wide Web Consortium, http://www.w3.org.

On the World Wide Web a popular programming language is JavaScript.[467] Most web-based advertising is done through JavaScript, unfortunately it is also the best tool for writing crud-ware. IT likes JavaScript because it allows web sites to be created easily and allows a high level of control on the remote web browser. Most web sites do not actually need JavaScript — it is a mere convenience. Avoiding use of JavaScript makes computer systems and the Internet much safer. At Leaping Fish, the Apache web server was chosen for both the external and internal web servers. The JavaScript language was forbidden on the external web server.

Whole-Disk Encryption

Encrypting an entire hard drive is a good way to guarantee that the information on the disk is only seen by authorized employees. It is a very good method for traveling employees who run the risk of having their laptop stolen or damaged beyond use. To use the data on an encrypted hard drive, the processor must first un-encrypt it. Un-encryption takes time; in a bad situation on the ICS network, time may be in short supply. At Leaping Fish, it was decided that only data on the IT network and data leaving the plant would be encrypted. The time lag to un-encrypt the data for the ICS network was considered too dangerous.

Policies and Procedures

Security policies and procedures in facilities where ICS networks are installed are often poorly written, poorly enforced, or non-existent. A successful policy or procedure must be easily understood, easily enforced, and easy to comply with. The policy must not impact safety, productivity, or be cost prohibitive. A committee consisting of representatives from the system administrators, plant engineers, management, and the common employees must work together to form adequate security policy and procedures. The SANS Institute has some excellent starts for policies and procedures. One policy that was suggested at the Leaping Fish

---

[467] http://en.wikipedia.org/wiki/JavaScript.

plant was that employees could be terminated if caught harming the ICS network or systems, intentional or not.

Security Training

In the world of computers, security training is ongoing and frequent. Staying up-to-date on the latest architecture designs, intrusion detection system (IDS) rule sets, and many other issues is a necessity for computer system and network administrators.

Patches

Patches repair vulnerabilities in operating systems and applications that could allow an attacker in or stop critical failures. The importance of patches should not be understated. Yet patches on ICS systems can be problematic. Patches should be downloaded onto an isolated server off the ICS network for testing. Results of tests should be distributed to plant managers and engineers. If approved, patches should be tested on backup systems before being implemented on production systems. Patches should be approached with a dose of paranoia. System vendors cannot test their patches for all occurrences, so it is up to system administrators to ensure that the patch is needed and safe. On systems with large chunks of the operating system removed and containing sparsely needed applications, most patches will not be needed.

Conclusions

The direction of IT today is not where ICS needs to go. Forcing ICS to follow the same technology route as IT will lead to high security risks for the nation's infrastructure; it will also lead to the same risks for corporate and government computer systems. Security is a complex issue that touches most aspects of ICS design and operations. Critical differences exist between IT and ICS.

Security for ICS often interferes with "ease of use" for an application or process. Wastewater treatment is a part of water infrastructure, critical to economic sustainability and national security. It is constantly under scrutiny for attack by jihadists who are likely at this moment planning an attack that will be very devastating. A critical failure of a wastewater treatment plant could sicken or kill thousands of people. The recent earthquake in Haiti that destroyed water infrastructure and resulted in outbreaks of dysentery and cholera serves as an example.

Current commercial off-the-shelf operating systems are very large and "clunky." They violate the security through simplicity principle and the internals of these operating systems can be purchased on the Internet. Despite the fact that IT systems call themselves "can't fail," this is not true. However, ICS systems are truly "cannot fail."

The current ICS trend of moving to slightly modified commercial operating systems and in some cases desktop operating systems will create even more security of the breaches and failures that we currently experience. However, the creation of a general purpose operating system for use in ICS networks would be a boon to critical infrastructure and its security. This new operating system should use micro-kernel architecture; other services should be "bolt on." Thus, if a graphical user interface is needed, it should be bolted on to the operating system, not be an integral part of the operating system. By using 'bolt on' components, unneeded functions such as games, movie players, and so forth, which can cause system vulnerabilities, would not be part of the operating system. Bolt-ons also reduce the overhead needed to run an operating system, which often means older or low-powered hardware can be used successfully in an ICS network. A needed bolt on will be a programming language and some type of structured query language (SQL) database. The programming language should speak Modbus and be able to interchange data with the SQL database.

The operating system should work on any Intel/AMD/VIA/ARM processor, especially the new generation of ultra low electrical power processors. A hard drive is not needed to function. The operating system should fit on a read-only media with changeable configuration parameters stored on a flash drive or other portable storage device. A simple terminal screen for control of the operating system should be part of the base operating system. This will yield best security, although it requires slightly more time to work with. The real trade off in security between ICS and IT systems is time.

The industry has slowly converted to convenience over security for the sake of saving minimal time, which is akin to passing a car on the freeway to take the next exit for the sake of saving 2-3 extra seconds. It creates a very dangerous situation unworthy of the risk.

Licensing for the operating system should be under the GNU General Public License (GNU) — free to use by any organization or person.[468] A foundation following the model of the Apache Foundation should be implemented for support and updates to the operating system. An operating system of this type would be easy to use, efficient and flexible, fast, open source, and very secure. However, it requires more skill to use than GUI driven systems such as Microsoft. Also, because of low profit, most ICS vendors would not admit such an operating system exists. For lack of the most concise illustration, ICS vendors have jumped onto the Microsoft wagon for substantially increased profits, similar to doctors prescribing drugs pushed on them by drug representatives for which they obtain a kick back. The end result will be that some wastewater treatment ICS will eventually pay a heavy price for using subpar, insecure systems, either through partial failure or potentially loss of life.

Technology constantly changes, and current upgrades and better methods of security are necessary; however, security will come at a price in time. The need for installing "Live" operating systems on general purpose computer hardware is here now if professionals truly desire to secure critical infrastructure control systems.

---

[468] Staff, "Gnu Operating System," GNU, http://www.gnu.org/licenses/gpl.html.

Tribal Water Symbol

CHAPTER 13: Transnational-Boundary Issues: Europe, China, Middle East

Executive Summary

Transboundary water resources, issues, and disputes are those that cross one or more international borders. The term 'water war' has often been used to describe disputes regarding water use. Although various experts emphatically deny that armed conflict has ever resulted concerning water disputes, the 1967 Israel-Syria war is an example that contradicts such statements.

The divergence between nations concerning economics, infrastructure, and political orientation has complicated transboundary water sharing. Poor use and management of already limited water resources provides evidence of problems at each level of government:

1. State level — lacking sufficient supplies,
2. National level — competing demands between sectors, and
3. International level — threats between nations sharing transboundary resources.

Examples of transboundary water issues include multiple entity competition for water, the stronger antagonist controlling water resources (through military or economic means), use of propaganda to justify control, threat of water terrorism, and economic development disputes.

During transboundary disputes regarding the Danube River in Europe, it was discovered using that the public consultation process and working with all stakeholders brought more rapid results. Several factors appear to have been the driving force for transboundary cooperation, at least in Europe:

- **A large gradient in economic development,**
- **Major political changes in Central and Eastern Europe after 1991,**
- **Transformation of legislation and administration of former East Bloc countries,**
- **Water pollution and environmental degradation,**
- **International River, i.e., used for navigation, and.**

From a historical setting, the mode of cooperation shifted from bilateral agreements to basin-wide agreements and ensured greater success.

Water and environment relation actions should likely be based on implementation of precautionary principles, utilizing best available techniques and practices, controlling pollution at the source, requiring the polluter to pay, and regional cooperation and information sharing. Also, the public participation and collaborative problem solving approach used in the development of the strategic action plan significantly shortened the time for preparation and approval. Additionally, the degree of cooperation among representatives of participating riparian states, and the importance given to public participation in developing the plan mark significant achievements in promoting regional cooperation in water resources management. Full success will ultimately be decided by the degree to which goals and operational strategies are implemented.

For conflicting areas such as China and its relation with Pakistan and India, as well as Southeast Asia, and for the Middle East, water-security issues threaten basic national interests. Both the quantity and distribution of water throughout these countries and their neighbors represent significant challenges to social and economic sustainability. Population growth increases demands on water supply, causing problems with the environment, salt-water intrusion, economic development, public health, and other issues. All of these nations are already under some form of water stress that minimally threatens economic sustainability from the individual fisherman to the country, threatening disruption of economic and agricultural activity in the most vulnerable.

Concerning China, despite cooperative efforts with other countries regarding transboundary disputes, it is clear its very survival, particularly its economic sustainability, is growingly threatened by water-security and water supply issues. About 23 percent of its population lives in western regions where glacial melt provides the principal dry season water source. This continually diminishing resource will create a growing competition among users. The Indus River system, with headwaters in Tibet, has become a significant problem that could potentially erupt into conflict. Because China, Pakistan, and India are nuclear armed, a solution to transboundary water issues for this area is critical. The Indus River has been an area of conflict between China, Pakistan, Nepal, Bangladesh, and India for centuries. The use and overuse of water, territorial claiming of water resources, damming and water distribution are resulting in water conflicts. Despite efforts from the International Law Association implementing the Dubrovnik rules leading to the Helsinki Rules, conflicts have continued. China's water related issues will likely continue to put pressure on the country as a whole, especially economically, as well as require additional focus on foreign relations and political discourse relating to transboundary issues and national security.

Specific regions such as the Mekong, Indus, and Ganges, will likely be more severely impacted with time in regard to water stress and being transboundary in nature will probably strain the capacity of Chinese institutions and policy frameworks. China's economic sustainability depends upon its water resources and water security, and its national security will be in jeopardy in event of severe water stress, forcing greater cooperation or potential hostility with its surrounding neighbors and even the U.S. because of strategic concerns over water and food security along with economic sustainability.

The Middle East, particularly Israel, Jordan, Syria, and Palestine, have a long history of irritants that fuel water wars. These issues have created violence on many levels. To understand the Middle East, particularly Israel and its relations with its neighbors, it is important to understand the role of water in the area. Recently, Prime Minister Benjamin Netanyahu declared in response to a suggestion by President Obama of the United States that there would be no

going back to the pre-1967 war boundary lines with Israel's neighbors. Many experts wondered whether the Golan Heights could be given up because it would leave Israel, particularly Jerusalem, indefensible.

More important than the strategic advantage of the Golan Heights is the water security it affords Israel. The eastern mountain ridge of the Golan Heights comprises the watershed of Lake Tiberias (Sea of Galilee), which provides Israel with 30 percent of its water supply. Syrian control of the watershed could contaminate the lake and enable Damascus to divert the water resources of the lake, cutting off water to Israel. The backdrop of Damascus's track record as a serial violator of commitments to other nations, including Turkey, Lebanon, Jordan, Iraq, and Israel stands in stark contrast to their promises to adhere to treaties. The belief of those in the UN, President Obama, and other global organizations and policy makers that Syria has launched a strategy of peace should be assessed against the background of the absence of comprehensive peace between Syria and its Muslim neighbors. Therefore, the comments of Prime Minister Benjamin Netanyahu to President Obama recently are able to be judged from a better perspective — partially as a stance to protect Israel's water security and national security interests.

An examination of the track record of security guarantees issued by the U.S., and by previous global powers, demonstrates that they do not possess automaticity or specificity for effective implementation. The vast majority of security guarantees have not been implemented; the ones that have been implemented failed miserably. As an example, the U.S. issued a presidential (Executive) guarantee in 1957 to coax Israel into a full withdrawal from the Sinai Peninsula. American failure to implement the guarantees when Egypt, Syria and Jordan declared a war on Israel in 1967 was a trigger for the Six Day War. Therefore, security guarantees have not constituted a credible insurance policy, but have instead produced a dangerous delusion, sacrificing long-term national security for a short-lived false sense of security.

In relation to this issue, Israel was initially provided a military advantage through capture of the Golan Heights, which is about 3,000 meters above sea level. It could be argued that with current military technology such as spy satellites, unmanned aerial vehicles, and so forth that this tactical advantage is no longer necessary. In contrast, the possible rupture of either energy supplies, in terms of electricity, fuel supply lines or communications, or other infrastructure and their cascading failure interdependencies, is likely not seen by the Israeli government as a wise decision to barter the strategic military nature of the Golan Heights away. If it were willing to vacate the heights, this would indicate that Israel could strengthen the relationship between the two governments, but only if Syria recognized Israel's right to exist. Both components will be necessary for a lasting peace. Conjointly, with the resistance of Hamas and Hezbollah to recognize Israel and their ties to Iran, the water issue will likely remain the primary obstacle to lasting peace.

For the Middle East and Southeast Asia, developing new resources will require technological solutions to increase water supplies such as desalination, water-water reuse, and so forth, but also, effective management of current resources such as transferring water from wet to dry zones is also necessary. Both types of measures will require significant financial investment. According to the U.S. State Department, billions of dollars (USD) of U.S. military aid has been given to Iraq ($6.5), Israel ($2.75), Egypt ($1.75), Pakistan ($1.6), Jordan ($0.3), Palestine ($0.1), and Yemen ($0.7) USD; additional aid is even larger in some instances. If this aid, even portions of it, were proportionately distributed for development of water resource programs and initiatives such as construction of a desalination plant on the Mediterranean, the development of these new water resources would enhance economic development, reduce unemployment, reduce citizen stress, improve public health, and overall, enhance security and stability of the immediate region. However, this is likely too idealistic because it would build trust and because it ignores the political self-interest factor of nations, politicians, and corporations.

Introduction

Transboundary water resources, issues, and disputes are those that cross one or more international borders. In this chapter three case studies will be examined to illustrate how transboundary disputes have been negotiated, the complex problems they involve, and how water resources have been developed and shared within regions. The term 'water war' has often been used to describe disputes regarding water use. Although various experts emphatically deny that armed conflict has ever resulted concerning water disputes, the 1967 Israel-Syria war is a specific example that contradicts such statements and will be discussed in detail herein. However, most water conflicts thus far have been controlled because stronger countries exercise control over weaker countries where the tension resides. Often termed hydro-hegemony, water-resource and security issues represent, to an extent, exploitation of a stronger group over a weaker group. The control has happened primarily through resource capture, in which countries acquire or annex land and construct infrastructure for control of the resource; containment, in which the stronger country may threaten economic sanctions, political isolation, or uneven agreements; and integration, in which combined water resources are shared and managed by multiple stakeholders.

The divergence between nations concerning economics, infrastructure, and political orientation has complicated transboundary water sharing. Poor use and management of already limited water resources provides evidence of problems at each level of government:

1. State level — lacking sufficient supplies,
2. National level — competing demands between sectors, and
3. International level — threats between nations sharing transboundary resources.

Domestically, transboundary water sharing conflicts are governed by legal regulations and enforcement. International transboundary water sharing conflicts are more difficult to cope with because such laws as the Fourth Geneva Convention are not enforceable at the country level without being prepared to go to war to achieve that enforcement. Transboundary water issues are quickly becoming the limiting factor in specific global regions for both political and economic sustainability. Experience has illustrated that revisions of transboundary allocation rights are generally contested when reassigned by political action. However, establishment of water markets by clearly defining property rights and compensation mechanisms could in some instances offer a more effective political option.

As examples of transboundary water-sharing problems that greatly influence regional and national security through a variety of factors, the Danube River System in Europe, China's transboundary water-sharing issues, and Israel's water disputes are discussed.

The Danube River – Transboundary Dispute Resolution

The Danube River represents the core, critical supply of water for central Europe, which includes all of Hungary, most of Romania, Austria, Slovenia, Croatia, and Slovakia, as well as significant parts of Bulgaria, Germany, Moldova, Serbia, the Czech Republic, and Ukraine. Other countries included are small parts of Italy, Switzerland, Albania, Poland, and Bosnia and Herzegovina (Figure 13.1). As with the rest of the world, a growing population base is placing greater demands on the river. The issues revolving around management have been complicated by the countries sharing the water that for years were enemy states.

Transboundary issues and disputes have revolved around three primary factors: political changes, severe economic changes, and climate. Despite historical hostilities, the riparian states of the river have established an integrated program for the basin-wide control of water quality, which is likely one of the first of its kind and also the most active and successful considering the scale of the system.

Politically, the collapse or Yugoslavia resulted in expatriation of hundreds of thousands and new states were established (Czech Republic, Slovakia, Slovenia, Croatia, Bosnia-Herzegovina, and others), which were pulled into the river agreements. Also, due to compliance with set environmental policies regarding water use in the Danube system, many of these countries have become members of the EU.[469] The Danube River transboundary problems, despite not

[469] Dr. Tindall served as a technical advisor for Romania for compliance issues revolving around environmental and water-quality contamination problems resulting from mine wastes in Romania's required compliance with EU policy regarding the

far distant political upheaval, have reached a more mature state than those of China and the Middle East; thus, a historical perspective can assist in describing how this system has overcome many issues.

Figure 13.1: The Danube River System and Riparian States.

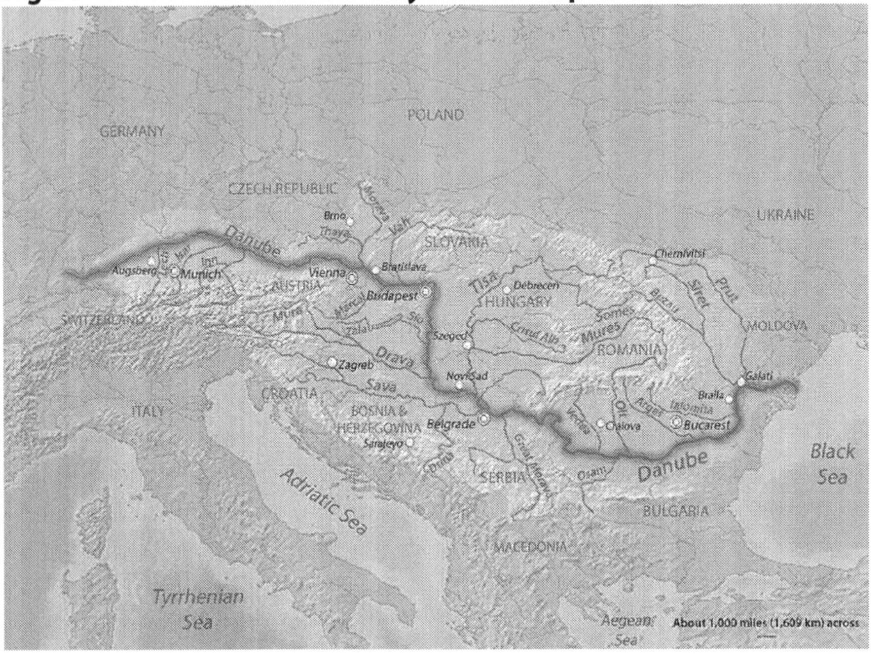

Prior to World War II, the European Commission of the Danube, with roots dating to the 1856 Treaty of Paris, was responsible for administration of the river. In the past, the primary concern was river transport, i.e., free navigation along the river for all countries. After the war, the East Bloc riparian who made up the majority of the delegates, shifted navigation control to the exclusive control of each riparian. This caused many problems, which were eventually resolved, primarily after the major political upheaval resulting from the breakup of the former Soviet Union. By 1980, navigation issues were yielding ground to environmental, pollution, and related issues in rank of importance. The large cities of Budapest, Belgrade, Bratislava, Vienna, and others were adding wastes from millions of residents, causing high pollution of various tributaries and

---

Danube. As a result of these efforts, Romania joined the EU in 2007.

the Danube River. This led to several policies or declarations that in 1994 became the Danube River Protection Convention.

The riparian states quickly learned that the environmental quality of the river depended on the environment of the basin as a whole and began work on a regional integrated approach to water-basin management.[470] Water quality became a driving force for cooperation and each state agreed to adopt similar monitoring systems and methods to assess environmental impact, govern state liability for transboundary pollution, define environmental protection rules, and define guidelines for development to preserve sensitive environmental areas. By 1992, an interim task force met in Brussels and adopted a plan that listed a series of actions and activities necessary to strengthen coordination between the governments and NGOs involved.

The environmental program established key principles for coordination and participation, making it unique in integration planning on this scale. The primary goal was to protect the environment, which was done by providing an operational basis for strategic and integrated management that focused on environmental issues. One primary factor of the plan that has made the outcome so successful was the recognition between internal politics among different sectors and political constituents within a nation in contrast to the strength and resilience of an agreement reached in the international realm. This effectually strengthened consultation procedures, allowing short-term goals to be met and major environmental threats to the basin to be addressed realistically utilizing joint problem solving. The most interesting factor of the strategic action plan was that it called for wide consultation during preparation with parties who would be responsible for its implementation. Effectually, it required public participation during development. Because of this, the Danube River is likely one of the most effectively management systems globally. Also, the concept of public participation rejects the principle that internal politics within nations should be treated as a geopolitical black box whose workings are of little relevance to international agreements, and instead embraces the vital need for input at all levels from all stakeholders for

---

[470] Staff, "Transboundary Water Basins in Europe," ed. Agriculture and Local and Regional Affairs Committee on the Environment (Parliamentary Assembly, 2004).

a plan to ensure the plan has the support of those who will implement it.

The public consultation process required each riparian state to choose a designated country facilitator to sponsor public consultation meetings and ensure public input and return feed back to the drafting group. The process also included training workshops to educate trainers. The consultation meetings included about 30 people from almost every sector, i.e., the government, universities, water, forestry, agriculture, industry, and so forth. The overall plan was adopted in 1994. However, it should be noted that the foundations date back to the Treaty of Paris in 1856 that established the European Commission of the Danube; major revisions next began in 1948 at the Belgrade Convention. Then, in 1985 a cooperative agreement concerning water management was signed by riparian states, known as the Bucharest Declaration. Since 1985, continual progress has been made to resolve disputes between riparian states.

Several factors served as the driving forces for transboundary cooperation for the Danube River. These include:

- A large gradient in economic development,
- Major political changes in Central and Eastern Europe after 1991,
- Transformation of legislation and administration of former East Bloc countries,
- Water pollution and environmental degradation, and
- International River, i.e., use for navigation.

From the historical setting above, the mode of cooperation shifted from bilateral agreements to basin-wide agreements, the establishment of what is now the International Commission for the Protection of the Danube River (ICPDR), and from a single objective approach to an integrated management approach. One of the latest major international agreements between the riparian states is the River Basin Management Plan that was agreed upon in 2009. Since 1948, it has taken 63 years for fruition of adequate transboundary dispute resolution that has required constant and consistent vigilance.

Through development and implementation of the strategic action plan, various principles and strategies appear important. Water and environment relation actions should likely be based on implementation of precautionary principles, utilizing best available techniques and practices, controlling pollution at the source, requiring the polluter to pay, and regional cooperation and information sharing. Also, the public participation and collaborative problem solving approach used in the development of the strategic action plan significantly shortened the time for preparation and approval. Additionally, the degree of cooperation among representatives of participating riparian states, and the importance given to public participation in developing the plan mark significant achievements in promoting regional cooperation in water resources management. Full success of such agreements will ultimately be decided by the degree to which the goals and operational strategies are implemented.

There remains competition for available water in some regions of the basin. Large abstractions of water combined with large season variation in flow still result in water supply shortages. However, the main conflict is between agricultural water supply and other uses. In some countries like Ukraine and Romania, the agricultural sector still requires more than 50 percent of total water consumption.[471] And, deficits in available water for consumptive purposes and pressures on the ecological system are increasing. Despite these issues, the Danube River management agreements represent one of the more successful transboundary dispute resolutions around the world, particularly because public participation early in the decision-making process helped facilitate cooperation and prevented conflict over management of international waters.

China-India-Pakistan Transboundary Water Issues

Water-security issues threaten China's basic national interests. Increasing drought conditions in some parts of China and disparate distribution of water resources, as well as economic interests and

[471] Ibid.

international political pressure are beginning to frame the Chinese government's position on this issue. Both the quantity and distribution of water throughout the country and its neighbors, including Pakistan, India, and Southeast Asia, represent significant challenges to China's future. Since the end of the last ice age, Himalayan glaciers have been melting; along with increasing population, it is anticipated that long-term declines in water availability will occur, as has been happening recently. The goal to maintain economic growth at about eight percent annually is threatened by water-security issues. Melting glaciers that provide a large amount of water to China's rivers and those of Southeast Asia are experiencing water-flow variability; other issues related to water quantity are also occurring, including desertification and salt-water intrusion along some coastal areas, which threaten both economic sustainability and food production. The Mekong River and fragile border regions along Northern Pakistan are demanding increased geopolitical communication with these neighbors, which are far from cordial.

China has been diverting water from sources originating in Tibet to aid their own water shortages which in turn leaves other neighboring countries with less water flow from source. One conflict (between China, Pakistan and India over the Indus River) has been aptly named 'war at the top of the world.' Can China and its neighbors manage the water problems within themselves or will it escalate into a form of the Jordan River conflicts between Israel and its neighbors, which resulted in war?

Many Asian nations are already under some form of water stress that minimally threatens economic sustainability from the individual fisherman to the country level, and the Asian continent, due to population, has the lowest per-capita water allocation of all continents excepting Antarctica.[472] As an example, in northern China, water use compared to availability is about four times the level in the south,[473] i.e., water availability in northern China is much less than in Southern China. Unfortunately, northern China is where most of the

---

[472] "Asia's Next Challenge: Securing the Region's Water Future.," (New York: Asia Society, 2009).

[473] Z. Shalizi, "Addressing China's Growing Water Shortages and Associated Social and Environmental Consequences," (World Bank, 2009).

factories that keep China's economic engine running were built. China's large size and proximity to ocean and desert regimes causes extreme cyclical climate change events and thus, disparate water distribution from severe droughts in the north to extreme flooding in the south. The extreme variability has increased soil degradation, resulting in desertification creep in the north and erosive soil loss in the south, resulting in loss of agricultural production. These climatic extremes are expected to increase maximum monthly flows along the Mekong river basin by 35 to 40 percent; minimum monthly flows are expected to decline by 17 to 24 percent.[474] This significant flux change will threaten and could disrupt economic and agricultural activity in the most vulnerable regions of the Mekong basin due to increased flooding during the wet season and less available water during the dry season. Additionally, coastal regions in these vulnerable areas could experience salt-water intrusion due to fresh water drawdown, resulting in greater effects on agricultural production.

Without the occurrence of another ice age that formed the Himalayan glaciers, they will continue to melt, analogous to tossing an ice cube onto the floor in the middle of a room, until the glaciers are gone, even without increasing global temperatures. Unfortunately, glacier melt accounts for about 70 percent of the summer flow in the Ganges river systems and about 60 percent of the flow in other major Asian river systems such as the Brahmaputra.[475] Inevitably, glacier flow will cease, resulting in catastrophic water shortages and extremely severe transboundary water-security issues that will likely lead to mass civil unrest, widespread starvation through reduced agricultural production, and war. Knowing the potential beforehand, how would policy among the transboundary water sharing countries avert these conditions? China's water and transboundary issues affect many countries, as illustrated in Figure 13.2, including Afghanistan, Pakistan, India, and all of Southeast Asia. It should be noted that both Pakistan and India are nuclear armed.

---

[474] B.C. Bates, and Kundzewicz, Z.W., Wu, S., and Palutikof, J.P., "Climate Change and Water," ed. Secretariat (Geneva: IPCC, 2008).

[475] T. Barnett, ADam, J., and Lettenmaier, D., "Potential Impacts of a Warming Climate on Water Availability in Snow-Dominated Regions," *Nature* (2005).

The Tarim River, as an example, which is Xinjiang's most important river system depends on glacial melt for about 40 percent of its annual flow and will likely be heavily impacted by seasonal flow variability. Overall, water distribution patterns, particularly related to precipitation, will likely become much more variable. The water-related issues will clearly spill over China's borders, especially in the major rivers and their systems, including the Indus, Ganges, Brahmaputra, Irrawaddy, Salwan, and Mekong. The major transboundary conflicts are likely to occur in relation to the Ganges, Indus and Mekong rivers, affecting Bangladesh, India and Pakistan, and Laos/Thailand/Cambodia, respectively.

Figure 13.2: Indus River and Southeast Asia primary rivers.

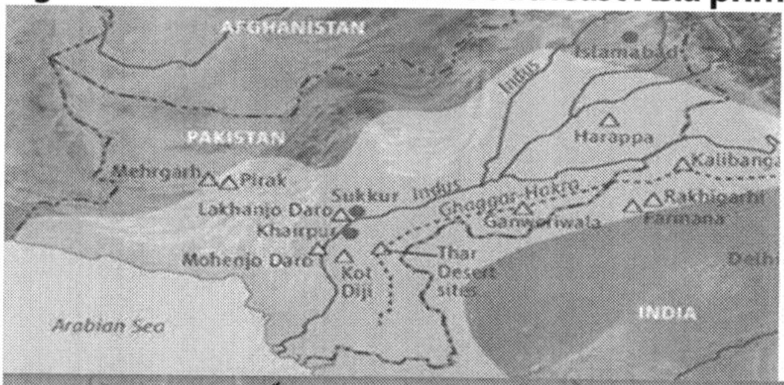

Indus river system left. Pakistan, India, and Southeast river systems bottom.

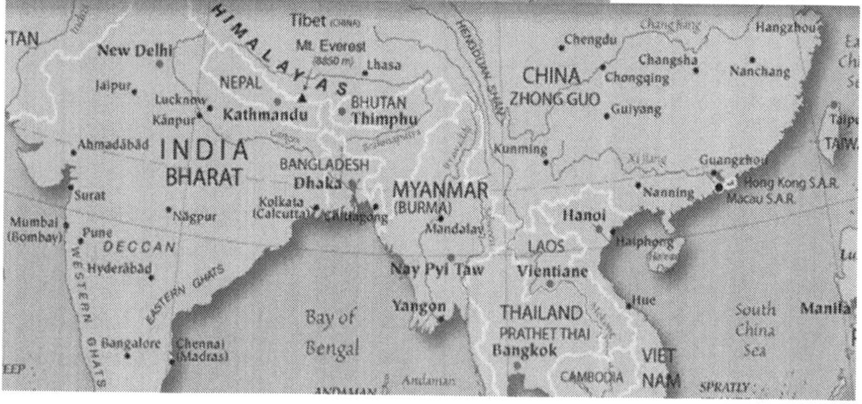

Since the late 1990s China has begun addressing both environmental and social issues through better cooperation and dialogue as a part of their new security concept and initiative, especially due to the destabilizing nature of water within China and on its neighbor states, which could potentially lead to conflict similar to that in the Middle East. As early as 2008, China began better

agreements with its neighbors and signed an agreement with the government of the Russian federation concerning reasonable utilization and protection of transboundary waters that specified the scope, contents and methods of bilateral cooperation, as well as providing legal foundations for further cooperation.[476]

Despite cooperative efforts with other countries regarding transboundary disputes, it is clear that China's very survival, particularly its economic sustainability, is growingly threatened by its water-security and water supply issues. About 23 percent of its population lives in western regions where glacial melt provides the principal dry season water source. This continually diminishing resource will create a growing competition among users. As water supplies grow scarcer there is the possibility of migration from scarce resource areas to more plentiful resource areas, resulting in unrest, possible ethnic tensions with the Han minority in western China, job loss and public health issues. During 2008-2009 in northern China, the worst winter drought in 30 years occurred, which affected about 40 percent of China's winter wheat crop. As with many countries facing resource shortages, a greater emphasis has been placed on disaster management and response capabilities, much of which will likely fall on China's military, analogous to what the U.S. has done with its National Guard.

Transboundary issues are only a part of China's water problems. The Yangtze River flows in China from Qinghai Province to the East China Sea and geographically separates North China and South China. It supports approximately one third of China's population and is the main water supply for agriculture, representing almost half of China's crop production. Additionally, analogous to the Mississippi in the U.S., the Yangtze serves as the major navigable waterway in China. It binds the inland and coastal ports together with other major cities into a transportation network in which Nanjing, Wuhan, and Chongqing are major hubs. The Yangtze River is also the main water supply for the industrial sector, with a recorded 40 percent of the country's industrial output through both the Gezhou Dam and the Three Gorges Dam.

---

[476] Ministry of Foreign Affairs, "China's Territorial and Boundary Affairs," (Beijing2008).

The river is a crucial lifeline that secures sustainable socio-economic development. The Three Gorges Dam, built across the Yangtze, helped to increase China's electricity supply, making it more affordable, and also helped to control catastrophic floods, thereby boosting agricultural production and the economy. The Three Gorges Dam has undergone much controversy; however, "It is necessary ... for the sake of the long-term stability of the national economy as a whole and the safety of the lower and middle reaches of the Yangtze," said Wan Li, chairman of the National People's Congress, China's nominal Parliament (1992). A report by the United States Department of Defense stated the dam would be a prime target for China's enemies because of the value the dam holds and the destruction of the dam from an enemy standpoint would be an easy way to win a war with China.[477] Other countries view the Chinese Dam projects as indirect deadly weapons, and if the Chinese continue their attempts to dam or redirect the southward flow of river waters from the Tibetan plateau, a war against South Asia is likely. In May 2007, the Asian Development Bank and Asia-Pacific Water Forum stated, "the majority of Asia's water problems are not attributable to an actual shortage, but rather are the result of poor water governance." This is only partially true as there generally is poor water governance throughout the world at large, but substantially it over simplifies the problem. At the 7th Asian Security Summit in June 2007, the Minister of Defense, based in Singapore, Teo Chee Hean, said, "Asia acknowledges the growing international water tensions and national conflicts, but, instead of competing over water, or food, or energy, we can increase our collective security by cooperating to harness alternative energy sources and increase food supply; while looking ahead, we need to build capacities that are capable of accommodating different modes of cooperation between different configurations of countries."

Within and without, China has enormous water-security concerns for which solutions will be hard fought and complex.

---

[477] "Asia's Next Challenge: Securing the Region's Water Future.."

The Indus River and China's Neighbors — Pakistan and India

The Indus River starts in Tibet, China, and flows through India and Pakistan, ending at the Arabian Sea (Figure 13.2); the river stretches 1,976 miles with the final flow entering the Arabian Sea at an approximate flow rate of 207 billion cubic meters annually. The Indus River is the main water supply to millions of people of China, India, and Pakistan. Water shortages in China, Pakistan, Nepal, Bangladesh, and India are driven by distribution patterns, population increases, and economic growth. This river has a history of conflict that is continuing to escalate. Dams and water diversions have been built along the Indus River to provide power and irrigation to provinces, but downstream users are experiencing decreasing supply, increased pollution, population displacement, and ecosystem destruction.

Water is the key component to survival. The Indus River has been an area of conflict between China, Pakistan, Nepal, Bangladesh, and India for centuries. The use/overuse of water, territorial claiming of water resources, damming, and water distribution are resulting in water conflicts. An example of water's importance is the 1948 dispute between India and Pakistan as the two countries were formed out of one big land mass, giving no defining water boundaries for either country. As a result, India stopped all water sources within its territory that were flowing into Pakistan. Pakistan, being down river from India, "was hit hard by the water shortage with enormous loss in energy sector and agriculture-related businesses, in addition to imminent food inflation. Instead of military retaliation, the Indus Water Treaty was formed to alleviate water conflicts by giving both countries control of three rivers from Jammu and Kashmir. However, despite efforts from the International Law Association implementing the Dubrovnik rules leading to the Helsinki Rules, conflicts have continued. Disputes between Pakistan and India have continued; in 1984, India built the barrage on the Jhelum River at the mouth of Wullar Lake and then, in 1992, the Baglihar Dam on the Chenab River; these, along with many more instances have maintained a constant tension between the two countries. And, because the headwaters of the Indus begin in Tibet, there is growing tension between three nuclear armed neighbors regarding these transboundary disputes. As water quantity diminishes, the trend of damming water resources continues as does the fight to control and profit from water resources. Depending on water shortage severity, the Indus Water Treaty is in jeopardy of failing.

China's water-related issues will continue to put pressure on the country as a whole, especially economically, as well as require additional focus on foreign relations and political discourse relating to transboundary issues and national security. Specific regions such as the Mekong, Indus, and Ganges, will likely be more severely impacted with time in regard to water stress, and being transboundary in nature will likely strain the capacity of Chinese institutions and policy frameworks. Not only does China's economic sustainability depend upon its water resources and water security, its national security will be in jeopardy in event of severe water stress, forcing greater cooperation or potential hostility with its surrounding neighbors and even the U.S. because of strategic concerns over water and food security, along with economic sustainability.

Israel's Water Disputes

Throughout history various irritants have fueled water wars. These issues have created violence on many levels: ethnic groups, religious groups, water-use sectors, states or provinces, and at an international level. Violence from water conflicts ranges from interstate violence and death along the Cauvery River in India, to California farmers blowing up a pipeline meant for Los Angeles, and toward much of the violent history in the Americas between indigenous peoples and European settlers.

Tactical, Strategic, and Water-Security Significance of the Golan Heights

To understand the Middle East, particularly Israel and its relations with its neighbors, it is important to understand the role of water in the area. Recently (summer 2011), Prime Minister Benjamin Netanyahu declared in response to a suggestion by President Obama of the United States that there would be no going back to the pre-1967 war boundary lines with Israel's neighbors. Many experts wondered whether the Golan Heights could not be given up because

it would leave Israel, particularly Jerusalem indefensible. However, the issue of water does not manifest itself only in the Golan Heights, which is a major watershed, but also in the valley below, where the Jordan River flows into Lake Tiberias, i.e., the Sea of Galilee (see Figure 13.3). The key elements that highlight the centrality of the Golan Heights in the national security policy of Israel also apply to the mountain ridges of Judea and Samaria, which are located at a much more strategically sensitive location than the Golan Heights. The military importance of the Golan Heights has increased during recent years due to the advent of ballistic technologies. The 1991 Gulf War and the proliferation of U.S. military bases and installations throughout the globe attest to the critical role played by topographic and geographic edge and depth respectively, and the strategic location for bolstering one's national security.

Figure 13.3: Water and political boundaries representing the real Middle East crises.

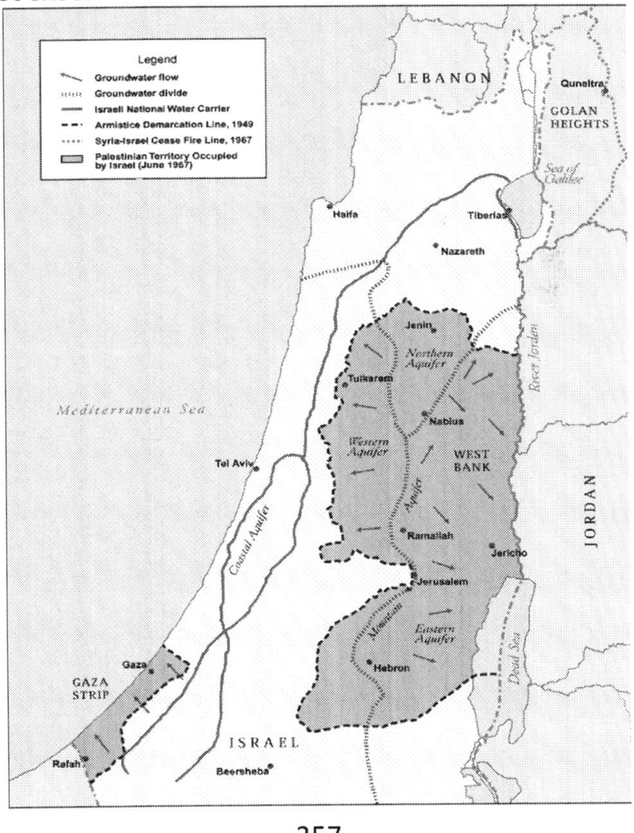

Although advanced high-tech military and early-warning systems enhance the capabilities of military forces, they cannot replace the unique contribution of a vital territory such as the Golan Heights. As an example, the high-tech of today will become the low-tech of tomorrow; in contrast, the high ground of today remains the high ground of tomorrow and no military strategist would recommend forfeiture. Israel's neighbors can and will acquire superior technological systems, but they cannot replicate the water resources or strategic nature of the mountain ridges of the Golan Heights and Judea and Samaria. Further, sophisticated military systems can be jammed, but no army can jam a topographical edge.

The importance of the Golan Heights to Israel's national security hinges on the eastern mountain ridge, which stretches between Mount Hermon in the north to the steep canyon of the Rokad River in the south. As a note, it was discovered this constitutes an effective natural tank barrier — it enabled less than 200 Israeli tanks to fend off the surprise offensive of 1,400 Syrian tanks during the 1973 Yom Kippur War, when Israel retook the Golan Heights. A withdrawal from the Golan Heights would deny Israel the key strategic military benefits they afford and would likely expose Israel to a plethora of lethal threats. Militarily, the Golan Heights and ridge, located 35 miles from Damascus, would deprive Israel of an effective posture of deterrence and could induce further hostilities in the region rather than reduce them, as suggested by President Obama and U.S. policy makers.

An examination of the track record of security guarantees issued by the U.S., and by previous global powers, demonstrates that the guarantees do not possess automaticity or specificity for effective implementation. The vast majority of security guarantees have not been implemented; the ones that have failed miserably. As an example, the U.S. issued a presidential (Executive) guarantee in 1957 to coax Israel into a full withdrawal from the Sinai Peninsula. American failure to implement the guarantees when Egypt, Syria and Jordan declared a war on Israel in 1967, was a trigger for the Six Day War. Therefore, security guarantees have not constituted a credible insurance policy, but have produced a dangerous delusion, sacrificing long-term national security for a short-lived false sense of security.

More important than the strategic advantage of the Golan Heights is the water security it affords Israel. The eastern mountain ridge of the Golan Heights comprises the watershed of Lake Tiberias (Sea of Galilee), which provides Israel with 30 percent of its water. Syrian control of the watershed could contaminate the lake and enable Damascus to divert the water resources of the lake, cutting off water to Israel. The backdrop of Damascus's track record as a serial violator of commitments to other nations, including Turkey, Lebanon, Jordan, Iraq, and Israel stands in stark contrast to their promises to adhere to treaties. The belief of those in the UN, President Obama, and other global organizations and policy makers that Syria has launched a strategy of peace should be assessed against the background of the absence of comprehensive peace between Syria and its Muslim neighbors. Further, Syria is a leader in narco-terrorism, prolifically abuses human rights, builds military systems of mass destruction, and denies Israel's right to exist. Transferring the Golan Heights to Syria would likely make them less constrained and allow them to dedicate even more of their military resources toward regional ambitions, upsetting, not binding, regional stability. Therefore, the comments of Prime Minister Benjamin Netanyahu to President Obama recently can be judged from a better perspective. The comments were not an insult to the President, but rather a stance to protect Israel's water security and national security interests. This is all aside from the Golan Heights' integral role in religious aspects, which will not be covered in this text. Determining the future of the Golan Heights without a grasp of critical facts is futile; their importance cannot be oversimplified if indeed sound transboundary water policy is sought.

Golan Heights Background

The Golan Heights were captured by Israel in the 1967 war and annexed in 1981. The Heights lay between the borders of Israel and Syria. More importantly, they prevent Syria from access to Jordan River water and to Lake Tiberias. As background, in 1966 the UN reported that Israel and Syria had produced 66,000 official complaints against each other regarding demilitarized zones between the countries borders. The decade leading up to the 1967 witnessed an

increased struggle over water; Syria initiated several water projects to divert the Jordan River; Israel promptly attacked them. The Syrian projects were likely in response to Israel's diversion of the water of Lake Tiberias by sending it 155 miles south to the Negev desert in 1956.[478] As demonstrated in the well-publicized discussion between Israeli Prime Minister Benjamin Netanyahu and President Obama, the issue of the Golan Heights will be an important part of any peace negotiations between Israel and Syria. Based on the water component, it is unlikely Israel will easily give up the Golan Heights, at least not without a guarantee of maintaining the current allocation of water to Israel and preventing Syrian access to that water.

In relation to this issue, Israel was initially provided a military advantage through capture of the Golan Heights, which is about 3,000 meters above sea level, but it could be argued that with current military technology such as spy satellites, unmanned aerial vehicles, and so forth, that the tactical advantage is no longer there. In contrast, the rupture of energy supplies, in terms of electricity, or fuel supply lines or communications and their cascading failure interdependencies, it is likely not seen by the Israeli government as a wise decision to barter the Golan Heights away. If Israel were willing to vacate the heights it could strengthen the relationship between the two governments, but only if Syria recognized Israel's right to exist. Both components will be necessary for a lasting peace. Conjointly, with the resistance of Hamas and Hezbollah to recognize Israel and their ties to Iran, the water issue will likely remain the main obstacle to lasting peace. Why?

The Jordan River begins in northern Israel and flows into Lake Tiberias, borders Jordan, and flows into the Jordan River basin, where it converges with the Yarmuk River. This basin supplies Israel, Jordan, and Syria with water, despite that Israel and Palestine utilize groundwater as a major supply. This basin supply has long been in dispute. In 1953, the U.S. sent special envoy Eric Johnston to attempt to mediate a negotiated settlement of Jordan River allocations.[479] The initial proposal from Johnston was based on a study prepared by Charles Main of the TVA at the request of the UN. Known as the 'Main

---

[478] A.T. Wolf, "Middle East Water Conflicts and Directions for Conflict Resolution," *International Food Policy Institute* (1996).
[479] Ibid

Plan,' it allocated 393 million cubic meters (mcm) annually to Israel, 774 mcm to Jordan, and 45 mcm to Syria.[480] Although the plan was initially adhered to by both parties, it was never ratified.[481]

During the 1960s both Israel and Jordan undertook projects that would divert water from the Jordan River for their own use, which was in excess of the Main Plan, later called Johnston's Plan. Israel began withdrawing 320 mcm for its National Water Carrier plan, while Jordan developed the East Ghor project and extended an irrigation canal from the Yarmuk River. Combined with skirmishes between Israel and Syria, these events helped initiate the 1967 war.[482] The Golan Heights and other territories Israel gained during the war improved its hydraulic geopolitical position; Israel acquired two of three headwaters of the Jordan River, riparian access to the entire Jordan River, and access to the Mountain Aquifer in the West Bank.[483] Thus, the war was a 'water war.' Although Jordan and Israel signed a peace treaty — the Jordan-Israeli Peace Treaty — water remains a point of contention.

Both countries have undertaken data exchange on water resources through the Joint Water Committee, which is comprised of three members from each country.[484] As a note, Dr. Tindall has worked very effectively with this aspect of the Middle East Peace Process, through the auspices of the U.S. Department of State, with Jordanians, Palestinians, and Israelis. While Jordan and Israel have cooperated for the most part, the relation with the Palestinian Authority remains highly contentious. The main source of concern between the latter two is the Mountain Aquifer located on the West Bank (Figure 13.3). The aquifer underlies the West Bank extending east to Jordan and west to the Mediterranean Sea and has three sub-aquifers: (1) Eastern; (2) Western; and (3) North-Eastern.[485] Latest estimates indicate Israel uses 340 million cubic meters (mcm) per year

---

[480] Wolf, "Middle East Water Conflicts and Directions for Conflict Resolution."
[481] Ibid
[482] Ibid
[483] Ibid
[484] R.M. Fathallah, "Water Disputes in the Middle East: An International Law Analysis of the Israeli-Jordan Peace Accord," *Journal of Land Use Environmental Law* 12, no. 1 (1996).
[485] Staff, "Treaty of Peace between the State of Israel and the Hashemite Kingdom of Jordan," (ILM, 1994).

of the 362 mcm supply of this aquifer, while the Palestinians use the remaining 22 mcm.

The water-security issues in contention among Israel and the Palestine were first addressed in 1993 in a meeting called the Declaration of Principles, which called for the creation of a Palestinian Water Administration Authority, as well as other issues to enable economic growth.[486] Both parties recognize the equitable distribution of the resource, but negotiations are complex. In 1995, further agreements were attempted in Oslo II where the parties agreed to basic water rights in the West Bank, the necessity to develop additional water supply, to coordinate the management of water and sewage resources and systems in the West Bank, maintain existing quantity use, and various other points.[487]

After Oslo II, both parties continued in negotiations, which stalled after 2000 due to the onset of the Second Intifada.[488] The Second Intifada, also known as the Al-Aqsa Intifada and the Oslo War, was the second Palestinian uprising — a period of intense Palestinian-Israel violence, which began in September 2000. Additional information may be found within numerous sources not listed here. The integrated water system that existed prior to this remains today, but the Palestinians have no control over or access to the water source. As an example, 75 percent of the Mountain Aquifer is allocated to Israel, even though it is on Palestinian land; approximately 20 percent of Palestinians in the West Bank are not connected to the water source and need to purchase water on the private market, as with many older systems, as discussed in chapter 15. Drilling new wells and utilizing other resources require permission from Israel for A (Palestinian inhabitants only), B (Israeli and Palestinians), and C (Israeli) areas.

New wells and other issues have been agreed upon, but are slow in development. However, many of the planned wells had adequate yield, but led to salt-water intrusion from the floor of Jordan Valley into the lower portion of the aquifer and were closed.[489]

---

[486] Ibid

[487] Ibid

[488] Ibid

[489] J. Selby, "Joint Mismanagement: Reappraising the Oslo Water Regime," http://www.ipcri.org/watconf/papers/jan.pdf.

A potential solution for this problem is a desalination plant at Caesarea on the Mediterranean from which water could be conveyed across Israel to the West Bank. However, costs would likely be about 5 percent, perhaps a little more of an average day's wage in the West Bank (presently $22/day USD). The cost could be lowered if the plant supplied Israel with water who in turn allocated additional aquifer water supplies to the Palestinians. Idealistically, the U.S. military aid given to these countries would be better spent on construction of the desalination plant.

Because of water issues around the world, most countries follow the old Harmon Doctrine, which allowed a state to use the waters on its territory without obligation to riparian neighbors. Fortunately, this law has slowly given way to reasonable sharing among riparian states that led to the Helsinki Rules, which have a better convention in international law and which paved the way for a binding convention to be taken up by the UN. In 1997, the UN General Assembly adopted the Watercourse Convention. Among other issues, the Convention states that nothing in the agreement shall affect the rights and obligations of a state arising from an agreement in force on the date it became a party to the convention.

The Jordan-Israeli Peace Treaty predates the Convention and, while Jordan and Syria have ratified the treaty, to be enforced requires 16 of 35 countries. The problem with the Syrian ratification was that the country stipulated that ratifying the treaty did not imply recognition of Israel and shall not lead to its entering into relations therewith that are governed by its provisions.[490] Consequently, Israel viewed this as a political response, which they also view as incompatible with the purposes and objectives of the Convention and cannot affect whatever obligations are binding upon Syria under general international treaty law or particular conventions.[491] Therefore, drafting articles on the law of transboundary issues are rarely enforceable, despite provisions of the Fourth Geneva Convention.[492] But, in cases of dire shortage, there is no adequate

---

[490] UN, "Convention on the Law of the Non-Navigational Uses of Internation Watercourses 1997,"(2005), http://untreaty.un.org/ilc/texts/instruments/english/conventions/8_3_1997.pdf.

[491] Ibid

[492] Ibid

way to enforce such civilities short of declaration of war whether the issue resides with human rights or water rights.

In summary, the issue of Israel's water disputes is highly charged and politicized. The potential solutions for the would-be expert lies in whatever political camp they are presently grounded, not the good will of Israel or other country necessarily. Furthermore, these individuals' and politicians' self-interests are oriented generally toward human rights concerns, animosity toward Israel, Israel's accused status of discriminatory water policy, and other issues. However, there are the matters of the strategic military nature of the Golan Heights, religious aspects, and water security because of the watershed that provides one-third of Israel's water supply and thus, Israel's national security. Past and present political solutions have failed and are wrought with insincerity and mistrust. Progress toward effective negotiations will require a neutral party, not a party that represents a country such as Johnston did the U.S., but an individual who is unbiased, knowledgeable about water use and issues, and non-political. Unfortunately, politicians have never been able to effectively settle such disputes and have proven ineffectual — in this case, putting forth the self interests of those they serve. A solution to this problem will require an individual who has a unique ability to build trust with all parties. More importantly, the person must be chosen by the parties involved, not pushed from the outside as was Johnston, despite the good intentions. In the biblical sense, a solution would require the wisdom of King Solomon and an individual not grounded in government or corporate bureaucracy.

Conclusions

Many well-documented case studies of transboundary water issues exist. Two examples in the U.S. include the Colorado River and in the Southeast U.S. between the states of Alabama, Florida, and Georgia. Even in peaceful settings, transboundary agreements have taken years to develop and adopt. The European case study presented in this chapter is analogous to these two. For the most part, the solutions to transboundary issues were developed during peaceful time and even then, required over 60 years to arrive at current practices and solutions that are constantly changed based on use, increasing population, and so forth.

Resolving a transboundary water dispute in a protracted conflict setting is, in actuality, the prior resolution of a political conflict and in such a conflict many self interests are held by the politicians involved, but are not representative of the people served. The history of the water disputes in the Jordan River basin and the Indus basin between India and Pakistan, where all parties have been deeply intertwined with a protracted political conflict, suggests that such states that provoke wars or engage in visceral issues of territorial sovereignty and the recognition of identities are not inclined to collaborate in highly technical matters that concern economic development and human welfare. There is simply too much posturing, not only from the parties involved, but also from the institutions and politicians who throw their alleged expertise into the ring, to supposedly benefit the countries in need. For example, some experts believe that an Israeli defense (on the ground of military necessity) fails regarding Israel's water policy and the Golan Heights, that the policy is disproportionate when viewed from the fundamental nature of water rights and what is termed as Israel's discriminatory water-use policy. However, this totally negates the strategic and water-security and supply side of the issue for Israel. The belief is simply that — not founded in facts; it is merely an objective for those whose interests are served by such expressions and are not conducive to effective collaboration between affected parties.

Understanding such matters would lead to the natural assumption that there will be no basin-wide accord regarding the Jordan River basin prior to completing final status negotiations between Israel, Jordan, Palestine, and Syria. And, for this to come about requires recognition of Israel as a state, as well as other important issues too lengthy to address. Another precondition for resolving transboundary water disputes is active support from a third party — a common assessment. However, what is lacking is trust of that third party, which has failed in the past, regardless of what country has put it forth. The negotiations should likely be done with a party, i.e., an individual, who can gain the trust of Israel, Jordan, and other stakeholders, and who has no political, geographic or country bias or agenda — only a hope to help people. No country or their ambassador(s) could likely fill such a task. The idea of a third party is as a sounding board that can develop trust between the individuals negotiating and that will not take sides in the issue. Institutional mechanisms have also failed in such negotiations although they can be a great help in qualitative analysis, but as with the negotiator, must be unbiased. Therefore, any successful and effective resolution of a transboundary water dispute will require that political and, in many cases, religious conflicts first are resolved. An impartial negotiator(s) is needed who can be chosen by the affected parties, not by other countries or organizations — working with local expertise on the problem will lead to quicker resolution if it can be achieved.

For the Middle East and Southeast Asia, developing new resources will require technological solutions to increase water supplies such as desalination, water-water reuse, and so forth, but also, effective management of current resources such as transferring water from wet to dry zones. Both types of measures will require significant financial investment. According to the U.S. State Department, billions of dollars (USD) of U.S. military aid has been given to Iraq ($6.5), Israel ($2.75), Egypt ($1.75), Pakistan ($1.6), Jordan ($0.3), Palestine ($0.1), and Yemen ($0.7) USD; additional aid is even larger in some instances. If even a portion of this aid were proportionately distributed for development of water resource programs and initiatives such as a desalination plant on the Mediterranean, the development of new water resources would enhance economic development, reduce unemployment, reduce citizen stress, improve public health, and overall, enhance security and stability of these regions.

PART III: POLICIES – EMERGENCY, ECONOMIC, AND LEGISLATIVE CONCERNS

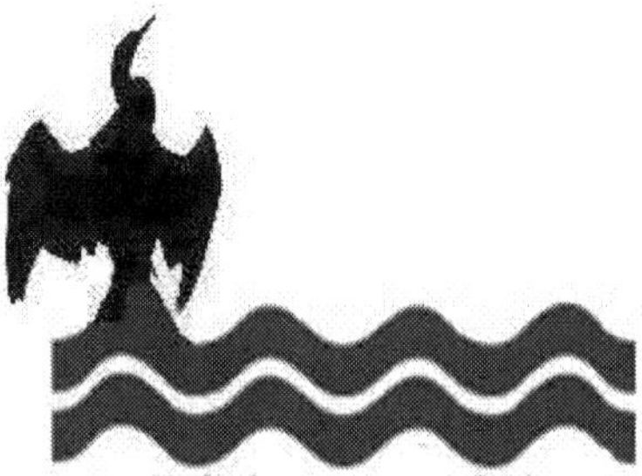

Tribal Water Symbol

CHAPTER 14: Emergency Preparedness, Incident Planning, and Response

William H. Austin CFO, CHS-III, MIFireE

Executive Summary

Expecting different levels of government, public authorities, and private sector interests to collaborate for the national good will result in disappointment. Why? When alleged collaborators have differing and unequal authority, funding, and power (operating doctrine and expertise), the politics of self interest generally rule. The trust and confidence between all levels of government and non-government collaborators generally decreases. This is the situation with water security in the United States today.

This chapter is not about writing emergency plans (the how-to is referenced in numerous locations) although some sources are mentioned. Our effort is more about shedding light on why the lack of information sharing between all levels of government and the private sector along with the infrastructure code of secrecy means most plans will not work after they are completed. Instant suggestions on what the security standards should be are not offered, even though there are no officially accepted federal or industry standards. Instead, it will be explained why this lack of standards continues to undermine the vast majority of the nation's water systems and local government emergency planning and complicate water security implementation in America. There is also an obvious difference in the federal approach to protecting water infrastructure compared to the approach of local and state governments — the low-probability high-consequence federal approach and the high-probability low-consequence local approach complicate collaboration and response. Are all the appropriate government officials intimately involved in the collaboration process? Who could be missed in collaboration efforts and why is that official (the local emergency management director, by any title) vital to coordinated success.

Introduction

This chapter is designed to create awareness about the value of collaboration and who should be collaborating in water security emergency preparedness efforts. First responders often focus on the hazardous materials angle of water-security. Health officials are concerned with sanitation and potability. The facility engineer will calculate proper chlorination and physical security measures of filtration facilities. The fire chief wants to maintain water pressure and constant flow rate of a system. Who could be missing in this critical effort?

Let us consider a few facts. Water is obviously critical to our existence. We drink it, cook with it, and clean with it. It's also used to transport commerce, it covers most of the world, and our body is over 90 percent water. Too much or too little water can cause death. Water is a natural force capable of saving crops or destroying entire communities — recent floods in spring 2011 in the U.S., primarily Missouri, are examples. However, it has only been the past eight to ten years that many have more carefully considered water and its security and requisite sustainability. Although water has always been part of our nation's critical infrastructure, it has only recently been recognized for its true value — to some extent. Emergency planners often fail to make the macro connection of water to critical infrastructure status, but "critical infrastructure is so vital to the United States that its incapacity would harm the nation's physical security, economic security, or public health. (United States Patriot Act of 2001, Public Law 107-56, Section 1016(e))."

There are nearly 53,000 community water systems in the U.S. The responsibility for development, management, and allocation of the nation's water resources is spread among federal, state, local, tribal, and private interests. The federal government has been involved in water resources development since the earliest days of the nation. From improvements to initially facilitate navigation and later to reduce flood damages and expand irrigation in the West, the federal government has been called upon to assist with and pay for a multitude of water resource development projects. In recent decades, it also has regulated water quality, protected fish and wildlife, and facilitated water supply augmentation. However, the federal role has limits. For example, Congress has generally deferred

to the states' primacy in intrastate water allocation. While local municipalities have largely been responsible for developing and distributing water supplies, the federal government in limited cases also has authorization to assist communities with water-supply development. Land-use planning and zoning are almost always within the purview of local governments; however, federal and state actions and interests may run counter to local interests and actions, and vice versa.[493]

Water is considered a tier 1 critical infrastructure component and the "the Patriot Act" definition was adopted by reference in the Homeland Security Act of 2002 (Public Law 107-296, Section 2.4), establishing the Department of Homeland Security (DHS). This means that under the concept of homeland security, the local government emergency management director (by whatever name) and designated homeland security officials at the state and Federal levels are key players and must be included in the collaborative efforts to protect our citizens. With this encompassing effort comes a brand new level of politics, responsibility, and need to communicate and share information with all the partners. But, "at the state and local level, there appears to be little that is positive about the relationship with federal partners. DHS continues to reorganize, change points of contact frequently, and brings to the table too much we are in charge attitude[494]."

Why is the subject of water security so volatile? A fairly small number of large drinking water and wastewater utilities located primarily in urban areas (about 15percent of the systems) provide water services to more than 75percent of the U. S. population. Arguably, these systems represent the greatest targets of opportunity for terrorist attacks.[495] Thus, although it is straight forward to focus on the issue, especially at the Federal level, the outcome generally is

---

493 CRS, "Congressional Research Service, 35 Years of Water Policy: The 1973 National Water Commission and Present Challenges," (Washington DC: Library of Congress, 2009).

494 DoD, "Unconventional Operational Concepts and the Homeland," ed. A Panel Report of the Defense Science Board 2007 Summer Study on Challenges to Military Operations and Support of U. S. Interests (Washington DC: Office of the Under Secretary of Defense for Acquisition, Technology, and Logistics, 2009).

495 Claudia Copeland, "Terrorism and Security Issues Facing the Water Infrastructure Security Sector," (Washington, DC: Library of Congress, 2009).

prioritization in grant funding with small providers feeling neglected or forgotten in the process, which is very similar in results to the Urban Area Security Initiative granting process, i.e., the larger cities get the most funding. The prioritization also means a lot of smaller systems and local governments will not provide the emergency planning attention their water infrastructure systems deserve due to lack of funding and/or responsible personnel.

Key questions include should protective measures be focused on the largest water systems and facilities; and who is responsible for additional steps since the federal government has direct control over only a limited portion of the water infrastructure sector?

No federal standards or agreed upon industry practices exist within the water infrastructure sector to govern readiness, response to security incidents, and recovery.[496] Additionally, analyzing security data on various water and wastewater assessments is difficult because of security issues created by releasing information that shows changes in security levels or applications. This safety and security process creates interference with operational readiness and preparedness of first responders attempting to deal with an incident and has a negative effect on situational awareness required by an incident commander.

What really defines the system must be clearly understood by all stakeholders involved in water security. Water supply was one of eight critical infrastructure systems identified in President Clinton's 1998 Presidential Decision Directive 63 (PPD-63) as part of a coordinated national effort to achieve the capability to protect the nation's critical infrastructure from intentional acts that could diminish them. ("The Clinton Administration's Policy on Critical Infrastructure Protection: Presidential Decision Directive 63," May 22, 1998; see (http://www.fas.org/irp/offdocs/paper598.htm.) And, in December 2003, President George W. Bush issued Homeland Security Presidential Directive/HSPD-7, which established a national policy for the federal government to identify, prioritize, and protect critical infrastructure as part of homeland security.[497]

---

[496] Ibid, p 5.

[497] President, "Homeland Security Presidential Directive/Hspd-7, Critical Infrastructure Identification, Prioritization, and Protection," (Washington DC: White House, 2003).

Water infrastructure systems include surface and ground water sources of untreated water for municipal, industrial, agricultural, and household needs; dams, reservoirs, aqueducts, and pipes that contain and transport raw water; treatment facilities that remove contaminants from raw water; finished water reservoirs; systems that distribute water to users; and wastewater collection and treatment facilities.[498] Defining the systems and analyzing potential security problems requires an emphasis be placed on specific processes to properly prepare for a natural disaster, act of terrorism, or technological failure. But, which process?

Funding for training and upgrading response capabilities at facilities and with first responders is beginning to make a difference. Although funding for security activities is always in short supply, research has shown that utilities in general have made little effort to address collection-system vulnerabilities due to the technical complexity and expense of securing collection systems that cover large areas and have many access points,[499] i.e., links and nodes in critical infrastructure terminology.

Also, many wastewater systems have reached the end of their useful design lives. Older systems are plagued by chronic overflows during major rainstorms and heavy snowmelt and are bringing about the discharge of raw sewerage into U. S. surface waters. The Environmental Protection Agency (EPA) estimated in August 2004 that the volume of combined sewer overflows discharged nationwide is 850 billion gallons per year.[500]

The Bioterrorism Act requires community drinking water systems serving populations of more than 3,300 persons to conduct assessments of their vulnerabilities to terrorist attack or other intentional acts and their abilities to defend against adversarial actions. In terms of water security, the act requires the EPA to protect the vulnerability assessments submitted by water systems and any information provided in them. The EPA is also required to provide information on potential adversarial actions that could threaten the

---

[498] Copeland, "Terrorism and Security Issues Facing the Water Infrastructure Security Sector."

[499] Ibid.

[500] ASCE, "2009 Report Card for America's Infrastructure," (Reston VA: American Society of Civil Engineers, 2009).

nation's water supply systems. Finally, the act requires the EPA to conduct research regarding prevention and detection of intentional contamination acts on water supply systems, methods that threaten water system infrastructure and physical security, and ways to provide alternative supplies of safe drinking water in the event of a natural or man-made act.[501]

Some experts view the physical destruction of a water system's components as increasingly more likely than contamination events because explosives are relatively easier to obtain than sufficient quantities of contaminants.[502] However, previously it has been shown this is an incorrect assumption — there is a high likelihood for either to occur.[503]

Water resources and water systems are viewed as vulnerable to terrorist attack for several reasons. First, they are vital to everyday life and economic activity — if disrupted or altered, the action can have a great impact on society and would garnish a great deal of publicity as a result. Second, they have played a prominent role in military history and terrorists often model their strategies from military-type operations, i.e., environmental warfare as an example. Third, water resources and water systems are typically easily accessible to the general public.[504]

These concerns highlight the utility of the systems themselves; what about external factors? In an open society such as the U.S., the vast size of the nation, combined with the complexity and diversity of infrastructure make it almost impossible to avoid an attack if terrorists plan and conduct one.

In addition, many state dam-safety programs do not have sufficient resources, funding, or staff to conduct dam safety inspections, to take appropriate enforcement actions, or to ensure proper construction by reviewing plans and performing construction

---

[501]EPA, "Requirements of the Public Health Security and Bioterrorism Preparedness and Response Act of 2002 (Bioterrorism),"(2009), http://cfpub.epa.gov/safewater/watersecurity/bioterrorism.cfm.
[502]Staff, "Security and Water," (Water Encyclopedia, 2009).
[503]J. Tindall, and Campbell, A., "Water Security - Nation State and International Security Implications," *Disaster Advances* 2, no. 2 (2009).
[504] Staff, "Security and Water."

inspections[505]. This situation clearly affects the quality of inundation maps submitted to the Federal government.

A dam's "hazard potential" is classified on the basis of the anticipated consequences of failure, not the condition of the dam. The classifications include "high hazard potential" (anticipated loss of life in the case of failure), "significant hazard potential" (anticipated damage to buildings and important infrastructure), and "low hazard potential" (anticipated loss of the dam or damage to the floodplain, but no expected loss of life).[506]

The 2009 American Society of Civil Engineers (ASCE) grade for dams is D, drinking water a D-, levees a D-, and wastewater a D-; absolutely dismal!

As of February 2009, initial results from the U. S. Army Corps of Engineers inventory show that while more than half of all federally inspected levees do not have deficiencies, 177, or about 9percent, are expected to fail in a significant flood event.[507] Levee failures in Missouri and along the Mississippi in the well publicized 2011 spring floods are examples.

Another odd twist is that states submit infrastructure classification information to the Federal government, which is not classified. Once the information is processed at the federal level it becomes classified (secret) information regarding what infrastructure qualified for the Federal list. Afterward, local and state government cannot then get the information to use for emergency planning. Also, droughts are another preparatory area; droughts of moderate intensity affect 10 percent of the United States at any given time.

From the emergency planning and homeland security perspective, if water problems are acute, agencies may not be sharing information, and significant portions of the water infrastructure are graded D or lower. Additionally, our nation always experiences a certain number of droughts, wastewater systems are old, and funding problems prevent proper inspections. Since readiness is about risk assessment, incident planning, and response, emergency planners should be really busy professionals. But are they?

---

[505] ASCE, "2009 Report Card for America's Infrastructure."
[506] Ibid.
[507] Ibid.

One could easily reason that our water infrastructure is in a very precarious position, even without threat of terrorist attack. The keys to successful solution for the current problems include several factors. The working relationships of critical stakeholders are of paramount importance; collaborative emergency response services are vital to the stabilization efforts; and a clear understanding of the big picture will be the public's test for evaluating correct emergency response.

Relationships

Similar to the concept of homeland security, the responsibility for maintaining, securing, and managing our nation's water infrastructure is spread among the various levels of government, the private sector, and some public authorities.

Local utilities have primary responsibility to assess their vulnerabilities and prioritize them for necessary security improvements. Most (especially in urban areas) have emergency preparedness plans that address issues such as redundancy of operations, public notification, and coordination with law enforcement and emergency response official's.[508]

Water utilities are dependent on electric power to treat and distribute power, and electric power is essential to collecting and treating wastewater (refer to chapter 3). Adequate and uninterrupted supply of water is necessary to support municipal firefighting.[509]

The National Strategy for the Physical Protection of Critical Infrastructures and Key Assets (NSPP) contains a list of the critical infrastructures, which includes drinking water and wastewater treatment. Critical infrastructure is also influenced by "geographic concentration" that is defined as the physical location of critical assets in sufficient proximity to each other that they are vulnerable to disruption by the same, or successive regional events.[510] For example,

---

[508] Copeland, "Terrorism and Security Issues Facing the Water Infrastructure Security Sector."

[509] Ibid, page 12.

[510] CRS, "Vulnerability of Concentrated Critical Infrastructure: Background and Policy Options," ed. Congressional Research Service (Washington DC: Library of Congress, 2007).

over 38 percent of the U. S. chlorine production is located in coastal Louisiana[511] and over 35 percent of U.S. freight railcars pass through Illinois, primarily around Chicago.[512]

To prepare for potential accidental releases of hazardous chemicals from their facilities, more than 2,800 wastewater and drinking water facilities, water supply systems, and irrigation systems already are subject to risk-management planning requirements under the Clean Air Act.[513]

Congress directed EPA to enter into a memorandum of understanding (MOU) with DHS to define the relationship of the two entities with regard to the protection and security of the nation in reference to wastewater and drinking water.[514] The fact this action was necessary signals operational and relationship problems.

For instance, the Department of Defense (DOD) does not really know what is expected of it and the homeland security community does not know what to expect from DOD. The transition of responsibility from supporting to leading roles among the various agencies involved and the handoff of these roles from one agency to another are not well understood among the interagency and response communities.[515]

Why is this situation a problem? Because the Federal Emergency Management Agency (FEMA) has statutory responsibility for national preparedness; however, it does not have directive authority to manage national preparedness. This creates the need for extensive collaboration.

The required preparedness collaboration seeks to assess risks, define roles and responsibilities, develop and sustain plans with associated tasking, identify capabilities and capability gaps, and determine resource requirements for operational execution of homeland security and emergency management missions.[516]

---

[511]USCB, "Alkalies and Chlorine Manufacturing: 2002," (Washington DC: US Census Bureau, 2004).

[512]Staff, "Rail Carloads Carried by State: 2005," (Association of American Railroads, 2007).

[513] Copeland, "Terrorism and Security Issues Facing the Water Infrastructure Security Sector."

[514] Ibid, page 11.

[515]DoD, "Unconventional Operational Concepts and the Homeland."

[516]John Morton, "The Effectiveness of Grants in Support of the National Preparedness

Morton's research also outlines how unresolved conflict over all-hazards risk and inadequate capacities for state/local-level operational planning play a significant role in the failure of the grant process. Keep in mind, the grant process mirrors the current status of initiatives to resolve the water security infrastructure problem.

Since 9/11, the Federal government's grant programs and their related analysis of risk generally have focused on high-consequence terrorist threats to urban areas with their concentration of populations and critical infrastructure key resources (CIKR). States and local jurisdictions normally resource operational plans based on high-probability incidents. In essence, the three levels of government do not yet have an effective structure and process to facilitate effective collaboration for agreement on prioritization of risk.[517]

This interaction points to a deeper conflict in agency relationships. The limitations of traditional organizational models and cross-sector coordinating structures to confront these challenges have given rise to Multi-Organizational and Networked Alliances (MANA).[518] These alliances organize horizontally with members joining and converging around areas of shared interest. As a means of engagement, local or regional alliances can be more attractive to private and civic sector actors than large, national level, government-directed models; alliances' horizontal framework is more responsive to their needs and concerns, and affords them a partnership position in the collaboration, rather than treating them as merely interested stakeholders. For government, the attraction lies in the ability to more efficiently access private and civic sector capabilities, resources, and cooperation to address mission priorities. The trade-off for all lies in the necessary give-and-take inherent in collaborative decision-making and action.[519]

System." Draft White Paper," (Arlington VA: Project on National Security Reform, 2009).

[517] Ibid, page 7.

[518] *D.J. Kaufman, and Dake, J., "Understanding and Advancing Cross-Sector Collaboration in Homeland Security and Emergency Management," CAN Analysis and Solutions (2009).*

[519] Ibid, page 2.

Emergency Service

For emergency planners, water security has always been a top priority, whether we learned from western movies or the latest round of water wars in Alabama, Georgia, and Florida — water's importance is all too obvious. Emergency responders and planners are also aware of the terrorist interest in water infrastructure since 9/11.

For example, by its very nature a treatment plant not only provides security from waterborne contaminants, but also facilitates chemical and biological attack. Although treatment processes may remove or neutralize an agent introduced into the raw water of a local system, the facility is the controlling point for system quality where chemicals are or can be deliberately and systematically added to the water. The plant lends itself as an ideal attack point for water downstream in the system.[520]

Clear wells and reservoirs provide disinfectant (typically chlorine) contact time and store system water. Unpressurized and typically only passively defended (usually covered, but not always locked), they are a relatively easy target for contamination. By design they provide contact time and mixing opportunity, and directly feed potable water into the distribution system, and therefore are critical points.[521]

Risks to water systems are commonly believed to be small, because some experts insist it would be difficult to introduce sufficient quantity of agent to cause extensive harm. Nevertheless, the Centers for Disease Control lists the following as Category 'A' biological agents of high concern: smallpox, anthrax, Clostridium botulinum toxin, tularemia, and hemorrhagic fever viruses.[522] Any of these agents introduced into a water system, in any quantity, would create an extreme emergency situation and involve every level of government in the response, stabilization, and recovery from the incident. Additionally, facility operators generally focused on vandalism or theft by disgruntled employees or customers, rather than what might be considered an unlikely terrorist attack.

---

[520]Donald C. Hickman, "A Chemical and Biological Warfare Threat: Usaf Water Systems at Risk," ed. USAF Counter proliferation Center (Air War College, Air University, 2003).

[521]Ibid, p 7.

[522]Staff, "Security and Water."

The typical water system emergency response plan outline confirms that the plan does not have to be one huge document, but rather components of procedures, check lists, operational manuals, and appendices that comprise the plan, including specific sections for different types of incidents. These plans are also typically heavy into mitigation security measures and preventive activities. Infrastructure protection is by its nature is based on prevention. The Federal grant process also favors preventive activity and hardening of the facility itself. But, the local government will likely stick to response and recovery activities, especially if the water distribution agency is a private entity or quasi-governmental organization. Adding to the philosophical distance in approach is the fact that many water systems have their own protective forces, which impact response, posture, structure, and policy of both the facility and the responding levels of government. These facts further emphasize the necessity of inclusive response planning.

The process of planning must include collaborative relationships, understood policies, procedures, and actions. Vulnerability assessment should be used to identify specific emergency actions steps are required for response and recovery. Alternative water sources are essential for emergency situations. A clear understanding of the incident command system that first responders will use and how it should interact with the facility is highly important. Communications with all agencies and responders should be clear, short, and convey valuable information that helps stop or stabilize the situation. Property protection probably will not be enough in a terrorist situation.

The purpose of an emergency response plan (ERP) is to provide a utility with a standardized response and recovery protocol to prevent, minimize, and mitigate injury and damage resulting from emergencies or disasters of human-caused or natural origin. There are two types of data needed to develop an ERP: detailed information about the risks to critical water-system facilities and knowledge of emergency response protocols, personnel, and resources.[523]

The EPA has developed "Emergency Response Plan Guidance for Small and Medium Systems," and "Large Water System Emergency Response Plan Outline: Guidance to Assist Community Water Systems

---

[523] Ibid.

in Complying with the Bioterrorism Act." These documents can be downloaded from the Water Security page on the EPA web site (http://ctpub.epa.gov/safewater/watersecurity).[524]

The Water Sector Committee under the Department of Homeland Security Critical Infrastructure Partnership Advisory Council (CIPAC) developed the water-sector plan that covers wastewater and drinking water. The plan focuses on four goals: (1) sustain protection of public health and the environment; (2) recognize and reduce risks; (3) maintain a resilient infrastructure; and (4) increase communication, outreach, and public confidence.[525]

The Water/Waste Water Agency Response Network (WARN) action plan is about utilities helping utilities and outlines ten key steps in formation of a WARN. The plan includes a sample agreement that supports the National Incident Management System (NIMS) criteria and is recognized by the Department of Homeland Security, Environment Protection Agency, and the states as a model for the water sector (www.NationalWARN.org).

The current voluntary standard guidelines were jointly developed by the American Society of Civil Engineers (ASCE) and the American Water Works Association (AWWA) with technical input from the Water Environment Federations (WEF)) are the result of Phase III of the Water Infrastructure Security Enhancements (WISE) program titled "Guidelines for the Physical Security of Water Utilities" and "Guidelines for the Physical Security of Wastewater/Storm water Utilities."

The plans and networking identified reinforce the need for an inclusive collaborative approach. The response and emergency service delivery are based on commitment, funding, and information sharing. The value of the plans and the planning process begin and end with the amount of trust developed in building the response capabilities.

The trust developed will directly translate into sound decision-making. For example, evacuation and relocation can help reduce the number of deaths and injuries, but, can also result in an increase in

---

[524] ———, "Security Guidance for Emergency Response Planning," (American Water Work Association, 2009).

[525] Copeland, "Terrorism and Security Issues Facing the Water Infrastructure Security Sector."

business interruption. In fact, massive evacuations can result in larger business interruption than would be suffered from an actual event.[526]

How critical is the point of collaboration and trust building? Absolutely critical because experts believe, the authors included, that the United States should expect future asymmetric attacks to focus on manipulating its populace — by attacking either critical infrastructure targets or the populace directly. The attacks would generally be tactical, but with strategic effect.[527] Since the demise of Usama Bin Laden, terrorist groups may feel particularly incited to plan a catastrophic blow. However, given their constant planning nature, that blow may not be immediate as some pundits believe.

Where are we going?

Although Federal standards are not the norm yet, the water infrastructure industry has made progress. With financial support from EPA, drinking water and wastewater utility and engineering groups developed three security guidance documents, issued in December 2004, that cover the physical design of online contaminant monitoring systems, and physical security enhancements of drinking water, wastewater, and storm water infrastructure systems.[528]

The Strategic Plan for Homeland Security, issued in October 2004, recognized the evolving role of the Department of Homeland Security. The National Infrastructure Protection Plan of 2006 states that resiliency is the capability of an asset, system, or network to maintain its function during or recover from a terrorist attack or other incident. The goal is resiliency; thus, the American Water Works Association (AWWA) and other water related and emergency response organizations are teaching that all emergencies are local and require a local response capability.

---

[526] Adam Rose, "Estimating the Total Economic Impacts of Terrorist Attacks: Computable General Equilibrium (Cge) Modeling of Resilience and Extended Linkages," (University of Southern California Center for Risk and Economic Analysis of Terrorism Events, 2007).
[527] DoD, "Unconventional Operational Concepts and the Homeland."
[528] Copeland, "Terrorism and Security Issues Facing the Water Infrastructure Security Sector."

As Dr. James Tindall points out, four key trends are parallel and interrelated and continue to drive changes for security: geopolitical, demographic and social, economic issues related to globally interrelated markets, and technological.[529] While the typical government emergency official should learn how to adjust and respond to macro trends, he or she is more likely to consider the limited knowledge base of the typical first responders and the constant change of personnel within ranks as a limiting factor in the planning process.

The Environment Protection Agency (EPA) has expanded its security activities in two ways. First, its focus has enlarged from the post 9/11 emphasis on terrorism to an "all hazards" approach emphasizing to water utilities that issues of risk identification and risk reduction also include natural disasters (which were the focus of much of the industry's attention before 2001) and protection of hazardous chemicals (see chapter 1). Second, the EPA supports the establishment of intrastate mutual aid and assistance agreements to facilitate flow of personnel and resources during response to emergencies.[530]

Hurricane Katrina, levee breaks in California and Nevada, and the 2008 [and 2011] Midwest floods have increased the recent debate about how to manage flood, coastal, and aging infrastructure risks, what is an acceptable level of risk (especially for low-probability, high-consequence events), and who should bear the costs to reduce these risks.[531] Hurricane Katrina also brought national attention to the issue of levee and floodwall reliability and different levels of protection provided by flood damage reduction structures — some of which were built by the federal government, but most of which have been constructed by local entities. Levee overtopping and failure contribute to approximately one-third of all flood disasters,

---

[529] J.A. Tindall, "Expected Key Trends Likely to Influence Global Security," *Global Security Affairs and Analysis (GSAAJ)* 2, no. 3 (2008).

[530] Copeland, "Terrorism and Security Issues Facing the Water Infrastructure Security Sector."

[531] CRS, "35 Years of Water Policy: The 1973 National Water Commission and Present Challenges," (Washington DC: Library of Congress).

and a large percentage of locally built levees are poorly designed and maintained.[532]

Understanding the Big Picture

As a nation, progress is being made to protect our water infrastructure. Some experts would argue it is not enough; others argue it's all that can be expected based on capabilities, politics, and funding. However, the entire infrastructure debate is about risk. The probability of terrorist attack or simple levee break is factored into decisions at every level of government. Once again the distance becomes obvious. The Federal government's approach is low-probability high-consequence and the local government's approach is high-probability low-consequence. This situation will not lead to a common understanding on priorities.

The 1973 National Water Commission report Water Policies for the Future presented 232 recommendations including two key concepts. The demand for water in the future is not predetermined and does not allow an inexorable growth pattern, but depends on policy decisions that society controls, and the level of government nearest the water resource problem and capable of adequately representing all interests should control water resource development, management, and protection.[533]

The largest Corps and Reclamation facilities also produce enormous amounts of power. For example, Hoover and Glen Canyon Dams on the Colorado River represent 23percent of the installed electrical capacity of the Bureau of Reclamation's 58 power plants in the West and 7percent of the total installed capacity in the Western United States.[534]

During the August 2003 electricity blackout in the Northeast United States, wastewater treatment plants in Cleveland, Detroit, New York, and other locations that lacked backup generation systems lost power and discharged millions of gallons of untreated sewage

---

[532] Ibid, p 38.
[533] Ibid, p 7.
[534] Copeland, "Terrorism and Security Issues Facing the Water Infrastructure Security Sector."

during the emergency, and power failures at drinking water plants led to boil-water advisories in many communities.[535]

The last presidential drought disaster declaration in the continental United States was for New Jersey in 1980. More recent drought declarations have been issued for U. S. territories in the Pacific. On October 20, 2007, the governor of Georgia requested a presidential drought disaster declaration because of prolonged exceptional drought conditions existing in the northern third of the state. No such presidential declaration has occurred in response to the request as of March, 2009.[536]

Vulnerabilities do exist, however. Large underground collector sewers could be accessed by terrorist groups for purposes of placing destructive devices beneath buildings or city streets. Pipelines can be made into weapons via the introduction of a highly flammable substance such as gasoline through a manhole or inlet. Explosions in the sewers can cause collapse of roads, sidewalks, and adjacent structures and injure and kill people nearby. Damage to a wastewater facility prevents water from being treated and can impact downriver water intakes. Destruction of containers that hold large amounts of chemicals at treatment plants could result in release of toxic chemical agents, such as chlorine gas, which can be deadly to humans if inhaled and, at lower doses, can burn eyes and skin and inflame the lungs.[537]

DHS has identified 36 highest priority infrastructure assets and over 2,500 next level assets on which to focus attention, and, where appropriate, investment-under the constraint that much of the infrastructure is owned privately and therefore not eligible for public funds.[538]

A likely consequence of higher temperatures in the West would be higher evapotranspiration, reduced precipitation, and decreased spring runoff. A recent controversial study asserts that water storage in Lake Mead on the Colorado River has a 50 percent

---

[535] Ibid.

[536] CRS, "Drought in the United States: Causes and Issues for Congress," (Washington DC: Library of Congress, 2009).

[537] Copeland, "Terrorism and Security Issues Facing the Water Infrastructure Security Sector."

[538] DoD, "Unconventional Operational Concepts and the Homeland."

probability by 2021 to "run dry" and a 10 percent change by 2014 to drop below levels needed to provide hydroelectric power under current climate conditions and without changes to water allocation in the basin.[539] Dependence on "just-in-time" centrally managed, networked supplies of water, power, food, communications, and transportation leaves the United States extremely vulnerable to an effects-based attack.[540] Compared to aerial attack (inhalation or skin contact), effective doses are easier to obtain in water (less dilution than air and directly ingested), and in many cases the materials are more stable (protected from ultraviolet and temperature extremes, although exposed to chlorine)[541].

All of these factors lead to a simple conclusion. They collectively point out the necessity for all key stakeholders in emergency preparedness to be trained, trusted, and included in the collaborative process. At the beginning of the "current status" section it was asked if someone was missing in this critical effort. The emergency management director (by whatever name) may be that official.

The ghost in the emergency management sector is often the emergency management director. Why? Often there is a questionable appointment to this position or it is a collateral assignment along with someone's full-time job. Although there are highly trained dedicated professionals serving, the leadership capability and competency need to be factored into the end product of the emergency planning process.

What has been done?

The EPA has supported two special initiatives since FY2006: first, a pilot program to design, deploy, and test biological and other contamination warning systems at drinking water systems, the Water

[539] T.P. Barnett, and Pierce, D.W., "When Will Lake Mead Run Dry?," *Water Resources Research* 44, no. W03201 (2008).
[540] DoD, "Unconventional Operational Concepts and the Homeland."
[541] Hickman, "A Chemical and Biological Warfare Threat: Usaf Water Systems at Risk."

Sector Initiative; second, the Water Alliance for Threat Reduction (WATR), to train utility operators at the highest risk systems.[542]

The Water Sector Initiative, initially known as WaterSentinal, it is a pilot project that could serve as a model for water utilities throughout the country. Its purpose is to test and demonstrate contamination warning systems at drinking water utilities throughout the country. So far, EPA has awarded grants to install and evaluate early warning systems in Cincinnati, New York, and San Francisco.[543]

The Infrastructure Security Partnership has prepared a guide for developing an action plan to provide a flexible, dynamic, high-level framework for use by all levels of government, service providers, and other organizations to create an action plan to help improve comprehensive regional preparedness.[544]

The guide for preparing an action plan is based on twenty nine assumptions ranging from the establishment of regional preparedness, information technology, infrastructure interdependencies, cyber security, resilience, investment tradeoffs, and a risk-based approach to identifying critical assets, and environmental protection. Particular emphasis is given to disaster response, recovery and restoration, integration of federal assets, law enforcement and public safety, National Incident Management System, private sector and nonprofit involvement, health care, special needs management, and the media[545].

The Infrastructure Security Partnership guide uses a seven-step action plan process that may be customized to suit specific stakeholder needs as follows:

TISP Seven-Step Action Plan Process Includes:

Step 1. Create a formal or informal regional cooperative initiative or partnership composed of key stakeholders,

---

[542]Copeland, "Terrorism and Security Issues Facing the Water Infrastructure Security Sector."

[543] Ibid, p 7.

[544]ASCE, "The Infrastructure Security Partnership. Regional Disaster Resilience: A Guide for Developing an Action Plan," (2006).

[545] Ibid, p 4.

ideally including the leadership of senior local/state and private-sector organizations.

Step 2. Develop and conduct an interactive, educational workshop to provide necessary information to key stakeholders on regional infrastructure interdependencies and disaster preparedness and security challenges.

Step 3. Develop and conduct a regional infrastructure interdependencies exercise that includes a scenario designed by members of the core stakeholder group and other interested organizations to reflect their interests and concerns regarding a major disaster.

Step 4. Produce a report based on lessons learned from the exercise that includes findings and recommendations that have been coordinated with/validated by the key stakeholders.

Step 5. Develop and conduct an action planning workshop with the exercise participants to prioritize and build upon the recommended activities in the exercises report and identify specific projects.

Step 6. Produce an action plan composed of these prioritized projects, using the framework provided in this guide, and coordinate it with the key stakeholders.

Step 7. Create working groups within the regional partnership-including lead government agencies and private-sector organizations-to undertake those short- medium- and long-term activities in the action plan that require a cross-sector cooperative approach.

FEMA's Flood Map Modernization Program, which remaps floodplains using modern technologies, is resulting in a

reexamination of levees throughout the United States to determine if they can still be accredited.[546]

Conclusions

This chapter emphasizes why existing emergency plans may not work. The attitudes of key stakeholders affect water infrastructure preparedness in various ways. These attitudes must be addressed or reconciled before there is any real hope of success. The public expects and demands safe potable water and although the individual may believe that the EPA and local health department will keep water safe, neither of these agencies is responsible for site security. Additionally, the EPA is regulatory in nature and public health agencies, like other first response entities, are generally involved only after an event has occurred. The need for sharing information has never been more important. At the same time, the importance of maintaining infrastructure security secrecy has never been higher. This situation creates a flawed process when response is based on multiple layers of government and the private sector.

Secondly, first responders (local government) are functioning with a plan (perhaps) that is generally underfunded and based on high-probability and low-consequence events. The facility operators are using voluntary industry standards where funding is limited and based on a slim profit margin. The state is also operating from a severely depressed tax revenue position (due to the current economic climate) and may lack qualified inspectors to check on infrastructure maintenance status. The Federal government is approaching the situation from a risk-based, low probability high-consequence point of view. These differences, while appearing benign, can have a dramatic impact on approach to preparedness for water infrastructure safety, security, and sustainability. There is much hope that massive failure will never happen because no single agency or level of government can guarantee their absolute readiness for an accidental event or planned terrorist attack.

Third, the lack of standards greatly affects water infrastructure security and its impact. Although voluntary industry standards have

[546]ASCE, "2009 Report Card for America's Infrastructure."

been developed based on extensive experience and analysis, the situation, size of the water provider, and the cost of compliance do not always make them tenable. Further, out of 53,000 water supply systems in the U.S., most are privately or locally government owned and 15 percent of the systems supply 75 percent of all the water needs to the nation. The need for risk-based priorities is therefore clear, but without some degree of uniform regulatory security guidance, entities likely will continue to have preparedness problems in smaller systems and municipalities.

Finally, throughout this chapter it has been pointed out and alluded to that a key stakeholder may be missing in the emergency planning process: The emergency management director (by any name) must be involved in and play a lead role in planning. If this responsible official does not exist at the local level, is another collateral duty assigned to someone else? Is a political appointment based on campaign support or filled by someone not adequately qualified for the position? If so, the security planning will be significantly hampered by the resulting lack of trust, and the plan will fail due to lack of execution and/or understanding. Who would be willing to jeopardize the security of an entire community by allowing this?

From the emergency planning perspective, ensuring water infrastructure security is very complex. Attitudes of the public, facility operators, first responders, and every level of government ultimately impacts success. Security becomes much more than a 3G (guns, gates, and guards) operation. The need to share information, even when it is classified between planners and first responders is a basic requirement for success. Collaborative, fact-based stakeholder attitudes and information sharing offers a unique opportunity for success. The opportunity will hinge on willingness and trust backed by belief in doing one's part of the mission in an expert and professional manner.

CHAPTER 15: Economics of Water

Executive Summary

The world is facing a global crisis for resources; energy prices are soaring, creating unexpected consequences for water-supply issues and commodity prices. An emerging water issue is the effect it has on city bonds. Municipal utilities face growing financial risks due to water scarcity, but the credit rating agencies that rate municipal bonds largely ignore the problem. The problems associated with water scarcity for cities and the bonds they sell to help build new infrastructure, etc., will produce risks for thousands of utilities that are managed by municipalities and counties and for those who buy the cities' bonds. This is particularly true for cities that are at risk of losing water supplies. The ten largest cities in the U.S. at risk of running out of water include Orlando, Las Vegas, Phoenix, Atlanta, Tucson, Ft Worth, San Francisco, San Antonio, Houston, and Los Angeles.

When discussing water versus the national economy it is important to understand three basic areas: (1) the relation between the overall economy and the water sector; (2) the physical, social, and economic nature of water; and (3) the pros and cons of alternative approaches to water policies for public use and policy issues related to an economic organization of water resources and their management.

The four primary types of economic benefits of water use include: (1) commodity; (2) water assimilation; (3) recreational; and (4) aquatic and wildlife habitats. Also, individuals obtain commodity benefits from water through use for cooking, drinking, and sanitation. Agriculture and industry gain commodity benefits by using water for production, whether for foodstuffs or manufacturing. This type of use represents private goods from water through production activities, but also represents rivals in consumption.

An economic organization of the water sector has generally been split into either market or government entities. Along with attempts to organize have come many market and government failures, many of which have related to economic structure and

irrigation. Almost every country relies on a mix of market policies and government interventions to manage water resources. In the U.S., while the capitalist or free market/competitive system is often viewed as the most efficient system for allocation of resources, market imperfections and fluctuations can accentuate income disparities. Current gasoline prices are an example. So, societies' public welfare goals often incorporate a broad range of social objectives that generally include ameliorating income inequalities between members in the society. For these situations, water projects can provide important investment strategies for both human welfare (drinking-water and food supplies) and infrastructure to support economic development. For lower income groups, public ownership of the supply is, therefore, beneficial. Even when markets fail, public sector intervention or non-market approaches may not always lead to a socially optimal solution. This was evidenced in 2009 with the bailout of American auto companies in which some government performance incentives resulted in a divergence from socially preferable outcomes in both allocation and distributional equity. In the water sector, a variety of problems are relevant to this scenario. They include the definition of products, externalities from public action, inequitable distribution of power, and private goals of public agents, i.e., self interests.

The outputs of non-market activities for water are difficult to define and the inputs that produced them are difficult to measure. Regardless of the issues, the economics of water is complex, the resource is extremely interdependent with other sectors, and due to scarcity in many areas around the globe, and development of supplies and pricing are currently primary focuses. Because of these issues, water is a national-security problem.

Pricing water is also difficult, initially stemming from increasing populations that need more; concentration of these populations in locations that over time are further removed from the resource; increased pollution requiring more costly treatment; and industrialization that has led to the connection of all homes connected to public water and sewer systems. The pricing of water must consider both the level and structure of prices. A pricing structure should consider at least four requirements:

(1) A price must be sufficient to recover costs. This implies earning a profit and covering costs for extraction, cleaning, and transportation, as well as water treatment. Ideally, this 'profit' should be used to maintain infrastructure and thus, be assessed over a period of years against estimated costs of maintenance and replacement.

(2) The price should be fair for all users. Each person should be able to acquire the water necessary, which means the water bill should be fair to the user based on volume used and not so high it represents a disproportionate share of household income. In many locations this requires subsidizing low-income households. Further, long-term planning is crucial so future generations are not adversely affected.

(3) Pricing should provide incentives for conservation. The price should also consider investment and incentives in water saving technologies and activities. It is important to note that social, rather than private marginal costs are more important in this issue and long-term costs are important, which of course includes capital and operating costs of infrastructure. Peak use periods, distance from source, etc., need to be priced according to the energy needed for conveyance and distribution.

(4) The price should be efficient and administratively feasible. Different meters for different users may be required; a marginal pricing on the administrative side requires knowledge about the monetary equivalent of external costs, which can be uncertain. Since many operators of these systems are engineers, they often lack such knowledge. Complex systems often lack transparency, which limits their usefulness for providing incentives. Simpler systems are desirable to promote the necessary incentives.

A primary principle in the economics of water is that there is a demand for water of differing qualities. Also, the largest costs in the water sector are borne by the development of storage, transportation, distribution, and treatment systems. Innovative and forward thinking approaches of water management are needed to ensure sustainability of such huge systems. Economic principles also must be explicitly integrated into management. Development of a basic framework that could serve as a starting solution would include numerous parameters such as:

1. Cost Recovery
2. Utilize/Develop Tools for Economic Analysis
3. Putting Costs and Benefits Into Proportion
4. Implement Pricing Policies for Droughts and Water Scarcity
5. Implement Analysis of Management and Economics
6. Assess a 'True' Value for Water.

The shorter the supply of a natural resource, the more important it is to have an institutional structure for allocating it efficiently among stakeholders, both present and future. The economic system views water as either a common property resource to be freely shared or, as a good to be priced and traded in the market. Neither approach ensures sound water management and economics because many functions, services, and values of water are not used or traded in the market. These include the value of aquatic environments as a habitat for biodiversity, recreational values of water, use as a transportation medium, role in waste treatment and manufacturing, water's function in displacing and transporting materials and contaminants, and more.

Because of these many issues, there has been much discussion recently about water being undervalued around the world. Many nations are focused on water issues, but many also lack the capital investment to develop and implement needed water systems for supply and treatment. Conceptually, water can be priced directly or indirectly. Direct pricing involves setting prices and charges payable from use, reuse, and disposal of water — by users. Indirect pricing relies on using a wide variety of mechanisms that reveal the cost of using water and associated resources. The latter is more difficult, but compares interdependencies with other sectors

and through economic analysis and other tools could suggest a more true value for water within a locale, region, or country.

It should be noted that externality charges work in both political and social contexts when there is reasonable acceptance of the principle of 'polluters and users pay.' In a social climate that supports economic development regardless of impacts across the water cycle and sector, an externality charge is difficult to implement. Thus, within such a framework, it is important that externalities associated with potable water, reuse, and wastewater be treated consistently. Typically, any framework used would be designed to facilitate a rational investment in potable water, reuse water, and wastewater, which incorporates the full costs of production and effects of the environment into account. For large projects, public investment is likely always a requirement due to total cost and environmental consequences. Failure to adequately address the economics of water will imperil national security.

Introduction

The world is facing a global crisis for resources; energy prices are soaring, creating both unexpected and expected consequences in water supply issues and commodity prices. The shorter the supply of natural resources, the more important it is to have an institutional structure for allocating that resource efficiently among users. Thus, useable fresh water is not fundamentally different from other diminishing resources such as precious metals, or oil and gas. To obtain a good grasp of the economics of water, we must first necessarily discuss the role of water in early civilizations and cultures and why water is 'the' crucial key for economic development.

In early civilizations, water played a relatively simple role. It was used for drinking, transportation, and provided hunting and fishing sources. As population increased, the creation of conveyance systems and piping of water through these systems created larger and larger cities. Basic urban infrastructure for water and sanitation was created and made scalable. Financing these systems was done incrementally with taxation and other funds. The incremental, yet steady population growth allowed good planning and adequate control. Water makes housing habitable in all cities and we find that

something as simple as water drives societal views toward the role of government, norms, and the market.

Water has always been important, but focuses on disparate distribution; status as a finite resource; increasing famine and food failures around the globe; emerging contaminants; and hotly debated topics such as water-rights issues have increased public and government awareness. The once great infrastructures in the large cities, such as New York, Beijing, Rome and elsewhere are failing. Coupled with the threat of terrorist attack and natural hazards against water and food systems a new awareness of water security has developed, especially in the U.S. and Europe. These failing infrastructures due to age and the physical characteristics of water are creating severe economic problems about how to maintain water sustainability, protect it, and continue to convey it. Water is heavy and awkward; it requires lots of energy to convey it through systems, and storing it in dams and reservoirs, for example, requires both structural strength and leak-proof systems.

From Constantine's cisterns in Istanbul to Hoover Dam in Nevada, human societies have faced the challenge of supplying adequate quality and quantities of water. Regardless of geography or societal type, culture or government, providing adequate water supplies to meet demands is the prerequisite for any enduring society. And, water serves a multifunctional role, which makes its economics difficult to understand in terms of complex interdependency with other systems. For example, water is a physical resource and the basis of life; without it, life does not exist. It is also a cultural resource and has religious significance in many societies. Water also fulfills roles as a social resource in terms of access, but also a political resource since its provision to citizens serves an important communication purpose. Today, as water grows scarce (unavailable in needed quantity), especially clean drinking water, it quickly becomes an economic resource. As a traded commodity and purchase around the globe by large corporations, it could well become a submission resource.

Economically, selling water has become commonplace and a way to make a meager living in many countries. One could be walking down the sidewalk in Paris, Las Vegas, Oaxaca, Sao Paulo, New Delhi, Moscow, Tehran, or other city and witness many individual vendors selling cold bottles of water during the hot summer. Larger corporations such as General Electric, Dasanti, and many others are also capitalizing on water by purchasing water rights in countries around the world. At a future time, water will be more valuable than oil. Consequently, there is a strong relation between water management, urbanization, housing, technology development, and economics. In regard to technology, given the great number of people around the globe who lack fresh water in adequate quantities, a technology invention of most value would be a low-tech, low-cost water treatment process. In some areas, it could be desalinization technology, in others, the ability to clean water or filtrate it from the air. The largest cities have been built near the greatest water resources and, throughout history, water infrastructure predated capitalism. It is central to urban planning and has been shown to be the key factor in economic sustainability. Without water, development of strong societies is not possible.

The development of water supply technologies has matched developments in sanitation and water treatment. As early as 2000 BC, Sanskrit writings recommended water purification methods. However, water economics is not only a matter of supply and sanitation; as technology and population increases, the need for law, policy, and finance develops as well. Initially, water was free and the greatest focus on water was for irrigation for agriculture. In ancient times, water was free because people did not need to earn it. As early as 3000 BC, Jewish law insisted water was a common property because it was provided by God and came from the heavens. These societies, noted as pre-urban, did not need to address whether making water clean cost money or labor. Other religions appear to share the same commonality with Jewish law. For example, Islamic law parallels Jewish law in this regard. The Arabic word for Islamic law is 'Sharia' which means "way to water" and the Quran gives guidelines about sharing water:

"Anyone who gives water to a living creature will be rewarded.... To the man who refuses his surplus water, Allah will say: 'Today I refuse then my favor, just as thou refused the surplus of something that thou hadst not made thyself."

As time passed, a hierarchy of water was developed, which is used in economics today. The hierarchy of water use is: (1) drinking;

(2) cooking and washing (household use); and (3) agriculture. The first two uses require better quality than water used for agriculture. Eventually, water became a community resource, with survival trumping ownership, and laws were passed regarding its use on commonality. Today, we see these concepts in play in transboundary water-sharing issues such as the Nile, Colorado, and Indus River systems. In areas such as Australia, water sharing became common among neighbors and in many areas, access to drinking water in times of scarcity is considered a basic need. However, in large megacities and other cities, these basic laws do not work. Consumption restrictions are passed as policy and enforced by law. Sadly, as the units of government become larger, the range of water bans, especially in times of scarcity, increases. This is one reason why nationalization of water in a country is a very poor idea and one that could lead to massive civil unrest and a security fiasco.

Once cities began to form, more and more rules were applied to water sources and supplies. Cleanliness was the first priority and activities such as doing laundry and making bricks near water wells were prohibited. Around the globe, the laws are ever expanding around the globe, and they influence agriculture, manufacturing, recreational, and residential use of water and its protection. A basic business financial model has developed to provide a set of economic relations for participating groups. The initial components included government contribution of non-recoverable capital costs, system improvements, and sustainability. This shifted free water to community water and gave rise to most city-sized distribution systems with the city government in control and to determine who regulates and sets prices for water. However, ultimately, it is the community or tax payers who pay for all such systems. As laws have changed and economics of ownership and rights have become clouded, tensions over water rights and water issues have increased, as explained previously. From poisoning wells in ancient times to civil unrest, disputes over rights and ownership, and threats of terrorist attack, the economics of water is beginning to affect society at greater levels.

A new issue is the affect water has on city bonds. Municipal utilities face growing financial risks due to water scarcity, but the credit rating agencies that rate municipal bonds largely ignore the problem. The problems associated with water scarcity for cities and the bonds they sell to help build new infrastructure, etc., will produce risks for thousands of utilities that are managed by municipalities and counties and for those who buy the cities' bonds. This is particularly true for cities that are at risk of losing water supplies.[547] The ten biggest cities in the U.S. at risk of running out of water include Orlando, Las Vegas, Phoenix, Atlanta, Tucson, Ft Worth, San Francisco, San Antonio, Houston, and Los Angeles.[548] The water problem is worse than most people realize and several large cities which are occasionally low on water will almost certainly face shortfalls within a few years. Also, investors who buy municipal bonds are blindly placing bets on which utilities are positioned to manage these growing risks and which could be an extremely poor investment. Likely legislation will be passed this year that will not allow credit rating agencies to ignore the problem and which can greatly affect the credit rating of a city.

To gain an adequate understanding of water economics, it is advantageous to consider historical water development trends in large cities. The economics of water were first demonstrated in Rome, which was arguably the first municipality. The Romans realized housing made cities and there was a great need for advanced water management to provide water. They realized that clean water and sanitation materially influenced city scaling. This is unlike today when the world's rapidly expanding cities create spontaneous communities with little regard to water services initially. Through a complex system of wells, cisterns, and storage basins, Rome was transformed. Aqueducts conveyed water where needed and increased the splendor and reputation of Rome. Rome was the first to provide public drinking fountains, and water was a priced resource. This infrastructure was not free and the price was passed on to the citizens in the form of taxes. Like cities of today, water requirements

---

547 R. Schoof, "Water Scarcity Affects Bond Value," *McClatchy Newpapers*(2010), http://www.stltoday.com/business/article_e14e7ea6-dca6-55cb-9b80-cd930279a4fb.html.

548 C.B. Stockdale, Sauter, M.B., and McIntyre, D.A., "The Ten Biggest American Cities That Are Running out of Water," *24/7 Wall St.*(2010), http://247wallst.com/2010/10/29/the-ten-great-american-cities-that-are-dying-of-thirst/.

rose faster than population as urbanization increased demand. Sanitation problems developed as waste built up. In response, the 'Cloaca Maxima' was built to eliminate Rome's waste water and it did; unfortunately, it flowed back into the water supply. The more the infrastructure grew, the more civic organization was required, and water management became a municipal activity to support citizens and a great workforce. All of this led to the true beginning of water economics; also initiated was municipal finance, which serves as the basic model used today.

As population and infrastructure grew, the Roman emperors needed more capital to administer a larger empire and so, invested heavily in infrastructure. Today, that infrastructure is referred to as critical infrastructure by Homeland Security (discussed in chapters 1, 3, 5, 6, 7, and 8 of this text). The aqueducts of Rome were paid for by the government, not by user fees, and became the basic model for infrastructure finance. After development of infrastructure, operating costs were paid by users. Today, water is about the only infrastructure owned by municipalities. Electricity, communications, transportation, and the others are primarily owned by private corporations who follow a similar finance model. Once the infrastructure is built, operational costs, improvements, etc., are paid by user fees. In Rome and other early cities, a free-rider problem arose whereby individuals with apartments and houses would illegally tap into the main water supply and get water for free; this was in 300 BC to early AD. Today, the roles are reversed: municipalities attempt to get water for free from farmers and they actually do to an extent. Tensions are battled in court where inevitably the deep pockets of the city outlast those of the farmer who is generally driven out of business. This creates a competition between the farmer and city in which the farmer usually loses, but at what sustainable cost? In developing megacities, slums usually spring up, but over time, their scale, longevity, and civility collectively legitimize them and they are brought formally into the surrounding community and pay their fair share. Initially though, extensive water and public health issues exist within these communities.

New York was perhaps one of the first cities to reinvent the basic economic model for water distribution within a municipality. Public wells were first constructed in 1667, but proved insufficient for

a growing population. In 1686, construction of eight water wells began. A combination of public funding and financial assessments of families who would be served by these wells paid for construction. Essentially, New York modified the basic Roman model and eliminated the 'free rider' problem by coercing such individuals of forced sales of property and/or goods to pay for services. As New York grew, its water supply did not, and this led to the development of slums, i.e., housing developments outgrowing infrastructure. The gap between water supply and water demand was temporarily solved by entrepreneurs and people with means who began to purchase water from springs outside town and from deeper wells — known as "Tea Water." This same process occurs today in the West Bank of Israel among the Palestinians. However, even the entrepreneurs could not keep pace with a growing population. Thus, New York managers began taking a serious look at water supply and sanitation using the Roman model. In 1774, the city approved a steam-powered waterworks that would pump water throughout the city similar to the aqueducts of Rome, but using power to overcome conveyance problems upslope. Such an ambitious plan required huge amounts of capital.

The city responded by issuing 'water works money' — the first paper money issued by an American city. The original work was interrupted by the Revolutionary War and languished for 15 years afterward. The crises of population growth forced action as demand overloaded supply capability. Epidemics had been linked scientifically to hygiene, which created political pressure and thus, the political commitment to spend tax money. In 1795, a yellow fever epidemic struck New York and tax payers demanded action. The city turned to privatization. Prominent politicians such as Aaron Burr and Alexander Hamilton joined with others to drive a public/private solution. Hamilton persuaded the City Council that the city should not build its own water works due to insufficient capital through loans and taxes. Given the challenges of the time, Hamilton's logic was sound and Aaron Burr in three days hurried through state legislature a bill which authorized the City Council to create the Manhattan Company that was mandated to provide New York City with clean drinking water. Burr directed ten percent of this company's two million dollar assets toward investments in water works. The company actually converted

public money to private profit — a model for many corporations today. The remaining money of the company was invested in local businesses. The ability to keep a chartered private company in its remit was a regulatory problem that still exists today. The company went from water to money for true liquidity and today is known as Chase Manhattan Bank. The company drove Tea Water pumps out of business as their monopoly grew.

A series of disasters finally illustrated the privatized infrastructure was a failure and the birth of public infrastructure was realized. Some of these disasters included the 1828 New York fire, the 1832 cholera epidemic, and others. Finally, a permanent Board of Water Commissioners was created and authorized to raise capital and condemn land to supply needed water. This was perhaps the birth of eminent domain. In 1838, 35 acres of land was condemned and developed into the Croton Reservoir that supplied 95 million gallons of water per day to the city. This capacity to supply necessary demand was exceeded after ten years; more importantly, construction of this reservoir displaced the Manhattan Company.

While it is clear that urbanization is a phenomenon of money, New York changed the basic financial and economic model for water that is now used in water infrastructure projects around the globe. Since a fully private monopoly cannot be adequately regulated (even today), the basic financial model is now one of government funding for non-recoverable costs and then, taxation to supply operational costs and pay off the construction loans and improvement and maintenance processes in infrastructure. This also allowed private firms to bid on maintenance and development of new water projects. However, we may yet again see the basic model change.

When water is plentiful in regard to demand, its policies and laws remain generally simple and little enforced. This phase is termed an expansionary phase. However, as populations grow, causing an expansion of economies, water sectors evolve into what is termed a mature phase.[549] At a certain point within the expansionary phase, the financial and environmental costs of development begin to exceed the economic benefits of the least productive or marginal uses of existing supplies. The mature phase is actually characterized

[549] A. Randall, "Property Entitlements and Pricing Policies for a Maturing Water Economy," *Australian Journal of Agricultural Economics* 25(1981).

by rising marginal costs of supplying water and the increasing interdependencies among users. During this phase, conflicts over scarcity and additional external costs arise. Conflicts can become so complex that elaborate management systems are necessary to allocate water among users' various economic sectors and resolve disputes. Thus, development of new water supplies and water-sector policies is difficult for several reasons. First, water is heavy and costs of conveyance can be high; in addition, economic and cultural characteristics that distinguish it from other resources make user rights difficult to address.[550] Secondly, water management is complicated administratively due to environmental, economic, technological, and political concerns.[551] As with most of life's issues, political considerations dominate water-resources use decisions. Despite this, most water-policy options are framed in terms of economics.

When discussing water versus the national economy, it is important to understand three basic areas: (1) the relation between the overall economy and the water sector; (2) the physical, social, and economic nature of water; and (3) the pros and cons of alternative approaches to water policies for public use and policy issues related to an economic organization of water resources and their management.

Water and the National Economy

As with the majority of issues in government and politics, politicians generally confront one issue at a time in a singular approach. This type approach limits solutions to water problems simply because it ignores unintended and unrecognized consequences relating to the interdependencies of the water sector

---

[550] R.A. Young, and Haveman, R.H., ed. *Economics of Water Resources: A Survey*, vol. II, Handbook of Natural Resources and Energy Economics, Vol. Ii. Amsterdam, Elsevier Science Publishers (Amsterdam: Elsevier Science Publishers,1985).

[551] Water management generally depends upon the government's ability to establish an appropriate legal and regulatory framework, thus, most water markets are based on a system of enforceable private property rights. The old west in the United States issued water rights that are still in place today and, although newer water rights are somewhat modified to the older ones, private water markets require both transferable and secure property rights, which often excludes other users.

with other areas. To fully understand necessary policies and implementation, all interdependencies must be addressed to comprehend the social, economic, and environmental impacts of water on a given region, sector, or group of people. This requires an understanding of how the water sector as a whole is linked to the national economy of a country. An understanding of the alternative economic policy instruments that influence water use across and between various economic sectors at all levels from the farm, to corporations, to local, regional, and national levels is also necessary. For too long, this has not been the case, resulting in failed water policies and extensive litigation.

The policies of various sectors and macroeconomic policies that are not specifically geared toward the water sector can have a significant strategic impact on water-resources allocation and aggregate demand in the economy. In the U.S. for example, as well as in other countries, the overall development strategy and implementation of macroeconomic policies, including fiscal, monetary and trade policies, directly and indirectly affects demand and investment in water-resources and water-related activities. The most obvious example is government expenditures and fiscal policy for flood control, agricultural irrigation, and dams. Trade and exchange rate policy to promote exports and earning more foreign exchange is a factor, but less apparent. For example, if a currency depreciates, the export of high-value, water consuming crops can increase. This is one reason virtual water is so important. Utilizing this example, if additional policy changes reduce export taxes on a crop, the farmer is provided with an extra incentive to invest in export crops and in their necessary irrigation. An example of this is the Syrian economy. In the late 1980s, a severe drought occurred. By 1991, the agro-industries had recovered. However, during the drought, the government was forced to import large quantities of wheat and barley, which drained foreign currency reserves. The lowered water levels and supplies also resulted in reduced hydropower generation that increased the need for thermal power, consequently lowering crude oil exports, all resulting in lowered economics or monetary returns across many interdependent sectors.
Another example in relation to regional economics is illustrated in the 1995 Texas drought, which spread from central, eastern, and

western Texas and New Mexico into Arizona and parts of California, Nevada, Utah, Colorado, Oklahoma, and Kansas. Cascading impacts of the drought were dramatic — water restrictions increased in many cities, forcing residents to cut usage about 25 percent; winter wheat conditions in 19 states were in very poor condition; wind and insect damage significantly affected crops; a shortage of hay throughout the region reached disastrous proportions, forcing ranchers to sell cattle at the lowest prices in ten years; and agricultural losses for cotton, wheat, feed grains, cattle, corn, and agriculturally related industries such as harvesting, trucking, and food processing in Texas alone reached five billion dollars.[552] Economically, reduced supplies of irrigation water led to decreased vegetable production with related job and income losses; food prices increased as much as 22 percent in response to the lower production levels for milk, meat, produce, and other foodstuffs; and prices for gasoline, diesel, and liquefied petroleum rose 15 percent above previous levels. Fires raged throughout the region and in Colorado alone burned 262,009 ha (647,440 acres). Total regional drought impacts were estimated at $10–15 billion, although it is difficult to quantify many social and environmental impacts.[553] This extended drought demonstrates the significant level of vulnerability, the diversity of impacts, and the effects such impacts can have on a myriad of water-security risks.

Other influences from water allocation in relation to national development strategies are also evident. Suppose, for example, that a government wanted farmers to grow rice, which requires significantly more water, instead of other crops. The government would likely subsidize the water-intensive inputs for this policy and by providing financial incentives to grow rice the government is influencing both the demand for water and private irrigation investment due to price policies. The increased demand for irrigation water for this crop has inter- and intra-sectoral, distributional, and environmental repercussions. In this instance, the agricultural sector is provided with an economic advantage for water access compared to the industrial sector (intersectoral). Also, the water used for rice production gains an economic advantage over water used for other crops

[552] D.A. Wilhite, and Vanyarkho, O., ed. *Drought-Pervasive Impacts of a Creeping Phenomenon* (London: Routledge Press,1999).
[553] Ibid.

(intrasectoral). Distributionally, farmers who grow rice and have more land and, therefore, access to water, gain over farmers with less land and water. There is also environmental repercussions since the increased pesticide and fertilizer use are likely to affect water quality overall.

In another example, in the western U.S., about 75 percent of the region's water is derived from higher elevation snow melt, most of which is under public jurisdiction. Allocation is varied. Rangeland management alters vegetative conditions and affects the rate of evapotranspiration, which affects both streamflow and groundwater recharge, demonstrating the effect of water use and allocation in non-agricultural sectors.[554] One must ask, "Do water market prices appropriately measure water values?" Consequently, it is important for water managers at all levels to understand and become involved in the decisions of other sectors, such as livestock, forestry, public health, rangeland, etc.

Witnessing the failures and successes of various countries with water-use policies, developing nations tend to implement fundamental changes in macroeconomic and sectoral policies that call for a greater reliance on markets, more open trade, and reducing producer and consumer subsidies (input and product markets). However, in sluggish economies such as the global recession that currently prevails, budget-reducing measures increase competition between and within sectors for funding new water projects. The overall economic, social, and environmental implications of choices need to be carefully addressed since there is a tendency for farmers to receive lesser consideration. As an example, local to national governments must choose between financing an irrigation or hydroelectric project: there is an added social opportunity cost of irrigation water for countries that are dependent on imported energy sources. Likewise, water scarcity may allow some farmers to produce on uneconomical lands such as steep watersheds or very arid environments. Consequently, a country could suffer twice: first, through potential reduced production compared to that possible with irrigation; and second, resource depletion and erosion that

---

[554] Saliba, "Water for Wilderness Areas: Instream Flow Needs, Protection, and Economic Value," *Rivers* 2, no. 4 (1987), http://www.fs.fed.us/rm/value/docs/wilderness_water_instream_flow.pdf.

could possibly shorten the lifespan of existing water management processes that include dams and reservoirs.[555] The latter is present in countries with very mountainous terrain such as El Salvador.

Due to population growth, in most countries, pressure has increased to modify investment allocations and to recognize and accommodate new demands for water. This generally leads to fewer capital investments in new water projects, elimination of irrigation subsidies, increased efforts to recover water costs, and increased emphasis on improving efficiency of existing supplies.

Physical, Social, and Economic Nature of Water

Because water is essential to life, policy makers around the globe treat water as more than a simple economic commodity and often reject competitive market allocation mechanisms, perhaps because in many cultures water is sacred and a symbol of ritual purity. Although only a small fraction of water use is actually consumed in drinking, the connection between water and human life is dramatic and the international community recognizes that access to water is a basic human right. Because society is partial toward technological solutions to solve water problems, in most countries water management has been relegated to the engineering domain. Because most water managers are engineers who are trained to solve technical problems, inadequate public policies are increasingly blamed for water-related problems. There is therefore, a strong case for implementing human behavior, social, and cultural aspects into water management decisions because people are the consumers; the issue is not simply a matter of conveying water from A to B.

Water is bulky and lacks mobility, especially on the large scale. Because it is so heavy, the value per unit weight tends to be relatively low as is seen in the pricing of water globally. Due to its weight, the cost of transporting and storing water is high relative to its simple economic value, i.e., the price charged per unit (about $4.00 per 1,000 gallons in the U.S.). Unlike petroleum, water is also difficult to identify and measure due to evaporation, recharge, and plant use. Thus, it is

[555] D.W. Bromley, Taylor, D.C., and Parker, D.E. , "Water Reform and Economic Development: Institutional Aspects of Water Management in the Developing Countries," *Economic Development and Cultural Change* 28, no. 2 (1980).

difficult to ascribe exclusive property rights and enforce them when compared to oil or other commodities. Additional problems related to physical properties also arise. A great many water management problems are site-specific, which eludes a uniform policy treatment. Generally, water consumption and quality requirements are tied to local populations and development, but water availability changes due to climatic variations and over longer cyclical periods, which can make supplies highly variable and unpredictable long term. The Hoover Dam and Colorado River System compact are good examples of this. Most rainfall is concentrated in early spring and snow pack is accumulated in the winter months (October – March), but there can be large annual variations. When precipitation amount is coupled with the inability to perform forecasting of significant climate change — attributable to natural and anthropogenic causes — concerns increase about long-term supply and sustainability in regard to increasing population.

Water projects, generally in the form of dams and related conveyance systems, that attempt to compensate for seasonal variability, including floods and droughts, typically require huge investments. As an example, when the Hoover Dam was completed in 1935, it cost $49 million; today it would cost about $790 million due to inflation, potentially $1 billion or more. This is a global problem; the economies of size are so large in these cases that unit costs generally exceed the range of existing demands. Conversely, it is a situation in which a single supplying entity is the most economically efficient organizational arrangement, but not a desirable security arrangement. Because there is no redundancy, failure could result in severe risks and unmitigated consequences. Worldwide, most economies of size for pumping groundwater are achieved at relatively small outputs resulting in multiple suppliers operating efficiently with greater redundancy. But, aquifers are usually hydraulically linked to rivers and streams, which means that part of a river's volume can come from these underground sources. As a result, the hydraulic linkage can be severely affected when an aquifer is heavily pumped, causing reduced streamflow to downstream water users and other problems.

Water-Use Economics

The four primary types of economic benefits of water use include: (1) commodity; (2) waster assimilation; (3) recreational; and (4) aquatic and wildlife habitats. Individuals obtain commodity benefits from water through use for cooking, drinking, and sanitation. Agriculture and industry gain commodity benefits by using water for production, whether for foodstuffs or manufacturing. This type of use represents private goods from water through production activities, but represents rivals in consumption. For example, one industry's use may prevent or preclude another industry from use of specific water supplies. A good example of this is the rival between agriculture and energy sectors which are the two largest users of water and compete for limited supplies. Government regulations and policies that focus on improving market access and fostering competition are important measures that improve both the productive and allocative efficiency of commodity use of water.

Waste disposal has become an increasingly important economic benefit. Water bodies have a limited capacity to assimilate contaminants and dispose of wastes; thus, disposal is a necessity. But, as it has grown in significance, so has the amount of water it uses. Often once water is treated it may be pumped back into streams and may move out of the region of its origin. This continually diminishes local supplies and increases supply costs long term.

In the past, recreational and aesthetic benefits of water as well as fish and wildlife habitats were regarded as a luxury and therefore not of concern to most governments. However, as populations grow, more people have focused their recreational activities around lakes, rivers, and oceans, and policies and regulations have grown with use. For the past three to four decades, many countries have developed niche tourist industries around water habitats. Examples include the Caribbean Islands, Dolphin shows and fish habitats at Disney World, city aquariums in San Francisco, Atlanta, Denver, New York, and in many other cities around the globe. Also, there are cruises on the Nile, visits to famous water falls in Hawaii and Brazil – the list is virtually endless. These activities have resulted in knowledge about human impact on the environment and its ecosystems and raised interests and concern about aquatic and wildlife benefits of water, both of which are related to commodity and recreational issues of water.

For the past decade, waste processing and recreational values of water have more or less become public goods — seen as non-rivals in consumption since one person's use does not preclude use by another. However, this has helped shape policy and regulations in these areas since non-rival goods require large amounts of resources to exclude non-entitled consumers from use. Also, exclusion costs are frequently high for water services such as navigation systems and flood control. Due to this high cost, non-rival consumption is generally better suited to the public sector in terms of ownership, provision, regulation, and intervention.

Pros and Cons: Alternative Approaches to Water Policies

— For Public Use

The economic organization of the water sector has generally been split into either market or government entities. Along with attempts to organize have come many market and government failures, many of which have related to economic structure and irrigation. Almost every country relies on a mix of market policies and government interventions to manage water resources. There are advantages and disadvantages to each. Any competitive market, almost without exception, has the potential to allocate resources efficiently among competitors and competing demands. Inevitably, producers and consumers, acting in their own self-interests, arrive at a price for which available supplies are allocated. If the price is too high, the producer cannot sell it to the consumer and vice versa. As with all commodities, profit guides inputs and outputs to combine them in the most efficient form and hopefully create the best product.

Generally, consumer wealth and preferences dictate expenditure patterns that encourage firms to produce commodities individuals are willing to pay for. The more desirable the commodity or the more needed, the more prices are forced upward, which allows producers to allocate resources in direction of greatest potential profits. Water is no exception. As a matter of fact, with the many industries purchasing water rights around the world, there will be a future rise in water pricing that will likely rival or surpass the cost per gallon of gasoline on a per volume comparison. Current water pricing is admittedly low, but will likely and inevitably, spiral beyond control. Just as water scarcity leads to a national security issue, so too will potentially spiraling prices of a resource that each person requires for life.

In the case of water, while the private sector has the potential to produce maximum benefit by bundling goods and services, the public sector also plays an important role. Primarily, the public sector can ameliorate income inequalities, promote development in disadvantaged regions, regulate private activities that harm the source/system, and regulate the resource to control profit-oriented monopolies — making good water affordable to all.

Generally, if water as a commodity meets the preconditions for a market system, government interventions can be minimized. This is because in competitive markets, a government's primary role is to establish rules and emphasize incentive structures. For water, one of the most important rules is property rights, i.e., water rights. However, all market economies experience shortcoming, e.g. market failures. A failure occurs because efficiency or economic criteria fail to satisfy national social welfare objectives or encourage behavior that does not meet efficiency criteria. In such cases, the public sector can intervene to influence water supply and allocation. Market failures affecting water resources include what is termed externalities — public goods and natural monopolies or, when efficient markets cannot meet society's equity criteria thus, requiring public intervention to compensate for distribution inequity. In a real sense, the choice becomes one of markets or governments — far from perfect or preferred.

Within the water sector externalities are inherent. The Colorado River is a good example: saline return water flows from irrigation of agricultural crops, affecting all downstream users, and the quality of the river water degrades with distance, impacting more and more users. This is an external cost to additional users which is typically not considered by the operator; therefore, governments attempt to procure funds from users through taxes, regulations, fees, subsidies, or technical standards. In this case, regulations would be implemented that control the salinity level of water moving off

property back to the river. As a regulatory agency, the EPA is in charge of enforcing water regulations; consequently, those who pollute the environment pay, not only for their production costs but also for externalities and fines.

Along the Colorado River system, water storage projects such as Hoover Dam and Lake Mead, as well as flood control programs represent public goods. Public goods are not adequately supplied by the market since private entrepreneurs cannot easily exclude non-paying beneficiaries and obtain a return on investment (ROI). As an example, for a flood protection plan developed for a river, it would not be easy to exclude those living along the river from the benefits of the plan. A common situation in the water market is a natural monopoly — when a firm experiences decreasing costs and increasing returns throughout the production process and, as a result,, obtains the ability to dominate the market. This allows under pricing of competing firms. An unregulated monopoly can reduce production and charge unwarranted prices. Such firms could include urban water supply systems, hydropower plants, river irrigation projects and so forth. The way to mitigate the undesirable effects of profit-oriented monopolies is through public regulation or public ownership, which usually benefits all with more moderate prices and innovation of technology to make the system more efficient.

In the U.S., while the capitalist or free market/competitive system is often viewed as the most efficient system for allocation of resources, market imperfections and fluctuations can accentuate income disparities. Current gasoline prices are an example – they are more easily affordable with a household income of $70,000 annually compared to a household income of $16,000 annually (minimum wage). So, societies' public welfare goals often incorporate a broad range of social objectives that generally include ameliorating income inequalities between members in the society. For these situations, water projects can provide important investment strategies for both human welfare (drinking-water and food supplies) and infrastructure to support economic development. For lower income groups, public ownership of the supply is therefore, beneficial.

Public intervention may not always be the answer either and denotes the complexity of the economics of water. Even when markets fail, public sector intervention or non-market approaches

may not always lead to a socially optimal solution. This was evidenced in 2009 with the bailout of American auto companies in which it was illustrated that some government performance incentives resulted in a divergence from socially preferable outcomes, not only in allocation, but also in distributional equity. In the water sector, a variety of problems are relevant to this scenario. They include the definition of products, externalities from public action, inequitable distribution of power, and private goals of public agents, i.e., self interests.

The outputs of non-market activities, especially water, are difficult to define and the inputs that produced them are difficult to measure. Examples are flood control projects, the amenity benefits of water storage reservoirs, and so forth. Additionally, public sector projects can result in many externalities, defined above, especially related to agriculture and irrigation.

Whenever there is a large monopoly, either privately or publicly owned, responsibilities to the public are generally not scrupulously or competently exercised and such monopolies provide specific individuals or groups with sufficient power over the economic welfare of the water user that procedures to protect the user, who has limited influence, are of primary importance. Internalities or goals of a public water agency provide the rewards, motivation, and penalties for individual performance. Counterproductive goals would include budget maximization, expensive yet inappropriate technology solutions, non-performance, and so forth. But, the most egregious acts would be when personnel are persuaded by money, gifts, etc., to violate rules in favor of one or a few and/or for personal gain. This happens too frequently. However, likely the best example comes not from the water sector, but from an intelligence agency — the CIA. Robert Baer, in his book "See No Evil," gave an accounting of this aspect in which national security decisions were being made by a few GS 12 to GS 15 grade-level personnel — the decisions they made were based on personal gain — how their individual stock portfolios would fare based on the intelligence decisions they made at the time. Lives hung in the balance, but they were concerned only about personal wealth — sadly, this behavior — preserving self interests, has become rampant throughout society, especially in government and political activities from the local to national levels.

Observation of many of the world's large irrigation projects illustrates a type of structural reform, especially in developing nations attempting to adjust and transform their economies toward a good trade regime that both modifies government involvement and increases market influence. Most success has taken place at the macroeconomic level, where the dominant supporting actions for agriculture have been non-price policies, but for non-agricultural sectors, the policy mix includes minimizing government involvement in pricing and marketing of inputs and outputs, privatization, and limiting government borrowing.

Regardless of the issues involved, the economics of water is complex, the resource is extremely interdependent with other sectors, and due to scarcity in many areas around the globe, development of supplies and pricing are currently a primary focus. Because of these issues water is a national-security problem. Addressing these problems has been difficult, but there are solutions. Generally, the immediate imperative in pricing water, at least in the private sector and to an extent the government sector, is to make as much money as possible. This ideology discounts the long-term interests, but it has become perfectly acceptable to pass on any external costs to others — those too weak to defend themselves, the collectivity, or to future generations. The inevitable result is to increase the extremes of wealth and poverty, while leaving a growing burden for future generations. Although stronger governments can curb some of these effects at the national level — given moral politicians who actually serve their constituents — there are no equivalent possible mechanisms for global control of water in any area of the sector.

Pricing Water

Pricing water is difficult at best. The problem has initially stemmed from increasing populations that need more, concentration of these populations in locations that over time are further removed from the resource, increased pollution requiring more costly treatment, and industrialization that has led to the connection of all

homes connected to public water and sewer systems. Overall, these factors have led to a drastically increased demand. Because of the social nature of water, privatization has been most successful in water treatment issues while public ownership and management has worked perhaps better for distribution and conveyance.

In theory, the market mechanism could be used to bring both demand and supply together. However, as mentioned earlier, several market failures justify government intervention. But, just how should government intervention be formulated from a socially optimal view? In addition to being bulky and lacking mobility, from an economic view, assignment of property rights is difficult. After all, precipitation is free and flows, and evaporation has no regard to geographic or property boundaries, so water may be said to be non-excludable. Therefore, water is generally labeled as a common-pool resource — a finite supply that must be shared in common for use over a specific area, be it a county, state, or country. Secondly, the renewal of water is disparately distributed and seasonal, implying uncertainty in supply. Climate change, resulting in periods of drought that could be followed by periods of heavy rainfall, creates discontinuity in supply, making association of economic factors difficult, hence the reason for dams, reservoirs and other storage systems and conveyance. Water is also not homogeneous — quality varies greatly. Thus, there is a demand for huge investments for supply and quality.

Investments are non-reversible. Once a project is developed and implemented we are stuck with it. Consequently, we must distinguish between demand for production and consumption. Failure to account for disparity in household incomes, gardens and parks, industrial mix, and other uses can result in forecasts of water use that may be greatly flawed and result in serious and potentially damaging consequences. Use due to geography, population density, community mix, income, age, etc., also influences economics of water use through economies of scale. Within this mix, the quality of water must also be considered since that used for drinking, washing, showering, irrigation, and manufacturing purposes can vary considerably. It should be noted that the majority of water use is for activities that do not require potable water.[556] Separation of quality

---

[556] Hutson, "Estimated Use of Water in the United States in 2000."

requires different costs for treatment, but to be efficient and effectively distributed also requires separate conveyance systems.

The supply of water also factors heavily into its economics. Two main sources of renewable supply are surface water (rivers, lakes, and streams) and rainfall. In contrast to surface water, groundwater is non-renewable — it can be recharged, but that rate of recharge is low. To an extent, waste water serves as a renewal source to surface water and is therefore and important element of a well-functioning water management system, i.e., the treatment and cleaning of waste water. While surface water is easier to obtain, it is also generally lower in quality due to pollution from agriculture, industrial, and other activities. During periods of drought, surface water sustainability can be rather low. Groundwater, being more non-renewable, is subject to a rapid rate of depletion. Due to disparate treatment, a sustainable supply of good quality water, at least on a global scale, has problems that include: (1) temporal and geographic variation in supply; (2) population growth and increased demand; (3) population density located far from supply source; and (4) overall reduced quality of water globally.

The supply of water must be considered against the backdrop of activities associated with the water industry, which include gathering, treatment, transportation, storage, and distribution. The wastewater side includes collection, transportation, and treatment. Both of these areas are capital intensive. Fortunately, investments in the water sector, such as dams, have long life spans — 50 years and more. Given the supply chain structure, water is a natural monopoly, and because the required investments are large, even one or two private firms, each with their own network, would be unlikely to have profitable operations in such an environment. The Manhattan Company, now Chase Manhattan Bank, serves as an example. Accordingly, the expense falls to the public sector and its consumers. However, the supply chain can be split into several parts in which large parts do not have the characteristic of a natural monopoly. This has happened globally and there remain questions about scope and scale of privatization components of this sector. Within the economics of water, supply and demand meet each other and, of course, water management.

The pricing of water must consider both the level and structure of prices. A pricing structure should consider at least four requirements:

1. **A price must be sufficient to recover costs. This implies earning a profit and covering costs for extraction, cleaning, and transportation as well as water treatment. In terms of a government entity, this 'profit' should be used to maintain infrastructure and thus be assessed over a period of years against estimated costs of maintenance and replacement.**
2. **The price should be fair for all users. Each person should be able to acquire the water necessary, which means the water bill should be fair to the user based on volume used and not so high it represents a disproportionate share of household income. In many locations this requires subsidizing low-income households. Further, long-term planning is crucial so future generations are not adversely affected.**
3. **Pricing should provide incentives for conservation. The price should also consider investment and incentives in water saving technologies and activities. It is important to note that social, rather than private marginal costs are more important in this issue, and long-term costs are important, which of course includes capital and operating costs of infrastructure. Peak use periods, distance from source, etc., need to be priced according to the energy needed for conveyance and distribution.**
4. **The price should be efficient and administratively feasible. Different meters for different users may be required; a marginal pricing on the administrative side requires knowledge on the monetary equivalent of external costs, which can be uncertain. Since many operators of these systems are engineers, they often lack such knowledge. Complex systems often lack transparency, which limits their usefulness for providing incentives. Simpler systems are desirable to promote the necessary incentives.**

A water bill it generally includes two parts. One part is the rate — the volume of water used for the billing cycle. The second part is a flat fee — it is unrelated to the amount of water used and may reflect the number of persons in a household, property size, and so forth. In some metro areas in the U.S., for example, when purchasing a new home, the more persons in the house, the more units (1,000 gallon increments) the home is allowed before meeting the next, higher, rate bracket. There may also be additional charges on the bill. This resulting structure has been influenced by the stakeholders involved — consumers, supplies, government, etc. Resulting pricing systems vary by location and depend on the relative weight of the various requirements. As an example, the efficient use of water may have a more urgent need than equity considerations. This is true for metropolitan water systems and transboundary issues. Regardless, price and rate structures employed around the world vary considerably.

Government intervention in the water sector is common around the globe, but to a necessary end to ensure supplying demand with at least some equity. Generally, this intervention is considered in the market and comes in the form of pricing policies, namely taxes and subsidies, regulation, and adopting new technologies. The classic solution for excess demand resulting from externalities is the introduction of a tax, usually referred to as a Pigovian tax.[557] Theoretically, a tax should reflect the externality associated with water demand and reduce it, but taxes have in many instances been problematic since the damage caused by excess demand for water is generally uncertain. Also, for practical policy making, goals are often associated with consumer response to a tax, which can be uncertain due to price elasticity of demand, making achievement of the policy goals a process of trial and error, at least initially. Taxation for lower income households is often considered unfair and is yet another problem for government intervention.

Subsidies also cause problems in the economics of water. Typically subsidies in the water sector are granted for investing in water saving technologies and other water conservation methods. But, there are also implicit subsidies since a price structure that does

---

[557] W.J. and Oates Baumol, W.E., *The Theory of Environmental Policy, 2nd Edition* (Cambridge: Cambridge Universit Press, 1988).

not satisfy the criteria for full cost recovery implicitly grants a subsidy to water users. The goal of a subsidy is to create incentives for efficient water use, which is often inferior to the same goal from a tax. This is because subsidies may reduce demand on a firm or organization, even an individual level, but total demand can remain sub-optimally high because firms that would not normally be able to compete survive through subsidization when they could not survive under taxation. The best solution is likely to totally phase out subsidies in favor of fair use taxes.

Given the nature of the water sector, regulations are inevitable. The EPA arose due to the requirement for sufficient water quality. And, because the industry tends toward a natural monopoly, regulations are required to avoid abuse of the power gained from such a position. Heath requirements for high quality water also require imposition of regulations, as well as the prevention of dumping and other forms of contamination. Therefore, given the investments and requirements, government intervention is likely warranted.

The True Value of Water — A Partial Solution

Water should be considered an economic good; however, studying its supply and demand is a perquisite for developing sound policies aimed at sustainability and, therefore, security. A primary principle in the economics of water is that there is a demand for water of differing qualities. However, around the globe, even though drinking water has virtually the smallest demand of water used, the supply of water for private use is uniform in quality - typically the highest quality and, therefore, costly to provide. There are likely substantial welfare gains through provision of a dual system water supply that can convey different quality water, one for drinking and hygiene, the other for lesser quality needs such as irrigation, manufacturing, etc. However, empirical evidence would be needed to prove this theory.

The largest costs in the water sector are borne by the development of storage, transportation, distribution, and treatment systems. Innovative and forward thinking approaches of water management are needed to ensure sustainability of such huge

systems. Economic principles also must be explicitly integrated into management. Development of a basic framework that could serve as a starting solution would include numerous parameters such as:

1. **Cost Recovery**
2. **Utilizing and Developing Tools for Economic Analysis**
3. **Putting Costs and Benefits Into Proportion**
4. **Implementing Pricing Policies for Droughts and Water Scarcity**
5. **Implementing Analysis of Management and Economics**
6. **Assessing a 'True' Value for Water.**

As stated, the costs of large water systems are enormous. To develop an initial framework as a guide for economics and management will require users to pay full costs of water services they receive, and for municipalities, member states, water boards, etc., to use economic analysis in a comprehensive management of their water resources to assess overall costs and cost effectiveness, as well as the costs of alternative measures for supply. These will be necessary for all sources of supply including river basins, natural geographical and hydrological units, dams and reservoirs, transportation methods, treatment and so forth.

Cost Recovery:

Water services must be priced to fully reflect the services provided — drinking water, irrigation, flood control projects, reservoirs for hydropower, etc. These costs could be broken down into several areas, each paying for various components of the services provided. As an example, user fees should cover operational and maintenance costs of water supply and treatment, as well as investment into infrastructure, both development and maintenance. User fees should also cover environmental and resource costs. In a real sense, polluters and other users would pay for natural resource use and environmental damage (pollution that harms fish and wildlife in rivers). This damage also includes the lowering of water levels in lakes and rivers that could harm ecosystems. These costs can be measured and should be included. As with any resource, scarcity should drive price upward. This is true in many areas since water use

restrictions with a subsequent rise in price are common, especially in the arid western U.S.

All water activities must be considered to implement these measures — recovering costs from only certain activities will not guarantee sustainability of supply. All users must pay in equal measure regardless of supply source. Pricing should reflect incentives for conservation measures, whether for reduced use or newer technology. Such principles will ensure conservation and therefore, economic efficiency, as well as reduce the burden on water suppliers; it will also help the environment.

Any policy needs flexibility for both the user and supplier. Cost recovery would initially begin with a good economic analysis of current water prices and the population pressure and impacts on the supply; likewise, each supplier needs to be mindful of their users, since culture, income, and other social variability affects use. The pricing mechanism should ensure fairness for all and not represent another government measure to rape the user of their fees and end up with failing infrastructure as we currently have in most large cities around the globe. Despite the mechanism, water pricing is difficult.

Tools for Economic Analysis:

General economics has illustrated a variety of tools that would be useful for the water sector, which include cost-benefit analysis; cost effectiveness analysis; and others. Cost-benefit analysis, while complex, compares overall costs and benefits of an initiative or project and can assess disproportional costing. Most of the estimated costs and benefits can be readily calculated, such as maintenance of existing systems, investment for newer sections of supply systems, and continued water treatment. A more difficult analysis is determination of the direct benefits, such as cost reduction of water treatment downstream should more or less pollution be discharged into a stream, the ecological and human health effects of emerging contaminants, cleaner water for a tourism industry, aquatic and wildlife health, etc. However, valuation methods can provide ways to estimate these costs and could be passed off to other groups as a synthesis of management. For example, anglers love to fish and are willing to pay fees to maintain a healthy aquatic habitat; additional fees could be paid through this system. Rather than be thought of as

singular, a comprehensive approach from all users and sectors should be considered for maximum efficiency and effectiveness in sustaining and managing water supply. Additionally, a cost-effectiveness analysis could assess the costs of alternative actions to achieve specific goals so that a more informed decision can be made of choices based on least-cost solutions and effectiveness.

Putting Costs and Benefits in Proportion:

Costs should be proportional to all users based upon location, community base, sector, etc. For example, those living far from the source incorporate much greater costs for transportation and distribution due to greater energy use; this should be accounted for and require higher costs. There should be a comparison of costs and benefits not only due to volume of water used, but also quality. Generally, costs should exceed benefits by a substantial margin, but without gouging the user.

Implement Pricing Policies for Droughts and Water Scarcity

Climates change continually and have repeating cycles of too much precipitation or too little. Thus, droughts and famine mitigation are a growing concern globally. Regardless of global region, an acute climate condition and resulting drought is not without concern or likelihood — it is a matter of when. Water stress or scarcity affects 44 percent of the world's population.[558] It is a situation in which demand exceeds a level of sustainable use. Droughts represent temporary declines in water resources and supplies due to less rainfall, but they can have lasting effects — a water supply needs time to recover from them. As population and energy costs continue to increase, water scarcity will be an ever prevalent problem on a global scale — no country or region is immune. Therefore, through management and pricing, utilizing economic tools is necessary in planning for drought and water scarcity situations. The ability to have forward looking, accurate forecasts for at least 7-10 years forward is necessary and is

[558] Tindall, 2010

available.[559] A primary goal is to conserve water and avoid unneeded losses; it is ultimately a 'user pays' system.

Implement Analysis of Management and Economics

Development of a sustainable management plan requires cost estimation of implementation of a variety of water sector measures. These include cost effectiveness to improve sustainability and health of supplies, i.e., water bodies, levels of contamination, forecasts of population growth, climate measures, and other measures. Such measures could include new regulations, new investment projects, improving existing infrastructure, negotiation of agreements with current polluters, and economic analysis methodology and cost accounting for all water use, infrastructure, etc. New investment and similar projects will entail costly investment. An economic analysis that assesses the cost effectiveness of alternative measures will be needed to ensure existing and future funds are well spent. Long-term forecasts for supply and demand are necessary as well and should be based on population growth by sector, i.e., people, industry, and agriculture, as examples. This should help identify future demand on supplies and the estimated impacts from climate change as well.

Assessing a 'True' Value for Water

Although a variety of factors are needed to determine the economics of water, it remains difficult to assess a true value due to externalities and other factors. Thus, any framework devised for management, economics, and sustainability should be integrated on business principles, and more importantly, with the scientific and technical analysis needed for development and implementation. All relevant impacts must be considered, and all stakeholders, including the public, need a voice. This is because water in many instances is an intangible product, not a commercial one. Thus, there is a good framework from which to begin.

---

[559] TinMore Institute provides extended precipitation and hydrology forecasts for 7 years forward for entire regions and countries (www.tinmore.com).

Case Study: Importance of Water Economics — Potential Critical Infrastructure Loss

If one considers the economy of water, what is the implication of loss of 50 percent of a water supply on regional economics? It is important to answer this question since most large water systems are not redundant and would result in dire consequences due to failure. Such a failure could result from a natural, man-made (terrorist), or technological hazard. Let us look at one from the view of a potential terrorist attack; a system failure that would have major cascading effects. Terrorists are certainly already well aware of this system — the Delaware Aqueduct. It conveys water from the Rondout Reservoir through the Chelsea Pump Station (see inset below - courtesy New York City DEP), the West Branch Reservoir, and the Kensico Reservoir, ending at the Hillview Reservoir in Yonkers, New York. This feed forms the bulk of New York City's drinking water supply. It was constructed between 1939 and 1945, and carries approximately half of NYC's 1.3 billion U.S. gallons per day water demand. The Delaware Aqueduct leaks up to 35 million gallons per day. Being 85 miles long and 13.5 feet wide, the Delaware Aqueduct is the world's longest continuous underground tunnel.

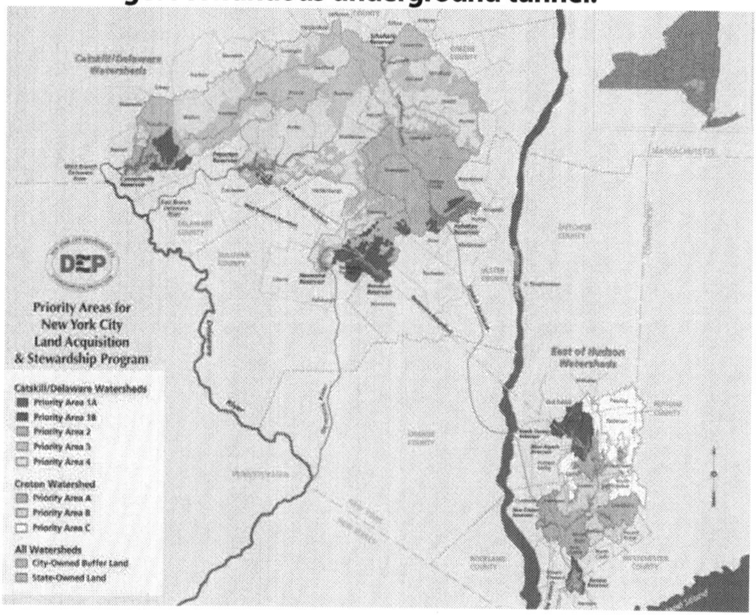

The aqueduct is comprised of three distinct pressurized tunnels through bedrock, built from 31 vertical shafts at depths from 300 to 1,550 feet below the surface. One of these tunnels, the Rondout-West Branch Tunnel (RWB Tunnel), conveys water from Rondout Reservoir in Ulster County, New York, under the Hudson River, to the West Branch Reservoir in Putnam County, New York. The RWB Tunnel is the Delaware Aqueduct's centerpiece. The aqueduct leaks so badly that it has been leaking, via a process called capillary rise, into homes (basements) and yards for years in the town of Wawarsing. There is no alternate system to provide redundancy to the Delaware Aqueduct, which means that if the water was drained from the Delaware Aqueduct's water tunnels for repair or if there were a terrorist attack, no other system is available to convey water to New York City — the city' water supply would be cut in half.

The average flow rate is about 2.9 m/s or 6.5 miles per hour; thus, water released from Rondout Reservoir would take about 16 hours to arrive in New York City. From a security perspective, the aqueduct represents significant vulnerability, either from a natural hazard or terrorist threat. For example, it is a perfect conveyance system for canister-type bombs filled with either explosives or bio-agents. Canister bombs (floating bombs) capable of carrying 15-20 kg or more of explosives or bio-agent could be released into the aqueduct and timed to explode at specific locations. Each canister could be filled with a mixture of air and explosives so that it would be carried within water flow — not floating on the surface. Other explosives devices could also be used with minimal logistical problems in terms of planning, transportation, and implementing an attack. These type devices are not unlike a self-propelled Autonomous Underwater Vehicle (AUV), but far simpler in design. On Thursday, June 4, near the Rondout Reservoir in Ulster County, an AUV dubbed ULIISYS, for Underwater Linear Infrastructure Investigation System, was inserted into the Aqueduct and removed 16 hours later near the West Branch Reservoir in Putnam County to survey leaks and damage to the aqueduct.

Weaker areas with the potential of creating the most damage would of course be where the aqueduct is leaking heavily. Two leaks in the Rondout-West Branch Tunnel, located at Wawarsing and Roseton, already threaten the aqueduct with significant water loss

and catastrophic collapse. Collapsing this aqueduct, regardless of cause, especially in several specific locations, would cut off half of New York City's water supply, possibly for months. The population of New York City proper is 5.3 million; the population for New York City metro areas is 19 million. What are the potential consequences?

How would failure of this system affect the overall economics and GDP of the immediate region? What then is the true value of water and the role of economics of water in sustainability of a populace? Fortifying this system would be the best management decision for long-term sustainability.

Conclusions

The shorter the supply of a natural resource, the more important it is to have an institutional structure for allocating it efficiently among stakeholders, both present and future. In this respect, usable fresh water is not fundamentally different from other scarce resources such as oil. The qualification of 'usable' is important since climate change and population growth, resulting in both low levels of replenishment and increased demand, seriously affect supply. What can be concluded generally is that water pricing is typically in favor of households and farmers, but also in corruption, resulting in an inefficient fresh-water market.

The economic system views water as either a common property resource to be freely shared or as a good to be priced and traded in the market. However, neither approach ensures sound water management and economics because many functions, services, and values of water are not used or traded in the market. These include the value of aquatic environments as a habitat for biodiversity, recreational values of water, use as a transportation medium, role in waste treatment and manufacturing, water's function in displacing and transporting materials and contaminants, and more. Consequently, society is accumulating many kinds of water debts that future generations will need to repay if the values and functions contributed by water to human health and welfare, the environment, sustainability, and security are to be restored. Watershed destruction, the depletion of water reserves, degradation of quality, accumulation of pollution in supply, and use of the oceans

as the ultimate sink for many wastes all represent depreciation of the natural capital of water resources.

Because of these many issues, there has been much discussion recently about water being undervalued around the world. Many nations are focused on water issues, but many lack the capital investment to develop and implement needed water systems for supply and treatment. The primary areas of emphasis in the water sector and economics are mechanisms that reveal the full cost of using water based on economics and the importance of potable water, reuse, disposal, and return of water to the environment as part of a comprehensive economic and management framework. A more optimal economic system would facilitate the long-term sustainability of water use and renewable water resources. It would also incorporate the ethical dimensions of water use, including equitable distribution and access, and apply fairness for stakeholders. Fundamentally, the failures of the economic system are not as much within the market mechanism as in the basic values that, almost unconsciously, underlie modern economics. Only the material counts in economics; the intrinsic values are difficult to buy or trade and are, accordingly, externalities, as are many other social, cultural, and environmental dimensions of society. Unfortunately, the immediate imperative to make as much money as possible ignores or discounts long-term interests, making it perfectly acceptable to pass along external costs to others, especially those too weak to defend themselves or collectively. The inevitable result is to increase the extremes of wealth and poverty while leaving a growing burden for future generations.

In terms of water, such a renewed and reoriented economic system would be able to account for multiple human and natural benefits of water and facilitate its management and sustainability.

The pricing of potable first-use water, reuse water, and treatment are important issues for both security and sustainability of a nation. Externalities or unintended damage to other users or the environment, which in turn has an impact on society and its future well-being, should be incorporated into frameworks developed for water management and economics. It is important to trace the cycle of extraction, storage, regulation, distribution, and use with the

return of water and wastewater to the environment as a means of identifying the potential set of externalities.

Conceptually, water can be priced directly or indirectly. Direct pricing involves setting prices and charges payable from use, reuse, and disposal of water — by users. Indirect pricing relies on employing a wide variety of mechanisms that reveal the cost of using water and associated resources. The latter is more difficult, but compares interdependencies with other sectors and through economic analysis and other tools could suggest a more true value for water within a locale, region, or country. Regarding externalities, not all are suitable for direct pricing. When causal links from action to outcome are tenuous and difficult to ascertain (examples are water use and quality), a charge to reduce water use is unlikely to reduce water quality problems. Ideally, such a charge would lead to a reduction in the economic activity that directly causes the water quality problem. For example, supply externalities that relate to extraction, regarding use and return could be, and likely are, the most straightforward to estimate.

Externality charges work in both political and social contexts when there is reasonable acceptance of the principle of 'polluters and users pay.' In a social climate that supports economic development regardless of impacts across the water cycle and sector, an externality charge is difficult to implement. Therefore, within such a framework, it is important that externalities associated with potable water, reuse, and wastewater be treated consistently. Such charges need to be implemented across all of these areas since excluding any of the three would create a distortion in inter-connected and interdependent markets. Ultimately, only by pricing to account for the full costs with an investment address both financial and environmental objectives.

Within the private sector, reuse projects are often driven by a need for water or a perceived marketing edge. Likewise, projects implemented by wastewater treatment utilities are generally driven by either a need to meet a reuse target goal and/or to avoid water based disposal per regulatory guidelines. As with pricing water generally, a potential outcome of pricing reuse water is over use. Thus, efficiency considerations must be addressed and a way provided for returning to full cost pricing needs to be in place.

Typically, any framework used would be designed to facilitate a rational investment in potable water, reuse water, and wastewater, which incorporates the full costs of production and effects of the environment into account. For large projects, public investment is likely always a requirement due to total cost and environmental consequences. Regardless of framework, transparency is the best beginning point for social choices. This requires explanations and rationale of pricing and the economic analysis and other mechanisms that set them. Failure to adequately address the economics of water will imperil national security.

Tribal Water Symbol

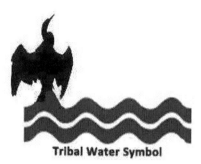

CHAPTER 16: Water Security – Policy, Governance, and Legislation

Executive Summary

The U.S. federal government has a long history of involvement in water resource development and management to facilitate water-borne transportation, reduce flood losses, expand irrigation for agriculture, and restore aquatic ecosystems. Globally, naturally scarce water supplies and increasing population have created new and harsher debates over water allocation, especially for threatened species. Water use and scarcity issues have increased state, transboundary, regional, and national tensions.

Critical questions arise about water and other resource and policy issues. What are the roles of local, state, Tribal, and Federal governments in water resources development and management? Who should pay, and how much? What agencies should be involved? Should existing projects be revamped or re-operated? The list is endless, but good policies can alleviate major future problems.

Within a management context, policy is generally presented as a formal, written policy statement. Policy analysis can aptly be defined as a systematic analysis of policy options. Alternately, policy management is a comprehensive umbrella term that concerns a specific effort to improve capacity to manage policy, perform good policy analysis, and facilitate cooperation in policy processes. Generally, policy development can be improved in two ways: (1) upgrading policy-making processes, which can involve improved policy process management and restructuring organizations; and (2) establishing improved broad-scope policies that guide the substance of discrete policies. Regardless of policy type or approach, specific circumstances will likely need specific process requirements. A problem with many international type policy process models is that they provide for the policy analysis phase in great detail, but do not provide guidance regarding events that lead up to the analysis phase.

Regardless of the water or other policy being developed, a variety of underlying issues separate to the policy itself and should be recognized. These include policy reform, political processes, time-frame opportunities, internal processes, process development, inclusion of multiple stakeholders, and other criteria.

Atop a policy sets a governance cycle, generally a four-step process, but one that can be highly complex in terms of execution. Governance cycles generally follow: (1) Review phase; (2) policy development phase; (3) reform phase; and (4) implementation and control phase. When implementing functions of the governance cycle, it is important to emphasize, especially for sectors as complex as water, fit within the country's national development framework and thus, with governing laws and consistent with the constitution. It is also important to begin with the macro level. Additionally, each phase typically contains subcomponents. Once the basic phases of policy development are accomplished, there must be a review cycle that will monitor and evaluate implementation of policy, which may need to be adjusted through time in terms of legislation, resources management, etc., along with cross-cutting issues such as intra-governmental cooperation and interaction.

Inclusive within policy development is defining and having a clear understanding of what policy is and what it is not, that it is dynamic, requires political endorsement (particularly for a national policy), and a specific process and style is necessary for writing policy. A policy will require the primary or main policy principles that provide an overall framework such as water use, water management, fostering participation, etc. The policy needs to be sufficiently detailed so that it covers a comprehensive range of issues that integrate the whole. It is also important to address global concerns, such as, water security and global systems for water-scarce regions. Perceptions of natural resources have changed greatly since the 1990s. Consequently, fundamental economic measures taken by governments to meet their water deficits will differ widely from the water rhetoric and declared water policy.

The hydrological nature of river basins pose just one group of problems for governments that need to deal with water scarcity because management of river basins by national governments and international institutions are subordinate to the national and international political economies of which they are a part. They are essentially segmented, closed systems. Hydrological models can make a significant contribution to the analysis of regional and global water problems.

Interdependent within global perspectives is the fact that water has become recognized as an economic resource, which contradicts user expectations and various religious texts that water should be a free entitlement. Within this environment, water that was free for agriculture is not based on user pay scenarios. Two economic principles — allocation and productive efficiency — are particularly relevant to water allocation and management because they comply with the sound principle of increasing returns to water. Unfortunately, the subject of the reallocation of water generally results in intense political reaction from those who perceive they might lose by the change.

Other factors that are of great importance globally are the close relationship between a national water gap and a nation's food gap. The greatest management challenge in attempting to steer the political economy of water is how to access sufficient water to meet staple food needs. This is a growing problem in the Middle East, Africa, the Midwestern and Southwestern U.S., and other countries. Water is a major factor of production in agriculture, and its relative availability in different climatic zones ensures that some economies have a significant advantage in the food staples production. The contrast in the capacities to produce food surpluses is given stark expression in the world trade figures. In the decades since the middle of the twentieth century, agricultural sectors of industrialized economies located in the temperate climatic regions have progressively increased their productivity in grain production.

All of these global issues, as well as environmental resources and development for sustainability, along with legal issues (particularly transboundary water sharing) create growing complexities for water security. Water policy, whether national or global, should reflect economic environments in relation to decreasing water supplies due to growing populations — most policies around the world are developed related to increasing allocations of water to agriculture, industrial, and residential use, despite limited real national water budgets.

Despite water needs and whether or not water resource conflicts may or may not arise, policies developed for the water sector should minimally be focused on improved productive and allocative efficiency and understand virtual water as a significant component of the water budget, economics of water, and trade. As a consumer of virtual water in global trade, it is necessary to link the water and food gap of nations, both within country, transboundary, and internationally. Greater cooperation among countries will become a necessity.

Introduction

The U.S. federal government has a long history of involvement in water resource development and management to facilitate water-borne transportation, reduce flood losses, expand irrigation for agriculture and restore aquatic ecosystems. Pressures on the quality and quantity of water supplies are increasing due to population growth, environmental regulation and ecosystem needs, emerging contaminants, agricultural water demand, green energy production (extensive volumetric use for corn for ethanol), climate change, energy production due to increased demand, and public interests that have been heightened due to water security. However, as with energy for which the U.S. has never developed adequate policy since about 1930, so it is with water — most water resource legislation deals with specific locations and regions, not at a national level.

Globally, naturally scarce water supplies and increasing population have created new and harsher debates over water allocation, especially for threatened species. An example of this is the California versus Delta Smelt issue. The Delta Smelt is an endangered species, small fish in the middle of a very large controversy in the Sacramento-San Joaquin River Valley. On August 31, 2007, California Federal Judge Oliver Wanger of Federal District Court protected the rare declining fish by severely curtailing human-use water deliveries at San Joaquin-Sacramento River Delta from December to June — these are the pumps that send water to Central and Southern California for agricultural and residential use.[560] The water shut-off

---

[560] B. Boxall, "A Small Fish Caught in a Big Fuss," *Los Angeles Times*(2011), http://articles.latimes.com/2011/feb/02/local/la-me-delta-smelt-20110202.

devastated the San Joaquin Valley and was the most drastic in California's history. Ironically, the 81 billion gallons of water that was not sent to the farmers was discharged into the Pacific Ocean — enough water for 85,000 acres of production agriculture. The shut-off also threatened 90,000 jobs, drove some farmers to bankruptcy (thus far), and increased food prices. For one of America's breadbaskets, the shut-off could potentially become a national-security threat by forcing dependency on foreign sources for food — a basic need of life. Once judge Wanger shut off the water, the governor of California, Arnold Schwarzenegger, stated he did not have the authority to turn the water back on — farmers turned to Congress and the Secretary of Interior Ken Salazar for help, but received none.[561] The water shut off, although initially helping the smelt, detrimentally affected the Delta ecosystem in other, primarily through destruction of agricultural crops, degradation of soil properties, and death of indigenous plant species that had adapted to the water supply. This battle is ongoing in the courts. Ultimately, the Delta Smelt controversy represents a horrific policy failure and lack of cooperation between local, state, and federal government entities and regulatory agencies if not outright senselessness. Biased analysis was presented from both sides of the issue within thousands of pages of documents and led to what some have called a 'congress-caused dustbowl.' Clearer is the mentality of inhumanity to humanity without presence of logic and reason that took precedence over facts, from which policy should be based and, in this case, policy was poor at best. If such a small fish that has no commercial value and exists only in California can cause such a large controversy, imagine what the outcome of reducing water flows between two states or countries would be. This case illustrates why good policy is so important.

Water use and scarcity issues have increased state, transboundary, regional, and national tensions. Within the U.S., the federal government has generally deferred to state primacy in intrastate water allocation. Additionally, climate change, snowmelt timing, and runoff issues have increased concerns about the reliability of developed water supplies, flexibility of existing management mechanisms, water security, and flooding. An excellent

---

[561] D. Stirling, "Blame 'Shortage' on Misguided Environmentalists," *Sacramento Bee*(2009).

example of the latter is the recent record flooding (May 2011) along the Mississippi River throughout Arkansas, Mississippi, and Louisiana.

Water legislation during the past several years in the U.S. has centered on project management and program issues, such as San Joaquin River settlement legislation, the Bureau of Reclamation's Title 16 water reclamation and recycling program, and sustainability of the Western U.S. water supplies, particularly falling water levels in Lake Mead and issues surrounding the Colorado River Basin. Additional focus has included oversight of the Bureau's Central Valley Project, including San Francisco Bay and Sacramento Rivers Delta management, and the Klamath project. Hurricane Katrina exemplified oversight issues and how to better coordinate federal activities, response, and rebuilding for water related and other issues.

Critical questions arise about water and other resources regarding policy issues. What are the roles of local, state, Tribal, and Federal governments in water resources development and management? Who should pay, and how much? What agencies should be involved? Should existing projects be revamped or re-operated? What should be done if an endangered species is affected by water use as in the Delta Smelt case? The list is endless, but good policies can alleviate critical and future problems. More importantly, valuable experience exists that is relevant to both future policy and strategy initiatives in this area, but also to policy process development in a regional and global context.

Perspectives on Policy Processes

Within a management context policy is generally presented as a formal, written policy statement. The interpretation and emphasis of policy is often communicated verbally, for example, through a press statement. From a working definition, policy is defined as a statement of intent. Policy articulates the basic principles to be pursued to achieve specific goals and actions. Therefore, policy reflects the values of a society, company, agency, etc., and is generally followed by pertinent project and program management actions related to implementation.

Policy analysis can aptly be defined as a systematic analysis of policy options.[562] Alternately, policy management is a comprehensive umbrella term that concerns a specific effort to improve capacity to manage policy, perform good policy analysis, and facilitate cooperation in policy processes.[563] In young democracies, policy development is about both technical policy analysis and institutional arrangements, known as capacity dimension. In process context, an emphasis has been placed on specific phases and elements such as evaluation, including continued focus on techniques.[564] Generally, policy development can be improved in two ways: (1) upgrading policy-making processes, which can involve improved policy process management and restructuring organizations; and (2) establishing improved broad-scope policies that guide the substance of discrete policies. The latter also involves application of policy analysis to overall policies, as well as process and organization restructuring and/or upgrading that serves policy development as a whole. internationally, process models are the norm in which the phases of agenda setting, policy formulation, policy adoption, implementation, and assessment are common. The authors inherently believe that a process model of policy development is more effectual long term since this type model has the advantage of easier metric development to both track and improve the processes involved. This type model also favors a larger macro approach that places significant emphasis on institutional factors. And, although complex, this type model can be simplified into several dimensions such as policy formulation, policy implementation, and monitoring and evaluation.

Regardless of policy type or approach, specific circumstances will likely need specific process requirements. However, to begin, a generic process model provides for both a comprehensive set of phases, as well as proposes specific requirements and key issues to be addressed during each of the phases. A generic model for water could include basic steps such as policy process initiation, process

---

[562] C.B. De Coning, "The Nature and Role of Public Policy," in *Improving Public Policy*, ed. F. and Wissink Cloete, H. (Pretoria: Van Schaiks, 2000).
[563] Ibid.
[564] J.E. Anderson, *Public Policy Making: An Inroduction*, 2nd ed. (Boston: Houghton Mifflin, 1994).

design, analysis, formulation, decision, statutory components, dialogue, implementation and strategy, and finally, policy evaluation. Each of these and their subcomponents are listed in Table 16.1.

Table 16.1: Generic Model Processes and Phases

Policy Phase/Process	Subcomponents
Process Initiation	Consultation with Stakeholders Rules and Requirements Mandate and legitimacy Preliminary objectives and goals
Process Design	Stakeholders agreement on process Institutional arrangements and MOU's Agenda and setting objectives Policy project planning Monitoring requirements and arrangements
Analysis	Consequences of design and forecasts Analysis of differing options Prioritization Set of value judgments
Formulation	Preparation of proposals Report format Confirmation
Decision	The decision making process Consultation with stakeholders and experts Mandated decision(s)
Statutory Issues	Legal draft Bills/Acts General and specific guidelines Negotiation
Dialogue/Participation	Communication strategy Dialogue Feedback Implementation
Implementation & Strategy	Operational Policy Planning (program, budget, priorities, projects, etc.) Monitor and manage
Evaluation	Objectives Management and evaluation Reports and follow up Improvements – how to?

A problem with many international type policy process models is that they provide for the policy analysis phase in great detail, but do not provide guidance regarding events that lead up to the analysis phase. Institutional arrangements, organizational change, and policy capacities at various organizational levels need to be carefully considered. However, other models such as governance frameworks, negotiation models, strategy and leadership concepts, power models, and others should be considered for employment in the policy development process as well.

Every policy must have a clear premise. For example, the Constitution of the United States begins:

> "We the People of the United States, in Order to form a more perfect Union, establish Justice, insure domestic Tranquility, provide for the common [defense], promote the general Welfare, and secure the Blessings of Liberty to ourselves and our Posterity, do ordain and establish this Constitution for the United States of America."

Is the Constitution a policy? Yes, although some would argue it is only a charter. Why? It articulates the basic principles to be pursued to achieve specific goals and actions and, in this instance, the policy interests and benefits the values of the American society. As a policy the Preamble explains the purposes of the Constitution and defines the powers of the new government as originating from the people of the United States, i.e., the purpose of members of congress, etc., is to serve the will of the people as a whole. The Constitution has several specific goals, all coinciding as a whole to achieve a specific, yet broad policy process. The "Constitution" as a policy guarantees other policies through articles, sections, and amendments. For example, "The Constitution gives the Senate a share in foreign policy by requiring Senate consent, by a two-thirds vote, to any treaty before it may go into effect. The president may enter into "executive agreements" with other nations without the Senate's consent, but if these involve more than minor matters they may prove controversial." The Constitution, as a policy, was thought out in great detail and implemented with clear strategy. It was so well-conceived that it is the world's longest surviving written charter/policy of government.

Developing a Water Policy

A policy would generally begin with a basic premise, as described in Table 16.1. For example, we could begin a water policy with the goal that "everyone has the right to have access to sufficient, clean water" as a preliminary goal and objective. What is necessary within the policy to ensure that this goal is achieved? There may be a need for a constitutional change, development of water-law principles, a national water resource strategy, and varied other components. However, the provision of water to meet environmental requirements and obligations is, according to the preliminary goal, a priority for the policy, although the mechanisms to achieve this may not be in place. To achieve this lofty policy goal, the generic process in Table 16.1 could be shortened and/or modified to basic phases such as water policy initiation, development of objectives, perhaps development of a regional or national water policy (this could lead to a water act, such as the U.S. EPA clean water act) and continued policy and legislative development, policy implementation, and ending in a water strategy of the appropriate scale, i.e., local, regional, or national.

As each phase of a water policy is outlined, specific criteria need to be explained. For example, there should be a distinction between water resource management and water services and why they should be dealt with separately, whether in the law or in policy and implementation. Likewise, although interdependent, a distinction exists between the hydrologic cycle and water supply and related sanitation and waste-water disposal. Often, one may wish to develop other sub-phases for the major phase for clarity and outlining goals, objectives, responsibilities, and so forth. If we were to look at a water law review process, for example, sub-phases might include public consultation, developing a monitoring process and committee, and drafting a new bill or legislation. Separate committees could be formed for each of these depending on complexity and relation to overall scope. Similar activities would be necessary for each phase as each team or committee drafts various sections of the policy for policy analysis and formulation, statutory issues, implementation, or other phases as listed in Table 16.1.

General Policy Development Observations

Processes used for developing policy can be remarkably similar for an array of sectors. However, the water sector is very complex and, regardless of policy goals, experts who have an extensive knowledge regarding the interdependence of all areas and not just surface complexities should be sought to assist in policy development. This means finding someone who understands the entire process, as well as how water relates to public health, energy, transportation, economics, critical infrastructure, and other sectors. By nature, policy is embedded in legal frameworks and reform processes. Because of this, care should be taken not to forego policy analysis and formulation as needed due to potential time constraints. All phases and components must be prioritized; this will help in systematic analysis of the entire policy. Other fields such as leadership and management, sound decision making, etc., need to be woven into the policy teams and overall process.

Regardless of the water or other policy being developed, a variety of underlying issues relate to the policy itself that should be recognized. First, reform of a policy is an ongoing and necessary process, but does not necessarily imply poor management. Second, developing a policy is primarily a political process often geared in self interests of a number of individuals, agencies, and other sectors interests — elimination of self interests generally results in the most effective policies. However, this is necessary to an extent since without a high-level political mandate, just as obtaining vision buy-in within a corporation, it may be difficult to undertake, follow through, and implement. Thus, developing policy is a people activity; the technical issues naturally work into the process. Third, depending on the nature of the project and scope, there are certain time periods when it will be easiest to make the reform and implement the policy. This could be due to climate change, political atmosphere, costs, or other measures. It is necessary to recognize the appropriate window of opportunity. Fourth, the policy process is an internal one. As an example, if the U.S. were to develop a national water policy, care should be taken to involve national experts within country, not from outside, since experts within country are more knowledgeable of political, social, cultural, and hydrological issues within the country, despite the fact a national U.S. water policy would almost certainly end in failure due to loss of sustainability. Fifth, the process of development is as important as the output to achieve long-term goals and effects. The process must promote the key values of the outputs. As an example, President Obama heralded transparency frequently during his presidency. However, a transparent, effective, and cooperative institutional agreement or arrangement is unlikely to be developed and delivered by a process that is closed, lacks transparency, and does not involve the average citizen. Sixth, a successful reform process will build a legacy for future generations — generally, for 20 to 30 years forward. This requires forward thinking to ensure the policy will stand the test of time. The U.S. constitution is an excellent example. In the end, whether in life, death, or politics, individuals are remembered for what they last accomplished — a legacy is a monument that shows the concern and ethics of the individual or entity. Finally, a policy process is a whole government/entity engagement. It typically involves multiple agencies, corporations, and others that may or may not be interrelated. Cooperation between at federal agencies requires political consent minimally; thus, policy issues can be politically contested, whether related to water or not.

Atop a policy sets a governance cycle, generally a four-step process, but one that can be highly complex in terms of execution. Governance cycles generally follow: (1) review phase, (2) policy development phase, (3) reform phase, and (4) implementation and control phase. When implementing functions of the governance cycle, it is important to emphasize, especially for sectors as complex as water, fit within the country's national development framework and therefore, with governing laws and consistent with the constitution. It is also important to begin on the macro level with policies that encourage more private sector involvement, decentralization, and so forth. The governance cycle is by nature dynamic and should not be constricted or rigid due to self interests. Each element within the cycle, while working with the whole, demands attention; some may require an immediate review before completion of the full cycle. Such reviews could and generally do lead to modifications of the policy, additional legislation, etc.

1. Review Phase

The review phase first considers the current status of the sector. As national experts weigh in, current strengths and weaknesses can be uncovered and addressed and problem areas recognized. Virtual snapshots of portions of the sector are developed prior to the next phase. A variety of subcomponents of the water sector can be addressed and could include water security, agricultural water use, environmental degradation, groundwater, surface water, user categories, supply and sanitation, infrastructure assets and needs, and many others. Once developed it will become clear there is an interface between the review phase and the policy development phase. One of the most important criteria is to identify the key policy areas and how they can best be developed and implemented to achieve the policy's objectives and goals.

2. Policy Development Phase

This is the most important phase of the reform or policy development process and generally has two subcomponents: policy principles and policy development. The first phase leads directly to the issues of development which are the basis for legislative and institutional reform for a national strategy or one of smaller scope and scale. As mentioned previously, policy in a simplistic form is a set of decisions that determine what and how activities will be executed in a given sector. Macroeconomic and sector policies are important issues that must be well understood to enhance policy development and are why it is requisite that at least several of the experts working in the development and other phases understand the interdependent complexities of the entire sector with other sectors, not just the surface issues. Political in nature, once adopted, policy provides the authorization for a government department's role in implementation, but should not be confused with strategy. The latter is a plan of how to implement the policy, although it will by nature have implicit elements of policy. If there is already an existing strategic plan, it should be reviewed and contrasted with new policy developments as they occur and modified as needed. Often, existing legislation makes policy impossible, which requires adherence to legal implications proposed within the new policy and also related policy of other sectors that are interdependent with the water sector.

This phase could consider major components such as water use, the environment, water resource development, economics of water, water services, legal aspects of water, and so forth. The first subcomponent, policy principles, should be a public participation process since they are the majority stakeholders in this sector. As the reader may recall, this worked well for transboundary issues of the Danube River in Europe. The policy development subcomponent will join policy principles, the latter being broader in scope. This stage will require senior officials from cooperating entities.

3. Reform Phase

The reform phase has three major subcomponents, which can vary depending on policy goals, and include legislative reform, institutional validation, and strategic planning of water resources management. This phase applies approved policy to existing legislation, institutional arrangements, water resources management, and other activities. It then looks at the implications of these processes within the overall policy.

Legislative Reform — reviews current legislation related to the sector, especially water resources management and current laws. Amendments to existing laws are generally necessary to successfully implement policy and may, on occasion, need to be rewritten. It is important to avoid piecemeal amendments as they typically reduce effectiveness of policy. This step also requires public participation.

Institutional Reform — this phase should outline the specific roles and responsibilities as well as the function and authority of each institution engaged in the sector addressed by the developed policy. It is natural to have tensions and competition between different government departments. An excellent example of this is the 16 members of the U.S. Intelligence Community. Existing legislative and institutional political environments have led to confusion and duplication of roles, both between departments and within different levels of government. A clear distinction between cooperating entities is necessary for success, which is best accomplished during policy formulation. The roles and functions of non-government organizations (NGOs) also need to be clarified. It is within this phase that additional skills need to be addressed other than water-related skill sets. An example is change management, which is a specialized activity within the institutional change process. This is not just about changing an institution, nor should it be; it is about helping people who work within each of the cooperating institutions gain a new vision of the role of the institution and their personal contribution and careers. As an example, the Central Intelligence Agency (CIA) and other members of the intelligence community are very good at what they do, but often conflict with each other because of the need to justify receiving funding for operations. Giving others credit for helping in specific tasks does not always sufficiently justify that funding. And, more importantly, it requires trust, which is typically lacking at the agency/bureau level and now more commonly and unfortunately at the individual personnel level. Thus, fully implementing change management for extremely critical sectors such as water, intelligence, and so forth, requires building trust among personnel from cooperating (and presumed competing) agencies and creating and sharing a vision with all personnel within all cooperating groups, agencies, and levels. Using an analogy to a watch, if any agency fails, comparable to a watch gear, the policy will fail, perhaps not quickly, but it will decline substantially in effectiveness long term.

Strategic Planning of Water Resources Management — the development of a national model for a water sector allows for greater and generally more effective strategic planning. This phase can be highly political, technical, and tension-filled. This is an integrated process that needs to be carefully planned.

4. Implementation Phase

This phase delivers the practical side of implementing policy and will determine what portions of policy to implement as tenable since most policies cannot be implemented at once. Occasionally, various policy options need to be tested through pilot studies or programs to determine best implementation guidelines and processes. For example, within the homeland security sector, certain states may be ready to implement specific processes before other states; the same is true of water security, the water sector, and other sectors. This usually is due to barriers to implementation that can be caused by such factors as economic feasibility, lack of coordination between cooperators that effectually block policy implementation, technology requirements, and related factors that render the policy inadequate, external factors such as public resistance, and so forth.

Utilizing these perspectives, a more specific rendering of policy goals and process flow is illustrated in Figure 16.1. Major components and subcomponents should be changed as needed, but Figure 16.1 will serve as a general framework for policy development. It can also be adjusted for sectors other than water.

Conclusions

Once the basic phases of policy development are accomplished there must be a review cycle that will monitor and evaluate implementation of policy, which may need to be adjusted through time in terms of legislation, resources management, etc. It is also necessary to recognize cross-cutting issues such as intra-governmental cooperation and interaction, which will require change management processes, creation and sharing of a vision, and trust building — a difficult process overall that requires patience. Unless this is done, cooperating entities will not be unified and will resort to working in isolation from each other. For example, water and energy sectors are heavily interdependent with each other and yet the U.S. agencies responsible for working in these issues remain mostly separate. The failure to have a policy for each sector is also a detriment, especially for long-term resource planning. Public awareness and participation is also extremely important in development of effective policy in the water sector — they are the majority consumer and stakeholder.

Inclusive within policy development is first defining and having a clear understanding of what policy is and what it is not, that it is dynamic, requires political endorsement (particularly for a national policy), and that a specific process and style is necessary for writing policy. A policy will require an overall description and reference framework. Ideally, it will contain primary or main policy principles that provide an overall framework such as water use, water management, fostering participation, etc. The policy needs to be sufficiently detailed so that it covers a comprehensive range of issues that integrate the whole. Figure 16.1 lists a variety of policy items; however, these should not be regarded as a comprehensive list since

there are other issues not listed that should be based on scale and scope of the policy, national circumstances, and so forth.

Figure 16.1: Policy & Goals Components (partial listing).

Policy Development & Goals
1. Policy & Reform
Policies
Reforms
Targets
2. Water Resource Management
Allocation & Monitoring
Coastal Programs
Channelization
Environmental Protection & Social Measures
Fish & Wildlife Protection
Flood Control & Protection
Flood Policy
Reservoir Development
River Basin Planning/Management
Water and the Natural Environment
Waterborne Transport & Inland Waterways
Water Rights
3. Improving Water Services
Decentralization
Emerging Contaminants
Federal Water Resources Coordination
Irrigation & Drainage
Public Participation
Private Sector Participation
Public-Private Partnerships
Reclamation Reform & Irrigation Policy
Water Pricing
Water Supply & Sanitation
4. Water Conservation
Awareness & Education
Cost Recovery (include User/Beneficiary Pays)
Water Resources Authorizations, Budget, and Appropriations
Regulation
5. Regional Cooperation
Promote Understanding
Transboundary Issues
6. Foster Participation
Concepts
Culture / Gender
Strategy
7. Improving Governance
Core Concepts
Building Capacity
Developing Synergy
8. Policy Implementation
Adopting the Policy
Building Skills
Partnerships
Resources
Sequenced Approach
Transition

In addition to looking at local, state, province, Tribal, and national water-policy issues, due to the critical nature of this resource, it is important to address global concerns as well; water security and global systems for water-scarce regions must also be considered. Perceptions of natural resources have changed greatly since the 1990s. In the late 1980s, most Middle-East economies believed that additional water had to be mobilized to meet the rising demands for agricultural, industrial, and domestic water. During this time, Israel utilized science and technology to change its approach and was able to cut water allocations to agriculture without reducing efficiency. The way Middle East countries and their economies have adapted to

water scarcity could serve as a framework for other countries despite their transboundary water issues. The primary issue in global policies, transboundary sharing, and related issues highlight the major political challenges associated with the adoption of any new policy since the livelihoods of all are generally affected and communities may not readily adapt due to political, religious, or cultural issues. However, fundamental economic measures taken by governments to meet their water deficits will differ widely from the water rhetoric and declared water policy.

Global policies, especially transboundary sharing, would include many of the issues discussed above, but more specifically, individual water-use needs that drive demand, and virtual water (the most significant factor for water-scarce regions). For example, it is much more energy efficient to move a ton of foodstuffs than 1,000 tons of water; world trade in food staples is the means by which water-deficit economies balance water budgets. A combination of virtual water and indigenous water enables national water needs to be met.

The use of hydrological models that forecast forward is a necessity, particularly for water-scarce regions. The hydrological nature of river basins pose just one group of problems for governments that need to deal with water scarcity because management of river basins by national governments and international institutions are subordinate to the national and international political economies of which they are a part. They are essentially segmented, closed systems. Hydrological models can make a significant contribution to the analysis of regional and global water problems. A model of global water — including soil water availability — would be helpful by assisting in the determination of the global agricultural system capacity to produce staple foods. At this stage, it is only possible to point to the need to research this grand topic. The TinMore Institute, a global resources think tank, has developed coupled models that can look forward seven years or more with at least 80 percent accuracy and relate hydrologic water, climate change, and economic factors effects on food production, energy use, other major infrastructure and sector needs, delineating specific shortages in water and cascading effects in other areas.[565]

[565] Personal communication, TinMore Institute 2011 (www.tinmore.com).

Interdependent within global perspectives is the fact that water has become recognized as an economic resource, which contradicts user expectations that water should be a free entitlement. Within this environment, water that was free for agriculture is not based on user pay scenarios. Two economic principles — allocation and productive efficiency — are particularly relevant to water allocation and management because they comply with the sound principles of increasing returns to water. Unfortunately, the subject of the reallocation of water generally results in intense political reaction from those who perceive they might lose by the change. The most important measure of the economic efficiency of water allocation and management in the Middle East is the extent to which small amounts of water are effectively used to mobilize elements of the economy to produce goods and services. These in turn generate foreign exchange with which to gain access to water and/or "virtual water." However, the process of reallocation has not yet been carried far enough in most Middle Eastern and other water-scarce economies, but it is becoming increasingly recognized that there is no alternative. The principle of productive efficiency is much more readily adopted than that of allocative efficiency because while increases in productive efficiency require investment and changes of practice, the introduction of more productively efficient water management does not generate political stress.

Other factors that are of great importance globally are the close relations between a national water gap and a nation's food gap. The greatest management challenge in attempting to steer the political economy of water is how to access sufficient water to meet staple food needs. This is a growing problem in the Middle East, Africa, the Midwestern and Southwestern U.S., and other countries. Water is a major factor of production agriculture, and its relative availability in different climatic zones ensures that some economies have a significant advantage in the food staples production. The contrast in the capacities to produce food surpluses is given stark expression in the world trade figures. In the decades since the middle of the twentieth century, agricultural sectors of industrialized economies located in the temperate climatic regions have progressively increased their productivity in grain production. Also, internationally, as an example, almost all the Middle Eastern economies were unable to feed themselves by the early 1970s. In contrast, the greater populations of China and India have been able to maintain per capita food availability, generally without the need to import food staples until recently — due to water scarcity. This has also led to water saving by importing food from other countries, taking advantage of that country's virtual water. Consequently, there is growing interdependence between countries for necessary food supplies, which is heightening national and international security issues and concerns.

All of these global issues, as well as environmental resources and development for sustainability, not to mention legal issues (particularly transboundary water sharing) create growing complexities for water security. As an example, constructive contributions to water scarcity and water sharing could be made by international specialists in water law by improving the legal basis for trading water internationally. This could significantly affect virtual water through increasing food prices due to shipment out of country.

Water policy, whether national or global, should reflect economic environments in relation to decreasing water supplies due to growing populations — most policies around the world are developed related to increasing allocations of water to agriculture, industrial, and residential use, despite limited real national water budgets. Additionally, self interests from individuals and communities allied with elite interests whose livelihoods or wealth depend on irrigation systems based on surface and groundwater can alter policy to the detriment of broad user consumption. A combination of these issues has led to a major dependence on world trade, which is both good and bad. Trade can increase GDP of a country, helping to provide jobs and increasing the economic status of the country as a whole. Contrasting this is the growing dependence on food with ever lengthening supply lines, creating significant detriments in times of manmade, natural, or technological hazards — a national security threat. As an example, the international market in staple grains has proved unpredictable — wheat prices rose rapidly in 1995 by about 60 percent as a result of a combination of anxiety about global stocks and the evident demand from countries such as China, which is now viewed as a possible long-term scenario. A water scarcity or supply issue in any of the countries providing grain to China could cause a significant disruption in supply, resulting in possible starvation, civil unrest, and public-health issues.

Despite water needs and whether or not water resource conflicts arise, policies developed for the water sector should minimally be focused on improved productive and allocative efficiency and understand virtual water as a significant component of the water budget, economics of water, and trade. As a consumer of virtual water in global trade, it is necessary to link the water and food gap of nations, both within country, transboundary, and internationally. Greater cooperation among countries, to maintain sustainability, will become a necessity.

Perhaps the most advantageous approach to enhance water security is a local, regional, national, and global dialogue to address pertinent questions such as:

1. How do we best develop flexible and adaptable transboundary water-sharing policies and planning for hydrologic, political, and socio-economic circumstances?
2. What are the interdependencies between water and energy, agriculture, ecosystems, conservation, and climate change? How should long-term planning and policy account for these issues to ensure that competing users of water, especially energy and agriculture, have adequate supplies to continue regional and national economic growth?
3. Given the critical importance of water, should a single U.S. agency be responsible for water security that could aggregate and manage these problems? What capacity and capabilities would be needed to address and manage national and international water-security conflicts, threats, and policies?
4. The primary threats to water security are population growth, terrorism, climate change (sustained droughts), and industrialization. These threats are often interdependent. What are the best methods for

developing comprehensive strategies to address these threats?

5. **How can we achieve stakeholder cooperation between the federal and private sectors for information sharing, vulnerability analysis, and risk assessment to improve security and sustainability?**

Few other issues impact the global community so directly as water security. Every individual is a stakeholder for ensuring the sustainability and thus, security of water supplies.

END

NOTES

NOTES